BERTRAND TAVERNIER ON
WARNING SHADOWS

"Reading *Warning Shadows* is an illuminating, rewarding experience. Giddins's approach is documented, sharp, intelligent, and exciting. He never recycles clichés, he questions the clans and the cliques, and he writes very well of actors and actresses. He rightly considers that an opinion (even repeated by many zealous disciples) is not a fact. Whether he talks of the good ideas of Pabst that make the construction of his *Threepenny Opera* better than the play, of Ford, Bing Crosby, Resnais, or Tati's *Trafic* ('a step to the side, not back'), he inspires a violent urge to rush to a cinema or to buy a DVD to see those films again. He made me discover many neglected films (*Overlord* and *The Garment Jungle*, to name a couple) and the beautiful black and white of *I Wake Up Screaming*, and newly appreciate underrated directors. Roland Barthes made a distinction between the subservient 'écrivants' and the priestly 'écrivains.' Clearly Giddins belongs to the second category."

BOOKS BY GARY GIDDINS

WARNING SHADOWS

HOME ALONE WITH CLASSIC CINEMA

GARY GIDDINS

W. W. NORTON & COMPANY

New York   London

For information about permission to reproduce selections from this book,
write to Permissions, W. W. Norton & Company, Inc.,
500 Fifth Avenue, New York, NY 10110.

For information about special discounts for bulk purchases, please contact
W. W. Norton Special Sales at specialsales@wwnorton.com or 800-233-4830.

Manufacturing by Courier Westford
Book design by JAM Design
Production manager: Devon Zahn

Library of Congress Cataloging-in-Publication Data

Giddins, Gary.
Warning shadows : home alone with classic cinema / Gary Giddins. —
1st ed.
p. cm.
Includes index.
ISBN 978-0-393-33792-1 (pbk.)
1. Motion pictures. I. Title.
PN1994.G475 2010
791.45'75—dc22

2009049298

W. W. Norton & Company, Inc.
500 Fifth Avenue, New York, N.Y. 10110
www.wwnorton.com

W. W. Norton & Company Ltd.
Castle House, 75 / 76 Wells Street, London W1T 3QT

1 2 3 4 5 6 7 8 9 0

FOR ELORA CHARLES

· ·

And in memoriam, NY:

The 5th Avenue Cinema
The 8th Street Playhouse
The Anco Theater
The Apollo Theater (42nd Street)
The Arcade / Studio One (Lynbrook)
The Baronet & Coronet Theaters
The Bleecker Street Cinema
The Brooklyn Paramount Theater
The Carnegie Hall Cinema
The Central Theater (Cedarhurst)
The Criterion Theater (Broadway)
The Criterion Theater (East Rockaway)
The Embassy Theater
The Green Acres Theater
The Harris Theater
The Hewlett Theater
The Little Carnegie Playhouse
The Loews State Theater
The Lynbrook Theater
The Lyric Theater
The New Amsterdam Theater
The New Yorker Theater
The Oceanside Theater
The Regency Theater
The Rivoli Theater
The RKO 86th Street Theater
The Selwyn Theater
The St. Marks Cinema
The Sunrise Drive-In
The Thalia Theater
The Times Square Theater
The Valley Stream Theater
The Warner Theater

I once saw a light, shining bright, deep brass and gold,
both young and old, dark and light, gold and bright . . .
and then it flickered back out of sight.
—SONNY ROLLINS,
Reel Life

One escapes into reminiscence as one escapes
into gin or sodium amytal.
—ALDOUS HUXLEY,
The Genius and the Goddess

The moment a person forms a theory, his imagination
sees in every object only the traits which favor that theory.
—THOMAS JEFFERSON,
letter to Charles Thomson

To meditate on shadows is a serious thing.
—VICTOR HUGO,
Les Misérables

CONTENTS

. . . .

ACKNOWLEDGMENTS

· · · · · · · · · · · · · · · · · ·

The essays in Parts Two and Three originated, mostly, in newspaper and magazine pieces published between 2005 and 2009; they have been variously revised—expanded, truncated, combined, and otherwise tidied up. Most were written for *The New York Sun*, a short-lived broadsheet (2002–08), with a political ideology that ran the gamut from *The Fountainhead* ("the world is perishing from an orgy of self-sacrificing") to *The Wild Bunch* ("next time, you better plan your massacre more carefully"), balanced by an intoxicatingly nonideological embrace of the arts in all their radical glory. Once you tossed away the first section, you could hardly believe how fine the second section was, day after day. It was a privilege to be a part of it, and to work with editors Matt Oshinsky, David Propson, and Michael Woodsworth, as well as Robert Messenger, who recruited me. (My earlier *Sun* pieces are collected in *Natural Selection*.) Several of the director essays were written for *DGA Quarterly* (the "Craft Journal of the Directors Guild of America"), which, as edited by James Greenberg, merits far wider distribution. Much of the material on Orson Welles, Sidney Lumet, and Ingmar Bergman was commissioned, respectively, for *The New York Times Book Review*, by the editor David Kelly; *Film Comment*, by the editor Gavin Smith; and the Criterion Collection, by the editorial director Elizabeth Helfgott. My thanks to all.

Warning Shadows is the second book I've done with my editor Maribeth Payne, and a much easier job than the first. I'm grateful to her for bringing it to Norton, along with everyone else there, especially her editorial assistants past, Imogen Howes, and present, Ariella Foss. I'm pleased to acknowledge production manager Devon Zahn, digital production work by Sue Carlson and Joe Lops, designer Jo Anne Metsch, and managing editor Nancy Palmquist. I am particularly grateful to Susan Gaustad, a wonderful copy editor who left her usual bailiwick in the textbook division to tag my repetitions and suggest several (I'd have written *many*, but she has a thing about that word) nifty solutions.

It is always a pleasure to express gratitude for the guidance and friendship of my agents Georges and Anne Borchardt, and their assistant Barbara Galletly. As this is my first book exclusively devoted to movies, I take the opportunity to thank the people with whom I routinely spend hours talking and arguing about them, Michael Anderson, Steve Futterman, and Mary Cleere Haran; Richard Schickel, from whose books, films, and conversation I've derived more pleasure than I can rightfully say; the late, lamented Alfred Appel Jr., who wore his erudition about everything so lightly that he invariably had me bowled over with laughter; Bertrand Tavernier, whose occasional correspondence invariably leads me to new channels; and Tom Luddy and Gary Meyer, whose inimitable Telluride Film Festival has intensified my immersion in film in the loveliest possible setting. I am grateful to the incredibly big-hearted team of Judy Schmid, who created and maintains garygiddins.com, and Lee Rothchild, who patrols the moat between it and me. Words cannot express my appreciation to CUNY Graduate Center President William Kelly, whose invitation to join his faculty has given me the forum to think and talk through ideas explored here and elsewhere. Little would have gotten written without the due diligence of my pistol-packin' assistant Elora Charles, and the three muses—my daughter Lea Giddins, wife Deborah Halper, and mother Alice Giddins.

GG
New York
September 2009

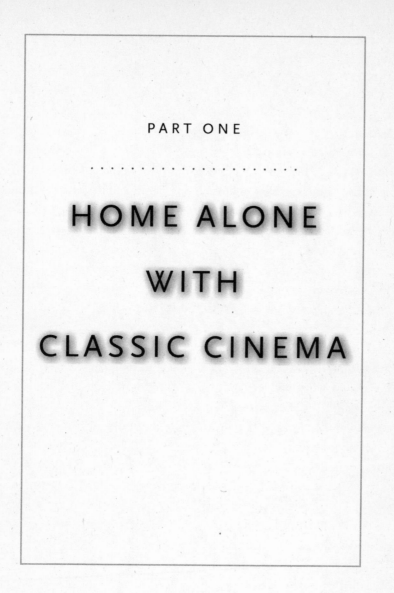

PART ONE

. . . .

HOME ALONE WITH CLASSIC CINEMA

YOU PAYS YOUR MONEY

PROGRESS ISN'T ALWAYS PROGRESS. Twenty-four hundred years of bookmaking have forfeited Codex for Kindle, and library for mail order. Massive advances in audio technology peaked with the acoustic LP only to find a near-universal acceptance of the $300 iPod with $2 earplugs. A century of cinematic exhibition took us from Radio City Music Hall to streaming laptops. In the pursuit of formerly communal entertainments and arts, we have peeled away from the mob, secluding ourselves as isolated spectators. "The huge and heterogeneous crowds" that once assembled in "movie palaces with their majestic marquees climbing five stories high" have, as David Nasaw writes in *Going Out: The Rise and Fall of Public Amusements*, dispersed, engendering a twenty-first-century mode of the gaslight cloister and hearth, when "the home—not the club, the saloon, the firehouse, or the theater—was the heart and soul of middle-class existence."

Those enormous flat video screens that François Truffaut made terrifying and desirable in his 1966 adaptation of Ray Bradbury's *Fahrenheit 451* are now in countless homes. They mesmerize us as shameless neighbors compete shamelessly in the name of "reality"; and Big Brothers on the left and right shout over each other's heads as if they had nothing in common beyond the need to flog consumer goods. Those who use their screens as monitors to watch movies, whether vintage or recently exhibited at the multiplex, and to surf the illusion of the whole webbed world are equally contented to be sheltered from the public square, relinquishing to memory and history the age of stately showplaces and the crowds that filled them. Those who do venture into the public square tend to be young people in pursuit of superheroes borne on special effects, families patiently lined up to sample the homogeneity of theme parks, sports fans, or angry mobs parroting paranoid book/movie plots (the president is *The Kenyan Candidate*, programmed to socialize America; universal health care is *Medical Farm*, complete with bolshie death panels). In the absence of a comprehensive

popular culture, American recreation is an ongoing struggle between the
inclination to go out and stay in. Staying in has had the edge for a long time.

PEEPING

BROADWAY SNAKES PAST 27th Street on one of New York's dodgier merchant strips. Though only a few blocks north of the splendidly open area
that includes Madison Square Park and the insuperable Flatiron Building,
Broadway narrows here, filtering the sun. The chockablock storefronts
are long oblong stalls, most serving as public entrees for wholesale import
businesses operated from offices above: a bazaar of party favors, souvenirs,
designer knockoffs, cut-rate perfumes, scarves, caps, wigs, jewelry. It's an
odd place to find a hotel, the Broadway Plaza, which now occupies 1155
Broadway, its lobby entrance as constricted as that of the neighboring storefronts. No brass plaque adorns its façade to commemorate the event, and
yet this particular site marks a significant episode in American cultural history. Here, on April 14, 1894, the commercial cinema was born.

Thomas Edison had begun working toward the pictorial equivalent of
his phonograph in 1887, having moved his operation to a plant in West
Orange, New Jersey. He assigned the problem to his assistant W. K. L.
Dickson, who within two years produced a device that could capture
and reproduce images from life—nothing more, at first, than vague appa-
ritions barely coalescing from the electrical ether, like warnings of life
about to be born. Indeed, the title *Warning Shadows*, appropriated from a
little-remembered marvel of German Expressionism made by an American director, Arthur Robison, living in Berlin (see Part Three), alludes to
a far older phenomenon: Plato's shadows in the cave, the eternal dichotomy between life as lived and projected—for what are movies but light
and shadow thrown upon a wall? By 1891, those images had become startlingly distinct: Dickson waving his hat in welcome, an assistant sneez-
ing, Eugen Sandow the muscleman flexing, dancers and boxers and circus
performers cavorting, a blacksmith at work. Dickson designed a building
to shoot films: the first movie studio, called the Black Maria, as dark and
forbidding from the outside as a paddy wagon. Celebrities postured in its
darkness to win a new kind of immortality.

Unable to project the images for a crowd, Edison perfected a peephole
machine, which he called a kinetoscope, or kinetograph. In 1893, his dem-

onstration of the prototype enchanted a group of businessmen who lined up to look into the eyepiece and see moving pictures, fluid as life: a wondrous amusement in an age starved for amusement. Within a year, the Edison Manufacturing Company licensed the Kinetoscope Company, a subordinate syndicate, to distribute the first twenty-five models: five to Atlantic City, ten to Chicago, and ten to a vacated shoe store at 1155 Broadway—at that time a Neo-Grec, three-story building, erected in the 1870s (it survived intact until the early 1990s), at the hub of New York's business and entertainment district.

On Saturday, April 14, 1894, as other members of the syndicate lounged in the store, smoking cigars, the brothers Andrew and Edwin Holland, who had worked with Edison on the phonograph, labored to get the place ready for the big opening on the following Monday. It's not hard, even now, to peer into the Broadway Plaza's entryway and imagine how it looked on that day: a bust of Edison in the window, floors waxed to a shine, the walls decorously lined with potted palms on pedestals, two dragon-shaped incandescent lights hovering from the ceiling, and, in the center, two back-to-back banks of five kinetoscopes, guarded by brass rails. Unlike the earlier phonographic salons, which offered free entry and nickel machines, the kinetoscope parlor charged 25 cents admission, for which customers could lean over a rail and peep at each of five moving pictures. For an additional quarter, they could see the other five. The higher price signaled a desire for respectable clientele, including "ladies." With all in readiness that Saturday, the men thought it would be a fine joke to admit the few gawkers milling outside, and collect enough money to buy a fancy dinner. They had as well opened the door to Oz: the ever escalating crowd kept them occupied until 1:00 A.M.

In 1895, kinetoscope parlors flourished around the country, while attempts were made to liberate moving pictures from the wooden box and isolating eyepiece. Edison would announce his Vitascope projector in 1896. But he had been beaten to the punch. In France, the Lumière brothers, Louis and Auguste, inspired by Edison, introduced a portable hand-cranked camera, called the Cinematograph, that could project images on a screen. In March 1895, they gave a demonstration of footage taken at their factory; on December 28, they presented a twenty-minute exhibition before thirty-three paying customers, at what must be accounted the world's first provisional movie theater—the Indian Salon, located in the basement of Paris's Grand Café.

That should have marked the fast demise of the peep show. The novelty was wearing off anyway, and neither Edison nor his increasing number of competitors could produce enough new and better films to draw crowds. Yet peep shows continued to dominate the new business for nearly a decade, now configured as coin-operated gizmos. The American Mutoscope and Biograph Company, which had recruited Dickson after he quarreled with Edison, played it both ways—screening and peeping. The premiere of the first all-Biograph program, screened at New York's Olympia Theater in 1896, with pictures like "Stable on Fire" and "Joseph Jefferson in a Scene from Rip Van Winkle," was a triumph complete with a Republican flag-waving demonstration to greet the image of its presidential candidate in "Major McKinley at Home."

The same company also introduced a rival to the kinetoscope, the coin-operated mutoscope, a hand-cranked machine in which each frame of a film was printed on a separate card. Turning the crank was like thumbing the pages of a flipbook. As the flow of pictures could be manipulated, the mutoscope became associated with mildly salacious material. In effect, it offered the 1890s equivalent of slo-mo and fast forward, and was immensely popular. Movie screenings, on the other hand, took place in various converted venues, usually as special events; many people, especially women, were afraid to enter a dark room that was lighted only by a flickering image. Penny arcades decided the issue: they became a huge business, as kinetoscopes and mutoscopes easily outperformed other mechanical diversions—fortune-tellers, weigh scales, candy dispensers, boardwalk games—in well-lighted, well-appointed emporiums. Some of these arcades were operated by the very men who later became Hollywood moguls.

Yet no entrepreneur thought to open a dedicated motion picture theater in the United States until 1905, when John Harris and Harry Davis converted a Pittsburgh store, installing 100 seats and projecting an uninterrupted daily showcase of moving pictures in surroundings no less reputable than those of a vaudeville house. They charged a nickel admission and called the place a nickelodeon. The movies had gone public. In 1907, *The Saturday Evening Post* estimated some 5,000 nickelodeons in operation, entertaining 2 million customers a day, a third of them children. That same year, Edison hired David Wark Griffith as an actor, who insisted on using a pseudonym so as not to damage his prospective reputation on the stage. Still, the furtive kick of the peep show refused to die.

The first time I saw Lon Chaney unmasked as *The Phantom of the Opera* was in a kinetoscope on Disneyland's Main Street. This was 1961, when a penny was worth the stooping and penny arcades had not yet morphed into pinball outlets, let alone video-powered Playlands. Shortly before that West Coast trip, I had found a marvelous penny arcade underground, in the subway at 42nd Street and Eighth Avenue. This arcade, which also sold stacks of 1940s and 1950s paperbacks and had machines that dispensed purplish-tinted, heavy-stock cards of cowboy stars unknown to me and my friends (usually signed "Cordially": Cordially, Johnny Mack Brown; Cordially, Bob Steele; Cordially, Ken Maynard), offered a row of mutoscopes that cranked scenes from ancient Westerns. Boring as they might have been on a thirty-foot screen, they were made compulsive by the act of peeping. A few years later, we found other peepshows on 42nd Street, women writhing on beds in their underwear, occasionally topless. This was the era of films about nudists playing shuffleboard, when true pornography was illegal, and the only use for cinema's first means of exhibition, beyond Disney nostalgia, relied on relatively innocuous voyeurism. Not even Edison could have imagined the trillions of nickels to be generated decades later by the brazenly ravenous appetites of peeping laptops.

SCREENING

DURING THE NICKELODEON era, most theaters were little more than adapted storefronts, but the fare, which had ranged from the marvelously frightening (a gunman shooting right at you) to the vaguely embarrassing (a middle-aged couple nuzzling), quickly took on complicated means of storytelling—not only Westerns, damsels in distress, and insanely chaotic comedies, but also public domain classics (Shakespeare and Jesus without words), delirious special effects, and stars: famous ones and movie-made ones, beginning with "the Biograph Girl," who in 1910 was hired away by Carl Laemmle and promoted by name—Florence Lawrence. In this period, 1905–15, the movies became a prime destination for going out. In the *Saturday Evening Post* article mentioned above, Joseph Medill Patterson, who went on to found the New York *Daily News*, wrote: "To-day the moving-picture machine cannot be overlooked as an effective protagonist of democracy. For through it the drama, always a big fact in the lives of the people at the top, is now becoming a big fact in the lives of the people at the bottom." The bottom was doing quite well: it had Charlie Chaplin.

D. W. Griffith's *The Birth of a Nation* (1915) wasn't the first feature-length film—that distinction probably belongs to Australia and Charles Tait's 1906 *The Story of the Kelly Gang.* Enrico Guazzoni's Italian-made *Quo Vadis* and Helen Gardner's *Cleopatra* (Gardner operated her own film studio with her husband along New York's Hudson River, and played the leading roles) were released in 1912—Griffith himself had made the hour-long *Judith of Bethulia*, in 1914. But *The Birth of a Nation* ran three hours, and its achievement, no less epically ambitious than its title, employed and surpassed every technique he had devised and perfected in the nearly 500 Biograph shorts he had made since parting with Edison. Its jubilant premiere, hailed by President Wilson despite its appalling racism and wretched account of history (many theater owners refused to show it), meant that nickelodeons could no longer encompass the movies.

Movies were now the most spectacular and expensive form of entertainment ever created. The shadows were bigger than life, not merely warnings of things to come, but rather prognostic, even prescriptive visions of how to act and dress and part your hair. They represented impulses beyond the courage and imagination of their audiences and required suitable structures to house them—nothing less than palaces, erected when American builders attempted to marry the geometrical opulence of art deco to the cheesier instincts of classical revivalism, which in picture-theater aesthetics included Mayan, Egyptian, Spanish, Chinese, and every other storybook style known to man. The grandest of them were sui generis cinematic churches, complete with balconies, organ lofts, and militarily outfitted ushers as sextons. Programs were distributed and souvenir booklets sold along with refreshments. Men were often directed to piss and smoke in subterranean closets, but women were invited to powder their noses in carpeted drawing rooms with mirrors, draperies, davenports, writing desks, telephones, and decorative sculpture. Ceilings had domes, roofs had minarets, screens had curtains, and pits had orchestras or chamber groups. The acoustics were as carefully designed as the sightlines. The chandeliered lobbies were grander than the halls of any exclusive club. Dozens of these theaters survived, neglected and run down, into the 1960s and 1970s, at which time most of those that weren't demolished were partitioned into multiplexes. Nothing in the history of America's long disregard for its schizophrenic architectural style is more disheartening than the wanton destruction of these magnificent tributes to art and monopoly.

The vast majority of picture theaters found a middle ground between Vatican excess and storefront efficiency, as they spread into every community. In violation of antitrust laws, the studios owned most of the theater chains, ensuring distribution of their product while minimizing competition from independent filmmakers and other upstarts. What a business!—production, distribution, promotion, and exhibition in very few hands. By 1929, in the United States alone, 95 million people—more than 75 percent of the population—watched movies each week in 23,000 theaters, almost all of which had recently converted their equipment to play talkies. Things could only get worse, and they did, beginning with the stock market crash and gathering steam with the rapid advances made by radio, which, beyond the purchase price (available on the installment plan), provided unlimited hours of free entertainment. Who needs pictures? Imagination's the thing. By 1935, more than two-thirds of American homes had radios, while the number of movie screens had diminished by a third.

The content of films had also changed. Movies talked, sang, and danced, with camerawork that was mobile and daring. Some were shot in Technicolor, a process that divided primary colors into discrete celluloid strips that, combined, practically vibrated off the screen; others emphasized extreme contrasts between radiant light and darkest pitch. They featured more stars than there were in heaven, including a few raided from radio. But the enforcement of the Production Code, ardently supported by the Catholic Church, mandated new rules amounting to rank censorship. From 1935 to 1938, the No. 1 box-office attraction was Shirley Temple, succeeded in 1939–41 by Mickey Rooney—the age of the precocious child. Thanks for the memories and farewell, Marlene Dietrich and Mae West.

The more ornate movie theaters had always offered live entertainment as well as the picture show. They continued to present second-rank vaudevillians and local talent in smaller venues, and prominent big bands, comedians, singers, and dancers in the palaces. The average theater devised more mundane bribes, including hams, dishes, twofers, and lotteries (a quarter of American movie theaters subscribed to Bank Night). The most durable incentive was the double feature—the addition of a low-budget B movie that occasionally had more snap and bite than the main, star-studded studio attraction. Double and even triple features, further enhanced by cartoons, travelogs, comedy or mystery or educational shorts, and trailers, became the normative way of seeing movies well into the 1950s. Two other moviegoing habits also remained fairly constant. Since the shows ran uninterrupted, as in nickelodeon days, people got into the habit of dropping in at any time and staying until the scene at which they entered replayed. At the same time, the studios created a hierarchy of distribution: a major film would open in a major city, gather reviews and word of mouth, and weeks or months later spread into the neighborhoods, where tickets were cheaper. By the 1960s, however, all was in flux as the studios went on the auction block.

TELEVISING

MOVIE MOGULS FEARED television even more than they had radio. The studios had ultimately made a lucrative peace with radio, after first trying to ignore it and banning its contract players from appearing on it. At some point, the public relations wizards realized that having a star promote a new film on, say, Bing Crosby's *Kraft Music Hall* (especially given Crosby's simultaneous status as a champion box-office movie star), with its tens of millions of faithful listeners, was more efficient than full-page ads in the *New York Times* and the *Los Angeles Times* combined and squared. The studios soon pleaded for radio time. They commissioned radio versions of hit scripts, with top stars repeating or taking over the lead roles. You'd think there would have been no hesitation in recognizing and seizing upon the even greater synchronicity of television, which metastasized faster than radio and required no imagination whatsoever. Instead, television was regarded as a new enemy, but not the main enemy. That role was played by the Supreme Court, which on May 15, 1948, declared that the five major studios were guilty of a monopolistic conspiracy to control film exhibition and impose block booking (sort of like Microsoft bundling stuff that no one wants onto hard drives), forcing them to accept a Consent Decree that meant selling off all their theaters—a boon to smaller studios and independents, and a spur toward freelancing by actors, directors, producers, and everyone else who had been indentured servants to the studios' infamous seven-year contracts.

The timing could not have been worse. Just three weeks after the court handed down its 7–1 decision, *Texaco Star Theater* (a radio staple with various hosts) made its Tuesday night NBC television debut, starring the peculiarly radio-frosty but telegenically warm Milton Berle. In early 1948, prime time was literally a wasteland, its broadcast hours desperately filled with quiz shows, wrestling, boxing, and basketball, often going dark by 10:00 P.M. Berle helped change that: within months, the number of households with television sets rose from a low six figures to 2 million. If that wasn't enough, the studios simultaneously knuckled before the House Un-American Activities Committee (Orwell couldn't have invented a better parody-proof name), sacrificing irreplaceable talent and ensuring a blandness in its A (but not B) product that Technicolor, Eastmancolor, Cinerama (an anagram of American, as the Scottish critic Gilbert Adair noticed), VistaVision, Cinemascope, 3-D, Todd-AO, Smell-o-vision, stereo, and other technological contributions, sublime or ludicrous, could not entirely counteract.

Television, however, gave the studios a long-term gift: the knowledge that their back catalogs were good as oil. If Hollywood was slow to pick up on TV production, several entrepreneurs realized that given the rush to fill broadcasting hours, nothing was more reliable and cost-effective than old movies. The movies of your youth—in your own home—for free, except for the cost in time consumed by commercial interruptions. Before television, movies had been rereleased to theaters, often as the bottom half of a double bill, but only those with profitable track records. Television could afford to be less discriminating.

It is no accident that the postwar baby boom produced enough film makers, critics, historians, biographers, teachers, and other obsessive fans to populate Rhode Island and then some. No other generation, before or after, was inundated with old movies all day, every day. Packages of Warner classics landed at one network or syndicate, RKOs at another, MGMs, Paramounts, and Columbias at others. Laurel and Hardy, Hopalong Cassidy, and Farmer Gray (aka Farmer Al Falfa) and their contemporaries enjoyed second acts that, for all the children of the 1950s knew, were first acts. *Million Dollar Movie* showed the same film sixteen times a week, creating nine-year-olds who could quote more lines from the scripts than the scriptwriters. *Shock Theater* indemnified horror as the most reliably lucrative of film genres. NBC's *Saturday Night at the Movies* revived movies not yet a decade old, including Alfred Hitchcock's *Vertigo*, which had died in theaters and is now routinely included on best-ever lists.

True, the films were almost always butchered, often to the point of incoherence. Yet the numberless glitches simply made the process of rediscovering them later in revivals and on home video more enthralling. Movies and television were ever intertwined. Not surprisingly, videotape, introduced in the late 1970s, took off—despite the VHS versus Betamax format war—almost immediately. The ability to own thousands of movies, uncut if often reformatted to fit the size of a television screen, created a new breed of collector, and helped kill off the art house and revivalist film circuits. For the first time, you could walk into the cinematic equivalent of a bookstore or record store, and peruse and partake in the history of movies.

At the same time, cable stations took up the slack of broadcasting old films—a custom abandoned by the networks, which had turned against black and white and anything else that wasn't au courant. The most important new channels were created by the Southern news magnate Ted Turner, and though he initially reaped deserved scorn for colorizing movies, he won cinematic immortality for programming pre-Code and silent pictures in addition to the usual classics on TNT, which led to the purest of movie channels, the commercial-free TCM. (The once equally beloved AMC, with its access to the Paramount archive and its annual Film Preservation Festivals, went down the drain of mediocre films, reformatted prints, and endless commercials, Mad Men notwithstanding.) Videotape allowed you to tape movies, along with everything else on television. The generation of young cineastes who had matured from Million Dollar Movie to the contemplation of filmographies in Andrew Sarris's enlightening text The American Cinema (1968) could now line up most of those films on their bookshelves. Amazing.

DIGITIZING

THE WAY MOVIES are shown affects our perception of them and the way they are made. The kinetoscope, nickelodeon, and palace altered the scope and ambition of movies as much as the introduction of sound and color. Television exerted no less influence. It helped to kill off the Production Code, as there was little beyond sex, nudity, extreme bloodletting, and overripe spectacle that movies could offer as a lure to get people out of their homes. Accordingly, the prime era of videotape, the 1980s and early 1990s, witnessed a startling upswing in the fortunes of public exhibition, which, for the first time since the crash, found the number of theaters rise beyond the 20,000 mark.

Television's influence went further. It reduced attention spans, so that filmmaking became obsessed with constant editing and close-ups, strenuously ominous music scores, bone-crunching sound effects, over-the-shoulder dialogues instead of medium-range two shots. Beginning in the early 1950s, the movies had increasingly gone widescreen, and television didn't know what to do about that: audiences didn't take to the idea of pictures smaller than their television screens as the price of replicating the widescreen aspect ratio. Stations would letterbox only the opening credits, followed by a full-frame format that either omitted the left and right sides of the picture or panned and scanned it—refilming within the original frame. Filmmakers began directing pictures so that they could be matted for wide-screen presentation in theaters and shown full-frame (with more information at the top and bottom) on television. Meanwhile, the decline of the revival circuit and the ready availability on videotape of foreign language films limited the ambitions of exhibitors. The audience for subtitled movies all but disappeared.

The new studios, bearing the brand names of the old studios while serving primarily as deal makers and distributors, focused on blockbusters for their most reliable audience: teenagers with an insatiable demand for the faux-Homeric pretensions of science fiction epics and live-action comic books. The sex and nudity were modified, the violence ramped up. By 2008, widescreen had conquered the format issue, to the degree that all flat-screen televisions were manufactured in imitation of the moviegoing experience. The Truffaut/Bradbury future had been first broached with the introduction of digitized music and images on video discs. The impact of the laser disc proved dramatically out of proportion to its market share. The LD was too expensive to gain a mass audience on the order of videotape, though it might have had a shot if it had been recordable. Yet for the first time, stay-at-home movie fans could watch films with remarkably precise images—60 percent sharper than videotape—in an accurately matted widescreen format with surround sound. As multiplex screens shrank and television screens grew, the line between movie theater and home theater narrowed. Videotape created collectors; laser discs created connoisseurs. Film lovers caught in the laser frenzy spoke McLuhan-like about the tactility of the image: the brilliance, the sensuousness, the movieness of movies, including bad ones. If a film *looked* good enough, maybe it wasn't so bad after all. In the initial blush of digitization, *Citizen Kane* and *Abbott and Costello Meet Frankenstein* weren't exactly equals—just brothers under the skin.

Lasers also pioneered enhancements to film literacy that carried over to

its successor, DVD, which did achieve mass appeal. Like the screenings of
the Depression, lasers usually came larded with extras, beginning with the
package—a twelve-inch jacket (the same as for the old vinyl LP) with artfully, often exuberantly designed cover graphics. The collectible jackets functioned like posters and lobby cards, telegraphing the pleasures to be found
on the disc, which, in addition to the movie, included a dizzying variety of
supplements, sometimes requiring not a jacket but a thick carton to contain
them. The quality of the film did not necessarily dictate the number of extras.
Africa Screams, another Abbott and Costello opus, came annotated with production history, outtakes, still photos, and publicity montages. *Gettysburg*,
a film made for television but given a limited theatrical run by Ted Turner
before airing on TNT, came in a long ("director's") cut with maps, essays,
eight-by-ten glossies of relevant generals, a pouch containing an "authentic
Civil War bullet," a CD of the score, a 130-page "leather-bound" companion
book, and the sentiment that "in some small way," this project might "bind
us together as a people." Other laser discs included complete scripts (each
page still-framed) or audio commentaries by directors and stars.

Most extras were designed to bring the audience into the filmmaking
process, turning us all into film students. We were now privy to material
once discarded to the cutting-room floor, alternate endings, how-to featurettes, and personality tributes. In a television interview, the great director Jean Renoir once apologized for the vulgarity of bringing up a technical
issue, which should be of no interest to the audience and might even mar
its absorption in his film. By the 1990s, when DVDs came along, consumers
practically demanded access to the set: Hollywood filmmakers heard the
siren call and began shooting supplemental featurettes during production.
By 2003, laser discs were long dead and DVDs outsold VHS tapes. Oddly,
for all its commercial success—or maybe because of it—DVD proved less
audacious in its ambitions than lasers, which had a more ardently collector-
oriented following. Political correctness filtered cartoons and blackface performers, while commercial dictates and legal complications did as much for
Vitagraph shorts, dozens of cult films, the complete Betty Boop, and even
(as of fall 2009) Orson Welles's *The Magnificent Ambersons*. The last had been
a highlight of the Criterion Collection, a project introduced in 1984, which
helped launch laser discs with its creative dedication, subsequently maintained for its state-of-the-art DVDs and high-definition Blu-rays.

Introduced in collaboration by Sony, Philips, and Panasonic in 2006,

Blu-ray is the new industry standard, providing the crispest picture ever, bringing to life previously lost extras in distant crowd scenes and overemphasizing rouge and powder to the point that Technicolored women often look ripe as fruit. Impressive as it is, Blu-ray has had a disappointing rollout. The declining economy is surely part of the problem: the new system demands of consumers that they buy a new machine, a high-definition television, and pay more for individual discs—a factor that, even among converts, discourages collecting in favor of renting. But research also shows that potential customers don't believe Blu-ray is a sufficiently dramatic step beyond DVD, or that it will be around very long, given the proliferation of format changes and format battles. They may be right. The studios are trying to perfect online streaming so that movies can be quickly and accurately downloaded to computers, and protected so that they can be copied only once to disc; a more likely alternative notion is to have computers wired to televisions—the latest generation of Blu-ray players are already outfitted with wireless Internet connections. No one knows how this will play out or how long it will take. In an era of pay-per-view movies on television, streaming movies—especially if they are synched with theatrical distribution—will requite the demand for instant gratification while bypassing retail middlemen, providing yet another incentive to stay home.

LAUGHTER AND TEARS

THE DVD ERA, which the essays in this book represent, doesn't exactly complete a circle begun with the kinetoscope. The latter required a stroll into town, and permitted only one solitary viewer at a time. Most DVDs are watched by couples, families, or gatherings of friends. Yet these relatively small circles have a closer connection to the isolation of the middle-class home, with its genteel entertainments, than the emotionally charged convergence of strangers at the Roxy. Have we traded up or down or laterally? If we long ago abandoned the habit of the weekly or twice-weekly visit to the movies, we now have a library of cinema; though hundreds of major films have yet to be released in any home video format, the available and growing selection is greater than most of us can accommodate meaningfully in a lifetime, even if we are paid to do nothing else.

During the early years of talking movies, the moguls thought that their silent archives were largely worthless, and that even the newest films—

including the hits, the prize winners—would have a limited shelf life. The wily old wizard of Paramount Pictures, Adolph Zukor, started out with penny arcades in 1903; he liked the idea of a business where you could keep charging for the same product, nickel after nickel, but he also knew that the product had to be constantly replaced. When the nickelodeon opened two years later, he wasted no time installing a projector in one of his arcades. Soon he teamed with Marcus Loew to create a huge theatrical chain. Then he moved on to distribution, then to production, creating Famous Players, which became Paramount, with its famous logo of a mountain peak rising beyond the clouds. He called his memoir *The Public Is Never Wrong*, but he didn't care about the public or movies, except as a game that allowed him to exercise his acumen as a businessman, a strategist, a power player. If he facilitated art, so be it, but he knew little of art and probably would have empathized with teenagers who won't watch black and white, let alone silent movies—relics of yesterday.

If DVDs testify to the endurance of cinema as art, they also underscore the differences between movie art and literature and music. Bad books become unreadable and bad music unlistenable. But many if not most bad movies, even some that were unwatchable in their initial release and for decades later, in the fullness of time become curios that allow us mild pleasures of performance, photography, dialogue, costume, set design, and documentary evidence of another age—not because the movies show us the way the world really was but because it lays bare the way it imagined itself to be. Genuine realism is also a bonus factor in the joy of excavating old movies, going back to the long-vanished locations in Brooklyn or Los Angeles captured inadvertently as the background for knockabout comedies. Bad films are often endurable in the way badly written novels aren't. In 1901, the ingenious cameraman Billy Bitzer, D. W. Griffith's right-hand man, attached a camera to the rear of a moving train and got a stunning three-minute shot of an entire Western community ("The Georgetown Loop"). Bitzer's impulse was the same as that of every child and tourist who ever took a camera onboard a train or plane, hoping to personally, permanently capture the details of everyday life.

Classic cinema is thus sometimes indistinguishable from old cinema, which is not to say that greatness is up for grabs or that discrimination plays any less of a role in evaluating movies than it does other arts; only that the standards are gentler and more flexible. Films once dismissed as routine now sometimes seem genuinely revelatory. Movies made an art of melo-drama and genre, and the passing decades are a boon to the appreciation of stylistic nuance that gives certain melodramas and genre pieces the heft of individuality. DVD has documented, in impeccable form, genuine interna-tional classics (as in the Criterion Collection), lost and forgotten silent mas-terpieces (as in the Kino Video catalog), and Hollywood staples and B films deserving reevaluation (as in the Warner Bros., 20th Century Fox, and other studio series). The more we watch, the more we are drawn into the essence of cinema, which includes overlooked and ridiculed works, as well as films that once played better than they do now. (Did people really laugh at Rich-ard Quine's strenuously witless *The Notorious Landlady* in 1962? Did they really dismiss as routine André de Toth's masterly evisceration of Nazism *None Shall Escape* in 1944? Significantly, the latter is not, as of this writing, on DVD; the list of unreleased gems is very long and very frustrating.)

DVD, and the home circle that circumscribes it, affects even our appre-hension of the acknowledged classics. The big loser is comedy. Laughter is augmented in a group—as though each individual wants to advertise his or her involvement in and understanding of the joke, creating a virtual pride of hilarity. Tears, on the other hand, embarrass us; yet the kind of button pushing that elicits them remains impervious to solitude. Comedy needs company, weeping doesn't. No one comprehended this better than Charlie Chaplin, who recognized that cinema isn't the natural habitat of classical comedy and tragedy, but was born for banana peel comedy and sentimental drama, which can be just as potent a mixture.

No popular artist since Shakespeare achieved greater universal renown than Sir Charles Spencer Chaplin Jr. (1889–1977), primarily for his enduring alter ego, the Tramp: the relentlessly caricatured and mimicked little man with big sensitive eyes, unruly hair, and square mustache, dressed in frayed black derby and tailcoat, ballooning trousers and oversized shoes, twirling a pliant cane as he saunters, herky-jerky and splayfooted, down a dirt road toward an unpromising horizon. As the centenary of his first one-reel shorts approaches (2014), Chaplin seems safely installed in the pantheon of immor-tals, yet like Shakespeare, his legacy increasingly belongs to the thinner if still populous ranks of the educated. In 2009, Warner Bros. and the French company MK2, which issued magnificent DVDs of the ten feature films and seven shorter films he made between 1918 and 1957 (sumptuously trans-ferred and supplemented by hours of ancillary footage from Chaplin's own archive), took a page in *Variety* to boast of 3.5 million in sales. Still, he must be sought out or "taught," along with his more arcane cinematic contemporaries, including Carl Dreyer and Jean Cocteau (both born the same year as Chaplin). Chaplin's art illuminates the virtues and vices of the DVD, which delivers his work into our hands to a degree unimagined by previous generations, while making impossible the theatrical experiences where collective laughter waxes in a ringing assault on the absurd and unjust.

With *The Kid*, in 1921, Chaplin invented a new kind of film—a new kind of art that balanced farce and drama, slapstick and tears, triumph and anguish. He was warned that he was courting disaster, that people came to see the Tramp to laugh, not to cry, and that if he made them cry, he wouldn't be able to get them to do a turnabout and laugh again. He concocted a customary plot for *The Kid*. The Tramp, saddled with an orphan, played by the implausibly adorable and talented six-year-old Jackie Coogan, finds love and purpose by taking responsibility for the boy, and battling social guardians to keep him. For seven reels, incidents of astonishing, resourceful comic irreverence (the Tramp teaches the kid various scams) are interrupted by scenes of wracking pathos. Sir Richard Attenborough (speaking in Richard Schickel's 2003 film *Charlie: The Life and Art of Charles Chaplin*) observes that with *The Kid* Chaplin denied viewers "the choice" to laugh or cry—"he took control of me."

Chaplin understood as well as Griffith that the hallmarks of melodrama—a sinkhole of clichés, chases, sentimentality, and happy endings, held in low repute by serious artists—could be fine-tuned as the basis for empowering cinematic expression. Chaplin, however, could do what Griffith couldn't: check the melodrama with ingenious comedy. And he could do what slapstick master Mack Sennett couldn't: check the comedy with affecting drama. If Chaplin's greatness as director-writer-actor-producer-editor-composer can be summed up in one word, it might be *balance*. He peerlessly weighs the scales of laughter and tears, while avoiding gross mawkishness and routine pratfalls. His masterpiece, *City Lights* (1931, and another presumed folly, coming four years after the synchronized dialogue of *The Jazz Singer*), is the ultimate example, effortlessly switching gears between inspired black comedy (involving attempted suicide, boxing, brutality, and jail) and the heartbreaking glare of reality: one of the screen's supreme comedies sends the audience home dabbing its eyes.

The poet Guillaume Apollinaire told the pioneering French filmmaker

Georges Méliès, whose creative period began in the Edison peep-show era and ended during the height of the nickelodeon, "You and I are in the same business—we both try to lend enchantment to vulgar material." *City Lights* is so enchanted it can withstand the viewer's solitude. But only in a crowd is the viewer borne away on waves of joy and sorrow and recognition. Chaplin was so sure of the crowd that when he made *Limelight*, in 1952, he presented the climactic comedy routine, performed by Chaplin's character, Calvero, and his partner—played by Buster Keaton—on a music hall stage, without recording the attendant laughter of the music hall audience. He believed that movie audiences would provide that laughter, and they did. Watching that scene on DVD is an unsettlingly quiet experience. DVDs allow us to see thousands of movies at will, and to see them repeatedly, stopping or jumping ahead to savor certain scenes, to form a bond of intimacy with movies that was previously limited to a small group of obsessive film lovers. Yet DVD and Blu-ray, however eye-popping, remain substitutes for the intended experience. We are at home alone with the movies, and progress is in the eye of the beholder.

PART TWO

DIRECTORS AND STARS

1

TOUCHED BY ERNST LUBITSCH

IF ERNST LUBITSCH had been conceived with "the Lubitsch touch," he might have looked like Cary Grant, spoken like Herbert Marshall, and moved like Fred Astaire. No such luck: Maurice Chevalier, an actor virtually remade by that touch, recalled him as a "droll, cigar-smoking cherub"—a kinder description than many. Dark and dumpy, Lubitsch had piercing eyes and an ironclad smirk welded around his omnipresent cigar. Renowned for directing large and small roles alike by precisely miming the desired gestures, he waddled when he walked and was thought to be generally clumsy.

Yet he invented a comprehensively detailed fantasyland occupied almost exclusively by adults, many of them attractive and sexually gifted, who glide stylishly through life, speaking softly and carrying a large repartee. As his characters make their way from one boudoir to another, balancing as best they can the distinction between seduction and love, romance and responsibility, we never feel that Lubitsch is envious or disapproving of his characters. If we could vacation in the films of any director, we might well choose his, if only for the clothes. As timeless as it is imaginary, Lubitsch's world is an outpost located somewhere between Ruritania and Hollywood, dotted with Epcot-like villages called Paris, Budapest, and Venice that are no more or less real than Sylvania—the setting for his first talkie, *The Love Parade* (1929).

In that film, Chevalier's lusty soldier pretends to explain why his accent is so very "Fraaanch," unlike that of other Sylvanians, as represented by the patrician Jeannette MacDonald (her film debut), the eccentric cockney dancer Lupino Lane, and the precocious Broadway babe Lillian Roth (all of seventeen). Chevalier's thoroughly facetious and pointless explanation is a rare acknowledgment of illogicality in an oeuvre that usually dispenses with rationalizations, apologies, or justifications of any kind. In *Trouble in Paradise* (1932), for example, the central figures are a couple of thieves and their semi-willing dupe; the leading men in *Design for Living* (1933) consent to a semi-chaste ménage à trios with the leading lady; the hero of *Heaven Can Wait* (1943) recounts to Satan stories of his unquenchable lust and is rejected from hell for having enjoyed life too much. Laughing well is the best revenge, and who's complaining?

But many did complain, never more vociferously than when Lubitsch unveiled his 1942 masterpiece *To Be or Not to Be*, a near-slapstick romance set against the Nazi invasion of Poland and starring Jack Benny and Carole Lombard. Decades passed before film lovers could agree that this burlesque was, in its way, as trenchant as the usual depiction of goose-stepping monsters and slaughtered innocents. Mockery and contempt aren't the least effective responses to absolute evil, and a Hitler who says "Heil myself" puts barbarity in perspective, at least to the degree that those who don't enjoy life enough are unlikely to value the lives of others. Lubitsch was nothing if not a humanist— the *pater familias* in a small pantheon that includes Jean Renoir, Leo McCarey, Yasujirō Ozu, Max Ophuls, and Carl Dreyer among its leading lights.

Lubitsch, the son of a successful Berlin haberdasher, was born in 1892, and found his way to Max Reinhardt's theatrical company as a teenager, playing a hunchbacked carnival clown avenging the murder of a dancing girl in an Arabian harem pantomime. Over the next few years, he starred in several short films as the stereotypical Jewish schlemiel, invariably saving the day. In 1918, he began to direct movies, starring Pola Negri, that combined melodrama, impish humor, and a sharp eye for the way cinematic storytelling proceeds from meticulous staging and rhythmic editing. Kino has issued splendid prints of several of these films, including *Sumurun* (1920), Lubitsch's adaptation of Reinhardt's harem ballet, reprising his role as the hunchback—his farewell to acting.

Kino's other titles are more indicative of his increasingly stylish and mocking social criticism: *The Oyster Princess* (1919), *Anna Boleyn* (1920), and especially *The Doll* (1919), which opens with Lubitsch constructing a dollhouse that turns into the actual film set, just as the mechanical doll at the heart of the story becomes a genuine woman. In 1922, Mary Pickford brought "the European Griffith," as he was called, to Hollywood, though she fought with him while making *Rosita*. It hardly mattered: Lubitsch took to America like bratwurst to cabbage. Charming everyone but Pickford, from actors to studio heads, he set out to raise the bar for sophistication. From 1924 through 1928, he attained new heights in a series of romantic comedies that, as Renoir observed, reinvented Hollywood with continental panache. Among these films (presently unavailable on DVD), two of the most ingenious are adaptations of Oscar Wilde's epigrammatic play *Lady Windermere's Fan* and Sigmund Romberg's operetta *The Student Prince*, each enhanced with emotional truths in the absence of the factors—wry dialogue and chest-thumping songs—that made the originals famous.

In 1929, Lubitsch embarked on a quartet of musicals for Paramount, now collected in a Criterion DVD set: *The Love Parade, Monte Carlo, The Smiling Lieutenant,* and *One Hour with You.* If the first is the most static, it is also the most prescient. At a time when film musicals were inert revues, often with a single unmoving camera facing the proscenium, and songs were recorded live on the set, crippling movement and spontaneity, Lubitsch created a fluid, funny gambol in which songs emanate from the story. These four musicals and a fifth, *The Merry Widow*, made at MGM in 1934 and the most gracefully polished of all, track his growing command of sound. Even *Monte Carlo*, the weakest of the lot owing to Jack Buchanan's ineffectual giggling in the kind of role elsewhere allotted to Chevalier, has an enchanting scene as Jeannette MacDonald sings "Beyond the Blue Horizon" emoting from a train window and accompanied by the train's whistle and chugging rhythms.

Yet if Lubitsch showed that sound did not have to demote cinema from visual poetry to mere theatrical documentation, he also proved that the lessons of the silent era remained indispensable. The Lubitsch touch is exemplified in the opening episode of *The Love Parade*. We see a closed door and hear an argument. Chevalier walks through the door and addresses us directly: "She's terribly jealous." A woman enters after him, holding aloft a telltale garter. She lifts her skirt to show her own garters in place, and then pulls from her purse a pistol. Suddenly, her husband bursts in, and she fires into her own chest. The distraught husband retrieves the pistol and fires at Chevalier, who, finding no holes in his body, gallantly attempts to help the husband, pointing out that the gun isn't loaded. They turn to the wife, now watching them from a prone position. The husband is so relieved he forgets his anger and takes her home. Chevalier shrugs and drops the pistol in a desk drawer, which is filled with a dozen similar weapons. Virtually every shot, master or insert, adds to the joke, and it is all played out in nearly complete silence.

In 1932, Lubitsch made his first nonmusical talkie masterpiece, *Trouble in Paradise* (also available from Criterion), which begins with another unforgettable silent bit, a garbage man hauling trash into a gondola—Lubitsch's way of telling us we are in Venice. Herbert Marshall and Miriam Hopkins play thieves who fall in love while conning each other. They target a wealthy heiress played by the inimitably lisping Kay Francis: "You are vewy, vewy clever," she tells Marshall, who seduces her while we watch a clock for more than a minute as time passes in successive dissolves, which lead to further clock-dominated episodes. When dialogue served no purpose, Lubitsch omitted it, shooting the characters through a window, speaking inaudibly. Watching *Trouble in Paradise* for the nth time, one continues to marvel at its clockwork precision.

By 1934, however, time seemed to be running out on Lubitsch's raillery, as Joseph Breen arrived to enforce the Production Code. Chevalier, who had originally become famous for a working-stiff persona until Lubitsch put him in a tuxedo, was shown the door along with Paramount's other erotic pinups, Mae West and Marlene Dietrich. That same year, the studio promoted Lubitsch to production chief, a disastrous move as he could not keep from offering directorial help. *One Hour with You* began as a George Cukor project, until Lubitsch began shooting retakes, eventually taking control of the picture. A few years later, Lubitsch was reborn, his spine stiffened not only by the code but by personal and professional disillusionment—he discovered that his wife was having an affair with his longtime writing partner, Hanns Kräly, as his films (including *The Merry Widow*) died at the box office.

The years 1938–43 were perhaps the richest in Lubitsch's career, and four of his most brilliant films from that period are available in excellent transfers: *Ninotchka* and *The Shop Around the Corner* (made at MGM, now on Warner Bros. DVDs), *To Be or Not to Be* (made at United Artists, now also a Warner Bros. DVD), and *Heaven Can Wait* (made at 20th Century Fox, now a Criterion DVD). Lubitsch's themes of romance between opposites, triangles, infidelity, and the deflation of pomposity remained dominant, but the vision had deepened—these films are at once funnier and more emotionally brittle than his earlier work.

Ninotchka (1939) was famously advertised with the tag "Garbo Laughs!"

Garbo had, in fact, laughed on screen before, but she had never elicited many laughs. As a dour Soviet envoy who says of Stalin's show trials, "There will be fewer and better Russians," she discloses subtleties of timing and timbre that are pure Garbo, yet unlike anything else she did before or after. *Ninotchka* endures as a nearly unique Hollywood take on the Soviet Union—a dark, knowing, yet humanistic satire, unlike the sentimental paeans made during the war or the fearful propaganda that followed. Billy Wilder, who co-wrote the screenplay, would attempt to recapture some of Lubitsch's conceits in later years, including his indulgent puncturing of Soviet agitprop (in his 1961 film *One, Two, Three*), but the Lubitsch touch could not be transferred. As Wilder told *Action*, the predecessor to the *DGA Quarterly*, in 1967, "If we were lucky, we sometimes managed a few feet of film . . . like Lubitsch, not *real* Lubitsch."

In *To Be or Not to Be*, the pursuit of a traitor determined to wipe out the entire Polish underground is centered on a theatrical troupe that, as one character notes, does to Shakespeare what Hitler is doing to Poland. Lubitsch generates suspense without neglecting sexual flirtations, beard-pulling pratfalls, and the inestimable vanity of Jack Benny's Hamlet. The marvelous character actor and Lubitsch favorite Felix Bressart stops the Nazis in their tracks by reciting the "Hath not a Jew eyes" speech from *The Merchant of Venice*, not as Shylock would, but as if the lines had just occurred to him in the theater lobby. We don't know whether to laugh or cry.

Still, the most emotionally intricate of Lubitsch's films is *The Shop Around the Corner* (1940), in which James Stewart and Margaret Sullavan, at their peak, insult each other into a mighty love, while their boss, played by Frank Morgan in an uncharacteristic mood of genuine distress (as opposed to his usual mode of puffed-up exasperation), learns that his wife "didn't want to grow old with me." The cuckoldry here is painful, even embarrassing, yet it unfolds in a mist of inspired humor; the boss's failed suicide is treated as no more pressing than the disposal of the shop's reviled "Ochi Chornya" music boxes. Death is annoying, but so is that ubiquitous Russian Gypsy song. Lubitsch's own death, at fifty-five in 1947, came much too soon. As Billy Wilder told *Action*, he left the funeral service in the company of William Wyler, commenting, "No more Lubitsch," to which Wyler responded: "Worse than that, no more Lubitsch pictures."

2

THE JOHN FORD CODE

FORD AT WAR

THE FILMS OF John Ford are endlessly scrutinized, and still there is no true consensus. As the received wisdom of one generation is supplanted by that of the next and the next, the battle lines are redrawn. Once enshrined as an expressionistic liberal, then reviled as a sentimental militarist, then resuscitated as a trickster whose movies say the opposite of what they appear to say, Ford usually kept his own counsel. He had no need to soothe his friendly critics or battle his detractors, though it could escape no one's attention that in his films, the good guys show far greater respect for enemy combatants than for journalists, who are usually depicted as lying scoundrels or complacent sheep.

Nor did he grouse overmuch about the butchery inflicted on his work by studio heads. Genius alone, as Orson Welles proved over and over again, does not secure financing. Ford (1894–1973), a shrewd studio insider, managed to make more than one hundred films between 1917 and 1966, a feat that can never be equaled, and those that survive (many silents are lost) contribute to an oeuvre so cantankerously individual that the voluminous Ford studies show no sign of interpretive exhaustion.

Warner Bros. has released two cartons containing thirteen Ford films, eight of them representing his long collaboration with John Wayne. All Ford pictures are not equal—there are, or course, masterworks and mutts—but all contribute to the sense of an artist who, usually in Western mode, managed the triple threat of mythologizing the American past, critiquing the American present, and documenting the artist's evolving perspective, which is alternately tormented, contradictory, sentimental, and cheerless. Ford's vision is held together by repetitions: the stock company of actors, the familiar subjects, and the replaying of scenes and gestures. These add up to a Ford code, the solution to which is ever in the beholder's imagination.

In several films, the code is grandly announced by the setting: Monument Valley, an anonymous Western moonscape and geological metaphor used as a kind of cyclorama with no more geographical specificity than when George Herriman used it to set his cartoon strip "Krazy Kat." In *Stagecoach* (1939), Monument Valley is New Mexico; in *The Searchers* (1956), it's Texas; in *My Darling Clementine* (1946), it's southern Arizona; in *Cheyenne Autumn* (1964), it's Oklahoma. Do any of Ford's Monument Valley films actually take place on the Utah-Arizona border? Ford exploited the location with a painter's eye—never more richly than in *She Wore a Yellow Ribbon* (1949), for which the heavens aided him and cinematographer Winton Hoch in capturing what is likely the most dramatic electrical storm on film.

Critics, who almost always begin as fans, develop a virtuoso skill for justifying their likes, for finding the depths in the shallows, for interpreting day as night, racism as brotherhood, patriotism as pacifism, male bonding as impotence, and every other reversal necessary to repatriate an artist whose politics obstinately get in the way. In Ford's case, that virtuosity isn't necessary. We have lived with his movies long enough to surmise that they have passed and will continue to pass the big test of time: they change, lending themselves to the concerns of subsequent eras while sustaining basic human believability. What *we* see in them is often not what the original audiences saw.

Take *The Wings of Eagles* (1957), a picture that burlesques and disparages the qualities it pretends to celebrate. The DVD box refers to it as "a soaring tribute to a courageous friend," "indomitable wife," and "cigar-chomping sidekick Jughead Carson"—enough to turn anyone's stomach and earn its dismissal as a minor, even egregious work. The opening credits intensify those negative assumptions. "Anchors Away" blares over a naval insignia and a dedication to the "men who brought air power" to the navy. The film is a biography of Frank "Spig" Wead, the flyer turned screenwriter and dramatist. But don't salute too quickly.

The first half hour isn't so much about Spig as it is a parody of the brawling military comedies he wrote in his early years (later in the film, Ford interpolates a parallel excerpt from the 1932 *Hell Divers*, based on a Wead story). The manly posturing is underscored with witless pie-in-the-face slapstick, the young cadets circling Spig (Wayne) like suckling piglets. They talk about women, but the only physical intimacy permitted them is in slugfests—Ford's code for the emptiness of military life, previously displayed in *The Long Voyage Home* (1940) and *She Wore a Yellow Ribbon*, and taken to a ritualized zenith in *Donovan's Reef* (1963). The episodic opening, strangely pathetic and distancing, is almost robotically predictable.

But the tone changes abruptly when Spig and his wife (Maureen O'Hara, caked in makeup) lose one of their children. Ford shows man and wife in two rooms in the same frame. She braces her arm with her hand—more Ford code—in the Harry Carey pose that Wayne revived in *The Searchers*, while Spig, alone in the dark, reluctantly goes to her, offering no solace. Spig's family is the navy. He attends a political conference in Washington, where the words "pacifism" and "disarmament" are scorned, and the conferees talk of the need for permanent war to keep voters asleep while they channel endless funds into defense. (This invocation of a military-industrial empire was shot three years before Eisenhower's warning.) Spig gets congressional permission for an army-navy race, yet we see his victory only through the eyes of his daughters, watching their absentee father in a newsreel. Meanwhile, Spig incites another slapstick brawl with the fellas.

The tone changes again as he comes home unannounced, bearing flowers and finding a note that indicates his wife is at a romantic rendezvous. He puts the children to sleep, without apparently learning their names, cleans the place, and then gallantly pretends all is well when his wife returns. This lovely, unusual, adult moment is but a prelude to the disaster that ensues when Spig wakes to his daughter's crying and breaks his neck on the stairs. The rest of the film is a series of further losses and missed connections. Even when Spig regains the use of his legs, there is little sense of triumph.

A comic routine concerning hospital visitors sneaking in liquor, previously used in *Fort Apache* (more Ford code), suggests the banal world in which Spig voluntarily encases himself, having driven away his wife. Nor is there relief in the money and acclaim he wins as a writer—hired by Ford himself, as broadly impersonated by Ward Bond. In the end, Spig gives no more of himself to his friends than to his family. As his "indomitable" wife is assaulted by a malfunctioning phonograph, spitting discs at her, Spig leaves her for good to rejoin the navy, from which he eventually expels himself in a wheelchair, hovering over the abyss between two ships. The genuine emotion of the climax is as bleak as the feckless humor of the opening.

This largely overlooked film, like many Ford works, comforts the audience with its patriotic music, heroic central character, and mindless fisticuffs. Its original audience bought in to those surface tactics and left with gratifying tears, or else found the humor and narrative strategy wanting, but few saw the film as a hard-boiled dissection of Spig and his way of life. Similarly, Wayne fans watched reporters favor legend over fact in *Fort Apache* (1948) and *The Man Who Shot Liberty Valence* (1962) and assumed that Ford approved, when, in fact, the films exist to expose the legends as fraudulent. In *Stagecoach*, an editor dictates a false headline; in *Cheyenne Autumn*, the reporters play a deadly game with truth and Wyatt Earp asks, "Did you ever, in your whole life, read anything true in that paper?" The only reporter Ford seems to admire is the Edmond O'Brien character in *Liberty Valence*, and he gets beaten to a pulp.

The Wings of Eagles takes on additional power when one remembers that the real Spig Wead wrote *They Were Expendable* (1945), Ford's magnificent World War II film, for which he shares his directorial credit card with Wead's screenplay—as he shared it with cinematographer Greg Toland for *The Long Voyage Home*, another examination of hopelessness and failure. Based on the life of Ford's friend Captain Robert Bulkley Jr., who in 1943 won the Medal of Honor, *They Were Expendable* stops well short of military success for the Allies or the Bulkley character (no medals of any kind are presented). Robert Montgomery's Brickley (the names were changed, though the people who inspired the characters played by Wayne and Donna Reed successfully sued for misrepresentation) never gets to prove the value of PT boats; his occasional victory invariably presages a greater failure—it's 1942 and the Japanese are in charge.

Significantly, Ford, who served bravely in the war, brooks no racial characterization of the enemy. The opposition is unseen and insurmountable—like the Arabs taking down members of *The Lost Patrol* (1934), Ford's influential World War I drama, which served as the plot device for the popular *Bataan* (1943). When reference is made in *Expendable* to Bataan, many filmgoers must have had that tortuous one-by-one massacre in mind. The image carries over to the conclusion as Brickley and Ryan (Wayne, second in command as he would be again in *Fort Apache*) are called home while members of their command are left—expendable—on the shore to face certain annihilation and worse. In the penultimate scene, Ryan sits near Brickley, who explains to the fresh-faced recruits that they are going home in order to return and finish the job. Ryan lowers his left arm around Brickley, cradling him in the most dramatic instance of physical contact in the movie. Yet the final shot is of those left behind, and "The Battle Hymn of the Republic" blaring on the soundtrack (the entire score is Mickey Moused with patriotic themes) can do nothing to undermine the panorama of unspeakable waste.

The cavalry films that followed, with great commercial success, extended Ford's view of war. *She Wore a Yellow Ribbon* plays a variation on the theme of troops left behind as the commander rides off, promising to return. He does and, using a ruse to scatter the Indians' ponies, averts war. This extraordinary film, which appears to promise yet never delivers a climactic battle, is a brief for pacifism and disarmament. It's a picture in which white settlers, traders, and soldiers are tortured and killed as Wayne, who describes his final assignment as "mission: failure," idly chews tobacco. The Indians emerge unscathed—even the belligerent Red Shirt (a character who would reappear in *Cheyenne Autumn*) is shown firing to the end, inflicting casualties on Wayne's command.

The contest between order and chaos centers Ford's political films, which, like the Westerns, are never entirely elegiac any more than they are entirely damning. The past is always dying and the present is always being born. The dauntingly elegiac *Young Mr. Lincoln* (see "Biopics" in Part Three) is racked with death: the monument that inspires Abe is Ann Rutledge's gravestone. The audience is primed to measure Abe's fate as a cataclysm of violence, the necessary death-in-birth pang of the nation Abe envisions. His political enemies may be shortsighted, bigoted, dismissive, and dumb—but they aren't evil, as they often are in, say, the films of Frank Capra. Even in his more mature political films, *The Last Hurrah* (1958) and *Liberty Valence*, Ford's lamentations for the passing of the old ways are balanced by grudging acceptance of the new.

Ford's underrated version of Edwin O'Connor's largely forgotten novel *The Last Hurrah* (available on a Columbia DVD) concerns the final mayoral race of a political boss, Frank Skeffington (Spencer Tracy), who uses blackmail and humiliation to guarantee support for a good and necessary bill. Skeffington's methods are deplorable, yet he is a beacon of realpolitik, defending

the interests of the shanty Irish against old-line plutocrats who put their support behind a compliant idiot. It's hard to think of a film with more idiots
than this one, among them the sons of Skeffington and his key adversary. But
the moral center of the film is also a simpleton, called Ditto (Edward Brophy's last and finest hurrah), whose saving grace is dogged loyalty. Skeffington steals a line from Tocqueville in describing politics as America's favorite
spectator sport, and Ditto is its most ardent fan: Ditto alone, climbing the
stairs to Skeffington's deathbed, occupies the closing shot.

In *The Man Who Shot Liberty Valence*, probably the most sentimental
Western ever made, the town of Shinbone, recently liberated from the
chaos of the outlaw Liberty Valence, holds a political convention. The loud,
unruly, comically overblown caucus represents the assumption of order,
and produces a political hack, Ransom Stoddard (James Stewart), whose
subsequent and apparently worthy career is based on the legend that he
killed Valence (Lee Marvin). A much older Stoddard returns to the fleapit
town that launched him to attend the funeral of an alcoholic ranch hand,
Tom Doniphon (John Wayne), who actually did shoot Valence. Stoddard
has become a parody of a politician, perfecting a my-good-man condescension for strangers, which crumbles in the last scene as he and his wife are
forced to face squarely the big lie that no one but he cares about. The sentimentality is not inherent in the material, but in Ford's treatment of it; he
mourns Stoddard's self-deception, Doniphon's obsolescence, and the rise of
a new nation that will be no less self-deceptive ("print the legend") and painfully remade than the old one.

Doniphon becomes Donovan in *Donovan's Reef* (1963), a thematic sequel
to *Liberty Valence* and *The Last Hurrah*, in which Lee Marvin appears as a
drunken but mostly benign brawler, while the New England plutocrats who
bedeviled Frank Skeffington return in the form of an imperious woman who
must be indoctrinated into the racial and ethnic enlightenment of a new-
found land—the new state of Hawaii. In this isolated paradise, Wayne's character is, again, the man who sets the community aright. Political expedience
is divided between two characters, a good doctor (Jack Warden) who can't
handle the implications of his own decency, and the ineffectual trickster governor (Cesar Romero) who serves as comic relief. This time, the mode is
screwball mischief and the politics are unabashed liberal tolerance, yet the
sentimentality is just as thick (and largely engineered, as in *Liberty Valence*,
through the music), underscoring the generational passing of a way of life.

Of the thirteen films assembled by Warner Bros., only *Mary of Scotland* (1936) is unwatchable. Katharine Hepburn delivers her lines in the singsong of high school dramaturgy, and her awkwardness is of a piece with the rest of the cast. As Elizabeth, Florence Eldridge expresses her distrust of Mary by looking at the camera and nodding like Oliver Hardy; other actors speak with exaggerated slowness to get across all the expository dialogue. This was shot during Ford's great love affair with Hepburn, which is thought to have triggered his breakthrough work during the next few years; evidently, he was too smitten to see what he was getting in *Mary of Scotland*. It is included in the *John Ford Film Collection*, along with the dated but still gripping *The Informer* (1935), the entertaining *The Lost Patrol* (Boris Karloff's religious fanatic is so over the top you wonder why he wasn't straitjacketed long ago), and two major late-Ford Westerns: *Sergeant Rutledge* (1960), the first film made about black regiments and misogyny (starring Woody Strode and Constance Towers), and the flawed but infinitely interpretable epic *Cheyenne Autumn*. The Wayne/Ford collection includes five masterpieces: *Stagecoach*, *They Were Expendable*, *Fort Apache*, *She Wore a Yellow Ribbon*, and *The Searchers* (too bad they didn't include Alan LeMay's fine novel instead of a facsimile comic book), as well as *The Wings of Eagles*, the exceedingly desolate *The Long Voyage Home*, and the bathetic but engaging and superbly photographed (by Winton Hoch) *3 Godfathers*. Ford contains multitudes, and so, in his vaguely wounded intransigence, does Wayne, whose performances riveted audiences long before critics were willing to concede the point.

FORD AT FOX

ANYONE WITH AN aneurism may want to think twice about *Ford at Fox*, a twenty-one-disc salute to John Ford's three decades or so at Fox and its successor, 20th Century Fox. I'm guessing it weighs fifteen pounds. After days of carrying it around, I notice enhanced biceps and labored breathing. Of course, the latter may reflect my susceptibility to these movies, which, just as sure as the turning of the earth, raise my sights, gladden my soul, worry my intelligence, jerk my tears, undermine my assumptions, and play havoc with my critical convictions. Well, damn the health risks: for lovers of cinema, *Ford at Fox* is one of the most magnanimous corporate gifts in memory. It's neither complete nor perfect, but taken together with the recent Warner Bros. collections, it puts within bookshelf reach most of this very great artist's surviving pictures. (Elusive Ford benchmarks include *Wagon Master, The Hurricane, The Sun Shines Bright,* and *7 Women,* but they will undoubtedly be along.) The Fox films, including five silent pictures, represent the years when Ford was at a peak of critical prestige, the years when he was associated with the mists of American history rather than the conventions (some of his own invention) of the Western. John Wayne's only appearance in this set is as a bit player.

Ford's first Fox film, *Just Pals* (1920), a charming Buck Jones melodrama, introduces several themes that echo through his mature achievements at Fox and elsewhere: they include a town idler who achieves purpose by protecting a child, uncertain parentage, misunderstood intentions, greed, the thin veneer of social order undone by short-fused hysteria, and the fragility of justice. For a director who drew on diverse literary sources, accepted many studio assignments, and lost countless studio battles, Ford was a defiantly consistent filmmaker. His perspective, however, is neither static nor predictable, and he specialized in presenting two opposing ideas simultaneously. A brass band blasts military tunes and our first impression is: Ford patriotic blarney. Yet his military films are among the most devastatingly critical portraits of wartime lunacy made in Hollywood. Few American artists have addressed the myths with which we justify ourselves to the gods and our children with more trenchant analysis.

Ford earns his patriotism by seeing through veils of vast sadness; he understood why America is worth dying for and even forgiving, which can be a tougher chore. Battle hymns and bugle calls cannot drown out the misery of the broken families, disappointed lives, abandoned women, and expendable men he documents. Although Ford saw action in World War II and made many war films, he rarely filmed battle scenes with large numbers of anonymous casualties. His films isolate the individual and mourn each individual loss. His Westerns similarly focus more on preparations for war and graveyard aftermaths than on massed attacks with legions of stuntmen biting the dust. The Indian attack in *Stagecoach* is an entertaining aberration.

In *The Iron Horse* (1924), when one of three old comrades is killed, Ford's camera focuses as much on the Indian behind the rifle as on his quarry. Ford particularized death. Typical of his two-handed exercises, the film sets up the Indians as an ominous enemy; yet the worst of them are manipulated by a white renegade in native drag, and the settlers are saved not by the cavalry, but by Pawnees. He makes the deaths of three reformed godfather-figures in *3 Bad Men* (1926) painful gestures of self-sacrifice. In the zestfully expressionistic *Hangman's House* (1928), a legionnaire announces he must return to Ireland to kill a man, and his comrades rise to toast him: "Viva le commandant!" But in the end, the villain burns to death at such length that even the avenger experiences remorse. In Ford's first major war film, *Four Sons* (1928), a relentless foreshadowing of imminent tragedy in no way mitigates its terrible power.

Ford's films often fall into small units within the larger genres (war films, Westerns, comedies)—units that may intersect with one another and are usually united by a star actor. The cavalry trilogy is measured against the growing confidence of the John Wayne characters; the five Maureen O'Hara films (including the sublime 1941 Fox film *How Green Was My Valley*) deal with requited and unrequited sexual relationships; the three with James Stewart are partial burlesques of Western legends. The Fox box includes some of the most important of these sub-category series. A Will Rogers threesome—*Doctor Bull* (1933), *Judge Priest* (1934), and *Steamboat Round the Bend* (1935)—consists of small-town idylls, anecdotal in nature, spontaneous in style: funny, nostalgic, gimlet-eyed displays of societies closed off by time, place, and prejudice. The heroic Henry Fonda quartet details successive American crossroads while exploring Ford's theme of the exiled savior: *Drums Along the Mohawk* (1939), *Young Mr. Lincoln* (1939), *The Grapes of Wrath* (1940), and *My Darling Clementine* (1946), the last a dark postwar rumination on the vulnerability of the community and the tribulations of personal commitment.

A particularly neglected Ford sub-unit is the Dan Dailey trilogy, which treats the military as a community of pompous knuckleheads that sucks the life out of its most dedicated men. Dailey was a former vaudeville hoofer whose signature gesture as an actor was an obsequious smile, begging for approval. The films he made with Ford begin with the deft comedy *When Willie Comes Marching Home* (1950), and grow increasingly bleak and homo-erotic in the misfire *What Price Glory* (1952) and the 1957 anti-epic *The Wings of Eagles*. In *Willie*, Dailey plays Kluggs ("like in juggs," he tells the gorgeous Corrine Calvert, as she deposits his identification in her décolletage), a good-hearted layabout not unlike the hero of *Just Pals*. He enlists the day after Pearl Harbor, but he ends up antagonizing everyone in town when he isn't sent overseas. He inadvertently parachutes into heroism, but even that adventure merely deepens the picture's aversion to home-front pettiness while priming the comedy. An extended joke regarding Kluggs and alcohol was repeated in *The Wings of Eagles* with more grotesque implications. *What Price Glory* is an ill-judged debacle about two World War I soldiers who compete for Calvert but prefer each other; as a sex substitute, they have ritual punchfests of the sort that recur in *Wings* and the Paramount comedy *Donovan's Reef*, in which John Wayne socks his friend and spanks his lover.

Ford at Fox includes half of Ford's work at that studio—nearly two-thirds of the surviving films. These were glorious years for him, and even minor works have privileged moments: *Pilgrimage* (1933) is a chilling portrait of maternal possessiveness (and an antiwar film that would make an instructive double feature with *Four Sons*); *The Prisoner of Shark Island* (1936) offers a disingenuous defense of Dr. Samuel Mudd and a prophetic brief on attitudes toward torture; the bowdlerization of Erskine Caldwell's marvelous *Tobacco Road* (1941) is an intriguing if obnoxious film for exposing a family deficient in all the virtues Ford celebrates everywhere else. The box holds twenty-four features, two wartime shorts (but not "Sex Hygiene"), and a good, if arty, documentary on Ford's relationship with studio chief and hands-on producer Darryl F. Zanuck.

The prints are generally first-rate—quality control failed only on *What Price Glory*, which is marred by a white border in the first nine minutes and a poor transfer. As to the selection, the most mystifying omission is *Submarine Patrol* (1938), which would have been a better choice than the hapless *Four Men and a Prayer*, from the same year. *The Iron Horse* and *My Darling Clementine* are offered in two versions, though only *Clementine* is supported by an informative featurette discussing the differences; *Wee Willie Winkie* is here in black and white and in a restored gold tinting. *Ford at Fox* also includes a museum-shop-quality 168-page book of photographs and facsimile brochures from the premiere engagements of *The Iron Horse* and *Four Sons*. Sorely missing is an essay explaining the selection process and discussing the films, particularly the two versions of *The Iron Horse*: why is the international version restored and accompanied by an unrevealing commentary track, when the American cut is longer and superior in every detail? On the other hand, discovering *Ford at Fox* on your own is surely the best way.

THREE BY HOWARD HAWKS

THE MOVIES OF Howard Hawks give as much pleasure as those of any filmmaker. But the price is often a heavy dose of didacticism, an endless if narrow discussion of what makes a man a man (taciturn virility and refusal to acknowledge death) and a woman a woman (getting along with men without depending on them). Add to that a curious paradox in which individualism is honored only within the context of teamwork, and Hawks (1896–1977) can sometimes pall. His dramas show little tolerance for outsiders, rebels, or eggheads. In his comedies, however, eccentricity is prized and conformity scorned, which is why I prefer *Bringing Up Baby* (1938) and *His Girl Friday* (1940) to *Only Angels Have Wings* (1939) and *Red River* (1948), despite the stunning and very different pictorialism of the last two. I keep hoping that the Rita Hayworth character in *Only Angels* will get the hell out of the jungle before Cary Grant's team turns her into an acceptable pod person, and that Montgomery Clift's "son" will put one right between the eyes of John Wayne's demoniacal "father" in *Red River*.

The Hawks films I treasure most are those that straddle the line between comedy and drama so successfully that they upend the formats that superficially define them. No one matches Hawks's legerdemain in this kind of alchemy. It isn't a matter of injecting comic relief into drama (as John Ford did), or switching from comic setup to dramatic denouement (Leo McCarey), or leavening tension with macabre mischief (Alfred Hitchcock), or deflating gravitas with sarcasm (John Huston), but rather beginning with an intrinsically irreverent attitude, so that drollery is the governing mode, interrupted by bursts of adrenalin-raising action relief.

Scarface, The Big Sleep, To Have and Have Not, and *Rio Bravo* follow the precepts of, respectively, the gangster, detective, adventure, and Western genres, yet Hawks and company approach them with a cheerful, sexual impertinence that resituates them in a separate terrain where they have more in common with one another than with the genres. They are connected not least by Hawks's frequent self-plagiarism; several memorable bits and lines in *Rio Bravo*, for example, were previously used in *Only Angels Have Wings* and *To Have and Have Not.* These echoes augment the agreeable familiarity and out-of-time constancy of Hawks's world.

Scarface (1932) and *Rio Bravo* (1959), his first and last masterpieces in the sound era, and *Air Force* (1943), one of his most effective—or least didactic— studies in group dynamics, form a cogent if unintended trilogy, tracing the evolution of his themes and storytelling techniques. *Scarface*, Hawks's contribution to the gangster cycle, came on the heels of *Little Caesar*, Mervyn LeRoy's episodic mock-tragedy of a megalomaniac, and *The Public Enemy*, William Wellman's lively wallow in charismatic brutality (both 1931). If Hawks's film lacks the psychological acuity of Edward G. Robinson and the improvisational zest of James Cagney, it triumphs through the vitality of his directorial style, broadly theatrical performances, literary wit, Jacobean violence, and musical authenticity—Hollywood's favorite Prohibition bandleader, the Coconut Grove's Gus Arnheim, can be glimpsed in the great nightclub scene.

Scarface is a farcical pilgrim's progress about an ape-like assassin, Tony Carmonte (a career-making performance by Paul Muni), who whistles while he works, murdering his way to the top, aided by a "portable" machine gun and a gang that includes a smooth, coin-flipping gunman (George Raft) and a simpleton "secretary" (Vince Barnett) who can't take a phone message. Tony's animal magnetism attracts Poppy (Karen Morley), though he would rather spend off-hours with his sister Cesca, played by an effervescent Ann Dvorak. All but Poppy wind up dead—most poignantly the secretary, a comic stooge who, though mortally wounded, turns back to double-lock a door before following the boss to safety.

A scene in a newspaper editor's office, added to mollify censors and not directed by Hawks, has the unintended virtue of justifying the film's stylized violence. *Scarface* is not designed to edify, except as an example of shrewd filmmaking, with its long tracking shots, chiaroscuro lighting, and visual shorthand (a gesture is worth a thousand words), including a motif worked out with co-writer Ben Hecht, in which each murder is signaled by a decorative X. All three of the key early gangster films make much ado about sexual confusion, as if it were a generic requirement, but *Scarface* merrily raises the stakes with homoeroticism, sadomasochism, narcissism, and incest. (The DVD includes a dreadful alternate ending, mandated by censors but rejected by producer Howard Hughes.)

In *Air Force*, Hawks limits the laughs to sweet-humored bits involving George Tobias and Edward Brophy. Dudley Nichols's screenplay, which tracks the bomber *Mary Ann* from San Francisco to Pearl Harbor, Wake Island, Manila, and the Coral Sea, is airtight, and Hawks's control of the material allows us to know all ten members of the crew, including the outcast (John Garfield) who changes his tune under the censorious gaze of Harry Carey's crew chief, plus several other important characters. The picture makes inspired use of two FDR speeches, but also spreads a lot of nonsense about fifth columnists in Hawaii. The benchmark cinematography by James Wong Howe, especially inside the bomber, emphasizes the gleaming reflections and shadings associated with portrait photographers like George Hurrell or Herman Leonard.

As a favor, William Faulkner, a frequent Hawks collaborator, wrote what the director considered one of the film's best scenes—the dying hallucination of the pilot, surrounded by his crew and imagining one last takeoff on the *Mary Ann*. The finest American novelist of the twentieth century was not its finest screenwriter. The scene is powerfully staged but disturbing, because we earlier witnessed the pilot (charmingly played by John Ridgely) in a farewell clinch with his wife, played by Ann Doran, who gave him a lucky pendant made by their young son. In an absolutely superb cameo, Doran suggests sexual urgency while uttering the quintessential Hawksian definition of a good relationship: "It's been fun, every minute of it, such good fun." So as the pilot dies, it's disconcerting to see that he thinks only of the plane, never mentioning wife and son. Of course, Hawks's love for this scene could simply reflect what critic Jean-Pierre Coursodon observed as his general disdain for marriage and children, the flip side of his admiration for good-time gals.

Or it might be interpreted as a comment on how war dehumanizes, especially if taken in tandem with the notorious line uttered by the always congenial George Tobias character, a Jewish Manhattan-chauvinist and swing band fan named Weinberg: having proved himself a softie by sneaking a dog on board, he remarks of a downed enemy plane, "Hey Joe, fried Jap going down." The climactic battle, incorporating actual Coral Sea combat footage, would seem to underscore that point, going on for a pummeling ten minutes, with inserts of burning Japanese sailors. *Air Force* is one of the very few good war films made during the war. Unfortunately, the DVD extras amplify period nostalgia and add no historical perspective—the *Mary Ann* and her crew were destroyed a year after the film came out.

Rio Bravo is a miraculous film, and Warner Bros.' two-disc DVD pays it and Hawks proper homage; it includes film critic Richard Schickel's indispensable 1973 documentary about the director, a commentary track by Schickel and director John Carpenter, and a new featurette that incorporates an interview with Angie Dickinson and recordings of Hawks taken from his published interview with Peter Bogdanovich. The pleasures of *Rio Bravo* are easy to talk about, harder to explain. After the astonishing four-minute silent opening, in which the two central characters and the main plot are elucidated, the film has three or four action scenes separated by long intervals of leisurely walking, verbose talking, and stock-character comedy, all played at a deliberatively slow pace. Yet it is a grand and mesmerizing entertainment, a character and genre study that creates its own world—emotionally, temporally, spatially.

Dean Martin's alcoholic Dude centers the story, motivating the action, but John Wayne's authoritative sheriff dominates the film. The ongoing joke is that Wayne's implacable sheriff—he literally stares a bad guy into stressed mumbling—would be dead several times over but for the help of the tattered Dude, Walter Brennan's hilariously cranky old gimp Stumpy, Ricky Nelson's callow but tuneful gunman Colorado, and, in her one indelible role, dazzling Angie Dickinson as Feathers, who seduces the sheriff with single-entendre directness. A nice touch is the morning-after scene, as Sheriff John T. Chance struts down the street with a definite spring in his step.

Martin idolized Wayne in real life, and his regard is a central element in the picture's overall appeal—his look of admiration and of pride when "Papa" tells him he did something "good." Wayne is flawless, at times balletic. Note the loving look on his face as he walks into the jail to tell Dude he's "getting a little touchy," and the sheepish look in the next scene, as he very slowly ambles over to Feathers, the one character who unsettles him.

Most filmmakers would have had her rush out after the climactic battle to embrace Chance, while Dude herds the bad guys to jail, ending the film on an action high note. Not Hawks: he added another eight minutes to amplify their quarrelsome relationship and closed not with the lovers but with Dude and Stumpy, strolling into the fantasy world of incandescent Hollywood, where everyone ends up content and whole.

4

FRANK CAPRA, TRUE BELIEVER

FAIRY TALES PLAY an ambiguous role in American culture. We accept those appropriated from the Old World, blithely passing them on to our children in cleaned-up versions. It's the home-grown moral mythologies and foundation stories on which we were raised that are so troublesome—not least because we are raised on their probity, on the belief that they are no less real than the symbols of religious faith. No filmmaker has shown a more acute appreciation for those American fairy tales than Frank Capra (1897–1991); and no one has done more to relocate them in the world most of us inhabit, as opposed to the Old West, outer space, or the urban underworld.

Capra's myths are not the tall stories of Pecos Bill, John Henry, or Paul Bunyan, but rather those that define our initial understanding of history: the founding fathers as Romanesque gods; the melting pot that welcomes and assimilates all races and creeds; the innocence we are forever claiming to have lost. We remember the Alamo, but not what actually happened there. As recently as the 1950s, elementary school students were instructed in Parson Weems's parable of George Washington's exemplary truth-telling, only to learn at a later date that the cherry tree belongs to the realm of Santa Claus and the tooth fairy. Capra knows the cherry tree is a lie, but he isn't convinced that it's a useless lie.

As John Ford also understood, we want it both ways: know the truth but print the legend. Capra's oddly stunted career illustrates the broad cultural ambivalence about who we think we are. Once upon a time, he had few if any rivals among American directors. Spinning variations on his signature story in which good triumphs over hypocrisy and greed, he created an alluring fable that surely helped his audience to make sense of and survive the Depression. For that, Capra received an unparalleled number of awards as well as the kind of faux-handwritten possessory credit associated with Walt Disney. Yet his reign was brief. Though his career lasted nearly forty years, ranging from ingenious silent comedies with Harry Langdon to a few undervalued postwar pearls, he was honored almost exclusively for the work of six years, 1934–39. After the war, during which he made a widely admired series of propaganda films, *Why We Fight*, Capra's view of life lost its appeal, and was often misremembered with the derisory epithet "Capracorn." His Christmas carol *It's a Wonderful Life* played to empty theaters in 1946, and his subsequent elaborations on old ideas seemed sentimental and remote. Put another way, our response to Capra's work mirrors his patented fable: we initially take it in with the happy credulity of a Mr. Deeds or Mr. Smith, and then ruefully return to it as cynics determined to cut the fable and the credulity down to size.

The power of a good fairy tale is that while it may be put to sleep, it can never be put to rest. The 1980s television resurrection of *It's a Wonderful Life* proved Capra's resilience. The 2006 *Premiere Frank Capra Collection* from Sony, collecting the five major Depression-era films he made for Columbia Pictures, confirms his ongoing relevance as well as the technical beauty of his work. (The delight of rediscovering them is vastly enhanced by outstanding prints; indeed, the digitalization of *Mr. Deeds* is so sharp it has the unfortunate side effect of highlighting the frequent use of process shots.) Not that we need to be reminded of Capra's dramatis personae. The culture has long since assimilated his characters—Jefferson Smith, Longfellow Deeds, and John Doe are part of the language. Yet seeing these five pictures all at once—*American Madness* (1932), *It Happened One Night* (1934), *Mr. Deeds Goes to Town* (1936), *You Can't Take It with You* (1938), and *Mr. Smith Goes to Washington* (1939)—underscores his obstinacy in attempting to reassert an American fairy tale involving the conquering rube, the smitten cynic, and the alternately malignant and benign mob. His ultimate faith in the mob—the little guys—in an era beset by mob violence is the essence of Capra's America.

Fairy tales evoke moral awakening. For Capra, that literally means the sleeping child in cynical adults—the dormant idealist who upholds the promise of American rectitude despite layers of corrosive distrust. Today, it seems evident that the real hero in *Mr. Deeds Goes to Town* or *Mr. Smith Goes to Washington* isn't the rube, who, Capra makes clear, is too dumb or innocent to survive alone. The person who saves the day is a hard-bitten city gal (Jean Arthur in both films), whose idealism is roused by love and who acts on it with a grown-up's knowledge of the way things work. Capra's theme is not that politics is tainted by money; he takes that as a given. He is concerned with a more intriguing paradox: idealism is corrupted by maturity, but in the absence of maturity, idealism is worthless. He offers a miniature allegory in the first of two excellent montages in *Mr. Smith*, as Jeff Smith (James Stewart) tours the capital and is moved not only by the monuments but by the very young and very old visitors who gullibly cherish myths Capra believes are worth cherishing. The film's plot turns on a contest between boys, who in effect appoint Smith to the Senate, and men, who, as the devious Senator Payne (Claude Rains) takes pains to explain, do work that boys cannot possibly fathom.

Capra departs from traditional fairy tale narrative in setting his stories in the present rather than a distant past. Otherwise they conform to a pattern that grants magical interventions on behalf of mortal heroes. He often refers to fairy tales in structuring his work, never more so than in his freely adapted version of the George S. Kaufman and Moss Hart play *You Can't Take It with You*, in which a lovers' spat is characterized as Cinderella spurning her prince. Her family's basement is depicted as a dominion of elves in smocks, making toys and fireworks and whistling "Whistle While You Work," aided by a crow who answers to the name Jim. As the prince Tony (Stewart) observes, this is a family Disney might have dreamed up.

Like all such tales, Capra's films rely on miraculous circles, rituals, and denouements. The circles are often embodied by rings of good people united by song—group-sing from which the snobs and crooks are self-exiled. Music plays an important role in setting things right. Capra's Depression classics not only capture the look of the 1930s, with their urban montages, masses of extras, wisecracking reporters, ruthless plutocrats, and rural Edens (Mandrake Falls and Bedford Falls are similar wombs of goodness), but also the sound of the era. This despite the fact that he does his best to avoid contemporary music; his 1930s have little relationship to the Swing Era—in *It's a Wonderful Life*, he uses jazz as a symbol of degradation.

In the virtually perfect *It Happened One Night*, which all but invented screwball comedy, singing "The Man on the Flying Trapeze" with a group of fellow travelers brings Clark Gable and Claudette Colbert together, *and* guns the plot by sending their bus off the road. In a performance of timeless candor, Gable constantly lectures her on trivialities—directly prefiguring *Seinfeld* in clamping on a word and stretching it into nothingness. He makes a big deal of her inability to dunk a donut, piggyback, or hitchhike, though she holds her own regarding the last. In song, however, they are at peace. In *Mr. Deeds Goes to Town*, transformation is achieved in a duet of "Swanee River" and "Humoresque"; duets also fuse the lovers in *It's a Wonderful Life* ("Buffalo Gals") and 1951's *Here's Comes the Groom* ("In the Cool Cool Cool of the Evening"). *You Can't Take It with You* has two important songs. In one sequence, James Stewart and Jean Arthur escape their families to sit on a park bench and discuss courage. Capra's courage is evident as he shoots the entire scene in one unbroken five-minute take, the camera never moving, trusting entirely to the actors to make it work. Their reward is to dance the big apple (a rare acknowledgment of contemporary pop) with some very hip kids. The movie's big number, though, is the more characteristic "Polly Wolly Doodle," which not only reunites the lovers but magically converts the soulless tycoon into a regular guy.

The distinctive sound of Capra films goes beyond music; it's there in the crowd noises, the drunken revelry, the alternating shouts and murmurs, the fast-talking rumor mill that feeds on fear and contempt and often leads to a courtroom climax, overseen by a benign judge (the nearly interchangeable Harry Davenport in *You Can't Take It with You* and Harry Carey in *Mr. Smith*) coyly suppressing his amusement at the will of the people. Rumors corrupt the body politic in *American Madness*, Capra's breakthrough film, and *It's a Wonderful Life*. In the former, malignant gossip precipitates a disastrous bank run, challenging the faith of the people's banker, charismatically embodied by Walter Huston, who declines from peacock energy to sodden deflation; ultimately, his faith will be restored as the mob reverses itself in a crescendo of American decency.

Another fairy tale convention recharged by Capra is the intercession of a plainspoken stranger. A starving farmer makes Deeds see the light; a destitute businessman shows up the tycoon in *You Can't Take It with You*. In *Mr. Smith*, Capra's most despondent and emotionally multifaceted film, however, not even a children's crusade can save Jeff Smith. The kids are mauled and possibly killed by thugs, causing Jean Arthur to call an end to Smith's filibuster. He can't beat the corrupt machine run by Jim Taylor (Edward Arnold in a superbly nuanced portrait); ninety seconds before the film ends, Smith collapses, destroyed. Yet in those last seconds, Senator Payne intercedes, bursting into the Senate chamber to confess his guilt. This is not an ending mandated by the Production Code; it's the point of the film. *Mr. Smith* is a parable of destroyed innocence, and a far more devastating portrait of American politics than most. The plot is launched when the Senate loses one Senator Foley, and corruption is exposed everywhere. The ninety-second turnaround fulfills the demand of Capra's fable: what's really at stake is not Smith, but those axiomatic American myths he embodies. Capra might have concluded the film with the mass of boys triumphing on Smith's behalf. Instead, he unleashes his brand of pandemonium over Jeff's unconscious body—it's a miraculous victory and beyond Jeff's limited oratorical powers. The kingdom will prevail, but it's a close call.

The cardinal in John Ford's *The Last Hurrah* asks where the best people are to be found. A monsignor tells him, "Not in politics." Capra knows this full well; despite the calamitous fade-out, he knows that Jeff Smith has no chance in Washington, a point underscored in his even more corrosive follow-up, nearly a decade later, *State of the Union* (1948, released on DVD by Universal). Capra's adaptation of the Howard Lindsay and Russel Crouse play tracks the pilgrim's progress of Grant Mathews (Spencer Tracy), an exemplary businessman turned presidential candidate and embraced by the devil's brood. Mathews, who is old enough to be Smith's father, is his reverse image—accomplished, pragmatic, unsentimental, ruthless when necessary, adulterous, and, still, a fantasy figure through and through. Mathews is a Republican, Capra-style: he supports the Marshall Plan, world government, and universal health care. "The wealthiest nation in the world is a failure," he says, "unless it's also the healthiest nation in the world."

However, his mistress (Angela Lansbury) convinces him to "play ball with anybody to get that nomination." In the climactic scene, a roomful of actors who specialized in rascality—Adolph Menjou, Charles Dingle, Raymond Walburn—salute him as one of them. This being Capra, and also a Spencer Tracy / Katharine Hepburn movie ("I'd rather be tight than president," she crows in a memorable drunk scene), he does a last-minute hokey-pokey back to idealism and the sanctity of marriage. But it's too late. The cat is out of the bag, the final plea to our better natures even more fantastic than in *Mr. Smith*. Did Karl Rove learn his stuff watching this film, with its invocation to keep the public divided? "Play on hatreds," a tactician insists. "Keep them voting in blocks!" Hillary Clinton cannot have found succor in the dying poll who praises his daughter for combining "a woman's body with a man's brains." Meanwhile, Hepburn's Mary, who is usually the smartest person in the room, says, "No woman would ever run for president—she'd have to admit she was over thirty-five," and in a fit of chagrin adds, "I'd give anything for one good smack in my south-end," to which Adolph Menjou lecherously replies: "I wish I could do something about that." As usual with Capra, the villain speaks the truth.

5

GUILTY: ALFRED HITCHCOCK

ALFRED HITCHCOCK HAS had the last laugh—a long, posthumous howl. Biographers and critics gnaw at his personal peccadilloes and professional limitations, yet he remains the most durably popular studio-era film director in the English-speaking world. Charlie Chaplin and Buster Keaton require fondness for silence, John Ford for Irish knockabout, Orson Welles for operatic amplification, Ernst Lubitsch for continental manners, Howard Hawks for didactic manliness, and John Huston for bemused pessimism. But Hitchcock—cold, sharp, irreverent, gripping, rarely poignant (his audience has no fear of ever tearing up)—continues to draw crowds across the board, generation after generation. His films have achieved something better than timelessness; the older they get, the more astutely they function as social critiques. They may be frostily schematic, but long after we know who did what to whom, we return repeatedly for the nuance, the humor, the stylishness, the daring, the frisson, and the sex, which is invariably delayed, frustrated, or undermined with perversity.

Consequently, most Hitchcock films have always been available on DVD. Yet their dependable sales record inclines companies to up the ante, most recently with packaging indicating that these are classics—in the way books and music become classics, to be stored on the shelves of all civilized homes. Universal has issued authoritative two-disc editions of *Rear Window*, *Vertigo*, and *Psycho*, complete with feature-length documentaries, various supplements, and one Hitchcock-directed episode each from his television series. At the same time, MGM has produced an enlightening eight-film loose-leaf folder called *Alfred Hitchcock Premiere Collection*, including three neglected films from his English period in stunning new transfers, and five from his first decade in the United States, all but one reflecting his uneasy but fruitful collaboration with David O. Selznick.

If you weren't around in 1960, the degree to which *Psycho* changed film-making and filmgoing may be hard to fathom. This was his low-budget picture, a return to black and white after the luminous color of the audacious, commercially unsuccessful *Vertigo* (1958) and the inevitable return to his most reliable plot device (innocent man on the run with woman of uncertain loyalty) of *North by Northwest* (1959). He shot *Psycho* with efficient techniques learned from television, and advertised it with a showman's bravado: no one would be admitted after the picture began. Hitchcock couldn't actually enforce a policy of restricted entry, but as word of mouth spread, audiences were willing to adjust the habits of a lifetime and line up at the appointed hour.

Psycho not only made people mind the clock, but also hastened the death of the double bill. When the film ended, your much-assaulted brain demanded light. On the other hand, you didn't want instant light. Hitchcock recognized that he couldn't send shaken customers home immediately after the mental/physical seizure of Norman Bates (Anthony Perkins's inspired career-killing performance, after which he could never again play a normal guy). The audience needed a few minutes to catch its breath, and in those days movies didn't end with six-minute credit rolls. So he added the sequence in which a comically adrenalized psychologist explains things the audience already understood, but appreciated having spelled out all the same. Maybe Hitchcock had a secondary motive as well: the shrink augurs the numberless critics who have long since explicated every gaze, gesture, and prop in his films.

Guilt is the central theme running through all of Hitchcock's work, and there is plenty to go around, far more than there is anything resembling innocence. Yet with *Psycho*, Hitchcock stepped beyond the typical gambit of making the audience associatively guilty by manipulating it to, say, root for violence or relish sexual indiscretion. He went for the jugular, exploiting his own voyeuristic obsessions, showing intimacies no one expected to see in a Hollywood movie: from Janet Leigh's brassiere (shot so close you can almost feel the texture) to the whirlpool of a flushing toilet, not to mention two relentless stabbings. At the moment Leigh's Marion Crane is assaulted, we have been caught ogling her in the shower.

In *Rear Window* (1954), James Stewart plays a hobbled New York photographer who spends the entire film staring at his neighbors through his apartment window, eventually happening upon a murder—a discovery so entwined with wishful thinking (what's the point of voyeurism if you don't see something you shouldn't?) that he seems to have all but willed the crime. In *Vertigo*, Stewart is a hobbled detective who, after being hired to stalk a woman, takes up stalking as his full-time occupation, turning one woman into another and watching as each tumbles to her death. *Rear Window*, with Grace Kelly providing languorous glamour, was a hit; *Vertigo* was a debacle. Small wonder: its circuitous story line and open-ended structure could induce, well, vertigo.

Yet *Vertigo* is now widely regarded as Hitchcock's masterpiece, and a frequent candidate for best-ever short lists. Gorgeously photographed by Robert Burks and scored by Bernard Herrmann, fastidiously art-directed by Henry Bumstead and Hal Pereira, and flawlessly acted, not least by the mannequin-like Kim Novak, it is Hitchcock's most ravishing and uncharacteristically emotional film. It was also his first attempt to regulate audiences. The ads vainly pleaded, "You should see it from the beginning!" If you didn't, you were completely clueless, but even seen properly, it was judged by many to be incomprehensible—so much so that the censors apparently failed to notice that the murderer gets away scot free. (Stewart's character is nicknamed Scottie.) Hitchcock also introduced his brassiere fetish in *Vertigo*: Scottie's ex-flame, played by the maternally purring Barbara Bel Geddes, designs bras for a living. To facilitate the film's extravagant romance, dreamy tempo, convoluted plot, burning obsession, and lethal impotence, Hitchcock sets up the story with a gambit popularized by Ambrose Bierce's story "The Occurrence at Owl Creek Bridge," in which a hanged man fantasizes his escape in the seconds before the rope breaks his neck. Scottie and a patrolman chase a thief over rooftops, the cop falls to his death, and Scottie is left hanging on to a gutter with bare fingers. Hitchcock's scrupulous editing shows there is no way he can survive. Yet in the next shot, he seems to have suffered no more than a sprain. The rest of the film plays out like the fantasy of a man falling into the void. It ends with him literally hovering over that void.

Plunging from great heights is frequently the fate of Hitchcock villains.

But the void is something else—a limbo between salvation and hell. In the climactic episode of Hitchcock's first signature film, *The Lodger*, a 1927 silent that opens the MGM binder, the eponymous lodger, suspected of being Jack the Ripper, hangs manacled from a fence, with a furious mob on one side and police on the other. Having cast the matinee idol Ivor Novello in the lead role, Hitchcock was obliged to revise Marie Belloc Lowndes's 1913 novel and make him "innocent." Even so, the lodger gets more than a whiff of brimstone, saved by sheer luck from becoming a vigilante killer on the trail of the real Ripper. *Sabotage* (1936) has plenty to recommend it, especially in MGM's restoration, including a set piece in an aquarium and amusingly judicious glimpses of Soho life. But it remains Hitchcock's most unpleasant failure owing to an unforgivably sadistic sequence in which a young boy is blown up. Rather than have the event reported after the fact, as in Joseph Conrad's *The Secret Agent*, the novel *Sabotage* is based on, Hitchcock trails the boy for ten minutes, encouraging our identification with him, and then cuts from the explosion to a cinema where the audience is laughing at Disney's *Who Killed Cock Robin?*, and from there to the boy's pet canaries —an instance of "wit" so misplaced as to verge on what François Truffaut called (in his book-length interview with Hitchcock, excerpted on the disc as an audio extra) cinematic malpractice.

Hitchcock recognized his error, and followed it with one of his most enchanting and underappreciated movies, *Young and Innocent* (1937), in which an innocent man on the run is aided by the chief constable's teen-age daughter (the uncannily assured Nova Pilbeam, who merited a longer career). Several unmistakable harbingers of later Hitchcock films—not least an ominous shot of massed seagulls—and edgily satirical characterizations, including an inept lawyer out of Dickens, *almost* allow us to overlook one of the biggest plot holes in any crime film. A woman of dubious morality has been killed, and the police never question her batty husband, an incompetent jazz drummer with a mean twitch. They are too engrossed with the purely circumstantial evidence pointing to the hero. Hitchcock's long, climactic crane shot, closing in on the telltale twitch, is as deliriously satisfying now as it was seventy-plus years ago.

Inevitably, Hollywood lured Hitchcock, a transition engineered by Selznick, whose general intrusiveness, habit of adding shots in postproduction, and conventional editing drove Hitchcock nuts. On the other hand, his story sense was undoubtedly helpful, and played a decisive role in the success of

Rebecca (1940, Selznick's second consecutive best-picture Oscar, after *Gone with the Wind*); *Spellbound* (1945, a psychiatric detective story with an explanatory dream designed by Salvador Dali); and the incomparable *Notorious* (1946), though Selznick's involvement here was uncredited and limited. *Notorious*, with Cary Grant as an unpleasant American agent, Claude Rains as a weirdly sympathetic Nazi apparatchik, and the luminous, never-more-heartbreaking Ingrid Bergman as the former party girl caught between them, is perhaps Hitchcock's most complex and rewarding romance in the years preceding *Vertigo*. The plot makes little sense, yet there is so much going on that the viewer is happy to grab at any MacGuffin—Hitchcock's famous term for an arbitrary plot device that spurs the action, in this case some kind of nuclear sand in wine bottles in beautiful Rio.

Selznick's interference took its toll with *The Paradine Case* (1947), the stylish but unfocused British courtroom drama hoisted on the petard of a miscast Gregory Peck, whose character, an allegedly brilliant attorney, is unreasonably obtuse. (Hitchcock had his last word on Selznick in *North by Northwest*, adding the middle initial O to Cary Grant's Roger Thornhill, creating the monogram ROT.) Significantly, the producer had no creative involvement with much of Hitchcock's best work during the war years, made on loan-outs—*Foreign Correspondent*, *Saboteur*, *Shadow of a Doubt*, and the eighth film in the MGM collection, shot at Fox in 1944, the often ignored *Lifeboat*.

Lifeboat is often relegated to Hitchcock's second drawer, but the DVD ought to generate a healthier evaluation. In faded television prints, this film always seemed to me terminally talky—too much patriotic pep talk, for which Hitchcock averted blame by turning its authorship into a shell game. John Steinbeck and the director share the title card, while Jo Swerling gets the screenplay credit. In fact, Hitchcock conceived the original story; Steinbeck, at the director's request, wrote a novella; and any number of hands massaged the script. Though initially admired, *Lifeboat* failed after the *New York Times*'s Bosley Crowther declared it propaganda for the Nazis, and a chastened Darryl Zanuck withdrew studio support. What a combination: obtuse critic, craven producer. Crowther's accusation is incomprehensible—if ever there was a detestable villain, it is Nazi Walter Slezak sending professional Brooklynite William Bendix to sleep with the fishes. The DVD, complete with commentary and brief featurette, restores one quality that makes the talk acceptable and compelling: the sensuousness of Glen Mac-

Williams's photography, which accentuates the resourcefulness of Hitchcock's camera placements and the rhythmic cutting in what is essentially a
tour de force, staged entirely in a lifeboat in a studio tank. If the patriotism,
as enunciated by Tallulah Bankhead and Henry Hull, twins in the realm of
throaty self-importance, dates the story, Hitchcock's masterly control of the
material, particularly his scrupulous development of the manipulative Nazi,
is riveting. Even his wartime propaganda survives to engross another day.
Guilt springs eternal.

6

THAT WILD SO-AND-SO
WILLIAM A. WELLMAN

FEW FILMOGRAPHIES ARE more disorienting, at first blush, than that of William A. Wellman: so many titles you've not seen, so many you've never heard of. But then your eyes focus more purposefully, and classics begin to leap from the list, suggesting (again at first blush) the work not of one artist but of a team of fast and furious workmen, turning out crackling entertainments in every genre other than musical comedy—though, just to be sure, a little research among the unknown titles shows that he even made one of those, *College Coach* (1933), about a singing footballer.

Had he made a dozen movies instead of nearly eighty, Wellman's stature would be vastly enhanced. A culled list would include the unavoidable mobster classic *The Public Enemy*; pre-Code Depression landmarks like *Night Nurse, Heroes for Sale, Safe in Hell*, and *Wild Boys of the Road* (1931–33); the consummate, caustic inside-Hollywood tearjerker *A Star Is Born* (1937); the mocking and frequently hilarious newspaper send-ups *Nothing Sacred* (1937) and *Roxie Hart* (1942); the innovative and heated Westerns *The Ox-Bow Incident* (1943), *Westward the Women* (1951), and *Track of the Cat* (1954); and two of the most credible films ever made about World War II, *The Story of G. I. Joe* (1945) and *Battleground* (1950).

Still, bring on those unknown or forgotten pictures. DVDs have mostly redounded to Wellman's credit, making available all the aforementioned films except *Safe in Hell* and *Westward the Women*, and the more we get to see of his work the more surprises it holds, good and bad. A self-proclaimed man's man director, who defined his personal story as that of a French Foreign Legionnaire turned World War I fighter pilot (for the Lafayette Escadrille, *before* the United States entered the war), he was by all accounts leathery, curt, physically brave, quick to take umbrage, and happy to bear the sobriquets "Wild Bill" or, as he remarked in an interview, "sonofabitch." So he ought to have been at his best with material like the biographically mythic *Buffalo Bill* (1944) or the 1950s perils-of-aviation dramas *The High and the Mighty*, for which he was inexplicably Oscar-nominated as director, and *Island in the Sky*. Yet to say that these erstwhile hits do not wear well is gross understatement; far from requiting nostalgia, seen today they induce unintentional giggles and stupefaction.

On the other hand, in the early 1930s, women's pictures—sexual melodramas so musty you wouldn't read them in hell's waiting room—were just the stuff to crank up Wellman's motor. If no breakfast scene is more sadistically enduring than James Cagney mashing a grapefruit in Mae Clarke's face in *The Public Enemy*, its polar opposite may be found in Wellman's neglected *Midnight Mary* (1933), when a smitten blue blood (Franchot Tone) rescues the delectable moll Mary (twenty-year-old Loretta Young, whose eyes seem to carry their own key lights) from the police, feeds her a late-night turkey leg, and courteously attempts to discuss sex. This scene shouldn't startle us now, when movie couples speak of nothing else. Yet, not unlike the grapefruit bit, it invites an oddly voyeuristic fascination—as though we are spying on a genuinely private, plausibly awkward tête-à-tête. Wellman was good at eliciting such offhanded intimacy, perhaps because he prized improvisation and single takes.

A characteristic one-two Wellman punch occurs near the end of the same picture, when the soiled dove, hoping to save her society suitor from her jealous gangster lover (Ricardo Cortez), wraps herself around the latter and whispers the pleasures she will proffer him if he stays at home. He grins lewdly, but decides to leave, whereupon she shoots him in the back. That much was predictable, but Wellman, who had a talent for singular deaths, gives the moment a gruesome twist by having the gangster's body slide down the length of a locked door as his henchmen try to get in—causing his head, with open eyes, to rattle in rhythm.

Midnight Mary, with its glossy photography (it was made at MGM), abrupt cuts, and a tricky scheme of horizontal wipes that suggests a cyclorama or comic strip, is a highlight of Warner Home Video's excellent DVD anthology *Forbidden Hollywood Collection, Vol. 3.* Unlike the previous volumes (*Night Nurse* is in the second), this one is director-centric: six concise, severe, tabloid-style Wellman films that move with a page-turning pulse. Even when the story is rubbish and the outcome as fated as a Batman movie (usually the case), Wellman's expeditious style, aggressively mobile camera, and empathic consideration for all his characters inclines the viewer to a willing embrace of raw melodrama. The story is nothing, the storytelling everything. In two of the films, *Other Men's Women* (1931) and *Wild Boys of the Road*, he shoots trains to maximize their power, and you feel their might as they clang toward and beyond the camera. But the tension is released in private and in close-up. In the former (with Mary Astor giving a seductively understated performance), the flare-ups reflect a tangle of sexual frustration and betrayal, played out in the living room. In *Wild Boys*, a growing mob of teenagers teem from the trains like roaches to battle the railroad thugs, but the most terrifying moments concern a rape and a grueling accident, and Wellman stays relentlessly on the victims.

Warner has done right by this package. In addition to vintage cartoons and a few episodes from a lost series of two-reel mysteries by S. S. Van Dine, it includes two documentaries: Todd Robinson's 1995 feature-length biography and talking-heads testimonial *Wild Bill: Hollywood Maverick* and a revised version of the Wellman episode from Richard Schickel's 1973 series *The Men Who Made the Movies*. Schickel's film is an energetic, autumnal interview with Wellman (he died in 1975, at seventy-nine), who, with his long narrow face, paper-thin lips, and white unruly hair, aged into one of his favorite 1930s character actors, the perpetually grizzled Charley Grapewin—except for those broad telltale vowels that betray his comfortable Boston upbringing. Wellman may have been a tough guy, but he was a well-bred one. He typically begins an anecdote with a cautionary "You won't believe it" and ends it with a cross-my-heart "really and truly."

Wellman flourished in the studio era as a nose-to-the-grindstone contract director, working quickly and decisively, intensifying scenes with tracking shots, confrontational performances, driving rainstorms (a Wellman signature), and ad-libbed bits of business, often to punctuate scenes. He also showed two abiding weaknesses—for sentimentality and comic relief. In his best work, the schmaltz is at least genuine. This extends to *Frisco Jenny* (1932), a shameless twist on *Madame X*, except that in the Wellman version the heroine (a brothel owner and killer) is prosecuted, not defended, by a man who doesn't know she's his mother, and she goes to the gallows rather than embarrass him. *The Purchase Price* (also 1932), an even more jaw-dropping saga, has Barbara Stanwyck's Broadway chanteuse ditch her married mobster boyfriend by assuming the part of a mail-order bride and marrying, sight unseen, a farmer in Montana. The mobster does right by them, but the locals—other than Stanwyck's farmer—are sexual and capitalist predators.

Wellman learned to mute sentimentality, turning it into harder stuff to delineate the injustice of *The Ox-Bow Incident* and celebrate the quiet valor of Ernie Pyle in *The Story of G. I. Joe*, a rare film about infantry grunts that allows them to keep their dignity without tears. His comic instincts also developed. One of his strangely amusing conceits was to set a scene in a nightclub with a songstress (Stanwyck, for one) of uncertain intonation. But he also fell for repetitious shtick, like the bunny-scrunching smile of Dorothy Coonan (whom he married) in *Wild Boys*, and the tongue-clucking in *Heroes for Sale* exchanged between Robert Barrat's grating communist turned heartless capitalist and Aline MacMahon's mockingly steadfast waitress. This is perhaps the only failing in one of the darkest and smartest movies ever made about the isolation of heroism in a world of personal and financial corruption. *Heroes for Sale* is truly a picture for the Obama era.

In 1937, comic relief morphed into full-blown comic brilliance in Wellman's and Ben Hecht's mordantly satirical *Nothing Sacred*—a tour de force for Carole Lombard, as the woman who pretends to be dying to get a free trip to New York so that the press can feed on her misfortune. Fredric March, Walter Connolly, and Charles Winninger also appear to have the time of their lives. If you watch *Nothing Sacred* (Criterion did a superb transfer) as a triple feature with *A Star Is Born*, made the same year, and *Roxie Hart*, you can hardly fail to recognize that in Wellman's view of divine justice, there will be deliverance for good-hearted whores, while public relations men are doomed to the deepest recesses of a raging inferno.

Wellman had plenty of time to develop his technique and ideas. Between 1923 and 1959, he opened at least one new picture every year, except for 1940 and 1957. In most years, he had two films, and in his most prolific period he turned out movies the way *Saturday Evening Post* writers produced short stories—thirty between 1928, when his *Wings* won the first Academy Award for best picture, and 1934, when the enforcement of the Production Code obliged him to change course. He worked around budgetary restric-

tions with blithe ingenuity, often making them work in his favor. For example, Wellman thrived on location shooting, but usually didn't really need it.

His masterpiece *The Ox-Bow Incident*, about the lynching of three innocent men, is a study in mob obedience to self-righteous hatred, a familiar
Wellman theme. The writing is taut—the film is only seventy-five minutes
—and the performances are empowered by casting against type. Dana
Andrews, a year before *Laura*, plays a "wrong man" with quizzical disbelief.
Henry Fonda is the laconic cowboy who knows better, having been unfairly
accused of rustling, but is too weak to avert the tragedy. Frank Conroy gives
the performance of his life as a malignant major still fighting the Civil War;
Jane Darwell's monstrously mannish Ma Grier puts paid to her Ma Joad persona; and the habitually uncredited Leigh Whipper (the first black member
of Actors Equity) steals his few scenes as an observant preacher.

But when Darryl Zanuck allowed Wellman to make the film, he restricted
him to studio sets. Though widely criticized at the time, the consequent art
direction by James Basevi and Richard Day turned out to be one of the film's
strongest components. Echoing the style of illustrations found in Western
novels and pulps of the 1930s and 1940s, the backgrounds in the scenes leading up to the lynching create a cunningly theatrical artifice that intensifies
the immediacy of the performances and the drama, and became part of the
shared memory of the way we remember the West. The clean, indifferent,
painterly settings foreground Wellman's great and abiding theme, evident
in all of his best pictures: man doesn't stand a chance, so he may as well do
the right thing.

7

THE ORSON WELLES DILEMMA

AFTER KANE

WHAT IS IT about Orson Welles that drives his chroniclers around the bend? Each emerges from the great man's messy life and messier legacy convinced that he or she has found the explanatory Rosebud. The mystery they feel obliged to explain is not how he survived as an independent filmmaker, creating remarkable films that were *not* mutilated by producers; but rather why the erstwhile genius of radio, theater, and movies, friend to presidents, and civil rights champion ended up as an obese television pitchman for cheap wine. Welles's chroniclers are either boosters or detractors, and they mingle like the sharks in *The Lady from Shanghai*, devouring each other.

The reputation of his onetime colleague John Houseman as a mighty, often courageous producer turned professional elitist and financial investment shill has been additionally muddied by his turn as an unreliable memoirist with an ax planted in Welles's skull. Pauline Kael's "Raising Kane," which concluded that *Citizen Kane* was really the work of its co-scenarist, Herman Mankiewicz, cashiered any respect she might have earned as a scholar, not because she got so many facts wrong but because she refused to correct or acknowledge them. In his psychological broadside *Rosebud*, David Thomson expressed the hope that Welles's *Don Quixote* not be released because, given its "tattered" legend, "actual screening would be so deflating." The British critic Clinton Heylin has written a defense of Welles, *Despite the System*, that is so violently ill-mannered as to render his good research indigestible.

We also have Welles's own many accounts of his life and career, most notably in interviews with his approved biographer Barbara Leaming and with Peter Bogdanovich (in the posthumously published collaboration *This Is Orson Welles*), which are charming, informative, and proof that Welles liked a good story as much as a good meal and a pretty woman. Frank Brady's *Citizen Welles* remains the most reliable one-volume biography (despite twenty years of subsequent research), but is out of print. Thus the white elephant in the room is Simon Callow's planned three-volume extravaganza, of which volume two, *Orson Welles: Hello Americans* (2006), covers just seven years—from the theatrical release of *Citizen Kane*, in 1941, to the completion of *Macbeth*, in 1948.

It hardly seems possible or desirable that Callow will finish his biography in one more volume. He has another thirty-eight years to go, covering much of Welles's best work, and many controversies to adjudicate. A glance at the contents page of *Hello Americans* suggests that Callow has already been too long at the well: the sedate chapter and section titles in his first volume, *The Road to Xanadu* (1996), have now given way to puns like "Welleschmerz," "Welles Afloppin'," "The Welles of Onlyness." Additional intimations of weariness are a string of minor errors, pointlessly long paragraphs, an obsession with insignificant details (he describes what has been presented as evidence of Welles's involvement in the Black Dahlia murder, before dismissing it as madness), and excessive excerpts from reviews and previously unexamined files.

Yet *Hello Americans* is a far more level-headed and illuminating work than its predecessor. In *The Road to Xanadu*, Callow often adopted a tone of ironic dismissal. Greatly influenced by John Houseman, he was determined to bring Welles down a notch, punishing him for his arrogance and self-promotion, challenging his every claim, trivial or significant. Although he doesn't acknowledge a change of heart in the new book, it is unmistakable. Having previously described Welles as little more than a bystander to the 1938 broadcast of *The War of the Worlds*, he now seems to regard it as a major Wellesian achievement. He accepts as fact ("famously" so) an anecdote regarding Welles, voodoo, and the death of the critic Percy Hammond that he had previously derogated as doubtful. He now relies frequently on the veracity of the Bogdanovich interviews, suggesting that Welles, like Jelly Roll Morton, was an inveterate liar whose most outrageous claims often turned out to be true.

Of far greater importance, Callow no longer defines the arc of Welles's career as a downfall. In the earlier work's munificent tribute to Houseman, he writes off Welles as "the uncontested great white hope of the American theater who came to nothing in the end." Now, having performed insightfully close readings of Welles's 1940s films—especially *The Stranger* (1946), *The Lady from Shanghai* (1947), and *Macbeth*—he is obliged to agree that Welles was more sinned against than sinful. He admits that Welles was never cut out for Hollywood and that his most fulfilling work may well have come in later years as a voluntary exile. He champions *Othello* (1952) and *Chimes at Midnight* (1965), a fondness that might surprise readers of *The Road to Xanadu*.

For here is the crux of the Welles conundrum, boiled down to one question: Which is the more impressive feat? A gifted young man is given a film studio, its technicians, and almost unlimited funds to make any movie he desires, and he comes up with *Citizen Kane*. A mature, experienced, stubbornly individual artist in middle age, working with little more than rent money and spit, makes *Chimes at Midnight*. The first film revolutionized cinema, yet merely hints at the sublimity of the later work. The question implies—as does *Hello Americans*—that the Welles debate has shifted ground. It used to center on the cause of his decline: was the fault in Welles, the stars, the system? Now the decline itself is in question.

The problem is that most readers cannot answer it, because *Chimes at Midnight* is unavailable—rarely screened and almost impossible to find on home video. *Don Quixote* has been issued only as a DVD import in a version edited after Welles's death, and *The Other Side of the Wind* has not been released in any form. The illuminating, impassioned documentary *Filming Othello* (1978), which has never been distributed in theaters or on home video, is the rare film of its kind to come up with a creative alternative to the standard use of talking heads: Welles assembled his heads at a banquet and let drink and camaraderie loosen their tongues. On the other hand, the recent "restorations" of *Touch of Evil* (1958) and *Mr. Arkadin* (1955) demonstrate that while Welles's cuts were far better than those released by producers, the films were always undeniably Wellesian.

Callow arrives at his more generous assessment with some reluctance.

Early in the book, discussing the butchery of *The Magnificent Ambersons* (1942) and the opposition to Welles's unfinished Brazilian film *It's All True* (1941–42), he denounces the suggestion, "widely promoted by certain of Welles's apologists, that he was the victim of a cynical and ruthless studio system." Yet a few pages later, he describes the indulgences at RKO as "aberrant," and concedes that "had he shot nothing else in his life" but the footage of *jangadeiros* in Brazil, "the surviving fragments would have marked him out as a supreme artist in film." By the time Callow details the demolition of *The Stranger*—which he provocatively and convincingly describes as a catastrophe almost equal to that of *Ambersons*—he has himself morphed into a scornful apologist. Even so, there is a hole in the grueling account of *Ambersons*, Welles's second film, the lost paradise of American cinema. The last third was not only cut but consigned to the flames. In Callow's account, the renowned Welles fury, the wounded indignation, is muted almost to the point of nonexistence. Welles abandoned a complete print in Brazil (now lost) and made no attempt to retrieve it. The reader expects him to howl, but he meekly moves on.

Nor can Callow explain Welles's political ambitions, which took him away from working as a director in film and theater for three years while he tried to reinvent himself as a Fred Allen–type comedian, liberal orator, and political columnist (for *The New York Post*). Welles's stand against racism was genuinely courageous (Callow tells it better and in more detail than anyone else)—his crusade on behalf of a black veteran assaulted by a police officer in South Carolina led to the arrest of the officer while hastening Welles's banishment from radio. Yet a man who signed off broadcasts with the breathtakingly insincere phrase "I remain, as always, obediently yours" was not cut out to be a man of the people. The sheer immensity of his needs undermines him. He must always do more, be more, take in more, give out more, grow ever larger. At one point, Callow can barely manage to juggle on paper all the balls Welles kept aloft in life: he directs and stars in *The Stranger* while writing his financially disastrous Broadway epic *Around the World in 80 Days*, broadcasting weekly, turning out a newspaper column, and dickering with Bertolt Brecht and Charles Laughton over producing *Galileo*. Slacking was not his problem.

Inexplicably, when Welles finally got to shoot and edit a film, *Macbeth*, with full studio support, he left the country right before the editing, delaying its release, refusing to promote it, and yet agreeing to cut two reels—

boasting that it was he who mangled it, not "some idiot" in Hollywood. The reader is stunned. Yet Callow is sympathetic. He sees Europe as a solution to Welles's uneasy existence at home, where critics and studios alike routinely rooted for his comeuppance. Welles's crime against Fortress Hollywood was his vaunted genius, which he was obliged to wear like sackcloth.

Callow has little new to offer about Welles's personal life, including his marriage to Rita Hayworth, to whom you might think any man would be delighted to come home at night or in the afternoon or in the morning or at tea time. Welles preferred the constant turnover of prostitutes at a producer's home. He appears to have completely ignored his two daughters, though he cast one as Macduff's son. Callow doesn't acknowledge reports that Welles wanted a girlfriend to star in *The Lady from Shanghai*, and not Hayworth. Nor does he add anything to rumors concerning Welles's alleged affair with Billie Holiday, though he makes a few meaningless references to one with Judy Garland. He does, however, inadvertently make a case for the one Orson Welles book we don't have: a collection of his writings—speeches (he was not above a Kane-like demagogy), essays, columns, scripts, memos, letters, and so forth. Callow prints enough of them to suggest that the genius had more genius than he knew what to do with.

THE TROUBLE WITH MR. ARKADIN

WHETHER ORSON WELLES'S *Mr. Arkadin* (1955) is a bad movie with great moments or a good movie with dire failings, it is, like much of Welles's work, mangled, contentious, and undying. Hailed and mocked in its day, *Mr. Arkadin*—released in at least six versions between 1955 and 1962, none approved by Welles—was largely disparaged by its writer-director, who, having lost control in the editing process, insisted that the experience was too painful to belabor. The butchery of *The Magnificent Ambersons*, he told Peter Bogdanovich, was nothing as compared with this. I don't blame him for trying to shake it off; *Mr. Arkadin* is a troubling film, and not all the troubles can be laid at the door of an impatient producer. Still, it's a favorite of mine, a film I've gone back to with abiding if equivocal pleasure for more than four decades.

Every flawed work by a master invites fierce debate: critical judgment rationalizes the defects, permitting entry into the pantheon, or folds its hand, leading to a limbo of culthood followed by an eternity of rejection. Filmmakers often postpone the verdict by shifting the blame to producers, a strategy that rallies the fan base but doesn't do much for posterity. No master has worked up more of a posthumous lather than Welles, who at times seems destined to join Jesus, Napoleon, and Lincoln as a biographical touchstone. Still, a work of art must finally stand on its own no matter who made it.

Criterion now weighs in with *The Complete Mr. Arkadin*, a triple-disc confidential report that doesn't solve the mystery of what Welles had hoped to create, but does—through sheer repetition—make a substantial case for the film as a representative Wellesian achievement. The highlight is a Criterion exclusive: a new "Comprehensive Version," edited by Stefan Drossler and Claude Bertemes, five minutes longer than its predecessors and likely to become the preferred edition. Relying, in part, on Welles's largely elliptical statements, it collates shots from previous versions, reorders scenes, and uses the best 35-mm stock available. Of the three versions included in this set (the others are the "Corinth" print, discovered by Peter Bogdanovich in 1960 and believed to be the earliest surviving release, and the 1956 European cut known as *Confidential Report*), the new one is the most fluid, dramatic, and logical. Still, it does not entirely supplant earlier versions, and the material itself is so interesting that the experience of watching all three is cumulatively rewarding, despite the fact that, as Drossler notes, "Eighty to ninety percent of the film is the same in each version." Criterion also includes the 1956 novel, which expands backstories and fills in plot holes. Welles played a shell game with its authorship, accepting or denying credit at whim.

One of Welles's primary gambits was the unveiling of a mystery, invariably concerning a fallen titan. Several of his films take the form of confidential reports, most notably *Citizen Kane*, though *The Stranger* and *Touch of Evil* also involve investigations, buried secrets, and spying. In *Macbeth*, the witches know the secret and Macbeth must find it out; in *The Trial* (1962), the state knows the secret and K must find it out. Welles began *Kane* with the Ivan Illych death of a protagonist; this may have inspired the variation devised by Graham Greene and Carol Reed in *The Third Man* (1949), which opens with the burial of Harry Lime, who isn't dead but soon will be. Welles, in turn, borrowed that gambit for *Othello*, opening with the general's funeral and flashing back to examine a man who, like Lime, is living on borrowed time. He did the same with *Arkadin*, beginning with an empty plane and then telling how an all-powerful tycoon fell into the void.

But this time he also came up with a plot device of his own, which he thought would achieve popular success: the detective as Judas goat. Welles's Arkadin, a mysterious potentate of finance, hires a seedy blackmailer to investigate his past, feigning amnesia. Obsessed with the good opinion of his daughter, who has just come of age, he needs to learn who if anyone can testify to his early years as a white slaver operating with a Polish gang in 1920s Warsaw. As the de facto detective tracks down each witness, none of whom give a damn about Arkadin, they are killed—until the only witness is the detective himself. The basic story could serve as a good, conventional thriller today.

Welles, however, tended to burn his fingers on convention. So he cast a minor stage actor, Robert Arden, as the investigator, Van Stratten. Arden delivered a performance so utterly charmless that the audience never identifies with him. What's more, Welles took pains to establish Van Stratten as a doppelganger for the pure villainy of Arkadin: "Maybe I'll wind up an Arkadin myself someday," he says. Welles also added a fairy tale subtext, in which Arkadin and his daughter, Raina (played by Welles's mistress and future wife, the winsome, copiously eyebrowed Paolo Mori), occupy an El Greco-meets-Disney castle and the ugly American Van Stratten liberates her from "the ogre" by inadvertently manipulating a parricide.

Are we still having fun? Welles also decided on a double-barrel framework. On the one hand, he followed the usual Raymond Chandler progress of the detective, scurrying from one interview to another, picking up threads of information. This allowed Welles to contrast the boorish Arden with some of the most accomplished scene stealers alive, all clearly inspired by their few minutes in Welles's spotlight: Akim Tamiroff (whose line readings salvage an otherwise impossible early scene), Mischa Auer, Michael Redgrave, Peter van Eyck, Suzanne Flon, and Katina Paxinou. They are all richly entertaining and surprising, as is Patricia Medina as Van Stratten's girlfriend, whose comment on Spanish penitents ("They must be awful sorry") is delivered with comic aplomb and whose intonation in the bumpy yacht scene recalls *Kane*'s Dorothy Comingore.

On the other hand, Welles chose to contort that narrative into an "intricate" system of flashbacks—which the producer negated in the cutting. On this point, I'm inclined to assume that Welles was a "weeny bit" (to borrow a locution from Redgrave's character) disingenuous. Most versions, including Criterion's Comprehensive one, restore some aspect of the flash-back plan, and there is nothing too involuted beyond a flashback within the enveloping flashback. *Citizen Kane* is intricate; *Mr. Arkadin* merely has Van Stratten narrating his story to Zouk (Tamiroff), switching from the pres-ent to the chronological past, until catching up to the present. The various versions of the film, Welles's interviews, and outtakes and rushes (some included among the Criterion extras) give no hint of anything more com-plicated than that.

Yet there are two interesting tricks played with time. An excellent scene in the novel in which Van Stratten tries to seduce information from a baron-ess down on her luck (he has a mother fixation absent from the movie) is, in the film, played between the baroness—an enchanting cameo by Flon—and Arkadin; this doesn't make sense, but is handled in a way that encourages us to suspect an intended flashback or at least an angle not quite worked out. Then there is the very first shot: an unexplained dead body on the beach. The editors have included it because Welles told Bogdanovich that he planned to start the movie that way; and it does explain the strange open-ing narration about an unsolved murder that almost toppled a European government (the portentous rhetoric anticipates Criswell's introduction in *Plan Nine from Outer Space*). The shot was almost certainly Welles's com-ment on the Montesi scandal of 1953, kicked off when a woman's body was found on the beach; members of the Italian government were implicated (as was Alida Valli, who played Welles's lover in *The Third Man* and may have perjured herself). The idea is supposed to be that the woman's death shakes up Van Stratten and rouses the Italian government to look into Arkadin, but it, too, isn't worked out.

One gets the feeling that other strands weren't thought through or, for that matter, filmed; how else to explain the dreadful recurring shots of a ceiling speaker in the closing scenes? The Comprehensive version includes two famous anecdotes told by Arkadin at a masquerade ball—one about a graveyard in which tombstones are marked with the dates of the deceased's longest friendship, the other about a scorpion and a frog. Yet it is natural to assume that Welles intended to choose one or the other. As it stands, Arka-din comes off as a stand-up monologist entertaining party guests. The first few times I saw *Mr. Arkadin*, I assumed that Welles's wig and beard, the kind of thing you expect to see in a high school production of *Faust*, were part of

Arkadin's masquerade costume, and was thus stymied by his wearing them throughout the film. I have made peace with his makeup; I now like the fantastic elements telegraphed by it.

Maybe this is an instance of critical rationalization. But even the film's most relentless detractor found, inadvertently, something he liked. Dwight Macdonald ended his evisceration by lauding Mischa Auer's delivery of the line "Feeding time!"—apparently unaware that Welles had substituted his own voice for Auer's and those of several other actors. I have scratched at the surface of the film's pros and cons. As for the novel, Welles surely had some involvement in writing it, even if the first French publication was assembled by critic and translator Maurice Bessy. (According to Criterion's notes, Welles wrote a serialization of the film for the *London Daily Express*; has anyone compared his installments with the novel?) For what little it's worth: In 1980, *Vogue* editor Leo Lehrman phoned Welles from his office after I expressed admiration for the novel. He asked Welles if he had written it. Welles: "Did he like it?" Lehrman: "He likes it very much." Welles: "Then I wrote it!" Followed by volcanic laughter.

DARK KNIGHT

ONE OF THE highlights of the 2008 Telluride Film Festival was the documentary *Prodigal Sons*, by Kimberly Reed, who endeavored to film the reaction of her family and friends as she returned to Helena, Montana, for her twentieth high school reunion. Her hometown had known her as Paul, the star quarterback of her class. Other than her rivalrous and mentally impaired adopted brother, Marc, no one seemed fazed by her "transition." Reed, however, had a shock in store for her when Marc set out to learn the identity of his birth parents: turns out his mother was Rebecca Welles, the daughter of Orson Welles and Rita Hayworth. Marc's uncanny resemblance to Welles haunts the film like a deranged doppelganger of genius—genius shorn of everything other than a small talent (he can play the piano by ear) and a terrible anger. Watching the fury bust out of him, one thinks of the power and limitations of DNA, and the bizarre fact that of all people, Welles should have left behind, unknowingly, an antithetical image—even a refutation, Cain for Kane—of the brilliance and prodigality that haunted his life and his reputation ever after.

There is a moment in Welles's *Don Quixote*, or rather the posthumous compilation of footage he shot for that uncompleted film, recently released on DVD by Image, when Welles, appearing as himself, receives an award from a convention of sherry manufacturers and is introduced as being "famous for his interpretation in *The Third Man*." Welles laughs his ho-ho laugh, and we can hardly fail to recall that he spent most of his life tilting at windmills and that his fame was only as valuable as the work it procured. *Don Quixote* is a big part of the legend—the unfinished work (one of several) to which Welles devoted the most time and from which he may have received the most pleasure. It began in 1955, when he shot tests, purportedly for a television adaptation, with Mischa Auer, who appeared in *Mr. Arkadin* that same year. A couple of years later, he began filming in Mexico with Francisco Reiguera as the knight of the mournful countenance and Akim Tamiroff as Sancho Panza. By 1958, the project had evolved sufficiently for Welles to tell the critic André Bazin that it was being improvised in the style of silent comedy (dialogue to be dubbed later), was set in modern times, and would run no more than ninety minutes.

During the next decade, Welles returned to his *Don Quixote* periodically when time and finances permitted, until Reiguera died in 1969, followed by Tamiroff in 1972. A wraparound narrative featuring child actor Patty McCormack was filmed but rejected, perhaps because she outgrew childhood. Welles began to speak of it as a private work, like a novel—it was his to finish as and when he pleased. He edited and dubbed or, more likely, test-dubbed several scenes, voicing Quixote and Sancho himself. But at his death, he left cans of film in several countries, and no script or memo to guide the material's organization.

In 1992, Oja Kodar, Welles's companion for many years and the executor of his estate, authorized the Spanish director Jess Franco, who had assisted Welles on the sublime *Chimes at Midnight* (1965), to assemble all the material he could gather and edit it into a film for a cultural expo in Spain and the festival at Cannes, where it generated near universal outrage. A DVD was issued in Spain and Brazil, with English and Spanish audio tracks, Portuguese subtitles, and short essays on the making of the film. Welles's *Don Quixote* has never been released in America until now—nor has there been much demand, since the contributions of Franco (who made good Eurotrash horror films in his prime) were regarded as indiscriminate butchery.

The problems with the Franco version are undeniable. The film stock looks worn and gray. Little attempt was made to carve a film from the hoarded footage (112 minutes are included), much of it repetitive and some of it tweaked with dreadful optical effects. The English dubbing makes Japan's giant lizard movies sound fastidious by comparison. For a narrator, the producers chose an actor who tried to mimic Welles. For Quixote and Sancho, they hired actors who are polar opposites from Welles, destroying all continuity between his dubbing and that of the others. Welles's own voice-over is uneven—he often sounds like Hank Quinlan from *Touch of Evil*, and in one odd passage, as Sancho discusses sainthood, Welles revives the faux-Irish accent he used in *Lady from Shanghai*.

Image reproduces the lame Franco print, right down to a reverse-frame glitch at the 39:50 mark (the only difference from the foreign release that I could detect is that the red lettering on the title card is monochrome in the Image transfer), but with no explanatory essay at all and without the Spanish and Portuguese. The company might have produced a worthy DVD, with a commentary track explaining the film's history and distinguishing between scenes that Welles cut and raw footage. Instead, it disingenuously promotes the DVD as *Orson Welles's Don Quixote*, with the subtitle "The Lost Dream Project," and advertises it as co-starring Welles, who appears with his camera for mere seconds, and Patty McCormack, who does not appear at all. (A fascinating scene that Welles shot with McCormack, set in a movie theater as Quixote slashes the screen to rescue a filmed actress in distress, has been viewed more than 14,000 times on YouTube and might have been included as a bonus.)

That said, I can't go along with the widespread judgment that this material is to be shunned as a worthless travesty. Given how long it has taken for even this to be made available on these shores, it is entirely possible that none of us will be alive when a more professional and creative version is offered—and even then, a best-case scenario will produce a speculative version of what Welles intended. This print is tough going, but there is much at which to marvel. The first half, once the deadly narration is finished, suggests Samuel Beckett, as the two principals jabber alone in the wilderness. The attempted comedy never quite jells (they extemporize for three minutes about a chicken wing), but many images are memorable. Someone could publish an impressively illustrated *Don Quixote* with captured frames from the film.

The second half is far more engaging. As in the novel, some of the finest scenes occur when Sancho goes his own way, and the highlight of the film is a twelve-minute sequence beginning with him wandering into a desolate town that promptly comes alive with the running of the bulls. Henry Fonda is there, a tourist with his camera. As the bulls enter the ring, two of them run smack into each other. The sequence is the kind of stuff all too familiar from newsreels, but never like this. It's a witting mini Welles essay on barbarism, much as *Don Quixote* is intended as his valediction of courage. A subsequent scene in which Sancho finds his master imprisoned in an oxcart and recalls the times they have shared, superbly played by Tamiroff, is kin to a parallel passage in *Chimes at Midnight*. Beyond these and other particulars, though, is the overall enchantment of watching what Welles could do in his spare time with a camera and a couple of actors. As a home movie, even the butchered *Don Quixote* has transcendent moments.

8

JOHN BRAHM:
THE EVIL THAT MEN DO

JOHN BRAHM IS not exactly a film school luminary, but he made his mark in 1940s Hollywood, showing a sharp eye and Freudian savvy during his seven years at 20th Century Fox. Most of his long, prolific career—he died at eighty-nine, in 1982—was spent elsewhere. Born in Germany, Brahm thrived for two decades as a theater director, until the collapse of Weimar. Then he moved to London, where he worked his way up the movie ladder as editor and writer, before landing a directorial assignment in 1935: a remake of D. W. Griffith's silent *Broken Blossoms*, from which Griffith had bailed. Two years later, he came to Hollywood to shoot programmers for Columbia, and two years after that Darryl Zanuck signed him to Fox. After Brahm's contract lapsed, he turned to television, where he directed dozens of episodes of key 1950s and 1960s series: crime, suspense, Westerns, science fiction—name a show and he probably had a hand in it. Meanwhile, his sporadic film work declined to camp exertions such as *The Mad Magician* (1954) and *Hot Rods to Hell* (1967).

In the mid-1940s, however, Brahm made at least four of the most stylish thrillers of the period, and for these he is justly, if somewhat esoterically, treasured: *The Lodger* (1944), *Hangover Square* (1945), *The Locket* (1946), and *The Brasher Doubloon* (1947). Brahm's name appears nowhere on the cover of a DVD set released by Fox, yet *Fox Horror Classics* is his work. It collects his two best films, *The Lodger* and *Hangover Square*, along with his Fox debut, a needlessly resurrected werewolf-in-the-family-closet saga, *The Undying Mon-*

ster (1942). If they had called it *Fox Suspense Classics*, the title would have allowed the inclusion of the surely worthier *Brasher Doubloon*, a version of Raymond Chandler's *The High Window*, in which George Montgomery's dim Marlowe is offset by a smart script and a ferocious Florence Bates. (*The Locket* was not an option; Brahm made it at RKO.)

The chosen films, which are bannered rather insistently as "A Terrifying Trilogy of Terror," are not without horrific touches, but they are concerned less with the dismemberment of victims than with the misery of human monsters who are not accountable for their depredations. Scotland Yard (as personified by a bored George Sanders) assures the strangler of *Hangover Square* that he isn't really to blame, and even Jack the Ripper (the eponymous lodger) is presented as more bent than evil—is it his fault that the Bible tells him to fillet fast women? *The Undying Monster* matches the others on two counts beyond the director's hand. All three films are gaslight melodramas, set at the turn of twentieth-century England, and all the villains are beside themselves—lycanthropy being the original schizophrenia. Unfortunately, it's a lousy denouement when everyone keeps muttering about mysteries beyond the ken of man and Scotland Yard vows to prove murder, only to find a wolfman at the door.

Brahm opens *The Undying Monster* with a superb tracking shot inside an old mansion, the camera circling a room at midnight, stopping for each of twelve chimes, then continuing its tour, gliding over sprawled bodies that, as the butler enters, rise and yawn. It's the only savory shot in a picture done in by bad writing and stupefying performances. As the Yard's forensics whiz, James Ellison is as Iowan as corn husks. Bramwell Fletcher all but announces, "I'm a red herring," playing the first hour as a rotter and the last minute as a concerned friend. Still, the professional gloss provided by Brahm and cameraman Lucien Ballard encouraged Zanuck to reunite them for the far more important and expensive update of Marie Belloc Lowndes's 1913 novel *The Lodger*. They were aided by Barré Lyndon, a British dramatist with crime on his mind (*The Amazing Dr. Clitterhouse*, *The Man in Half Moon Street*), composer Hugo Friedhofer, and Laird Cregar—a brilliant young, hulking actor and master of psychotic mood changes.

Cregar, whose film career lasted only five years, didn't need tufts of hair to show that the moon was full or the testosterone rising. His eyes, enormous yet slightly slanted ovals, were bay windows into his soul. His voice, a velvety baritone, measured his tenuous grasp of reality with unnatural understatement. He had already displayed his talent in diverse films, including comedies, but it was his performance as a deviant cop in *I Wake Up Screaming* (1941) that alerted audiences to a disturbingly new movie personality. *The Lodger* is his peak achievement, a courageous display of Grand Guignol venting, mired in homoerotic incest, desperate longing, and religious dread. Cregar chose to go all out, and Brahm let him, shooting him from below and above so that he either hovers or cowers. Everyone else is shot in a flat light, but when Cregar's character appears, the black and white contrasts increase and the images resonate as if willed by the Ripper.

Brahm also underscored the parallel forces in Lyndon's script: increasing discord between Eros, represented by Merle Oberon's music hall performer, and Thanatos; between those facing the future (Oberon's character) and those with only a misspent past (a marvelous vignette concerning the slatterns, Jenny and Wiggy); between healthy misgivings and delusional greed— the Ripper's landlady needs the rent money, which allows her husband to ignore his own liability for their reduced station. The climactic chase is full-bore expressionism, with Cregar's hunted killer climbing spider-like through lacy chiaroscuro, his half-moon eyes strangely illuminated, the entire crushing finale shot from his point of view. The ending, which involves a standoff that is silent except for the Ripper's panting, is masterful. *The Lodger* was a huge hit, and Zanuck wanted another just like it.

What he got was even better—Brahm's masterpiece—but at the cost of Cregar's life. Cregar had urged Fox to buy Patrick Hamilton's 1941 novel *Hangover Square*, but when he saw that Lyndon's script shifted the setting from modern London and Brighton to the gaslight era that Hamilton, as the author of the twice-filmed play *Gaslight*, did so much to popularize, he refused to appear in it. A contractual suspension changed his mind, but while preparing for the role, he embarked on a zealous diet that he hoped would save him from a career of crazed heavies. As a result, his face was slightly gaunt and his bulk occasionally receded into the folds of his costumes. Though always focused and frequently inspired, especially when making transitions between his George Harvey Bone, benign composer (his music, provided by the brilliant Bernard Herrmann, includes a climactic ten-minute concerto), and Bone's murderous alter ego, Cregar lacks the sullen charm and aggressive certainty of his best work. He feuded with Brahm, and died before the film opened—at thirty-one, of heart disease induced by the relentless dieting.

Cregar's frustration apparently did little damage to Brahm's concentration: his control of the material is immensely skillful, not least in an unforgettable bonfire sequence. Bone is as much drawn to fire as the Ripper was to the soothing, cleansing darkness of the Thames. Brahm and Lyndon, clearly, were drawn to undemanding metaphors, mining them without abusing them. Commentators often assume that the film of *Hangover Square* was backdated to 1903 to mimic the look of *The Lodger*. That seems not entirely fair. Hamilton's compellingly perverse novel, with its canvas of hysteria and dissipation, of sexual manipulation and political fury, simply could not have been set in modern times with a war going on—unless it was situated in an Axis country. Even so, this is a violent, morally contentious film in which the audience is fully complicit. The killer is tormented by a femme fatale—played by the lovely, undervalued Linda Darnell, whose character, Netta Longden, goes up in flames, as Darnell herself did twenty years later. Her demise is not only inevitable but hotly anticipated. Netta's crime against decency, if not the law, often registered as a capital offense in wartime Hollywood movies, when so many women were left to their own devices. She is a ruthless climber (worse, a bad singer) who toys with the affections of a great if lethal composer while bestowing her favors on a mustachioed fancy man. Of course she has to go. The audience is primed to feel a lot less concerned for her than for Bone, who exits in his own vainglorious, blazing inferno.

9

MICHAEL CURTIZ'S DORIS DAY PERIOD

ANY LIST OF the most enduring films of the Hollywood studio era is likely to include a few by the Budapest-born director Michael Curtiz (1886–1962), who was among the top contract directors at Warner Bros. for an unmatched twenty-eight years. Stylistically, his work is distinguished by aggressive visual compositions (signature shot: two characters shoulder to shoulder, facing forward), forceful acting, quick cuts, fluid camerawork, shadow play, location inserts, romantic and period realism, the kind of speed that results from keeping a story on track and free of distraction, and, above all, a shameless mastery of emotional manipulation.

Curtiz's best films operate on the principle that the audience must be busy all the time—either absorbed in verbal confrontations and elaborately staged fights, or chuckling or, when all else fails, weeping. No one could jerk tears like Curtiz, though many of his most lachrymose scenes are neither sad-sad nor happy-sad, just gratuitously sentimental. Think of *Yankee Doodle Dandy* (1942), which is fictional in plot and characterization but scrupulously researched in setting, jargon, music, and theatrical lore. The script presented him with a third-act problem: several plot points but little music until the finale. What to do? He filled in for the absent musical numbers with crying numbers, three in a row—a marriage announcement, a birthday present, and a dead father, though only the last can logically justify the suds.

Less proficient directors who tried to imitate Curtiz in juicing up hopeless scripts learned how difficult it is. Roy Del Ruth, in the scurvy *West Point*

Story (1950), the first James Cagney musical since *Yankee Doodle Dandy*, desperately attempted to justify his ministrations by choking up the big finish, and failed. In the equally noxious, even more cliché-packed *I'll See You in My Dreams* (1951), Curtiz incited blubbering whenever he damn well pleased; a closing testimonial scene, complete with inserts of character actors who've mined their marks throughout the film, is almost a parody of biopic insincerity, but nonetheless effective. Curtiz's film, unlike Del Ruth's, was a big hit in its day.

Both films are now on DVD. *The West Point Story* is part of Warner Bros.' *James Cagney: The Signature Collection*, which also includes Curtiz's *Captains of the Clouds* (1942), an American analogue to Michael Powell's British film of the same year, *49ᵗʰ Parallel*. Each is a recruitment poster staged in Canada, though only the Hollywood film indulges in the hero's redemptive death and general misogyny. Its theme, in Tokyo Rose shorthand, might be: "Your women cannot be trusted, so forget them and join the army." The other films gathered here are three William Keighley wartime epics, *The Fighting 69ᵗʰ* (1940), in which Cagney dies to redeem himself in World War I, with Pat O'Brien larding sanctimony as Father Duffy; the intermittently amusing *The Bride Came C.O.D.* (1941), with Bette Davis striving for lightheartedness; and *Torrid Zone* (1940), the politically indifferent and consequently lively Banana Republic retelling of *The Front Page*, in which Cagney, O'Brien, and Ann Sheridan seem to be having mucho fun.

The West Point Story is distinguished only by Cagney's arch, stiff-backed dancing (when he isn't throwing punches), Virginia Mayo's walleyed beauty, and Doris Day's impervious energy, magnetism, and voice. Day gets a worthier showcase in *The Doris Day Collection*, vol. 2, which includes her first two films, both directed by Curtiz: the mildly enchanting *Romance on the High Seas* (1948) and the vitally sadomasochistic *My Dream Is Yours* (1949), a high-water mark in Curtiz's long series of show business movies. The other pictures, in declining order of interest, are Del Ruth's *On Moonlight Bay* (1951), an essential postwar parable, as illustrative of that confused era as any noir, with its semi-feminist expositions and clashes between radical youth and frightened middle age; Del Ruth's more conventional if spirited sequel, *By the Light of the Silvery Moon* (1952); Curtiz's *I'll See You in My Dreams*, in which Danny Thomas impersonates the lyricist Gus Kahn as a sexually recalcitrant squirrel; and Jack Donohue's *Lucky Me* (1954), entirely unlucky but for the wasted oomph of Day and Phil Silvers.

When Curtiz is celebrated at all, which isn't often, it is for his "serious" amusements: his early exercises in horror, Errol Flynn swashbucklers, and those putatively isolated triumphs *The Sea Wolf* (1941), *Casablanca* (1942), and *Mildred Pierce* (1945). Yet almost from the time the Warners imported him, in 1926, on the basis of a prolific and now forgotten career in Hungary and Austria, he displayed a stubborn fascination with American entertainment. Indeed, his first Hollywood spectacle, the mostly silent *Noah's Arc* (1929), contrasts a contemporary backstage fable with the biblical flood. Curtiz left few aspects of showbiz unexplored, from Al Jolson minstrelsy (*Mammy*, 1930) to Elvis Presley minstrelsy (*King Creole*, 1958) to nonmusical films that examine radio technology (*The Unsuspected*, 1947) and the showmanship of sports (*Jim Thorpe—All American*, 1951). *Yankee Doodle Dandy* and *White Christmas* (1954), patriotic odes, respectively, to FDR and Ike, sustain evergreen status, but Curtiz touched on jazz, nightclubs, operetta, vaudeville, and Broadway in more than a dozen other films of varying value, including *Young Man with a Horn* (1950), *The Story of Will Rogers* (1952), *The Best Things in Life Are Free* (1956), and *The Helen Morgan Story* (1957).

If one theme animates Curtiz's work, suggesting a stronger thematic hand than is usually credited to a studio pro who didn't generate his own projects, it is the plight of the outsider, alienated by nationalism or class. Curtiz's backstage idylls invariably dramatize the fragile and temporary triumph of the entertainer. In band singer Doris Day, he found a vessel for his obsession, signing her to a personal contract. Yet he allowed her to prevail in only one film, her first, *Romance on the High Seas*, a bubbly mistaken identity farce by the Epstein brothers (who wrote *Casablanca*), punched up by I. A. L. Diamond.

Romance has a deserved cult following. The Jule Styne / Sammy Cahn score includes Cahn's derisive parody "I'm in Love" (the title is the entire lyric) and two classic Styne melodies, "It's You or No One" and "It's Magic"—the latter was Day's breakthrough hit on records. The film has sumptuous photography and set design, an all-too-rare specialty number by Avon Long (whose stage work stretched from *Porgy and Bess* to *Bubbling Brown Sugar*), comedy cameos, amusing dialogue mining white jive talk of the 1940s, balloon-mad Busby Berkeley choreography, and a cheerful gloss on the money-burning paranoia and tipping practices of the super rich. Day, fourth-billed, is radiant and imperturbable.

Day's subsequent films with Curtiz are less benign. She ends up in platonic isolation in *Young Man with a Horn* (1950). As composer Grace LeBoy in *I'll See You in My Dreams*, she invents and controls Gus Kahn's career, but at the cost of any recognition of her own talent (the film treats her mostly as a song plugger, ignoring her published ragtime pieces). *My Dream Is Yours* represents Day's deepest work with Curtiz. It begins deceptively as a gently satirical look at the banality of radio and the popularity of crooning, with Curtiz characteristically exploring studio architecture and the sponsor's domination. Then it takes a careening left turn, the first of two.

Lee Bowman, repeating his role from the 1947 *Smash-Up*, plays the arrogant, alcoholic singer Gary Mitchell, to whom women are fillies in a stable. Mitchell betrays his agent, Doug Blake (Jack Carson, the film's top-billed star), who goes to New York to create another radio phenomenon. Through a "live" jukebox trick, Blake hears Martha Gibson (Day), the widowed mother of a young boy, and brings her to Hollywood, where she is shunned for being too "jazzy." Mitchell, however, makes a play for her, and Martha gives in to him—a shocking development in 1949, leading the audience to two erroneous presumptions: that she will ultimately change him and marry him. Each member of the developing triangle is calculating and self-involved, and the picture is surprisingly cagy in keeping the involvement between Martha and Gary largely off screen, unknown to Blake or the audience. Amid familiar gender reversals (Blake is mocked, by the incomparably mocking Eve Arden, for his apron-wearing kitchen duties), Martha flourishes while Gary goes on a binge and is blacklisted. Blake falls in love with her; she hardly notices.

In one of the strangest digressions in a Hollywood movie, the film's point of view suddenly becomes that of Martha's unconscious son, who dreams a Friz Freling–animated sequence in which Bugs Bunny meets Martha and Blake, who dance to Liszt in humiliating bunny suits. (A friend of mine commented: "Is the kid on LSD?") In the end, Martha gives up Gary—the film's main flaw is in emphasizing Gary's monstrousness without allowing us to see whatever it is that enchants Martha—and instantly turns to Blake as a door-prize husband: gratitude and security in the absence of love and sex, a future as bleak as those bunny outfits. The new songs by Harry Warren and Ralph Blane are low-grade, especially compared with the old songs in the score, but the Technicolor effects of Ernest Haller and Wilfred Cline are vibrant, the lower precincts of the entertainment world are knowingly displayed, and Day provides exactly the right ambiguity with a sunshiny, maternal-erotic smile that gives nothing away.

10

ANTHONY MANN OF THE WEST

ANTHONY MANN'S MOVIES are often celebrated for their formal logic and psychological astuteness, as well as their intelligent use of space, perspective, and lighting, but the main thing to be said about them is that they are infinitely entertaining and beautiful to behold. In recent years, many of his best films have been released on DVDs in appropriately striking transfers, ranging from the fierce black and white chiaroscuro of *The Furies* to the deeply saturated colors of *Bend of the River* to the muted tones and majestic vistas of *El Cid*. Mann's greatest work suggests—usually from the first shot, establishing the landscape and the hero's link to it—a masterly confidence that puts the story and characters front and center.

Mann had a curious if not unique career, rising from the deepest crypts of Poverty Row to the crest of profligate spectacle. Despite the dearth or gush of bank notes, he remained focused and stylish in examining his key themes, which are contained in two interrelated questions: What is heroism, and what binds the individual to society? These are big issues, and Mann approached them through the most reliable of cinematic filters, the genre movie. Yet unlike directors who worked in several genres simultaneously, Mann tended to focus on one before moving to the next. His work falls into four key periods, each reflecting his financial clout at the time. In the first, from 1942 to 1946, he learned his trade on minimal budgets, grinding out ten programmers. Even so, his pictorial and dramatic abilities produced savory moments, including a purview of low-rent vaudeville in *The*

Great Flamarion, a valentine to wartime sentimentality and Frances Langford in *The Bamboo Blonde*, and a violent dream of feminine insecurity and aggression in *Strange Impersonation*.

Between 1947 and 1950, Mann found his forte in B crime thrillers of the sort later designated as noir (see "Crime/Noir" in Part Three). In eight terse movies that require no apology, he helped to define the form, collaborating with like-minded craftsmen, including screenwriter John C. Higgins and cinematographer John Alton. In pictures like *Railroaded*, *Raw Deal*, *T-Men*, *Desperate*, and *He Walked by Night* (signed by Albert Werker, but mostly directed by Mann), he focused on urban bottom-feeders, emphasizing sudden brutality and the sadistic pleasure it affords its perpetrators—exemplified by John Ireland's character in *Railroaded*, who perfumes his bullets. At this stage, Mann found greater interest in his villains than his heroes, who project a stolid anonymity. He also brought noir shadows and moral upheavals to the French Revolution in *Reign of Terror*, and explored location shooting in *Side Street*, in which city skyscrapers are filmed as though they were the canyons of the old West.

Then everything changed for Mann. Suddenly, he embraced the Western with astonishing poise, rivaling John Ford in producing some of the most original and consistent work in the idiom during the 1950s—chiefly a quintet with James Stewart that reestablished Stewart's career, recasting him from the bumbling, decent character he had created in prewar films to the loner with a secret and a pathological need for revenge. Mann maintained a stable of supporting actors (most frequently Harry Morgan, Charles McGraw, and J. C. Flippen), and found his own look: craggy mountains and desert sands instead of Ford's Monument Valley. Other directors explored parallels between urban paranoia and Western lawlessness—Robert Wise, Andre De Toth, Sam Fuller, Budd Boetticher—but Mann did the most to change the look and feeling of the A-list Western, giving it a raw, contemporary urgency that the others usually explored on the B end of the bill.

The 1950s were arguably the greatest years of the Western—the period in which generic formulas were at once sustained and destabilized through psychology, revisionism, high style, and the kind of grandeur that follows when the most durable cliché's are reframed against classical paradigms. Consider Mann's *The Furies* (1950), a baggy reworking of the Oresteia fraught with incestuous father-daughter enmity, miscegenation, vengeance, and startling violence, played out in an agora stretching to the horizon and encompassing endless cattle pastures, mountainous outposts, a city strip with saloon and bank, and communities of squatters. Yet ponderousness has no place on this Ponderosa. Mann knew his Aeschylus well enough to gun the plot, goading it with efficiency and brio, confining the poetry to visual effects that make the story memorable and, in two instances of sudden violence, awful—but in a good, Greek way.

Even Brian Garfield, in his anti-auteurist, anti-revisionist, foolishly ornery encyclopedia *Western Films*, concedes that while *The Furies* reminds him of the 1950s joke about adult Westerns—the cowboy still loves his horse, but now he worries about it—it remains "larger than life, and completely absorbing." Darkly, vividly photographed by Victor Milner, every shot of the film is framed with purpose, advancing the melodrama (tragedy was virtually unobtainable in the time of the Production Code) and underscoring its revenge and doppelganger motifs. All the performances are good, and three—Barbara Stanwyck as the daughter, Walter Huston (his last) as the patriarch, and Judith Anderson as the ill-fated interloper—are magnificent. *The Furies* is long overdue for reassessment.

Criterion's munificent edition of *The Furies*, coupled with *James Stewart: The Western Collection*, which includes *Winchester '73* (and two other Mann Westerns, *Bend of the River* and *The Far Country*), encourages a look back at 1950, the seminal year when Mann made his mark on the genre with three films shot between August 1949 and March 1950. Of these, only *Winchester '73*, his first Stewart picture, was a critical and commercial success, but it would not have come to pass had Mann not already shot *Devil's Doorway* at MGM. That powerful study of legally racist iniquities visited upon Native Americans, in this instance a Medal of Honor recipient played by Robert Taylor, might have had the distinction of being the first film to revise the Hollywood portrayal of Indians. However, MGM—caught in the rivalry between outgoing studio chief L. B. Mayer and rising mogul Dore Schary— shelved it as unfit family entertainment (to date, no DVD release either), until Delmar Daves's *Broken Arrow*, also starring Stewart, made a fortune with its pious treatment of Indian injustice that summer.

Stewart had seen an early cut of *Devil's Doorway*, and was impressed by its visual power. He requested Mann to direct *Winchester '73*, a film that had been in preparation for years as a Fritz Lang project, and it opened nine days before *Broken Arrow*, reviving Stewart's career as a tougher, more neurotic hombre than he had been in the best of his prewar pictures. Meanwhile,

Paramount rolled out *The Furies* in Arizona, where it was filmed, on the same day in July that Fox opened the much ballyhooed *Broken Arrow*, completely overshadowing Mann's film, which was predictably overlooked by the critics and the public.

By any standard, 1950 was a big year for Westerns. In addition to the influential *Broken Arrow*, it saw the release of two John Ford monuments: *Rio Grande*, the third and most sanguine of his cavalry pictures, and *Wagon Master*, an alternately sadistic and elegiac tour de force, parsed to Sons of the Pioneers cowpoke songs and without a marquee star in sight. Sam Fuller made his second Western, *The Baron of Arizona*, that year, and the veteran Henry King, always at his best when knitting samplers of Americana, made *The Gunfighter*. In the long run, though, it was Mann's approach to the Western that had the greatest immediate impact, as he revivified some of the genre's moldiest devices: the journey traveled by the hero and an unlikely sidekick, the faltering patriarch, the passion for vengeance—which, in Mann films, is almost always animated by depredations in the past that are never shown on screen.

The best and most telling of the extras Criterion includes with *The Furies* is the original novel by Niven Busch. A long-forgotten generational saga with a subtext of miscegenation that had to be laundered for the movie, it is a reminder that the themes of fratricide and patricide that haunt Mann's best work, as well as the infusion of Freudian motivations, were introduced to the Western by Busch as the novelist behind David O. Selznick's production of *Duel in the Sun* (1946) and as the author of the story and screenplay for Raoul Walsh's *Pursued* (1947). Both of those films concern murdered fathers, fratricidal obsessions, and pasts that won't let go. *The Furies* pushed the envelope, but *Winchester '73*, with which Busch had no involvement, also reflected his themes.

Indeed, the *Winchester '73* script, by Robert L. Richards and the redoubtable Borden Chase, could justifiably have been called *The Furies*. In the film of that name, the phrase refers to the cattle baron's ranch, and the theme of familial slaughter is played out symbolically—no one actually kills a blood relation, the test for intervention by the mythological Furies. *Winchester '73*, however, is premised on the aftermath of a patricide and details the murderous hunt of the "good" brother (played by Stewart) for the "bad" (Stephen McNally). Here and in the four subsequent Mann-Stewart Westerns (including *The Naked Spur* and *The Man from Laramie*) as well as in Mann's

1958 Gary Cooper Western, *Man of the West*, the Furies are in the maddened eye of the protagonist. Generational murder is either a stain that fratricide must expunge, as in *Winchester '73*, or a necessity to cleanse the son, as in *Man of the West*.

Mann symbolizes the hierarchy of familial conflict by placing pursued and pursuer at different levels of mountainous terrain, usually ending in a fall from the heights, as when Lee J. Cobb's demented patriarch tumbles to his death in *Man of the West*. The staging of the mountain battle in *The Furies* recalls the storming of the cathedral in *The Hunchback of Notre Dame*, as boulders are dropped on the attackers, or the assault on El Sordo's mountain stronghold in *For Whom the Bell Tolls*—in the bead Mother Herrera (Blanche Yurka, doing a Mexican Madame Defarge) draws on the Huston character below and in its ghastly finish, with the gratuitous hanging of Juan (Gilbert Roland).

The last scene of *The Furies* suggests, at first, an aberrant softening, as the chastened Vance (Stanwyck) and her appeased husband, Rip (Wendell Corey), ride home talking of the children they will have. But what kind of home will they really enter? The Judith Anderson character, whom Vance permanently disfigured with a pair of scissors, is drinking herself to oblivion in the bedroom. Also living on the premises is the deadly El Tigre (Thomas Gomez), who hanged Juan, Vance's lifelong friend and probable lover (in the novel, Juan and Vance are married when he is taken out naked and hanged). So are the Herreras, including the mother who avenged Juan by killing Vance's father. The marriage of Vance and Rip is less a love match than an accounting deal drawn up in hell.

Winchester '73 hyperbolizes the idea of the Western by fetishizing the eponymous gun. The villain Waco Johnny Dean (Dan Duryea), who dies in a glorious frenzy of mincing dance steps, flirts wolfishly with a dance hall hostess (Shelley Winters), but his eyes really go glassy with desire when he sees the Winchester. The first twenty minutes depict an impossible shooting contest out of Robin Hood or Fenimore Cooper's *The Pioneers*, presided over by a giddily flamboyant Wyatt Earp—a daring turn by Will Geer, twenty years too old and fifty pounds too paunchy, but just right all the same. (In the 1960s, Stewart would go him one further, with an even more outrageous Earp in Ford's *Cheyenne Autumn*). By the end of the violent roundelay pivoted on the Winchester, the Furies are finally unleashed on a mountain: the bad son plummets, and the good son returns to the ministrations of an aging sidekick and a woman of dubious virtue.

For his second film with Stewart, *Bend of the River* (1951), and his first in color, Mann used Technicolor landscapes to delineate the nature of the men who either settle or defy it. The personality split is made explicit when Stewart's Glyn saves his ostensible double, Arthur Kennedy's Cole, from hanging. Both have a secret past as murderous border raiders during the Civil War, but Glyn is determined to prove he has evolved. *Bend of the River* is the most watery of Westerns, its main set pieces staged in a creek and a river and aboard a steamboat taking provisions to a settlement. The cinematography, representing the pinnacle of Irving Glassberg's career, is sumptuous, dappled with reds and deep blues and frequently shot at night, taking in wilderness, town life, and river life.

Bend of the River created a paradigm for the next three Mann-Stewart Westerns—*The Naked Spur* (1953), a five-hander of mutual suspicions and betrayals played out on a rocky peak (the naked spur of the title); *The Far Country* (1955), in which Stewart plays a guide reluctant to take responsibility; and *The Man from Laramie* (1955), in which his vengeance-bent ranger has to contend with another fatally charming doppelganger played by Arthur Kennedy. In *Laramie*, in a characteristic burst of violence, a rancher's corrupt son shoots Stewart point-blank in the hand, as the camera speeds in for a close-up and Stewart lets out a roar ("You scum!") of agony and astonishment. Mann's morality is concerned less with the conflict between good and evil than that between niceness and corruption. In *Bend of the River*, one villain says of another that he seemed like a nice guy. The leader of the settlers responds, "He was until he found gold." The three non-Western films Mann made with Stewart in the 1950s suffer from a surfeit of niceness with too little opposition, especially given the sugary support of June Allyson in *Strategic Air Command* and *The Glenn Miller Story*—the latter a shameless travesty of wartime nostalgia in which characters repeatedly acknowledge each other's goodness.

At the same time, Mann made two relatively dour films starring Robert Ryan, who played the doppelganger villain in *The Naked Spur*. The Korean War film *Men in War* (1957) and the barnyard romp *God's Little Acre* (1958) are complementary existential parables, one tragic and the other absurdist, in which a plot of earth, whether as a battle objective or a farmer's dream, is ultimately revealed as nothing more than dirt. Salvation is won by refusing to surrender to doubt or futility. This is also a theme in Mann's most emotionally hysterical Western, *Man of the West* (1958), in which a reformed outlaw (Gary Cooper) has to destroy the criminal family who raised him before he can cement his place in society, if in fact he can—the film ends on a note of secluded ambiguity.

With *Cimarron*, the 1960 remake of Edna Ferber's melodrama about the opening of Oklahoma (released as a Warner DVD that does justice to the Cinemascope frame and Robert Surtees's photography), Mann set out to show the Western hero easily surviving the outlaws only to be done in by politics and finance. The picture takes on miscegenation, racism (against Indians: there isn't a black performer in the cast), and anti-Semitism, but Mann walked off the project—Charles Walters replaced him—when forced to abandon location shooting and accept a revised script that favored the hero's wife at the expense of the hero. He was fired early on from *Spartacus*, after tangling with producer-star Kirk Douglas. Still, these two films served as transitional episodes culminating in his triumphant direction of the most successful of producer Samuel Bronston's road show exhibitions, *El Cid* (1961), filmed in Spain with some of the grandest sets, natural and man-made, since D. W. Griffith's *Intolerance* (see "Biopics" in Part Three). Mann's second Bronston money pit, *The Fall of the Roman Empire* (1964), had the distinction of helping to kill off the era of elephantine epics, but remains a treasure of a kind that can never be replicated in the age of computer graphics. If *Roman Empire* loses much of its grandeur on a television screen (those thousands of extras seen in long shot might as well be computer graphics), it re-creates the Roman forum with palpable plasticity. It also boasts a tighter, better chariot race than the one in *Ben-Hur*, created by the same man—stunt legend and second-unit director Yakima Canutt.

After *El Cid*, Mann was king of the hill; after *Roman Empire*, he was a freelance looking for agreeable projects. *Heroes of Telemark* (1965), a World War II adventure, did not fill the bill, and he died, at sixty, in 1967, while shooting *A Dandy in Aspic* (1968, taken over by its star, Laurence Harvey), pursuing the hottest genre of the decade—spy films—to explore his obsession with how men behave in moments of crisis and stress.

11

SAM FULLER'S PULP CINEMA

ARISTOTLE, OF ALL people, is cited in the first two films written and directed by the poet of pulp Samuel Fuller. He is quoted by the theater manager in *I Shot Jesse James* ("No one loves the man whom he fears") and dutifully recited by the child-fiancé in *The Baron of Arizona* ("Dignity consists not in possessing honors, but in deserving them"). Aristotle and Fuller: as Dracula might have said, "What music they make."

Of course, the incongruity is quietly hilarious. No storyteller was less Aristotelian than Sam Fuller, the self-mythologizing, bantamweight film-maker who once insisted on smoking cigars two inches longer than those of Darryl F. Zanuck. Fuller had little use for the Greek's primary theatrical principle—the one about a beginning, middle, and end. He preferred to start in the middle and end in a circle of futility, especially in his peerless war films, such as *The Steel Helmet*, which closes with the legend "There is no end to this story," or *The Big Red One*, which begins and ends on the same chord of lethal error.

Nor did he pay much mind to traditional ideas of tragic stature and denouement. Fuller's heroes are grifters, military retreads, prostitutes, gunmen, renegades, and misanthropes; early on, he made a film (*Park Row*) lauding members of his first profession, journalism, but he later sentenced the journalist-hero of *Shock Corridor* to a straitjacket. Madness is a recurring theme in Fuller's pictures. As he sees it, madness is separated from socially condoned behavior by a fabric as thin as the one between crime and salvation. In *Pickup on South Street*, Thelma Ritter plays a self-righteous informer, honored as such by the very people she sells out. When she tells an immoral Commie, "You'd be doing me a big favor if you'd blow my head off," he does her the favor, thereby triggering his own destruction.

In retrospect, it's amazing that Fuller had the Hollywood career he did. Thriving on his own terms from 1949 until 1964, he wrote and directed seventeen films, most of which made money. Then he slipped into a long turnaround of failed, butchered, and unreleased projects, reinventing himself as cinema's grizzled anecdotalist-prophet, offering his own aesthetic principle. ("The film is like a battleground," he barks in Jean-Luc Godard's *Pierrot le Fou*. "Love, hate, action, violence, death—in one word, emotion!") Refusing to say die, Fuller rebounded and completed his masterpiece, *The Big Red One*, in 1980. It, too, was butchered; but the documentarian and film critic Richard Schickel later restored fifty minutes for a triumphant premiere at the 2004 New York Film Festival.

Fuller is a favorite of baby-boom filmmakers, who saw his pictures as kids and never forgot the experience. (My first was *Merrill's Marauders*, one of the most grueling movie memories of my childhood; my father observed that his three-years' service in the Philippines was less exhausting than watching Fuller's trek through Burmese swamps, re-created in the more verdant Philippines—see "War/Agitprop" in Part Three.) Yet much of Fuller's work, especially the early pictures, was a long time coming to DVD. At long last, thanks to Criterion and 20th Century Fox, we can now see seven of his first eight pictures, covering the years 1949–55. After that, Fuller took a breather, reemerging with no fewer than three independently produced films in 1957. Criterion's no-frills Eclipse series has issued *The First Films of Samuel Fuller*, collecting *I Shot Jesse James* (1949), *The Baron of Arizona* (1950), and *The Steel Helmet* (1951), and except for a brief distortion at the 102-minute mark of *Jesse James*, the transfers are clean and sharp. Fox has added *Fixed Bayonets!* (1951) and *Hell and High Water* (1954) to its earlier releases of *House of Bamboo* (1955) and *Forty Guns* (1957). Other available titles include *Pickup on South Street* (1953), *Merrill's Marauders* (1962), *Shock Corridor* (1963), *The Naked Kiss* (1964), the much banned and battered inquiry into racism *White Dog* (1982), and the restoration of *The Big Red One*. Still unreleased on DVD as of 2009 are *Park Row* (1952) and such later expressions of Fuller's lurid impudence as *Run of the Arrow* and *China Gate* (both 1957), *Verboten!* and *The Crimson Kimono* (both 1959), and *Underworld USA* (1961). Only *Hell and High Water*, a submarine misfire, is expendable. The others are genuine depth charges—vital, original, outrageous, and prescient.

Born in Worcester, Massachusetts, in 1912, to immigrant Jews, Fuller worked as a New York crime reporter at seventeen. He wrote pulp fiction (his novel *The Dark Page* is back in print), served with distinction as an infantryman during the war (Silver Star, Bronze Star, Purple Heart), and then nosed around Hollywood for years writing scripts. The independent producer Robert L. Lippert offered him his own film, and at the end of a decade (1940s) renowned for resplendent directorial debuts (Welles, Huston, Minnelli, Wilder), Fuller made his mark with a B picture in an overcrowded genre: *I Shot Jesse James,* a psychosexual, sympathetic look at Bob Ford, the "dirty little coward" who murdered the absurdly romanticized outlaw. From the first silent close-ups of two men, one with sweat on his upper lip, preceding a master shot that reveals them facing off during a bank robbery, to the eerie finish, in which a dying Ford declares his love not for the woman cradling him in her arms but for James, the film reflects the unmistakable vision of a man marinated in the quick fixes, vain sensationalism, and tattered truths of hard-nosed newspapering. Fuller found many of his best stories and characters during the war, but he learned his style in the tabloids—which is not to say that he wasn't a natural filmmaker.

Fuller was an intensely pictorial director. His obsessive close-ups stem from the belief that if you look long and deep into faces, they will reveal nuances not found in the script. His long takes, which in fight scenes required actors to do the work of stuntmen, elaborate the plot with a dizzying sense of spatial dynamics, sometimes obliging a performer to throw a punch at the camera. (Imagine what Fuller might have done with 3D.) His abrupt cutting between elaborate masters and invasive close-ups—surely it was from Fuller that Sergio Leone learned the power of shifty Cinemascope eyes—creates a visual dissonance, emphasizing an obsessive need to show the action outside while implying the tumult inside. Among his predecessors, the director Fuller most recalls is D. W. Griffith, who is mentioned only in passing in Fuller's posthumous memoir, *A Third Face* (published in 2002, five years after his death at eighty-five). They both had an eye for *tableau vivant* arrangements of characters, a penchant for drumming up suspense by interlacing opposing actions, and a predilection for punctuating emotional flare-ups with full-screen faces. Griffith all but invented these techniques, spurred by practical considerations, but that's beside the point.

Like Griffith, Fuller was more obsessed with race than any other director of his generation. He dealt liberally and candidly with black/white racism (*The Steel Helmet, China Gate, Shock Corridor, White Dog*), while elaborating on the compassionate exploration of prejudice between Occidentals and Orientals that Griffith had explored in *Broken Blossoms*. Fuller tackled Japanese-American relations repeatedly. In *The Steel Helmet*, he broke Hollywood's silence about Japanese interment camps; in the resplendent *House of Bamboo* (shot in Tokyo with a blasting of colors to rival that of Ozu's *Floating Weeds* or Kurosawa's *Ran*), he contrasted the healthy affair between a Japanese woman and an American military cop with the fatal friendship between two deeply closeted male gangsters. He brought the fear of otherness home in *The Crimson Kimono*, which was advertised with a poster that screamed: "*YES*, this is a beautiful American girl in the arms of a Japanese boy!" Yet the most profound tie between Griffith and Fuller is one of narrative attitude. Each man thrived on pulp. Griffith preferred a melodramatic, sentimental kind that flowered at the turn of the twentieth century, mixing gothic and penny dreadful conventions. Fuller brought the age of *Black Mask*, comic books, and scandal sheets alive with an energy that perfectly complemented what he habitually called his "yarns."

The true pulp imagination involves more than an appetite for gutter tales. James M. Cain (who, like Fuller, favored circular plots and *in media res* openings) was a moral Puritan compared with William Faulkner. Yet *The Postman Always Rings Twice* is archetypal pulp, which is not the case with the far more depraved *Sanctuary* (not to mention *Light in August*)—despite Faulkner's admitted desire to roll in the muck. Similarly, most classic noir films of the 1940s and 1950s, whatever their literary origins, were filmed by craftsmen who polished the material to a glossy sheen, hoping by virtue of their artistry to graduate to a better class of picture.

Not Fuller. You cannot fake a pulp imagination. No film school graduate can replicate dialogue that flowed from his typewriter, including the left-field borrowings from Aristotle. Choosing memorable Fuller lines is like assembling a bouquet: "It's you she's sorry for, but it's him she wants." "If you die, I'll kill ya." "Don't shoot! I'm out of bullets." "Now I know what I was looking for—a woman who loves me for who I am." "I'm your Itchiban, not him." "Each man has his own reason for living and his own price for dying." "In your estimation I am a . . . a female, but first I am a scientist and a good one." After Jean Peters comes up from a deep kiss and tells Richard Widmark, "I really like you," Widmark says, "Yeah? Why? Everybody likes everybody when they're kissing." Yet dialogue is the least of it. Fuller's tabloid resourcefulness extends to music (the orchestra "shoots" Jesse James with three brass chords before Bob Ford fires a shot) and photography (a thunder clap and lightning flash accompany Vincent Price's entrance in *The Baron of Arizona*). Then there are the wrinkles in the plots, with their mounting ironies, sudden breakouts of hitting or kissing or shooting, and pure storytelling orneriness. The true man of pulp can have his cake and eat it twice.

In the 1950s, Fuller wanted to make a film about a criminal syndicate run by ex-army personnel in accordance with military regulations. The project fell apart, so Darryl Zanuck, who admired and sponsored Fuller, suggested he remake a 1948 film, *The Street with No Name*—in Japan, if he preferred. Fuller simply adapted his military gang yarn to the basic plot device of the 1948 Fox film (FBI agent infiltrates gang) and the underworld of picturesque Tokyo, which, in *House of Bamboo*, is mysteriously ruled not by Yakuza but by Robert Ryan with the aid of sexually maladroit henchmen and jitterbugging "kimono girls." On the ground, the movie makes no sense. But in the higher frequencies of pulpland, where Sam Fuller operates, it is spellbinding. You can either fend his films off with invocations of logic and good taste, or give yourself up to his mania for truth, justice, and the American way.

12

AKIRA KUROSAWA'S DEEP FOCUS

OLYMPIAN

Spectacle in American movies gets little critical respect. It is too much associated with sanctimony, bad history, inflated romance, and special effects rather than with serious ideas and epical grandeur. In the postwar years, Hollywood studios—hammered by the loss of theaters and the rise of free-agent actors and television—fought back with spectacle as a corollary of lavishness: wider screens, longer running times, deeper cleavages, massed extras, star cameos, and colossal stories involving Christ, Moses, Rome, and D-Day. Successors to Griffith and Selznick bet their dividends on the usual trifecta of piety, star power, and visual gimmicks.

Another possibility existed: humanist spectacle springing from a capacious, Homeric scrutiny of mankind. In this realm, cinematic opulence is an extension of the artist's vision, not the producer's calculation. This vision may demand a large canvas, but it isn't defined by size: it's a way of seeing, as clear-eyed in the hero's tent as on the battlefield, an approach exemplified by the Japanese filmmaker Akira Kurosawa (1910–1998), whose influence spurred the imagination of a generation of American directors. In Kurosawa's work, the Olympian view predominates, whether the subject is as large as war and kingly succession or as pitiful as modern man caught in the labyrinth of urban blight. He knows that all we need to know of Achilles is that he is proud, not how he got that way. Pride dominates the human condition, generating action, whereas motive is conjectural, generating contemplation, which isn't nearly as cinematic. As a character in Sam Peckinpah's *The Wild Bunch* says, "I don't care what you *meant* to do. It's what you did I don't like."

The Criterion Collection, which has released most of Kurosawa's films on DVD, recently invited us to revisit what is arguably the greatest of all action films: the endlessly imitated, never equaled, 207-minute *Seven Samurai* (1954), in a deluxe three-disc presentation. Only dedicated enthusiasts will access all the deep-background material, including a two-hour conversation with Kurosawa (shot in 1993), two documentaries, two critical commentaries, trailers, artwork, and written essays. The prize is the restored print, a vast improvement on the previous edition: bright blacks and whites replace faded grays; the scratches are removed; the soundtrack resounds. The upgrade is more than warranted.

Other films (including a few by Kurosawa) contain more skillfully choreographed action and sharper dialogue. But none so movingly combine sweeping spectacle with the inspired delineation of character. The plot is simple enough to suit a one-line treatment (farmers hire professional warriors to defend them from marauding thieves), and the structure consists of two acts: recruiting the warriors, battling the thieves. Yet *Seven Samurai*, set in sixteenth-century Japan, encompasses the Homeric-Tolstoyan canvas of war and peace, honor and shame, good and evil, class warfare, gender iniquity, generational fear, and changing times. Its comedy ripens in the quotidian interaction of social opposites.

If a great epic must focus more on observation than psychology, the psychology it does present must be so astutely drawn that little explanation is required. Kurosawa found precisely the right technology to serve that vision: multiple cameras and a telephoto lens. Shooting action sequences with three cameras guaranteed him full coverage without having to shoot and match different takes. The telephoto lens enabled him to stay out of the actors' way while creating an absolute directorial omniscience. The narrator looks from on high, yet can zoom in for the kill. Kurosawa's mastery is always at the service of characters—in *Seven Samurai*, they are highly individualized samurai and farmers whom we return to with increased pleasure and understanding. Even minor figures are drawn with lucidity and originality, not least the women: the hidden daughter who seduces the apprentice samurai, the old matriarch who sets out to butcher a fallen prisoner. Most remarkable is Rikichi's abducted wife (Yukiko Shimazaki), first glimpsed in a burning brothel from which she calmly exits, smugly inhaling the fresh air, content to let the brigands burn—until confronted by Rikichi. Like Hidetora, the lord in *Ran* who cannot face the son he disowned, she prefers the holocaust to the reality of her disgrace.

Looking back after half a century, during which the proliferation of samurai and other martial arts films achieved a virtuoso athleticism, we can't help but notice that the swordsmanship in *Seven Samurai* is relatively inexpert. Yet in what other film do we so come to love its ancient warriors? When Kurosawa's samurai novice stares worshipfully at the reticent master, Kyuzo (played with reclusive cool by Seiji Miyaguchi), we smile at his naiveté—and share in it. Kyuzo's professionalism (which inspired James Coburn's knife thrower in John Sturges's 1960 nonepical rehash, *The Magnificent Seven*) is as appealing as it is deadly.

Kurosawa's most steadfast actors, Toshiro Mifune and Takashi Shimura, have defining roles in *Seven Samurai*, embodying opposing tonalities of the spectacle—Mifune an obstreperous trumpet, Shimura a shrewd oboe. Their respective expressions of blowhard irreverence and wise assurance mandate the film's shifting tempo and incarnate Kurosawa's shrewd economy. We learn all we need to know about their characters in emblematic moments. Mark Twain once observed, "Action speaks louder than words but not nearly as often." He would have no complaints about *Seven Samurai*, in which Mifune's character discloses his secret, humble origin in four words. "This baby is me!" he says of a farmer's infant, handed him by its dying mother. No less efficient is Kurosawa's comment on the mounting impersonality of warfare. His samurai are cut down by muskets, a weapon they have not been trained to resist.

In the 1950s, Japan was perhaps the least likely country to revive cinematic spectacle as an empowering art. Hollywood had the wealth and technical means; the Soviet Union had the panoramic tradition of Eisenstein. Japan, digging itself out from the rubble of firebombing and nuclear attacks, was known for a cinema of domestic realism—most notably the chamber films of Ozu and Mizoguchi. In claiming the sixteenth century as an adaptable setting for his themes, Kurosawa restored a forgotten age to Japanese history and gave the West a novel reflection of itself. Kurosawa single-handedly internationalized Japanese cinema with his eleventh film, *Rashomon*, in 1950.

Based on stories by Ryunosuke Akutagawa, whose use of the distant past anticipated Kurosawa's, it is a fiercely stylized film that combines Noh Theater with startling camerawork and lighting: the sunlight-dappled forest and the rushing of foreground characters against the far horizon became Kurosawa trademarks. In the West, the film seemed obviously Japanese; in Japan, Kurosawa's vitality and violence seemed all too Western. He was eventually criticized in both hemispheres for his alleged lack of authenticity.

Indeed, he often looked west for material, conceding the influence of Griffith and Ford, and adapting Shakespeare three times (*Macbeth* as *Throne of Blood*, *Hamlet* as *The Bad Sleep Well*, *King Lear* as *Ran*), as well as Gorki (*The Lower Depths*), Dostoevski (*The Idiot*), Ed McBain (*High and Low*), and Dashiell Hammett (unacknowledged for *Yojimbo*). Kurosawa switched between stories set in the past and present day, including several films dealing with the medical world and industrialism (the two come together in *High and Low*). Yet most of his films derive from Japanese sources, and all suit his thematic concerns and objective visual style, predicated on a love of spectacle.

For Kurosawa, history is a cycle of violence and corruption, interrupted by rare heroic figures who stem the tide and give cause for hope. The circularity of his vision is echoed by the shape of his career: the masterworks of his late period replay ideas found in the two dark stories that triggered *Rashomon*. The bandit who challenges authority in Akutagawa's "In a Grove" ("Am I the only one who kills people. . . . You kill people with your power, with your money") augurs the thief in *Kagemusha* (1980); the servant who steals to avoid starving in Akutagawa's "Rashomon" employs the justification that devastates almost every character in *Ran*. Both characters are embodied in the twisted kidnapper of *High and Low* (1963). The allure of Kurosawa's seven samurai warriors soured by the time of *Yojimbo* (1961), and vanished from the lavishly colored yet desolate landscapes of *Kagemusha* and the awesome *Ran* (1985).

Ran, which is as much a critique of Lear as an adaptation of its central dilemma, set again in the sixteenth century, is surely Kurosawa's supreme spectacle and one of his greatest films. (Packaged as a two-disc edition, *Ran* features one of the most eye-popping transfers in Criterion's catalog.) We marvel at the ingenuity of his widescreen compositions, saturated color, and rousing dramatic peaks, notwithstanding the copious bloodletting and severe denouement. Yet we *expect* a sumptuous grandeur in this kind of film. Those qualities are more surprising and disturbing when found in the corrupt mire of contemporary Tokyo. In that sense, Kurosawa's modern films are among the purest expressions of his humanism, particularly *Ikiru* (1952), his meditation on a dying bureaucrat and one of the few great films (another is Leo McCarey's neglected *Make Way for Tomorrow*) about aging and death; and *High and Low*, a thriller in which a moral quandary (should an executive ruin himself to ransom the mistakenly kidnapped son of his chauffeur) triggers a grim study of class division and irrational hatred.

Kurosawa created a new kind of hero in *Ikiru*. Watanabe (an indelible performance by Takashi Shimura) is part Ivan Illych and part Bartleby, and Kurosawa allows him a triumphant end, quietly rocking on a snowy swing in his unexpectedly fashionable hat. Yet his triumph is told through the recollections of inebriated bureaucrats who resent and deny his achievement. Drawing a line in the sand of municipal inefficiency, Watanabe is a samurai for another day. Both *Ikiru* and *High and Low* are structured with Kurosawa's patented two-act narrative: (1) Watanabe finds the answer to a wasted life and (2) acts on it; (1) *High and Low*'s industrialist surrenders to a tormentor who (2) is pursued through the rings of hell. This way of telling a story enforces its clarity, as does Kurosawa's unfashionable preference for action over motive.

Kurosawa's Olympian view did not sit well in the early 1960s, the height of the empathetic *Nouvelle Vague*. Rarely, in those years, did an epical vision, free of sentimental pandering, make its way into American films, although there were some—Anthony Mann's *El Cid*, Orson Welles's *Chimes at Midnight*, and Stanley Kubrick's *2001* come to mind. A decade later, however, Kurosawa's ability to locate the grand manner in ordinary and extraordinary lives found an enthusiastic reception among young American directors. Without his example, it's hard to imagine such prodigious visions as Francis Coppola's *The Godfather*, Martin Scorsese's *Raging Bull*, Philip Kaufman's *The Unbearable Lightness of Being*, and Steven Spielberg's *Schindler's List*. One measure of a towering artist is that he makes other artists raise their sights.

RED HARVESTS

CRITERION HAS RELEASED glistening new transfers of two catalog staples, *Yojimbo* (1961) and its sequel, *Sanjuro* (1962), suitably boxed together. Like the first two *Godfather* films, they enhance each other. *Yojimbo* (bodyguard) was Kurosawa's international blockbuster, and the character of Sanjuro (the bodyguard's alias), an ultimately infallible freelance samurai, endures as Toshiro Mifune's most popular role. Indeed, if neither film is ranked with Kurosawa's masterworks, one reason is that they so success-fully turn the screws of boys' life adventures—violence, revenge, comedy, suspense. Seek elsewhere for sex and romance. It is no more possible to imagine Sanjuro in an erotic clinch than on a horse with a six-gun.

Oh wait. That's precisely how Sergio Leone envisioned Sanjuro when he remade *Yojimbo* as *A Fistful of Dollars* (1964), though he, too, dispensed with amours. Yet despite Leone's fidelity to Kurosawa and Clint Eastwood's chin-scratching in the Mifune manner, the Japanese films remain essentially untouchable as character studies. Sanjuro may work as more of a fantasy figure than the monarch in *Ran*, the clerk in *Ikiru*, the manufacturer in *High and Low*, or the doctor in *Red Beard* (1965), but he is no less a being of univer-sal application. *Yojimbo* holds up a mirror to the West, presenting a Japanese reflection of our most familiar wish-fulfillment hero: the tough, unsenti-mental, yet good-hearted rebel who wanders into a strange town and cleans it up by killing most of the residents.

Kurosawa employed impeccable, if unacknowledged, source material. Dashiell Hammett's first novel, *Red Harvest* (1929), has a shadowy movie history. A milestone in crime fiction, it thumbs its nose at the legions that attempt to adapt it: for all the countless treatments and scripts, it has yet to be filmed. Upon its publication, Paramount bought it for producer Walter Wanger, who, had he trusted the book, might have got the jump on 1931's *Little Caesar* and the whole Warners gangster cycle. Instead, he replaced Hammett's operative with a dopey newspaperman and framed the plot as a vehicle for singer Helen Morgan. The result, *Roadside Nights* (1930), is now valued only for preserving the legendary nightclub act of Clayton, Jackson, and Durante—it was Jimmy Durante's first talkie.

Red Harvest may be too novelistic to suit the movies: if the laughably high body count is cinematically apt, the profusion of characters, gin-soaked dia-logue, and sequential mysteries are more of a challenge. Yet it introduced or at least popularized three concepts that movies have gnawed on for decades, without attribution. The first is the detective as avenging angel, often trans-posed to the West—in *Shane*, *Bad Day at Black Rock*, *High Plains Drifter*, the television series *Have Gun, Will Travel* and its urban retread, *The Equalizer*, among many others. The second is the link between business and crime: the town's thugs are brought to power when legitimate capitalist interests are corrupted by greed—an abiding Marxist critique so commonplace that it is hardly noticed in films as diverse as *Mr. Smith Goes to Washington*, *The Roaring Twenties*, *This Gun for Hire*, *Force of Evil*, *On the Waterfront*, and *The Godfather*.

The signal concept, however, is the one that gins the plot: the stranger pretends to hire out to all sides, manipulating them into mutual self-destruction. This device, coupled with one or both of the others, marks a film as a *Red Harvest* baby, a category brought to fruition in *Yojimbo* and then diminished by various degrees in such variations as *A Fistful of Dollars*, *Miller's Crossing*, and *Last Man Standing*. Ironically or underhandedly, take your pick, Kurosawa—who sued Leone for stealing his film (*A Fistful of Dollars* was released in America with no writing credits)—not only denied the Hammett connection but expressed surprise that no one before him had thought to exploit a rivalry between two "equally bad" sides. Actually, Homer had hit that one out of the park.

Kurosawa borrowed more than just concepts. The scene in which one gang blows up a rival's stronghold and butchers the unarmed leaders is taken straight from *Red Harvest*. More to the point, the character of Sanjuro has several points in common with Hammett's detective. He won't work without a client and advance payment; his morality is far from mercenary, and he takes orders from no one (least of all clients); he is physically vulnerable; and he has no name. Hammet's Operative takes a new alias every time he checks in to a hotel. Sanjuro's moniker vaguely refers to his age—thirty going on forty. Still, *Yojimbo* is quintessential Kurosawa, and an inspired example of solving the problems of adaptation. Unlike the American avenger, who sets out on a mission or is summoned, Sanjuro relies on chance. He throws a branch in the air and goes where it points. Having taken that road, he immediately overhears a family arguing about war, honor, and work—the film's only acknowledgment of the farmers who are striving to make do beyond the snake pit of a town. The image of the wife, working heedlessly at a loom, stands in marked contrast to everyone else in the film.

When Sanjuro arrives on the main street, he stops at a restaurant, where the proprietor, pointing through window slats, identifies the characters and sets up the plot. The rest is Sanjuro's chess game. Hammett's Op had to contend with four warring factions plus the industrialist behind them. Kurosawa sensibly reduces the parties to two, each with his own businessman trying fecklessly to pull their strings and ending up either mad or dead. In the end, Sanjuro steps over the bodies, waves to the few survivors, and leaves.

A year later, by popular demand, Sanjuro returned in the eponymous sequel, this time as a wilier observer who sees through the fakery of his opponents and accepts, with payment, the responsibility of mother hen for a group of credulous young noblemen all too eager to walk into a trap. *Sanjuro* is a funnier film, and the mode is intimate rather than epic. The powerful officials are as corrupt and desiccated as ever, but the supporting cast includes a traitor who sides with the good guys after a hot meal, and two ladies who are not going to let a massacre or two disrupt their tempo and repose. Kurosawa offers two of his finest conceits: the river of camellias to signal attack and the unforgettable climactic one-stroke duel, which produces an arterial gush that has corrupted any number of filmmakers who prefer gush to character.

An interesting question posed by the diptych is: Which story comes first— does *Sanjuro* follow the events of *Yojimbo* or precede them? The point is intriguing because the themes of the films are contradicted by their style. In *Sanjuro*, the samurai learns that the best sword stays sheathed, and appears to have attained a wisdom far removed from the bloodletting of *Yojimbo*, suggesting a chronological follow-up. Yet the comic bourgeoisie, chamber-like style of *Sanjuro* feels like a precursor to the grandeur of *Yojimbo*, where the hero undergoes a resurrection and satisfying triumph. Conversely, if *Sanjuro* has the look of a trial run before the stateliness of *Yojimbo*, then we must assume that the notion of resisting violence has itself been resisted— that Sanjuro's renunciation merely reflects his temporary foul mood after an unpleasant killing.

The new prints are a great improvement on earlier editions. The aspect ratio has been corrected, contrasts are more vividly defined, and the imposed English titles and preface removed. The translation is presumably more accurate and certainly wittier, with the addition of lines like "I'll make sashimi of them." The question "So that's Tazaemon, the drummer?" now reads, "Hey, is that your nitwit mayor?" and a yelped "Mother!" is suitably changed to "Mommy!" The sound does justice to Masaru Sato's bravura Japanese-percussion-meets-avant-garde-jazz score, and the extras include the usual commentaries and trailers as well as excerpts from the illuminating series *Akira Kurosawa: It Is Wonderful to Create*.

13

MEDIEVAL INGMAR BERGMAN: GOD IS IN THE HOUSE, MAYBE

THE COMBINATION OF high-contrast black and white cinematography with extreme close-ups—a stylization that, in this country, flourished in the noir years, reached an autumnal apogee in *Raging Bull*, and recently enjoyed a fleeting revival in *Good Night, and Good Luck*—achieved Nordic apotheosis in the middle-period films of Ingmar Bergman (1918–2007). The pictures he made between 1957 and 1963, from *The Seventh Seal* through *The Silence*, have a gleaming, raven, fixed look, the images as doted on as the gown in *The Virgin Spring*, sewn by fifteen maidens. However bleak humankind's prospects in an indifferent universe, the pictorial opportunities were ravishing. This paradoxically stark yet luscious visual approach helped win Bergman brief art-house hegemony, and continues to secure his films a respectful if by no means reverent reception.

The handsomeness of his work is itself dramatic, compensating for the occasionally sluggish pans, logical lapses, and "wither God?" meditations. These heirlooms from a distant shore are not beyond criticism, just impervious to it. We may speak of each shot in an Antonioni movie as a perfect photograph, but we don't really mean it; that is, we never really feel we are in a museum instead of a movie theater. But perusing middle-period Bergman can be an experience not unlike strolling through London's National Portrait Gallery and spotting the originals for dozens of vaguely recalled paperback and classical music album covers. Just as the museum originals restore luster absent from cheaply reproduced covers, Bergman's films restore the contextual power of those endlessly reproduced stills. The films are the best antidotes to the clichés of visual quotation.

The Seventh Seal (1957), in particular, is often honored more for its cultural stature than its prevailing vitality. Those who attended its first international rollout and were changed forever by the experience are now second-guessing their attachment to a work so firmly ensconced in the realm of middlebrow allusions. Its Eisenhower-lookalike Reaper, emblematic chess game, and Dance of Death have been endlessly emulated and parodied. Worse, *The Seventh Seal* quickly assumed, and has never quite shaken, the reputation, formerly attributed to castor oil, of something good for you—a true kiss of death. A movie that's good for you is, by definition, not good for you. So it's a relief to set aside the solemnity of cultural sanction, along with the still frames that have adorned greeting cards, and return to Bergman's actual film, restored to its original glossy look on a Criterion DVD: a dark, droll, quizzical masterpiece that wears its fifty-something years with the nimble grace of the acrobat Jof, who is the film's true prism of consciousness.

Not that its cultural importance should be forgotten. As the film that launched art-house cinema (along with Bergman, leading player Max von Sydow, and distributor Janus Films), *The Seventh Seal* holds a place in movie annals as secure as that of *Potemkin* or *Citizen Kane* or any other earthshaking classic you care to name. Other imports had found appreciative audiences in the United States before Bergman's film passed through customs, including Kurosawa's *Rashomon* in 1951 and Fellini's *The Nights of Cabiria* in 1957. But the effect of *The Seventh Seal*'s American debut at New York's Paris Theater, in October 1958, reinforced eight months later by the opening of Bergman's *Wild Strawberries*, was transformative. With that one-two punch, cinema catapulted to the front line of a cultural advance guard that—shoulder to shoulder with modern jazz, abstract painting, beat writing, Theater of the Absurd—sought to undermine the intractable mass taste promoted by Hollywood, television, and the Brill Building.

Everything about Bergman's work startled American filmgoers: the stark cinematography and unsettling imagery; the scorching beaches and bleak glades; the fastidiously blocked compositions and credible invocations of the distant past; the magnificent company of actors; the taut plotting and elliptical dialogue—all handled with psychological astuteness, deft symbols, mordant wit, and equal attention to religious-ethical concerns in a possibly godforsaken universe, and familial conflicts in an undoubtedly sexual one. At a time when the films of Carl Dreyer were largely neglected, Bergman advanced a Scandinavian aesthetic that rivaled and in some respects trumped that of the novelists Knut Hamsun and Pär Lagerkvist, proving to a generation of eager movie lovers that cinema is a global pursuit of infinite promise, worth living for and talking about late into the night.

The Seventh Seal opens with a gorgeously baleful sky and a gliding eagle, almost frozen against the gathering clouds. A fourteenth-century knight and his squire, lately returned from the slaughter of the Crusades only to face the slaughter of the Black Plague, are asleep on the beach. A long shot shows the sea and sky and rocky shore as though uncovering the world for the first time. The grim insinuations of this glossily disarming start are promptly borne out in the appearance of a decomposing face and a recurring skull that could not be more symbolically playful if it had "Memento Mori" stamped on its cranium. As one of the film's several mischievous artists and performers observes, with archness worthy of Alfred Hitchcock, "A skull is more interesting than a naked woman."

In 1958, American reviewers emphasized the film's foreignness, its cerebral artiness. In his enthusiastic *New York Times* notice, Bosley Crowther described it as "essentially intellectual" and "as tough—and rewarding—a screen challenge as the moviegoer has had to face this year," which evokes all the appeal of an algebra problem or a firing squad. Few called attention to the film's comic sensibility or its affinity with other movies and cultural strategies of the period, which in retrospect are harder to miss.

Bergman uses as his central narrative device one of the oldest and most persistent paradigms in Western culture: the questing, idealistic hero (tall, gaunt, easily awestruck) and earthy, practical lackey (squat, well fed, ironic). The Don Quixote and Sancho Panza template has endured numberless variations, reversals, and buddy-buddy deviations, from d'Artagnan and Planchet to Vladimir and Estragon, from Mutt and Jeff comedy teams to singing cowboys and their dumpy sidekicks. Bergman's version, as played by the craggy and prematurely aged (he was all of twenty-eight) Max von Sydow and the square-jawed Gunnar Björnstrand, promises, briefly, to be a conventional riff on righteous master and trusty servant. But a rude scowl from the latter indicates an unbridgeable gulf between them. Their most memorable conversations are not with each other.

The knight, Antonius Block, seeks proof of God or the devil, and gets no satisfaction from a strangely clueless Death (Bengt Ekerot), who may be the hardest-working man in eschatology—playing chess to harvest one soul, sawing down a tree to claim another. Block, the chessman, hopes to win his reprieve from Death by beating him through "a combination of bishop and knight," though he knows better than most how utterly inefficient are the combined forces of religion and the military. "My indifference to man has shut me out," he laments. Unlike the blithe entertainer Jof (Nils Poppe), whose family he apparently saves by diverting Death's attention, Block is not permitted visionary glimpses of God's beneficence, but he sees man's villainy, cloaked in religious avowal, everywhere. When Death finally arrives to claim him and his group, only Block blubbers in prayer. In contrast, his squire Jöns insists on his right as a man "to feel to the very end the triumph of being alive."

Jöns, the caustically plain-speaking singer of bawdy songs, is one of Bergman's (and Björnstrand's) greatest characters. Stronger than the knight because he is more confident in his agnosticism, he is not indifferent to man. He is, instead, contemptuous of military deliverance ("Our crusade was so stupid that only an idealist could have thought it out") and religious pageantry ("Do you really expect modern people to take this drivel seriously?"), and doesn't need a diversionary ploy to save Jof from the perfidy of men. Jöns gets many of the best lines, which resonate with the kind of verbal incongruities that Samuel Beckett had recently unleashed, especially as he tries to console the cuckolded blacksmith, who tells him, "You're lucky you believe in your own twaddle." "Who says I believe it," Jöns replies: "But I like giving advice. I'm a man of learning."

In the end, Jöns and Block share the same fate, chained hand to hand in the Dance of Death that only Jof can see. Jof and his wife, Mia (Bibi Andersson), and their child escape the holocaust, after inviting Block to participate in a sacramental meal of milk and wild strawberries. We don't know for how long they will be spared, but more than any of the other characters, they are us, neither courageous nor craven; they are devoted more to family than to God (or to the gods of war) and consequently live in God's grace. The angelic Mia is one of five women in the film, of whom only the libidinous chicken-gnawing Lisa is caught in the Dance. Five centuries before movie magazines, Lisa had set her cap on the closest thing she could find to a matinee idol, the actor Skat, and seduces him while his partners Jof and Mia sing a song about the devil shitting on the shore. The other women are the knight's Penelope-like wife, risking plague to welcome him home; an alleged young witch, bound for the stake, who takes the fanatics at their word, embracing the devil they insist lurks everywhere; and the silent maid (Gunnel Lindblom), saved from one rape but perhaps victimized by others. These three do not fear death—the last two welcome it with evident relief—and are absent from Jof's explicit vision of Death's humiliating dance. Is it because they embrace Death that they are spared that mortification (for they, too, have been reaped; we have seen the witch's final throes and heard Death's promise to harvest them all), or are they absent from Jof's vision simply because it *is* Jof's vision? He had never seen the wife or the witch and had shown only a benign indifference to the mute maid.

Bergman's religious symbolism, which distinguished *The Seventh Seal* from his previous films and marked many of those to follow, paralleled a turnabout in the work of his fellow Swede Pär Lagerkvist, a man no less attuned than Beckett to existential paradox. Lagerkvist, whose dramatic work Bergman had directed as recently as 1956, had been Sweden's most celebrated writer for nearly forty years when, in the 1950s, his concerns took a sharp turn toward religious inquiry, in a series of short novels beginning with *Barabbas* and *The Sybil*. His primary theme must have registered with Bergman: Did God create man or did man create God, and does it matter once the bond of faith is accepted? Having lost faith on the eve of apocalypse, Block, like Lagerkvist's pagans at the dawn of Christianity, needs God to show Himself.

Bergman acknowledged a correlation between his vision of the Middle Ages and the mid-century fear of atomic devastation. As an ardent filmgoer, he could not have been unmindful of the ongoing welter of End of Days scenarios, sublime and ludicrous. *The Seventh Seal* opened in Stockholm in February 1957; in the preceding two years alone, apocalypses, holocausts, plagues, eschatology, and resurrection had informed, among many other films, *Kiss Me Deadly, Ordet, Night and Fog, Invasion of the Body Snatchers, Godzilla: King of the Monsters, Forbidden Planet, The Wrong Man, Moby Dick, It Came from Beneath the Sea, The End of the Affair, Night of the Hunter, The Burmese Harp, Land of the Pharaohs,* and *The Ten Commandments.* Dozens more were on the way, including a few about Jesus, the most egregious of them starring Max von Sydow.

Yet of those films only *The Seventh Seal* maintains throughout a peculiarly modernistic insistence on doubt. It embraces doubt the way most of the others embrace piety, futility, or melodrama. Only *The Seventh Seal* achieves uncanny timelessness by convincingly recreating the time in which it is set. No self-respecting Egyptologist is likely to use a still from *The Ten Commandments* in a historical study. But in 2008, John Hatcher illustrated his "personal history" of *The Black Death* with Renaissance artworks plus a shot of Bergman's Dance of Death, which feels entirely appropriate. Nor have the film's moral concerns dated—its disdain for religious persecution, trumped-up wars, and the deals most of us desperately make with Death to delay the inevitable. Meanwhile, Jof and Mia ride off into the sunset, with their infant acrobat-in-training son: for the clowns, there is no final curtain.

The Virgin Spring (1960)—its gleam fully restored in Criterion's DVD, which is bolstered by comments and reminiscences from Bergman (audio), actors Gunnel Lindblom and Birgitta Pettersson (video), fan Ang Lee (video), scholars Birgitta Steene (audio) and Peter Cowie (print), and scenarist Ulla Isaksson (print)—arrived midway in the middle-period cycle, as the second and last of Bergman's medieval tapestries and the first of his films photographed by his longtime second-in-command, Sven Nykvist. The plot is so tidy and generic (revenge is mine, if that's okay with you, Lord) that it found an audience even as critics dismissed its technique and concerns as passé. Raging censorship battles regarding the rape and murder of the virgin didn't hurt.

The story is based on an old Swedish ballad, *Tore's Daughter at Vange* (included in the DVD booklet), in which Karin, the vain and spoiled daughter of a farmer, rides late in the day to church, richly adorned. Three herdsmen rape and murder her, and a miraculous spring flows where her body is abandoned. The killers ask for shelter at her home, revealing their foul deed by offering for sale Karin's clothing. The father, Tore, butchers them and prays for forgiveness, vowing to build a stone church.

Isaksson's screenplay makes many alterations, of which the most significant concern conflicts between nascent Christianity and lingering paganism, personified by the dark and wild-eyed Ingeri (Lindblom, whose finest moment is her vengeful bark "Ha ha!"). As a pregnant and abused foster child jealous of Karin (Pettersson), Ingeri wills the catastrophe. In line with movie and box-office conventions, the key plot change saved the miracle for last, after Tore (Max von Sydow) begs forgiveness. *The Virgin Spring* is the only Bergman film in which God isn't silent; He takes Karin, but gives back a spring. The moment when Tore lifts his daughter's head and the rivulet begins to gush is memorable, though perhaps not as picture-perfect as Tore wrestling with a birch tree. A particularly nice touch has Ingeri as the first to accept the spring as a sign, devoutly cleansing her face in it. For a true pagan, one superstition is as good as another.

The Virgin Spring moves at a deliberate pace, but not one of its eighty-nine minutes falters. Bergman not only framed his shots as souvenir post-cards (Here's our last supper! Wish you were here!), he filled them with religious symbols, rituals, allegorical side steps, fairy tale replications, woodcut chiaroscuros, and medieval observations. When Karin wants to examine her features, she looks into a water barrel, asking her hovering mother to get out of the light. The overall structure reverses God's rainbow sign, beginning with the invocation of fire and ending with purifying water. But when action is called for, it's delivered. Karin's rape and murder are made singularly appalling by mechanical details (one brute holds her legs out so the other can position himself), oppressive silence throughout the ordeal, and Karin's final, terrible, dazed glance back at those who inexplicably took her innocence, sense of self, and life. Similarly, Tore's vengeance, though illogically staged, is no more in doubt than Viggo Mortensen's Übermensch triumph in *A History of Violence*, which bears a more than passing resemblance. Tore is trying to live the life of a peaceful, Christ-abiding farmer, and his wrath is made the more horrible because it involves killing an abused and innocent boy.

Bergman's middle period divides his early, more naturalistic work from his mature, psychologically fragmented masterpieces of the mid-1960s, including *Persona* and *Hour of the Wolf*. After *The Silence*, he tried color for the numbingly unfunny satire of artists *All These Women*, but soon mastered saturated color with distinctive certainty in such benchmark films as *Cries and Whispers*, *Autumn Sonata*, and *Fanny and Alexander*. If *The Virgin Spring* seems like a minor endeavor in his development—stylistically and thematically regressive—it stands out as peculiarly characteristic of its time. It was not the only 1960 film to bring a new, graphic, sexually animated violence to world cinema. At a time when young French and Italian directors were propagating the self-reflective New Wave, breaking with the standard grammar of filmmaking, veteran directors were gnawing at the conventions of censorship, and their grueling violence was almost always directed toward women. Alfred Hitchcock, who had rarely indulged in explicit bloodletting, unleashed *Psycho*; Michael Powell, who had tempered his most violent conceits in ballet and opera, went for the jugular in *Peeping Tom*; and Luchino Visconti sacrificed a prostitute on the alter of rape and murder in *Rocco and His Brothers*. The year after Bergman received an Academy Award for *The Virgin Spring*, Vittorio De Sica, the most charmingly empathic of naturalists, won one for Sophia Loren for surviving rape in *Two Women* (best foreign picture went to Bergman again, for *Through a Glass Darkly*, in which another Karin seduces her brother and loses her mind).

The horrific content of *The Virgin Spring* outlived its religious-ethical concerns in two straight-out slasher films: Wes Craven's *The Last House on the Left* (1972) and Aldo Lado's bloodier yet more stylish and morally intricate *Night Train Murders* (1975). Lado, a specialist in the Italian *giallo*, goes far beyond Bergman in implicating the audience in obscene crimes while whetting its appetite for vengeance, but his film can only endure as a cult item for those with strong stomachs, because the religious factor, for which Bergman was mocked, is absent. *The Virgin Spring* holds the imagination because in addition to its vivid beauty, it acknowledges the truism that even if we don't believe in God, we can't help but wonder what in heaven's name He's thinking.

14

SERGIO LEONE:
HEROES, VILLAINS, AND IDIOTS

SERGIO LEONE'S CAREER is a parable of genius and ambition. To the industry born (his father directed and acted in dozens of silent films, many of them starring his mother), he began working at age seventeen, in 1946, as an unpaid assistant to Vittorio De Sica on *The Bicycle Thief*. During a long apprenticeship, Leone served as assistant director on various Italian and American epics. His reward for taking the reins from an ailing director and completing, without credit, a sword-and-sandals picture was the chance to direct his own film in the same genre, *The Colossus of Rhodes* (1961). Three years later, he made a bargain-basement Western that became an international event, *A Fistful of Dollars*.

Leone had realized every filmmaker's dream. Working with unknown actors and a $200,000 budget, he electrified a generation with the force of his visual style, remaking a fading genre into an expression of 1960s irreverence and disillusionment. Continuing in the Western idiom, he nursed a desire to become David Lean and demanded ever-larger budgets and longer running times. Yet despite the immense profits he generated, he was thwarted by censorship and cuts, especially by American distributors. His last film, the four-hour gangland saga *Once Upon a Time in America* (1984), was slashed by ninety minutes, rendering it incomprehensible. When he died from heart failure at age sixty in 1989, he had directed only seven films. Not until recent years have the English-language versions been restored to their intended length.

Seven films. Not a large legacy, but one that saved the Italian film industry when Hercules and friends wore out their welcome, and put an indelible mark on movies everywhere, not least on the American Western as practiced by Sam Peckinpah, Don Siegel, Robert Altman, and Clint Eastwood. Now his oeuvre is finally available in what appear to be authoritative DVD transfers. MGM's *The Sergio Leone Anthology* collects four of his five Westerns, accompanied by commentary tracks and companion discs with supplementary materials. In addition to *A Fistful of Dollars* and the much superior follow-up *For a Few Dollars More* (1965), it includes the 2003 restoration of *The Good, the Bad and the Ugly* (1967), now weighing in at three hours, and the 2006 restoration of *Duck, You Sucker* (1971), which is thirty-seven minutes longer than the version originally seen in American theaters. In addition, Warner Bros. has brought out a spruced-up print of *The Colossus of Rhodes* in its "Cult Camp Classic" series. Paramount previously released definitive editions of *Once Upon a Time in the West* (1968) and *Once Upon a Time in America*.

The qualities that made Leone's pictures jump off the screen in the 1960s continue to startle: visuals that play foreground against background as extreme close-ups alternate with sweeping vistas; excruciatingly slow rituals that precede rapid bursts of violence; and comical immorality that marries the good, bad, and ugly (a Leone construct that quickly became a cliché). And, of course, there is the ingenious Ennio Morricone music, so relentlessly mocking or sentimental that it is difficult to tell when he's being sincere or ironic. One of the happy oddities of Leone's career is that *A Fistful of Dollars* did not play the United States until 1967, three years after it blanketed Europe. The delay allowed the film to open when antiwar fever was ramping to a peak and youth culture was assuming a dominance that Hollywood had yet to acknowledge.

Leone's quiet man in a serape, jeans, and battered hat, eyes squinting with disbelief at the madness all around him, mouth locked on a homemade cigarillo, was the ideal fantasy figure for a generation—a soulful killer who defies authority, an anti–John Wayne (who that very year, 1967, was directing *The Green Berets*). Small wonder that Clint Eastwood bounded into stardom. He created the first merciless killer as a witting Christ figure, resurrected from the dead to rain payback on the idiots in charge of everything—a theme Eastwood amplified in most of the Westerns he later directed, and took to rigorous theological fulfillment in his autumnal non-Westerns *Million Dollar Baby* and *Gran Torino*.

The Western was a European tradition long before Leone. In Germany, the pathfinders and Indians of Fenimore Cooper had been adapted and idealized in novels by Karl May two decades before the fiction of Zane Grey. At least two dozen Italian Westerns rolled out of Cinecittà before *Fistful*, but they had been mostly cheapjack imitations of the Hollywood tradition. The first thing one notices in Leone's Westerns—actually the fourth thing, after the striking visuals, relentless violence, and uncanny music—is the absence of almost every stock figure and convention of the genre. There are no or very few instances of Indians, cattle and cowboys, infallible heroes who kill out of necessity, farmers, ranchers, able law enforcers, mountains (except way off in the distance), children, and schoolmarms or other women who aren't whores.

Leone's West is a flat, endless terrain, marauded by greedy gunmen and the hero who kills them and makes off with the loot. Death is both a sport and a pastime—in *The Good, the Bad and the Ugly*, Eastwood's "Good" and Eli Wallach's "Ugly" are partners in a lynching scam. Good turns Ugly in for reward money, then shoots the rope before it breaks his neck. As for moral distinctions, consider the film's thirty-minute prelude, in which they and Lee Van Cleef's "Evil" are introduced in sequential vignettes that show each man killing three other men, though only Evil kills children. In *For a Few Dollars More*, the marijuana-addled Indio (Gian Maria Volontè) murders a mother and infant just to anger his real target. Frank, the hired assassin superbly incarnated by Henry Fonda in *Once Upon a Time in the West* (giving new depth to cold blue eyes), reassuringly smiles at a young boy before shooting him. In these films, climactic shootouts are staged like bullfights in huge, spherical arenas as the opponents circle each other, the widescreen camera fixated on their panther movements and vigilant eyes. No woman ever claims the winner.

Leone's misogyny is unavoidable and constant: in *Once Upon a Time in the West*, the future of America is in the maternal hands of the water-bearing former whore played by Claudia Cardinale. In his cosmology, she represents the pinnacle of womanhood. After Tuesday Weld is publicly raped in a bank in *Once Upon a Time in America*, she apparently has no choice but to become a whore and a moll. In *Duck, You Sucker*, a passenger in a Pullman stagecoach with the interior of a three-star hotel suffers a protracted rape for insulting Rod Steiger's peon bandit, an assault made especially cruel by Leone's feckless attempt to inject humor. Yet there is a strong kernel of guilt in his movies, usually involving women, and it comes out in his flashbacks.

The flashback is one of cinema's technical contributions to the arts, replacing traditional memoir narrative and Joycean memory streams with time-bending recollections that flash backward and forward. Without the precedent in film, it is difficult to imagine its particular use in fiction like Faulkner's *The Sound and the Fury*, or plays like Miller's *Death of a Salesman*. For Leone, the flashback carries Freudian weight—animating action and belaboring motive. In *For a Few Dollars More*, the villain is driven mad by the recollection of a woman who shot herself as he raped her; in *Once Upon a Time in the West*, the hero exists only to avenge the killing of his family; and in *Duck, You Sucker*, a professional anarchist relives his execution of the traitor with whom he had shared a ménage à trois. The ultimate flashback film, *Once Upon a Time in America*, is a chain of opium-stirred memories and fantasies, a metaphor for a life suffocated by the weight of the past.

Although all of Leone's films hold interest, not all are successful. *The Colossus of Rhodes* is pretty much what you expect, but rewards a visit for the Western-style horse chases; the femme fatale, whose curtain line is "Funny, I wanted so much but I die without getting anything"; and the hollow-body Colossus, with a head that contains medieval catapults that pour molten lead on enemies, as in *The Hunchback of Notre Dame*. The scene in which Rory Calhoun climbs out of the statue's ear and fences with soldiers is pure Leone whimsy. *Duck, You Sucker*, his most serious attempt at a political statement, founders on uneasy 1970s comedy overlaid on the Mexican Revolution as Rod Steiger's accent wanders all over Latin America, prefiguring Al Pacino's Cuba-speak in *Scarface*. The film can't make up its mind about the revolution, which destroys Steiger's children but turns him into a human being.

Leone turned down *The Godfather* to pursue his dream project, a story not of Italian mobsters, but of a Jewish gang that worked its way up from petty crimes in Prohibition New York to labor and politics. Inspired by particular episodes in Harry Grey's memoir/novel *The Hoods*, Leone focused on the friends who betray each other and created his most painful and ecstatic film. *Once Upon a Time in America* lacks the upbeat adrenaline of *The Good, the Bad and the Ugly* and the eulogistic majesty of *Once Upon a Time in the West*, but it is his most deeply felt work—a tapestry of nimble set pieces that capture the vanished immigrant life of the Lower East Side and an elegy for lost time, set to a Morricone score.

Leone made his regard for Morricone clear in the credits of *For a Few Dollars More*, holding his name for a full twelve seconds, twice the length of the director's credit. In subsequent films, he encouraged Morricone to write music in advance to establish mood. Much of *Once Upon a Time in America* unreels to Morricone's clarinet arrangement of the 1924 song "Amapola." The film isn't always logical, but then logic is not Leone's strong suit. In *The Good, the Bad*, a Union commander, beset by spies, detains Eastwood and Wallach, and when Wallach says they want to enlist, the officer instantly spills tactical secrets. Leone will not allow coherence to block the route to action. In *Once Upon a Time in America*, logic is mooted by opium, but reveries are allowed their full emotional toll. For all the violence and treachery, it is a masterpiece of sentimental affirmation.

15

SIDNEY LUMET'S FAMILY PLOTS

IT ISN'T DIFFICULT to find thematic and stylistic precedents for *Before the Devil Knows You're Dead* (2007) in Sidney Lumet's filmography. Yet that effort circumvents the main point. Taken on its own, this picture reflects the dynamism, clarity, wit, and bravado of a man in his prime and palpably energized by his craft. What it does not suggest is the autumnal meditation of an eighty-three-year-old director offering his forty-fourth film on the fiftieth anniversary of his first. Still, just as any discussion of Lumet must resort to numbers, any accounting of his latest picture must acknowledge its place in what has become, thanks not least to his unbowed work ethic, a challenging labyrinthine oeuvre.

Before the Devil Knows You're Dead derives much of its vitality from a smart original script by Kelly Masterson and a quartet of engaged, at times startlingly candid, performances by Philip Seymour Hoffman, Ethan Hawke, Marisa Tomei, and Albert Finney. At least four thematic strains, each pushing at the line that divides realism from parody, place it squarely in the Lumet canon. First, it's a family film with a family that makes the Tyrones (*Long Day's Journey into Night*, 1962) and Popes (*Running on Empty*, 1988) look as content as the Brady Bunch. If Masterson hadn't taken her title from an Irish toast ("May you be in heaven half an hour before the devil knows you're dead"), she might have opted for Philip Larkin's "They fuck you up, your mum and dad." In this story, mum and dad reap the whirlwind.

Other familiar Lumet strains include manipulation and betrayal (*The*

Deadly Affair, 1966; *Network*, 1976; *Prince of the City*, 1981; *The Verdict*, 1982; *Q&A*, 1990); the canyons and getaways of New York City (too many movies to enumerate); and crime (ditto)—albeit crime without police. Six people wind up dead, but the police are conspicuously irrelevant and absent. The film's attitude toward them is encompassed in a delightfully emphatic moment, when dad (Albert Finney) contemptuously backs his car into a police vehicle, crushing it, then drives on, his own battered trunk serving as a souvenir as he takes it upon himself to solve the film's central crime and administer the coup de grace.

This may be Lumet's most completely satisfying work since *Q&A*, and it's a lot more fun than *Q&A*. Although the narrative style requires a tricky shuttling back and forth in time, it is eminently comprehensible. The plot may feel familiar in retrospect, but it keeps you guessing through the two-hour duration. Lumet controls the material admirably, judging the overall tempo and the setups for a series of dialogues that run the gamut from sexual disharmony to hysteria to inquisitional hammering to phlegmatic confusion. The most powerful sequences focus on two brothers and build from cruel camaraderie (the older one calls the younger a "faggot" and a "baby," unaware that bro is boffing his wife) to a nose-to-nose face-off and near-execution.

But every scene indicates deliberation. Consider the confrontations between Andy (Hoffman), the alienated older son who plans the robbery that will destroy them all, and Gina (Tomei), his unfaithful wife. In the film's sexual prelude—a Brazilian vacation that represents Andy's half hour in heaven—they are doubled by a mirror as they rut into orgasm. During Andy's breakdown in the front seat of a car, they are photographed as if in different worlds, without a single two-shot to connect them. When Gina leaves him, they are staged in a deep-focus slant, Gina in the foreground, seated on her luggage.

Lumet's trademark long takes, exclamatory zooms, and disconcerting edits are not much in evidence. Maybe because the narrative incessantly calls attention to itself as the pieces fall into place and episodes are formally designated with titles (e.g., "Andy: The Day of the Robbery"), he felt that his directing style should be invisible. Even so, there is a fine calculated use of light and dark throughout, underscored by odd color schemes; the cinematographer is Ron Fortunato, a frequent Lumet collaborator in recent years. A bar that the younger brother, Hank (Hawke), can't stay away from is bathed in violet. Hank's apartment at night is suffused in blue. Lumet cuts from dank interiors to pale sunlight—from the 47th Street Diamond District to a sleazy hallway in its midst, from a deceptively verdant suburban back-yard to the chrome and glass of a car.

Lumet's ability to get actors to go to the wall for him gets explosive results here. The principles abandon every veil of vanity and modesty. The occasional nudity (rather more frequent on the part of Tomei, who at forty-two is an advertisement for healthy living) is less striking than the overall physical breakdowns, as the characters degenerate from one scene to the next: Hawke's face etched in ever-deeper crags, Hoffman's bloated in hope-less pastiness, Finney's turning quite monstrous, hovering over a staggering deed before fading, along with the film, into white. All of which is reason enough to glance, yet again, at the Lumet tally.

Lumet eludes his admirers as easily as he does his detractors. Attempts to pigeonhole, mock, or honor him with the supercilious praise we accord an entertainer or canny technician are routinely undermined by his best work, which exudes vibrancy matched by assurance, efficiency, and an unerring sense of time and place. Affectionate assessments, on the other hand, are punctured not by merely bad and disappointing films, but by those that are borderline or over-the-border silly—pictures too bizarre to qualify as hackwork (*The Appointment*, 1968; *The Wiz*, 1978; *Power*, 1986; *A Stranger Among Us*, 1992), however much they may indicate that Lumet hires out too easily.

A comprehensive evaluation of his corpus would have to take note of his more than three dozen television shows, from his contributions to *Studio One* in 1948 through the nine episodes he wrote and directed for a captivat-ing series he created in 2001, *100 Centre Street*—a revelation to anyone who has acceded to jury duty and something of a closed circle for the director who first made his way in the movies with *12 Angry Men*, in 1957. Between those poles are any number of projects, highly regarded in their day, that hold new promise now, if only we could see them; to cite one readily avail-able example, there is the indelible 1960 production of *The Iceman Cometh*, with Jason Robards and Myron McCormick.

Attempts to reduce and divide Lumet's work into a Chinese menu format (Column A: good; Column B: not) are unsettled by revisits. Fifty years is a long time to captain actors, writers, photographers, and so forth, and time plays havoc with memory and assumption. Several of Lumet's presumed failures or overlooked films offer moments of intelligence and insight, often enough to trigger unexpected pleasures. While a consensus has calcified around his chronicle of the 1970s and early 1980s (the period of *Serpico*, 1973; *Dog Day Afternoon*, 1975; *Prince of the City*; and *The Verdict*), a tour of Lumet's earlier work suggests a no less vigilant understanding of political and sexual upheavals of the 1960s. *The Fugitive Kind* (1960), *Fail Safe* (1964), *The Hill* (1965), *The Deadly Affair* (1966), and *Bye, Bye Braverman* (1968), among others, have grown, not shrunk, in stature.

His second, easily teased film, *Stage Struck* (1958), manages to overcome the clammy shadows of Zoe Akins's ludicrous play, *Morning Glory*, and Susan Strasberg's misguided performance as the logorrheic Eva Lovelace to offer an affectionate memento of 1950s theater. There was no reason to remake it at all (the original Katharine Hepburn film, from 1933, has the advantage only of brevity and the relatively restrained star), but Lumet used the material to structure a tour of midtown and adapt the long tracking shots he had mastered for live television, giving many scenes—notably the party at which Eva does Juliet—a fluid aplomb. When he followed it with good plays, he did them justice: does anyone expect to see a better *Long Day's Journey into Night* than Lumet's film with Katharine Hepburn and Ralph Richardson, or a more judicious *Orpheus Descending* than his *The Fugitive Kind*, with Marlon Brando and Anna Magnani?

Lumet's long takes and political commitment rise to the occasion in *The Hill*, an oddly neglected film that, preceding *Cool Hand Luke* by two years, emerged as one of the first films to flippantly attack authority. At the time, it may have looked like the usual prisoners-versus-evil-warden melodrama (with Harry Andrews bringing real nuance to the role of the obsessive jailer), but now the specific references to the mounting frustrations of the 1960s are impossible to ignore. Ossie Davis's performance as a black soldier who impersonates the stereotype foisted on him—addressing the commandant in his underwear, filching a cigar, and protesting the conditions at the "hotel" (a World War II encampment for army reprobates)—is one of the glories of black acting in a period otherwise dominated by Sidney Poitier. Moreover, Lumet avoids the mythologizing that *Luke* savored; his hero, played by Sean Connery, is no better or worse than he seems. The elaborate takes, from an opening dolly shot covering the entire encampment to a five-minute dressing down of the prisoners, heighten the tension and electrify the actors.

Another film that merits reconsideration is *The Deadly Affair*, based on an early John le Carré novel and notable for the bleached, drearily autumnal colors by Freddie Young; the counterintuitive musical score by Quincy Jones, built around an Astrud Gilberto bossa nova record that has a diegetic presence in the story; and splendid performances that underscore sexual betrayals over issues of espionage. The long takes dramatize the tortured marriage of James Mason and Harriet Andersson, among them a deep-focus staging along a diagonal, as in *Before the Devil Knows You're Dead*. In one remarkable scene, Lumet closes in on Simone Signoret, who plays a concentration camp survivor who needs to explain herself—not unlike Thelma Ritter in Sam Fuller's *Pickup on South Street*, only Signoret's character finagles biography and deception. As always with Lumet, the politics are personal and the locations are smartly chosen.

One Lumet film that has maintained a steady audience is his stylistically resourceful lost-soul-seeking-salvation courtroom drama *The Verdict*, which recently graduated to a DVD double-disc Collector's Edition. A hit in 1982, *The Verdict* enjoyed a robust post-theatrical life, its critical and popular acclamation boosted by countless television broadcasts. Yet it may be the last major Hollywood film produced with little or no concern for home video, neither the then-burgeoning VHS phenomenon nor television itself. It is a movie made for movie theaters, shot with autumnal colors in long, medium-distance takes, frequently involving two characters in conversation as a third stands apart, silently observing. Lumet's panache invites the viewer to take in tableaux in which environment is crucial. No gratuitous reaction shots or musical cues interrupt to tell us what to think or how to feel; the prudent use of close-ups is almost Bressonian in its economy and control.

The wonder of *The Verdict* is that it claims our attention at all, given the familiar nature of its premise. An ambulance-chasing lawyer, blinking his way through the hell of alcoholic dissolution, takes an impossible case against the archdiocese of Boston, the hospital it runs, a corrupt judge, and a legal firm that operates with the principles of the CIA or KGB. It comes as no surprise that the lawyer and justice prevail. Haven't we seen this film a hundred times in the eighty years since Theodore Dreiser established the standard for the American courtroom thriller? Yes and no. Most have faded away, while *The Verdict*, Otto Preminger's *Anatomy of a Murder* (1959), and few others hold their ground.

Everything works, despite a few six-lane plot holes. The sheer filmmaking joy of talented people working at the peak of their powers rewards a return or three to the plight of Frank Galvin (Paul Newman), his treacherous lover Laura (Charlotte Rampling), his protective friend Mickey (Jack Warden), and the opposing attorney (James Mason), whom Mickey characterizes as "the prince of fucking darkness." Lumet's long history of capturing unflinching, original, inspired performances achieved no greater pinnacle than his work here. Mason's timing, silences, and dynamics in support of memorably skewered, mellifluous line readings brings Ed Concannon, the satanic counsel, to life with so much energy that we forgive him his trespasses. Rampling, whose facial bones enact mini-dramas that echo the lines she doesn't have, is the most touchingly defective femme fatale in recent memory. Warden's Mickey, Lindsay Crouse's witness, Milo O'Shea's judge, and Julie Bovasso's nurse, among others, are captured in performances with no false bottoms, all in support of David Mamet's elliptical dialogue and the lead performance by Newman, which makes the plot holes almost immaterial.

Much as great homely actors can make their features light up with sexual appeal, handsome ones may allow their features to congeal with failure and decay, and makeup has nothing to do with it. Newman's chiseled good looks sag. He emits seediness in his posture and walk, slow death in his pallor, hygienic indifference in his long and matted hair and greedy inhaling of a Breathalyzer. All this sounds like customary technique, but it doesn't look or feel like it. When Galvin is thrown out of a funeral, he turns toward the camera, one brow lifted, the famous face distorted for a few seconds like a mask gone awry. As he takes hold of himself, the features snap back into formation, but never in a way to indicate contrivance. A certain dissonance remains until the end.

A disconnect exists between the very lack of vanity in the actor and the character's narcissism. Galvin fell from grace in his profession because he rejected the immorality of his firm, but his sense of self is almost piously remote from reality. Offered a low but not unreasonable settlement in the case at hand, he neither bargains to make it better nor consults with his client on whether they ought to accept it. In a move that would and should get him disbarred, he tells the prelate that if he accepts, he is "lost"; he's determined to stage a courtroom redemption, no matter the consequence for his clients. That he ends up alone is inevitable; his refusal to take Laura's call may be some kind of poetic justice, but it also allows him to stew in solitude not unlike that mandated by drink. The script even gives Laura an opening for forgiveness. When she learns that Galvin is in New York, in search of the witness who will win his case, she pointedly declines to inform her masters. But *The Verdict* isn't about Laura or Laura and Frank; it's about Frank and the hollowness of even the most noble of resolutions to find justice.

Lumet, in his commentary, credits the actors and the writing for most of the film's felicities, but *The Verdict* is a director's movie first and last, and in a way that we are not likely to see again any time soon. The opening credits are scored to the sounds of a pinball machine, as Galvin plays disconsolately, his profile framed by a window. There is no music at all for the first four and a half minutes, only the ambient sounds of bereavement, and when John Mandel's concise brass chords are finally heard, they are neutrally transitional. Scene after scene is staged against windows and doors, under arches, and on ornate staircases, and the big moments are daringly static. The camera awaits Galvin and Laura as they enter his apartment, waits as he turns on the light and they kiss—more than a minute passes before the first cut, which indicates an emotional change. Other key moments are related with parallel objects: a letter that reveals Laura's perfidy followed by an envelope that reveals Galvin's identity to a reluctant witness.

The conference with Galvin, the judge, and Concannon is filmed as a three-shot, and when the judge taunts Galvin with a question, Lumet allows us to see the answer in the judge's response—no need for a line or a star insert. The crucial scene in which Galvin attempts to cut a deal on the phone is handled in a single medium-distance four-minute take, and it is riveting. Today it would be cut eight different ways, with each telling gesture (like Galvin's what-the-hell shrug to Mickey) getting its own insert. Most impressive is Galvin's ad hoc summation: one camera movement that slowly descends from wide view to a close-up of the lawyer, just before he turns from the jury and walks back to his seat. As the verdict is read, Lumet uses a short crane shot that quickly levels off as it zooms toward Galvin. *The Verdict* is one of those movies that are so intelligently made they invite rather than dictate the audience's participation.

Before the Devil Knows You're Dead similarly takes no notice of current events, but it, too, suggests a political subtext. The plot is based on the familiar noir situation of a character drawn into a conspiracy, making one mistake that demands the commission of others, until the bodies begin to mount. The analogy to Iraq or Vietnam or Korea, wars in which, as Andy remarks, the shit of one incompetent bungler lands on the shoes of others, is made more forceful by the general lack of innocence, the hunger for aggression—the rank fantasy of a victimless crime in which everyone wins.

Andy, who sets the death knell in motion, finds solace in heroin administered in an upscale East Side apartment (the Chrysler and Empire State Buildings dominate the window view) by a wraith-like gay man, toting a gun and wearing a kimono. In a trance-like state, Andy mumbles, "My mother is dying." "Bummer," the dealer says. The disaffection is contagious. When Gina, in a farewell taunt before leaving Andy, tells him that she has been fucking his brother every Thursday afternoon, Andy gives her cab fare.

Masterson's script, unlike some that Lumet has brought to the screen, takes pains to close the gaps of illogic. The questions that arise—why don't the sons borrow money from their parents? why do they continue to haunt the bar where the plan was hatched?—are effectively resolved in the delineation of the characters. Yet there is one suspension of disbelief required at the end, following a bloody shoot-out that leaves one man dead and Andy in the hospital. Andy obviously killed the other guy—the victim's sister witnessed it all—and once again the police are conspicuously absent: no inquiry, no hospital guard. Of course, the presence of a police guard would hamper the stunning climax and the ultimate expression of dissolution. Suffice it to say that only dad retains passion and purpose, and he needs a bit of privacy to totally fuck up his oldest son.

16

THE MAGICAL UNREALITY OF
LECH MAJEWSKI

READING LECH MAJEWSKI'S resume can give you a headache. A prolific poet and novelist, painter, composer-librettist and director of operas, and director, writer, composer, producer, and cameraman of video and films, he has released eleven movies (not including Julian Schnabel's 1996 *Basquiat*, which he co-wrote and co-produced), from 1978's *Zwiastowanie*, completed a year after he graduated from Lodz Film School, to 2007's *Glass Lips*, assembled from a thirty-three-part video installation called *Blood of the Poet*, which debuted at the 2006 retrospective of his work at New York's Museum of Modern Art. Born in Poland in 1953, Majewski has lived in America since 1981, working on both sides of the Atlantic, often financing his own projects and collecting many prizes. Yet few here know him or his work, a situation Kino International has sought to remedy by releasing four of his films on DVD. They are packaged individually, but if you are seduced by one, you will likely go back for more. Although Majewski prefers languorous tempos—his films sometimes play like museum exhibits, a sequence of tableaux—and repeats favorite symbols from one picture to the next (snow, bleeding Christs, grazing roes, spilled milk), the films are strikingly distinctive.

They might be viewed as high-tech gimmicks, but that would sell short their intellectual discernment and emotional urgency. In *Gospel According to Harry* (1992), a middle-class American family lives in the American desert (filmed in the Polish desert). *The Roe's Room* (1998) is an opera in which off-screen voices detail the imagined goings-on in a Polish apartment. In *The Garden of Earthly Delights* (2003), an abbreviated love affair, set in London and Venice and filmed by the participants, blends art history and science into a discussion of metaphysics and becomes a disquisition on cinema itself. And in the unnerving *Glass Lips*, the most incisively cruel and perversely optimistic of these four films, a madman's memories and imaginings are rendered with hallucinatory visuals and sound effects but without dialogue or much music.

Majewski's films are the sort about which mainstream reviewers remark, "not for every taste." Nor is *The Dark Knight* for every taste. The taste required here is for symbolism and allusion. His films are often entrancingly beautiful, erotically charged, grotesquely violent, efficiently acted (frequently by amateurs, in the Robert Bresson tradition), and fastidiously staged. They intend to mesmerize, to lure viewers into a zone where the real and unreal interact not to belabor the exertions of surrealism but rather to explore the monotony of life pitched on the edge of hysteria and ornamented with a common fund of resonant signs. By combining familiar icons and mythologies (religious or secular) with personal conceits (when a Majewski fridge door opens, snow will gust from it), he encourages viewers to find evidence of their own symbolic baggage. In short, these movies are novel, but they ring bells of recognition and familiarity. Even the repetitive, minimalist music (composed by Majewski and his collaborator, the pianist Jozef Skrzek), fashionable though it is and occasionally interrupted by Germanic waltzes, is sufficiently anonymous to spur connections. It's neither memorable nor intrusive, but it does the job. What is memorable, maybe indelible, is the imagery. Majewski often uses digital equipment that renders a stable but finite glow, suggesting the lighting on paintings in great museums. The result is at once distancing and inviting—don't touch, gaze.

Gospel According to Harry is the most accessible of the films on offer from Kino. It is an absurdist comedy with a famous cast, including Viggo Mortensen and Jennifer Rubin as Wes and Karen, a childless couple living a dreary existence, with all the electronic comforts, in a desert. Karen vacuums the sand, but it's everywhere, including her insides, making sex painful. Her mother complains of Wes's laziness, and Wes's father attempts to sell him life insurance. The American president drops by to deliver platitudes about a kinder, gentler world, while a foiled assassin is cruci-

fied nearby. The eponymous Harry is an IRS collector. The film is divided
into biblical episodes, drifting between Old and New Testaments (Exodus,
Judges, the Annunciation, Kings, the Crucifixion, Numbers), and some of
it is funny. Much of it, though, is heavy-handed, larded with wise-guy conceits reminiscent more of the forced irreverence popular in the 1960s movies of Robert Downey than the dislocations of Robert Bresson. The best
scene is the first: a black eminence strews the desert with trinkets, as dunes
drift aggressively by and clouds mark the sundown like inkblots. The next
morning, the trinkets have flowered into plastic-wrapped television sets.
That's the level of subtlety.

The Roe's Room represents a marvelous advance. The symbolism is no
more subtle, perhaps, but the concerns are larger, the concept more original, and the resonances of the allusions more universal and penetrating.
Except for a few exterior shots at the end, the entire film is set in a modest apartment occupied by a stamp-collecting father, a nourishing mother
(milk flows from the table like a fountain), and a son (Rafal Olbrychski) who
looks like a Giotto model stuck in the wrong century. The son reconfigures
their existence with his imagination, turning city life into pastoral disarray.
The story is fixed to the four seasons and reflects the son's alienation, sexual desires, religious restraints, and oedipal conundrum. In one sequence, a
beautiful naked woman comes to his bed, then breaks into the father's desk
to examine his stamps—yet the son tells us this scene is his father's dream
and that she is really reading evidence that "we are naked and unprotected
in a dream," and the father will awake to "realize that no one belongs in
dreams." As seasons pass, a tree grows through their living room floor and
ceiling, leaves burst through the walls, weeds cover the floor (the father cuts
them with a scythe), and two roes graze and make it their home.

When the father dies, the son is lured into a world epitomized by the
girl in a window across the way, and only the mother shuffles back to the
roe's room, which may now be her room. All this is conveyed without dialogue and with very little lip-synching to the operatic commentary, which
is mostly quotidian ("During dinner, I noticed no one looked at me"), made
sumptuous by the vocalist representing the son: Polish countertenor Artur
Stefanowicz. A choir (on-screen), two sopranos, and a tenor (voiced by the
actor playing the father, Mieczyslaw Czapulonis) are also interwoven, but
the countertenor sustains the piece's mood and tempo. The visual style

follows the rhythm of the music, with most of the shots lateral pans from right to left.

Majewski's most recent films represent greater progress and are more powerful. In *The Garden of Earthly Delights*, Claudine, an English art historian dying of throat cancer (superbly played by Claudine Spiteri) falls in love with an engineer and obsessive film recorder. Both are working on doctoral theses—she on Bosch's triptych, he on hull design in modern ships. They move to Venice, which has never been captured more comprehensively in a feature film (and yes, that includes *Don't Look Now* and *The Wings of the Dove*), even if Majewski's "pen" is little more than the semi-professional cameras wielded by himself and his two actors. The film begins with the engineer, Chris (Chris Martin), jumping into the lagoons to work off his grief, and cuts back and forth from their affair as he documented it to the present, in which he films himself viewing the tapes, using edits and optical tricks to make a record that serves as testimony to the power of art over death.

Most of the talk is about metaphysics and art, and it is good talk (though pedants will note that Claudine offers an unreliable interpretation of Jan van Eyck's *Arnolfini Portrait*), especially concerning Claudine's conviction that Bosch shows that "entry into paradise is possible here on earth," if good and evil are neutralized. To prove her point, she and Chris re-create sexual positions and symbols in the painting. Yet as her illness worsens, she lapses into a rant against modern evils, and whenever their lovemaking is interrupted by outsiders, they instinctively cup their genitals as if enacting the expulsion from another garden. Still, they bravely court ecstasy, as Chris demonstrates the temporality of her body by amassing the elements from which it is made. Majewski knows his Descartes and the right questions, and he doesn't pretend to have answers. The film ends with digital static.

Glass Lips begins with another mythological genesis—the baby abandoned on a mountain—and cuts to an alarm clock that works backward, as does an inmate in an asylum who backs out of his room, past another inmate frozen in a "Heil Hitler" posture. Nurses lower his arm, but it pops right back up. There is much comedy here, sublimely judged in a film that is essentially given to pathos. The mad poet Sebastian (Patryk Czajka) ruminates and elaborates on his appalling childhood with an abusive father and sexually stimulating mother. The images here are the most inspired and relentless in any of these four films: the boy tied into an elaborate cat's cradle when the parents leave the house, the father eating dog food in his office on the 365th floor while his wife hovers in the air outside the window, a ram slaughtered in a courtyard littered with inflatable dolls and pornography, a reenactment of Abraham and Isaac, even the rather passé closing at a rejuvenating pool (Thorne Smith did that much better in his novel *The Glorious Pool*, never mind *Cocoon*). The images are so resonant, the control of the material so sure, that you never miss the dialogue. Talk would be intrusive.

17

EDWARD YANG'S FAMILY TIES

EDWARD YANG, WHO died much too young, at fifty-nine in 2007, was a filmmaker of extraordinary intelligence who may have had the strongest claim, among directors of his generation, to a place on the Mount Rushmore of humanist cinema. He combined the equable humor of Renoir, the discriminating patience of Ozu, and the pictorial ingenuity of Antonioni. And like them, Yang was a virtuoso whose hand was generally visible. His magnificent *Yi Yi* (*A One and a Two . . .*) vibrantly orchestrates the harmonies, discords, and cadenzas of family life, employing contrapuntal parallels and tempo variations that range, in effect, from half-time to double-time. So it may be worth pondering the writer-director's aberrantly tone-deaf attempt to find an English title.

The colloquial Chinese title means "one-one" or "individually," signifying, according to Yang (whose notes are included in the booklet of Criterion's DVD), "the film's portrayal of life through each individual member." The English title, *A One and a Two . . .* , omitted from the DVD cover, derives from "what's always muttered by jazz musicians before a jam session." It was intended to indicate, Yang said, that what follows will not be "tense or heavy or stressful. Life should be like a jazzy tune." Jazz musicians, however, do not count off tunes with conjunctions—that's strictly Lawrence Welk—and the film is brazen with tense moments. So what goes on here? Both titles are evasions, the artist attempting to fade into his art. If audiences leave with "the impression of having encountered a 'filmmaker,'" he writes, "then I'd have to consider the film a failure."

In that sense only is *Yi Yi* a failure. The film is nothing if not sumptuous. Abetted by a skillful crew, including cameraman Weihan Yang and sound technician Duzhi Du, Yang frames his "simple" story with stunning pans of Taipei and Tokyo and an infallibly inventive visual motif incorporating reflective surfaces (windows, mirrors) and an acute regard for the meaning and constraints of architecture. No less impressive is the sound design. Turn up the volume to take it all in: a multidimensional soundscape, capturing ambient subtleties that distinguish apartments from hotel rooms; urban white noise and the unquiet quiet; isolated footfalls and hallway echoes; and the anonymous buzzing and clicking of a plugged-in world. Against these natural and unnatural sounds is a scenario featuring three languages (Chinese, Japanese, and English) and a diegetic musical score that makes witting use of Beethoven, Gershwin, and the Shirelles. In *Yi Yi*, technique and substance are as inseparable as in an Art Tatum piano solo. That's one reason it succeeds in blending the anxieties of soap opera with the temporal ambitions of an epic. A three-hour deconstruction of a family whose members spin into discrete orbits, *Yi Yi* is alternately funny, moving, nerve-wracking, and surprising. It demonstrates that even in the best of circumstances communication is limited, but respect for privacy is not the least-healing balm we can bring to family dynamics.

Centered on the big events in an average upper-middle-class life, *Yi Yi* begins with a wedding in the Jian family—a union delayed by the well-meaning if oafishly superstitious groom (Xisheng Chen), who was waiting for his horoscope to mandate a lucky day. His forbearing bride is in her third trimester. How lucky or not the day proves to be is central to the film's meaning. Other events of the day find NJ Jian (the groom's brother and principal character, played with a charismatic solemnity by filmmaker Nianzhen Wu) running into a woman he abandoned thirty years ago, and Grandma Jian (Ruyun Tang) suffering a stroke and lapsing into a coma. A doctor advises the family to take turns talking to grandma, in the hope of reviving her. With this narrative masterstroke, grandma becomes a stand-in for God, as each member of the family speaks aloud to the void (NJ compares it to praying) and hears unnerving echoes. Forced to confront the emptiness of her life, Jian's wife (Elaine Jin) runs off to a guru's mountain retreat. NJ, whose computer business is in financial trouble, finds his own guru in Ota (Issey Ogata), a rather sententious Japanese programming wizard, whose tentative command of English underscores the profundity of his seeming wisdom. Meeting with Ota in Tokyo, Jian also rendezvouses with his old flame Sherry (Suyun Ke), married to wealth in the United States and given equally to romantic proposals and hysterical outbursts.

The two Jian children provide greater emotional ballast, discovering for the first time the romantic complications NJ is merely trying to relive. Ting-Ting (Kelly Lee), a teenage girl, is enticed by an unhinged Romeo called Fatty (Yupang Chang); she is the only family member who takes sustenance from her comatose grandma, whose condition she blames on herself. She ultimately expunges her guilt in a brightly lit fantasy scene worthy of a Kenzi Mizoguchi ghost story. Yet the film belongs to her eight-year-old brother, Yang-Yang, one of the most appealing children in movie history, played by Jonathan Chang with a sly authority that surmounts mere cuteness (though there's plenty of that). Yang-Yang is the director's stand-in, an "avant-garde" artist (as his Dickensian teacher mocks him) who tries to photograph mosquitoes, producing pictures of empty rooms, and more effectively shoots the backs of people's heads: "You can't see it yourself," he explains offhandedly, "so I help you." Yang-Yang is too self-possessed to converse with grandma, yet he delivers the eulogy at her funeral that unites the others in wonder. Smitten by his teacher's daughter, a swimmer, Yang-Yang attempts to overcome his fear of water by submerging his head in a bathroom sink. Edward Yang is not above manipulating the audience. He knows that when the film dares to suggest that Yang-Yang drowned, viewers will react as readers once did to the death of Little Nell. When Yang-Yang later slips through the front door ("Why are you wet? Is it raining?"), the sun rises once again.

Yi Yi is strangely prudish about sex—the assignations are unconsummated. NJ remarks that no one thinks twice about jumping into bed, but he and members of his family do. In lovemaking begins responsibility: the adulteries indulged in by the family in a neighboring apartment trigger a grisly murder. Yet this prudishness helps make possible the film's well-earned epiphany. When NJ's wife returns, he assures her that nothing has changed in her absence. But something has changed. He tells her, "Even if I was given a second chance, I wouldn't need it." This is affirmation, not surrender.

Yi Yi isn't flawless. Keili Ping's piano music infects the score with a New Age banality. The mother is conveniently sent off to the mountains, a way to keep one less ball in the air—why no scene at the retreat? For that matter, why no final reckoning with Ota, whom NJ's company betrays? The shoe-horned murder adds nothing except a touch of genre that the film otherwise bravely eschews. Still, Yang hits few bad notes. He shows how Westernized Taipei is, with its fast-food and bagel shops, computer games and movie madness, but he hasn't gone Hollywood. This is a film that breathes with unforced life, even as it works through conventional plot points. The perfectly framed and unedited master shots respect the actors and their characters. Ting-Ting and Fatty attend a concert of a Beethoven cello sonata and we watch them listen for a minute, a voyeuristic moment even more intimate than their two-minute tryst in a hotel, silently staring at each other from across an antiseptic room.

18

HOUDINI ESCAPES!
FROM THE VAULTS! OF THE PAST!

FOR NEARLY FIVE years, beginning in 1918, Harry Houdini—the most famous magician since Merlin, most fabled escapologist since Jonah, most resourceful publicist since Barnum—tried his hand at filmmaking. He starred in one fifteen-chapter, five-hour serial and four feature-length films (a rumored fifth feature, *The Soul of Bronze*, probably was not made and almost certainly wasn't distributed), at times involving himself as the producer, writer, and director. Houdini displayed little cinematic aptitude, yet the viewer who plunges, handcuffed or not, into Kino's three-disc DVD tribute, *Houdini the Movie Star*, may surface with the showman's grim, stocky, square-faced, curly-haired, gimlet-eyed glare forever locked in memory, like an unshakable specter from the past. Houdini was no actor, but he had presence. At times, he resembles a more muscular, Hungarian-looking cousin to the mute magician-comedian Teller. With this set, Houdini's real-life flirtation with spiritualism is rewarded after all: the legendary illusionist retakes his corporeal self on celluloid—once again, bound for glory.

Maybe Houdini planned it this way. Born Ehrich Weiss in Budapest, in 1874, he died on Halloween 1926 in Detroit, the victim of a college student who tested his supposedly indestructible abdominal muscles by pounding them. In *The Man from Beyond* (1922), which he wrote and produced, Houdini appears as Howard Hillary, a first mate left for dead on the abandoned deck of his ship, moored in the Arctic Sea in 1820. As the years pass, Hillary becomes encased in a block of ice, standing erect like Frankenstein's monster. The discovery of his frozen visage startles two survivors of another Arctic voyage in 1920. They chip him out, give him a cup of thawing java, learn his backstory from a conveniently placed letter, and decide it would be best not to tell him that the clock has moved forward a hundred years. Hillary had (almost) perished to aid his beloved Felice, and his saviors don't think he'll be able to handle the knowledge that Felice didn't enjoy an equally cryogenic transition.

So they take him to New York, to the home of the mysteriously absent Dr. Crawford Strange (Albert Tavernier). Hillary still thinks he's in the 1820s, failing to notice little things that might upend the deception—such as bulb-like appurtenances that have replaced candles. As it happens, the daughter of Dr. Strange, who at the very moment of Hillary's arrival is preparing to wed a sneering scoundrel named Trent (Arthur Maude), is also named Felice. Since Felice I and Felice II are both played by vaudevillian Jane Connelly (whose only other movie role was as the mother in Buster Keaton's *Sherlock Jr.*), Hillary is understandably agitated. The medics helpfully take him to a sanatorium, place him in a straitjacket, and nail him to the ground. The denouement involves vamping by Nita Naldi (who vamped Rudolph Valentino in *Blood and Sand* the same year), a telltale rat, a secret cellar, and an ambiguous rescue from the precipice of Niagara Falls. It also tips its hat to Houdini's fellow spiritualist Arthur Conan Doyle, who was gratified—despite Houdini's constant debunking of mediums, including Mrs. Doyle (who rather imprudently claimed to have channeled Houdini's dead mother).

The point, though, isn't that there are more things in heaven and earth than can be dreamt of or defrosted. The point, as stated in the prologue of James Cruze's flatly directed (and overly dependent on title cards) *Terror Island* (1920), a cross between *Treasure Island*, *20,000 Leagues Under the Sea*, and diverse colonialist adventures, is: "While melodrama is not taken seriously by all spectators, it is of interest to know that Houdini, world-famous for his exploits as a self-liberator, actually performed the amazing feats here pictured." In short, the producers concede that this is the lowest sort of hokum, but who cares? Houdini had been a phenomenon for two decades: his movies existed only to get him into bondage from which to wriggle free.

Oddly enough, this conceit may be more entertaining now than it was to his contemporaries. His most effective stunts are of the Douglas Fairbanks variety, demonstrating his fearless athleticism. But the ones for which he was famous—writhing out of a straitjacket while hanging upside down, breaking out of a safe on the ocean floor, undoing the straps of an electric chair seconds before the zap—have a cinematic veracity on par with radio ventriloquism. Maybe these stunts weren't simulated, but they could have been and a few were—including the only surviving snippet from *The Grim Game* (1919), in which an authentic midair plane collision was turned to advantage by splicing that frightening footage to a shot of the hero, Harvey Hanford, emerging triumphant from the rubble. Contrary to production claims, Houdini did occasionally use a double, Bob Rose, who later became part of John Ford's team. Usually, Houdini was unmistakably the fellow at risk, but we don't really see what he's doing. One minute he is bound; the next, he isn't.

It doesn't matter. The pleasure of watching these films parallels the journey of the time traveler in Houdini's iceman cometh saga *The Man from Beyond*. Hillary leaps forward a hundred years. We leap in the other direction: to a world of hat wearers, when the clichés of penny-dreadful fictions were remade to accommodate technophobia, when genetics were so mysterious that bloodlines were constantly up for grabs, when immigrants were demonized and xenophobia was acceptable foreign policy—a time much like our own, but without the hats. In *Terror Island*, Houdini, as "noted philanthropist and inventor" Harry Harper, battles superstitious savages led by Chief Bakaida (Frank Bonner), who "glories in the fact that he can 'spik Ingrish,'" and the "meanest man in town," Job Mordaunt (Wilton Taylor), who is so mean he laughs when a little waif skins her knees. (Job's son is played by Eugene Pallette, the fat, frog-voiced, bad-tempered foil in 1930s screwball comedies.) In Houdini's half-hearted but thematically interesting final film, *Haldane of the Secret Service* (1923), he plays Heath Haldane, the scourge of counterfeiters, who is menaced by the Yellow Peril, which turns out to be under the command of a white man in YP drag.

The most remarkable Houdini film is the 1920 serial and box-office success *The Master Mystery*. An hour is missing, filled in with brief summaries, but they aren't necessary: in every chapter, the bad guys overpower Quentin Locke (Houdini's only alphabetically imaginative alter ego), and leave him alone to escape their increasingly desperate constraints. In one situation, he has to finesse an intricate tangle of ropes before an acid slick reaches his prone body—prefiguring Goldfinger's castrating laser. Yet the overarching plot is far from simplistic. It charts the convoluted offenses of a monstrous criminal who—are you seated?—violates the antitrust laws! Part of his plan requires infecting his enemies with Madagascar Madness, which has the same effect as laughing gas. He is aided by an "automaton," a year before Karel Čapek coined the word "robot." It isn't the first mechanical man in film (Georges Méliès invented one in 1897), but it may be the first with star potential, a cross between Gort and Robbie, with googly eyes and womanly hips. The final chapters could double as an old Sid Caesar sketch, as each character turns out to be the secret child, parent, or sibling of the others—happily averting incest while enriching all the principals.

The Master Mystery united Houdini with two men who, like him, did their best work away from movies. The chief writer was Arthur B. Reeve, who helped invent detective pulp fiction and true-crime reportage; his ripping novelization of *The Master Mystery* reads like the Hardy Boys on peyote. The producer was trumpet virtuoso and dance band leader B. A. Rolfe, who inspired Louis Armstrong to perfect the instrument's upper register. Armstrong cited his own 1929 "When You're Smiling" solo as his homage to Rolfe. An on-screen essay in *Houdini the Movie Star* notes that the film elements are below Kino's usual standards, but this collection requires no apology. In addition to the virtually unknown and unseen films, the set includes every scrap of newsreel footage, an Edison recording of Houdini's voice (he sounds like a carny barker), and other related oddities. Kino ought to have included an essay summarizing Houdini's life for those to whom his name is an undefined cliché, but even without it, this collection succeeds in bringing life to the long-ago hero of a long-ago time.

19

JOAN CRAWFORD IS DANGEROUS

ANYONE IMPERVIOUS TO the mild but genuine pleasures of *Sadie McKee* (1934), the earliest of five movies collected in *The Joan Crawford Collection, Vol. 2* (Warner Bros.), is probably immune to the genius-in-the-system artisanship that buttressed old Hollywood. Not being immune myself, I respond like Pavlov's or Louis B. Mayer's dog, synapses cued to every calculated stimulus, as Sadie works her way through three lovers and a four-chamber roundelay of the classes: surviving old money, underclass chicanery, and the nouveau riche, to emerge as—in the words of the bilious plutocrat who is the last man standing—"honest working girl."

Sadie McKee is, in the jargon of its day, absolute hooey, but it is the hooey of master craftspeople, working together like apprentices in a Renaissance studio, each one a specialist in light or fabric or hands or eyes, held in balance by the master's supervision. In this instance, the master was director Clarence Brown, who guided Crawford's renovation from the flapper of silent pictures to the talkies' perennial Cinderella. His second-in-command, Oliver T. Marsh, photographed a dozen Crawford vehicles through the 1930s (three with Brown as director), never more lovingly than in *Sadie McKee*. They accentuated each angle of her picture-perfect face, all eyes and mouth, making it gleam like well-polished silverware.

Lying in bed and listening to her unstable boyfriend, Tommy (Gene Raymond), sing "All I Do Is Dream of You," Crawford gets a seventeen-second close-up, as if the camera had gotten lost in its gaze. Elsewhere, the camera has plenty of distractions—including delectable bits by Jean Dixon, who says of Tommy's singing, "With a voice like that, he's sure to sit on his own lap." Akim Tamiroff giggles about a $1,000 tip, and Ethel Griffies mimes spinster outrage as a nosey subway rider. There are almost enough songs to qualify the film as a musical, including "After You've Gone" rendered by the 1920s crooner Gene Austin. Tiny in life, Crawford was magnified by the camera to colossal and eventually monstrous dimensions. The monstrous years are touched on at the end of this quintuple feature with Charles Walters's unforgivably entertaining *Torch Song* (1953), by which time Crawford's lipstick no longer followed the contours of her lips and her characters no longer followed the rules of humble humanity. If self-parody became her, *Sadie McKee* is a reminder that there was something worth parodying—something intrepid, insubordinate, and incorruptible.

The theme uniting all five films is that Crawford's character not only learns to do the right thing, but helps others to do it as well, except for those who are completely irredeemable, whom she has no choice but to kill. Crawford had few if any rivals in the arena of justifiable homicide. She kills Torsten Barring (a wondrously slimy Conrad Veidt) in George Cukor's *A Woman's Face* (1941) when she realizes, rather late in the game, that she would rather not help him murder a child who stands between him and an inheritance. She also offs Sheriff Titus Semple (a wonderfully megalomaniacal Sidney Greenstreet) in Michael Curtiz's *Flamingo Road* (1949, and based on a trenchant 1942 Robert Wilder novel that merits resurrection) because it makes things easier all around. In each case, she may serve a little time, but Melvin Douglas's rich doctor or David Brian's rich political boss will be waiting.

In *Torch Song*, the road to love requires the humiliation of her beloved, a blind pianist and war hero (Michael Wilding) who is beating the hell out of "Tenderly" when she stealthily appears in his living room, like a mantis about to bite the head off its mate. Crumpled by her derision, he does right by overcoming his pride and conceding his love for her. In *Sadie McKee*, do-gooding is rampant. She gets Tommy, who abandoned her on her wedding day in favor of a blond chanteuse (Esther Ralston singing hilariously if unintentionally off-key), to see the light on his tubercular deathbed. She had already cured the alcoholism of her insanely understanding millionaire husband (Edward Arnold) and brought to heel the plutocrat (Franchot Tone) who will be husband number two. That's how it was in the Depression: so many millionaires competing for a shortage of working girls.

Which leaves the set's unsavory stowaway—there's one in every box—*Strange Cargo* (1940), directed with less than a full measure of attention by Frank Borzage in the same year he made his romantic wartime masterpiece *The Mortal Storm*. Set on Devil's Island, the film tracks the escape of several remorseless killers, including one played by Clark Gable, who emerges from thirty days in the hole with his hair rakishly brushed and stubble scrupulously trimmed. They are accompanied by a dance-hall entertainer of unspecified talents, played by Crawford, and God, played by Ian Hunter. This film is always referred to as an allegory, which might hold water if Hunter's character were a symbol of or stand-in for God or Jesus; but he isn't—he is the Unmoved Mover Himself or a close associate with the same powers, including universal predestination. Unsurprisingly, the Catholic Legion of Decency was less forgiving than the Gable-Crawford fans (this was their eighth and final film together) or Borzage apologists. The Legion demanded a few alterations but ultimately backed off with a harrumph.

Why God intervenes in a penal colony when He could be doing so much more at, say, Auschwitz, which also opened the same year, is a mystery, but not a compelling one. The one true allegorical touch is that He fails to convert the German prisoner—Germans are beyond even His powers. I don't think we are meant to read anything into the fact that two convicts are named after French novelists, Flaubert and Verne. Still, it fits in with the theme of the other films. Gable's Verne not only does right, finding God (as his Blackie did a few years earlier in *San Francisco*), but turns himself in, confident that when he is released, Crawford, also converted, will be waiting —an honest working girl.

Except for a smooch between the stars, not much fun is had in *Strange Cargo*, but the other films in this set are filled with bonbons generated by Crawford. In a 1938 letter to Gerald Murphy, F. Scott Fitzgerald memorably described the difficulty of writing for her: "She can't change her emotions in the middle of a scene without going through a sort of Jekyll and Hyde contortion of the face, so that when she wants to indicate that she is going from joy to sorrow, one must cut away and then cut back. Also, you can never give her such a stage direction as 'telling a lie,' because if you did, she would practically give a representation of Benedict Arnold selling West Point to the British."

Indeed, there are moments when Crawford doesn't frown, but puts on a frown, and doesn't pout, but puts on a pout. Hearing a rumble of thunder at the beginning of *Flamingo Road*, she looks as though the weather had it in for her personally. Yet she is almost always absorbing—the bad acting has a disarming way of opening up the process of filmmaking with a kind of you-are-there candor. And quite often, the acting isn't bad at all; sometimes it's incandescent. Crawford is genuinely alert to other actors, something Cukor made the most of with his extended two-shots of her and Douglas, and her and Veidt. She is also very handy with props. In *Torch Song*, she does five minutes of mime, alone on a Sunday morning trying to imagine herself as a blind person. Unfortunately, that's also the film in which she does the notoriously pointless and inept blackface number "Two-Faced Woman," wearing what Debbie Reynolds once described (in *That's Entertainment!*) as "tropical makeup." What were they thinking: outlandishness as a substitute for youth? The next year (1954), Crawford made the witch-hunt Western *Johnny Guitar*, and not long after that, we would learn what ever happened to Blanche Hudson.

20

BETTE DAVIS,
BIGGER THAN LIFE

THE USUAL CRITICAL line on Bette Davis recalls Stephen Colbert's hard-ball question concerning the former commander-in-chief: "Great president or the greatest president?" In the many documentaries and featurettes included in Warner's *The Bette Davis Collection, Vol. 2*, the talking heads palpitate with platitudes—eyes welling, voices shivering, cheeks reddening as if in communion with Baby Jane Hudson herself. In an addendum called *All About Bette*, Jodie Foster pitches her entire narration on the verge of tears. The screen's Greatest Actress? That's the least of it. Davis is portrayed as a combination of Mother Courage, Athena, Edith Cavell, and Sarah Bernhardt on one stump, defying the gods and the brothers Warner not to give her better parts. Had she not walked out on her contract in 1936, she would never have won the right to shrivel away in pancake and bald wigs, and today's film actresses would not be luxuriating in the ostensibly ready supply of powerful scripts and ennobling roles.

At the time she stormed off, Davis had been relegated to a diet of generic trash, often cast as a gangster's moll or gutter viper. So it was quite a triumph, after losing her suit, to return in 1937 and win the lead in *Marked Woman*, the earliest film included in the Warner box. She plays a prostitute who brings down the mob, nursing a grievance because the gang lord killed her sister and carved a crucifix on Davis's cheek. Directed with uninspired efficiency by Lloyd Bacon, *Marked Woman* is notable as the one picture in the Warner gangland cycle centered on women; the men are invariably scurrilous, cowardly, or pious. But the film is rarely as shrewd as its final shot, in which Davis and the other "hostesses" disappear into a fog bank, leaving the prosecutor, based on Thomas Dewey, to nurse his dreams of Albany. Loosely based on the Lucky Luciano trial, it has a smashing performance by Eduardo Ciannelli as the reptilian mob boss and a memorable turn by Lola Lane as a disconsolate hostess who also sings. Humphrey Bogart, shackled by sanctimony, does what he can with the Dewey role. Davis's part is based on the tabloid darling Cokey Flo Brown, whose testimony put a crimp in Luciano's plan to launch the A&P of brothels. Of course, she does it without the coke and the prostitution. Indeed, she is so bright-eyed and bushy-tailed that we don't gag at learning that she's putting her kid sister through college.

The next year (1938), Davis enjoyed a genuine breakthrough in the first of her three films with William Wyler, *Jezebel*. Wyler seemed to recognize her for what she was: a magnificent gorgon, a whirlwind of short-fused energy, and a bowstring waiting to be plucked. In their subsequent films, *The Letter* and *The Little Foxes*, the material is almost as taut as Davis. *Jezebel* is Southern-fried malarkey, but never as languorous, smug, or racially oblivious as *Gone with the Wind*. From the moment Davis whirls through a ball in an inappropriate dress, even Henry Fonda is outclassed—and forget George Brent, who has the best line: "I like my convictions undiluted, same as I do my bourbon." The rest is Bette Davis opera. She lands a vigorous slap, goes into seclusion, emerges to instigate a duel, and ultimately gives her all to fight yellow fever. If Davis gave no sense of the soiled dove in *Marked Woman*, she replaces the idiocies of *Jezebel* with diva largesse, a commitment verging on devotion.

Jezebel kicked off the great period in Davis's career, which lasted a mere seven years, notwithstanding two indelible reprises. This was the era, from 1938 to 1944, of the "woman's picture"—multigenerational sagas in which Davis torments others and is tormented in turn. When she isn't killing and betraying, she is succumbing to age, disease, and death. Too bad Warner didn't include such primo examples as John Huston's blistering psychodrama cum social critique *In This Our Life* (1942), or her initial championship bout with Miriam Hopkins, Edmund Goulding's *The Old Maid* (1939). Instead we get her glorified supporting role (top-billed and built-up) in a tiresome adaptation of Kaufman and Hart's *The Man Who Came to Dinner* (1942).

William Keighley directed this faithful if weirdly expurgated version of the play, in which "a Joan Crawford fantasy" becomes "a Ginger Rogers fantasy," "a brassiere worn by Hedy Lamarr" becomes "a sweater worn by Lana Turner," and "lavatory" becomes "locker room," among a thousand other minor alterations. What matters here is the belief that if the action *appears* fast, funny, and irreverent it *is* fast, funny, and irreverent. Not true, and not even a crate of penguins and Jimmy Durante, who brings much-needed energy to the third act, can cut through the self-satisfaction, emphasized by Monte Wolley's enchantment with his every line reading. The only surprise is that canny Ann Sheridan, with her well-timed eruptions of temper, steals the film from Davis, who—except for one big speech and one close-up of girlish laughter—is reduced to furniture.

Miriam Hopkins similarly won her rematch with Davis in Vincent Sherman's *Old Acquaintance* (1943), which is about two friends who write novels and inexplicably love John Loder, the dreariest actor of his generation. (Where is George Brent when you really need him?) Hopkins's character is so loathsome that generations of audiences have cheered the scene in which Bette finally throttles her and says, "Sorry." To be sure, it is a winning moment. But whereas Hopkins entertains, Davis relentlessly telegraphs her character's decency and genius with the same misjudged gesture: she plays the whole film casting her eyes down with an air of thoughtfully patient superiority. She's so bloody superior you wish someone would throttle *her*. The one genuinely natural performance is provided by the very young Gig Young. *Old Acquaintance* is a piss-poor yet oddly engaging antique.

The end of the war coincided with Davis's decline, which she halted in 1950 with *All About Eve* (Fox). A decade of inferior work followed, before she grabbed hold of the title role in *What Ever Happened to Baby Jane?* (1962). This is the best film in the box, and the best evidence of the nuance, insight, originality, and humor that define Davis at the height of her sacred-monster powers. *Baby Jane* was greeted as a horror film in its day, but it endures for its consistent wit in contrasting the torturous relationship of the Hudson sisters (Jane and her crippled sister, Blanche, played by Joan Crawford with hand-wringing masochism) with those of a dull suburban mom and daughter (Anna Lee and Davis's real-life daughter, Barbara Merrill) and a lumbering bottom-feeder and his tiny cockney mum (played to perfection by Victor Buono and Marjorie Bennett). Adapting the eerie sensationalism of *Sunset Boulevard* at a time when talkie queens had reached the age of battle-ax madness and murder, it was directed by Robert Aldrich with an unerring eye for everyday Grand Guignol. The film wastes time with repetitive horrors and suspense, but its heart is in its scathing portrayal of vaudeville ("I've Written a Letter to Daddy"), television ("Iliad, the classic dog food"), and movies (the next two hours). The pitiless puncturing of age and delusion is whetted on masterly comic timing, as in the exchange between Davis and Buono: "I wonder if you can guess who I am," she says. "Can you give me a hint?" Davis's admirers often observe that she lacked vanity in her willingness to look ugly and incarnate evil. What her vanity could not abide was playing small. In Baby Jane Hudson, she created a gargoyle for all time.

21

THE SERENITY OF ALICE FAYE

LOOSELY SPEAKING, THE great musicals of the 1930s were made at War-ner Bros., Paramount, and RKO, the great musicals of the 1950s were made at MGM, and the great wartime musicals were made at 20th Century Fox. The Fox musicals are often dismissed as clichéd escapism. One reason is that they can least afford the offhanded treatment traditionally accorded movies by early television and revival houses—the butchered 16-mm prints, scratched by projectors and faded by time. If the colors don't pop off the screen to engulf the senses and the tempo is undone by commercial inter-ruptions, the Fox experience is fatally compromised.

The best of them were built around Alice Faye, an actor so comfortable in her own skin that she never had to rouse herself to rouse us. Instead, she invites our gaze, encouraging the voyeuristic impulse of women no less than men, to look her up and down and marvel at the way she fills out a sump-tuous wardrobe, carries herself, delivers lines, and reacts, often with unex-pected irony. Faye's plain beauty—broad flat face, pug nose, eyes slightly too wide apart—offers a comforting tableau of protective generosity, even when mordant, even when suppressing an erotic yawn at her erotically chal-lenged or inconstant beaus. If any film series requires DVD redemption, it's Faye's musicals, which are well served by *The Alice Faye Collection*, a four-volume set that includes *On the Avenue* (1937), her breakthrough film; *Lillian Russell* (1940), an undernourished dud with a few memorable moments; and two Technicolor spectaculars, *That Night in Rio* (1941) and Busby Berkeley's near-masterpiece *The Gang's All Here* (1943), all handsomely restored. The best of the uneven extras, which include a few stodgy featurettes and an informative commentary by Miles Kreuger, are two shows from the radio series Faye starred in with Phil Harris, her husband of fifty-four years.

Faye was a musical Garbo, without the mystery or ennui. Often characterized as the girl next door (in what neighborhood would that be?), she provokes the deep pleasure of unrequited familiarity. Yet if these qualities ought to ensure her ongoing reputation as a ruler of her genre, they also isolate her. The songbirds that preceded, rivaled, and followed her were, each in her own way, live wires. If they didn't dance, they belted, and if they didn't belt, they emoted full bore. Faye did none of that: she was almost always exquisitely languid, a mistress of understatement, especially when singing. The archetypal Faye moment is usually set at twilight, as she positions herself against a wall or column, tilting her head slightly as the camera comes in for a nearly invasive close-up, and she lends her warm and hale but undemonstrative contralto to a ballad. A passive dish served in Technicolor splendor, she allows us to devour her face, her makeup, her eyes—nothing more, but it's quite enough. Faye was one of the finest movie vocalists of her day. Along with Bing Crosby and Fred Astaire, she inspired songwriters, turning their work into hits that became standards. Unfortunately, she was not permitted to capitalize on them.

Fox studio head Darryl F. Zanuck, a little man with an oversized cigar and relentless appetite for self-aggrandizement and fleshly proofs of his power, may have been one of the few people who, like Fitzgerald's Monroe Stahr, understood "the whole equation" of filmmaking. Yet synergy baffled him. He refused to allow his stars to plug his pictures on radio unless they made direct reference to him, and refused to let them make records, perhaps fearing that success in another medium would weaken his control. This put Faye at a disadvantage, although even when she did record film songs, in 1936 and 1937, her dimly arranged versions fared far less well than others—she was regularly covered by no less than Billie Holiday. After her stardom crested, she was contractually barred from recording: in 1943, she introduced "No Love, No Nothing" (*The Gang's All Here*) and the wartime anthem "You'll Never Know" (*Hello, Frisco, Hello*), but the recorded hits were scored by Ella Mae Morse and Dick Haymes.

Still, Zanuck made her a film star before he drove her out of the business. Ridiculously young when she made her way from chorus line to featured parts onstage (she lied about her age at thirteen to join the Chester Hale Troupe), Faye soon became a protégé of Rudy Vallee, who faded from filmdom as she rose, initially in the guise of a Jean Harlow replica. Zanuck allowed her to be herself: normal, quietly intelligent, droll. He also had the insightful idea of complementing her rectitude with the liveliest wire of all, Carmen Miranda. With her flashing eyes, rolling midriff, eloquent arms, unremitting energy, English-mangling temper, and costumes that no one else would dare wear, Miranda was the volcanic id, setting in relief Faye's sometimes heartbreaking cool. Though they have few scenes together, they mesh the exotic and the plebeian.

Roy Del Ruth's *On the Avenue* puts its best foot forward with an opening ten-minute stage number featuring Faye and the lunatic Ritz Brothers; rubbery-faced Harry Ritz sings a parody of "Cheek to Cheek," introducing his brothers ("Dr. Matzohball, who invented the maypole") and dancing in lockstep with them. Faye is third-billed, which means she loses Dick Powell (no loss) to a gorgeous if stiff-necked Madeleine Carroll, while stealing the film from both. Between her close-ups and her reading of the line (see for yourself) "I love plumbers. And garbage men," she takes all the marbles. The plot, leavened by Irving Berlin's score, revolves around a family of zany plutocrats and a denouement that explicitly prefigures *The Philadelphia Story*.

Faye is miscast as the eponymous faux-operatic Gay Nineties star in *Lillian Russell*, a film devoid of coherence and drama, and censored to within an inch of Russell's life. Faye honors the costumes and sets, but there isn't much else to see, though it is perversely fun to find Henry Fonda, who did not lightly surrender a scene, reduced to a stooge by old pro Helen Westley. Eddie Foy Jr. does his usual impeccable Eddie Foy Sr., and Weber and Fields do themselves. Plot was not a Fox strong suit. Stir the plots of every Fox musical in a barrel and you won't have enough gruel for a single Deborah Eisenberg short story. Yet you wouldn't say that Fox favored style over substance; in Fox musicals, style is all.

This becomes clear in the Latin trilogy, beginning with *Down Argentine Way* (1940), which Faye abandoned because of illness (Betty Grable took over, and it made her a star). *Down Argentine Way* also represented a watershed in Hollywood's depiction of Latin Americans, at least for the duration. Upon its release, the Coordinator of Inter-American Affairs, Nelson Rockefeller, intent on revving up the Good Neighbor Policy, complained to Zanuck that the picture belittled Argentines as gigolos and worse and showed one character speaking Spanish with a Mexican accent. Zanuck agreed to reshoot the offending scenes before releasing the film in South America. The extra expense was worth it. With that film, three-strip Technicolor and Carmen Miranda triumphed, and Fox went all the way with them. Faye returned for the much improved follow-ups, *That Night in Rio* and *Week-End in Havana*, both in 1941.

Director Irving Cummings made up for *Lillian Russell* with *That Night in Rio*, recycling an old Maurice Chevalier vehicle that in the new version gave Don Ameche twin roles: one gets Faye, the other Miranda. The stars are shiny and bright, and the music, especially the Brazilian numbers by Miranda and her Banda La Lua, are lively enough to overcome the comic relief, but the real star is the photography by two of Technicolor's primary innovators, Leon Shamroy and Ray Rennahan. Every shot is painted with cartoon-like precision, as green areas are suddenly disrupted by touches of red or white or yellow, the chromatic design creating a luster that, along with the percussion, sexy dancers, and costumes, underscores the cheerfully carnal elation of adults at play.

By contrast, *The Gang's All Here*, which hasn't looked this good in years, takes an entirely different approach to the saturated hues of Technicolor. Shot by Edward Cronjager, a gifted Fox veteran who had recently proved his color bona fides with Lubitsch's *Heaven Can Wait* (1943), the film has a darker grain, as though the color stock were combined with monochrome. The deeper hues are balanced by a constant refrain of black. Faye sings "No Love, No Nothing" against a black background in profile, looking like a porcelain cameo. The big Berkeley set pieces are among his best and most notorious: the ten-minute "The Lady in the Tutti Frutti Hat" (note Alfred Newman's dissonances in the lead-in), the single-entendre coupling of giant bananas and supine strawberries conducted by Miranda, who is posed in one of the great matte effects of all time; and the twenty-minute finale, interrupted by a brief plot diversion, so that the film can finish in song.

The great achievement here is that Berkeley directed almost the entire film with the scrupulous dislocation and theatrical hyperbole that characterizes his musical numbers. Once derided as over-baked and inept and then rediscovered as fashionably campy, *The Gang's All Here* weathers its years with true grace. More than most musicals of its vintage, it is rather timeless, because it undercuts the suffocating morality of most 1940s films. For all the superficial merriment, the film plays up a core of real dissatisfaction in the insincerity that animates its central relationships. Benny Goodman swings and sings (twice), and even Eugene Pallette is invited to croak in the big finish, which has a curiously misanthropic edge, equal to the film's utter devotion to artifice and parody.

Faye never starred in another musical after *The Gang's All Here* (though she made an ill-advised return for the 1962 evisceration of *State Fair*). In 1945, she appeared in Otto Preminger's undervalued *Fallen Angel*, falling for Dana Andrews's grifter and making a man of him, but her scenes—and a song (she was replaced by Dick Haymes, this time on a jukebox number)— were cut, and she left the lot, never to return. She once recalled that Zanuck said something to her so vile that she knew she could never work there again, though she wouldn't repeat what it was. For the next eight years, she and Phil Harris enjoyed a top-rated radio series, in which a frequent butt of the humor was Zanuck, a producer forever trying to lure her back to the fold. DVD succeeds where Zanuck failed.

22

EDWARD G. ROBINSON, SEE

No one knew more than the spellbinding Edward G. Robinson about how to hold and control a scene. He didn't need directorial coddling—a star-struck key light, an invasive close-up, fail-safe blocking. From the director's perspective, he was a point-and-shoot actor: point the camera, call for action, and let him go. He was at his best in a medium shot with other actors, listening and reacting, then closing in for the kill: the trademark index finger pointing like a saber, the casually authoritative stance, the eyes that squint or widen, command or plead, twinkle or forewarn. He did a lot with his eyelids: eyelids at half-mast were not a good sign. His round, thick-lipped, putty face could brighten like paternal sunshine or shut down in implacable contempt or stall with crafty desperation or pontificate with ingenuous wisdom; his short, stumpy, erect frame could sport a tailor-made as smartly as Cary Grant. A homely yet vain peacock of a man who was never allowed to win the girl, he could even play beautiful—not handsome, but beatific, inspired, lit from deep inside. His voice, a favorite of mimics even now, was far more supple than the scowling bray of his indelible Caesar Enrico Bandello, with his punctuating "see," death-scene invocation, and nutty threats: "Listen, you crummy, flat-footed copper! I'll show you whether I've lost my nerve and my brains!" He modulated that voice up and down, and when he played a pipe-chewing or cigar-puffing bloodhound, as in *Confessions of a Nazi Spy* (1939) and *Double Indemnity* (1944), words spilled out with a seemingly unpracticed assonance.

If Robinson couldn't play the lover, he stretched in other directions. He could be hilariously funny—no one ever combined stupidity and arrogance better than Eddie G, as in Lloyd Bacon's informal trilogy of criminal screwballs *A Slight Case of Murder* (1938), *Brother Orchid* (1940), and *Larceny Inc.* (1942), in clover with more than a dozen of the most shameless scene stealers ever to mount a stage. No one could better incarnate a full heart, human decency, good sense, and natural intelligence, as in *Dr. Ehrlich's Magic Bullet* (1940), *Our Vines Have Tender Grapes* (1945), and his weird swan song as a dying man, *Soylent Green* (1973). And no one, but no one, could better personify pitiless, barbaric evil, born of pride and fear and utterly banal in its ambition, as in *Little Caesar* (1931), *The Sea Wolf* (1941, as Wolf Larsen, quoting Milton as if he were Satan's soul mate), and *Key Largo* (1948), in which he conveys the stink of pomade, cologne, cigar smoke, and moral rot. Small wonder that he was called on to play dual characters, his rubbery face modulating between kindness and derision in *The Whole Town's Talking* (1935) and *The Prize* (1963).

Robinson rarely failed to take charge of the action, drawing attention with his confident reserve, needing little recourse to overacting or physical shtick, though he had a repertoire of prefab techniques to lean on when bored or distracted. By the 1940s, he didn't have to do much: the bullfrog visage, sonorously taut inflections, easy smile, and perfect posture were enough—the cocked finger served as exclamation. The years 1944 to 1949 represented a peak, the last in his long career. This was the period of *Double Indemnity, The Woman in the Window, Our Vines Have Tender Grapes, Scarlet Street, The Stranger, The Red House, All My Sons, Key Largo, Night Has a Thousand Eyes*, and *House of Strangers*. But Robinson, in his posthumous memoir, didn't see it that way. For him, *Double Indemnity* signified the indignity of third billing; and he recalled the other films in terms of political arguments on the set or the insufficient status of his co-stars. He quarreled with Orson Welles on *The Stranger* and claimed to sleepwalk through two Fritz Lang gems, *The Woman in the Window* and *Scarlet Street*, shot by Milton Krasner and co-starring Joan Bennett and Dan Duryea. One wouldn't suspect any of this from watching the films. Robinson rivets the other actors as easily as he does the audience; in scene after scene, the eyes of his co-stars are glued to him.

The Woman in the Window (1944) was released on DVD as part of an MGM noir collection along with *The Stranger*; Phil Karlson's fine, sleek heist thriller *Kansas City Confidential* (1952), a non-Robinson vehicle though he would have been perfect in the Preston Foster role as the elusive gang leader; and *A Bullet for Joey* (1955), one of several post-McCarthy films Robinson made in penance for his left-wing politics. Here you can see him on automatic pilot, exiting the jerry-built sets as though he couldn't wait to go home (he did not like working with George Raft, who wears his pleated trousers midway between waist and neck), yet still managing to give the film what little buzz it has. *The Woman in the Window* has much in common with *Scarlet Street* (1945), but is tonally and thematically quite different—as much about voyeurism and middle-aged boredom as the wrong turn that can undo a respectable life. Robinson's splendidly named Richard Wanley has peaked as an assistant professor. As an amiable club man, content in his sexless marriage, he concedes he is willing to watch a burlesque stripper, but only if she comes to him.

She does, in the person of Joan Bennett's Alice Reed, a high-priced call girl and photographer's model who prides herself on her ability to read people. In Lang's world, there are no wrong men, innocently accused; instead, there are suppressed men who, when the ego is distracted even momentarily, break loose. A perfect description of the noir universe and Lang's place in it may be found in a letter written to a Jewish friend by the dying Octavius Augustus in John Williams's bravura 1973 novel *Augustus*: "Perhaps there is but one god. But if that is true, you have misnamed him. He is Accident, and his priest is man, and that priest's only victim must be at last himself, his poor divided self."

Lang sets up Wanley's dilemma with two preludes: a fragment from a classroom lecture on the gradations of homicide, with shadowy bars holding him in place; and the vacation leave-taking of his wife and children, which prefigures a similar scene a decade later in Billy Wilder's *The Seven Year Itch*. From the moment Alice's reflection appears in a gallery window as Wanley stares at her portrait, virtual reality gives way to the real thing, and poor Wanley is doubled by mirrors, especially those in her fun-house apartment, including a wall-size mirror surrounding a fireplace decorated with a Greek key. Perhaps the middle-classness of it all inclined Lang to a lightly sardonic touch, evident not least in the denouement. The dream framework is often assumed to be an add-on mandated by censors, though the whole film proves otherwise. Lang himself, in a typically ambivalent display of generosity to one of his characters, insisted on the dream structure, over vehement protests from the producer-scenarist, Nunnally Johnson. Lang didn't think Wanley deserved self- or other-inflicted capital punishment. And given Robinson's sympathetic performance as he inadvertently puts one foot, then the other, in quicksand, who would disagree? Still, the dream can also be interpreted as the kind of reversal in which salvation is fantasized, followed hard by death. Much of the story takes place in Wanley's absence, and people don't dream episodes in which they do not appear. Maybe he dies fantasizing his deliverance. Either way, it's a mischievously inspired ending.

No less rewarding is Kino's glistening release of *Scarlet Street*, a film that had fallen into the permanent purgatory of public domain cheapies, until Kino found a near-pristine print in the Library of Congress. Lang had been importuned into making it to cash in on the success of *The Woman in the Window*, and found another way for Robinson, this time an agreeably pathetic milquetoast, to commit an impulsive murder and get drawn into the web of the darker and more vividly imagined characters incarnated by Joan Bennett and Dan Duryea. Robinson remembered *Scarlet Street* and his work in it as "monotonous." In fact, his worm-that-turns ranks among his most powerful, witting performances, matched every step by Duryea's rancid pimp (his euphemistic catchphrase is "for cat's sake") and Bennett's luminous, cellophane-wrapped streetwalker who drolly tells Robinson, "You *are* clever," when he guesses that she is an actress. Lang catches Robinson in one of his most memorably off-kilter moments: wearing a frilly kitchen apron and holding a large carving knife at his side, while meekly answering to his scarily masculine wife. Who but Robinson could so convincingly open the picture by gratefully accepting a gold watch from the imperious tycoons retiring him and close it, ragged and terrified, shuffling into homeless oblivion? One of Lang's formalistic American triumphs, *Scarlet Street* exemplifies his fastidious control on a sound stage, fashioning—with Milton Krasner (coming into his own, midway in a long career)—a sordid stand-in for Greenwich Village, painting nights with bottomless blackness and glaring reflections. A matchless study of male impotence and desperation born of missed chances, *Scarlet Street* also packs a nasty, painfully funny rabbit punch on the subject of art and authorship.

In contrast, *House of Strangers* (1949), which Fox has released in its own Film Noir series, is an unmistakable A film, directed by Joseph Mankiewicz with lots of talk, some of it pretty good ("My husband died happy,"

"Your husband was happy to die") and made better by a high-powered cast that surrounds Robinson's patriarch: Susan Hayward, Richard Conte, and Luther Adler. The story riffs on King Lear while prefiguring *The Godfather*, and offers a singular instance of a sexually liberated woman who comes out on top. Robinson's self-satisfied banker explains that the New World is vertical, unlike the horizontal Old World, and so sexually advanced that "someday they'll find a way for husbands to have babies." The period décor is nailed with scrupulous detail, and the location shooting is startling in its realism. Yet dry lighting (favoring grays over extremes of light and dark) and direction date the film, despite its virtues, while the oily muck of *Scarlet Street* simmers with devious freshness.

The Stranger (1946) is usually dismissed as a Welles sellout, something done to prove to the studios that he could turn out a profitable programmer. Not likely. For one thing, it is filled with the privileged shots and jokes we expect only from Welles, or in this instance Welles in tandem with uncredited screenwriter John Huston and over-the-top composer Bronislau Kaper. The latter's score inserts pounding Rachmaninoff piano chords as foreign to New England as Welles's Nazi, Franz Kindler. True, the opening reels of a South American chase were cut and destroyed. True again, Kindler's eyes are so shifty they seem to be on rollers. True also, Kindler greets an erstwhile comrade, Meinike (Konstantine Shayne), with the most shameless expository speech in the history of dramaturgy. But: the opening and closing sequences are delightfully stylized (note Meinike's reflection in a camera lens); the film is never dull, not even sluggish; Russell Metty's photography is often ravishing; Robinson's Nazi hunter is all-American gemütlich, especially in colloquies with a rotund ex-vaudevillian, Billy House; and the marriage between Kindler and a Supreme Court justice's daughter (Loretta Young) is a Freudian banquet. I'm guessing that Huston came up with the idea of Meinike's "all highest" turning out to be God, and having him pray that God give Kindler strength. God does, and Kindler strangles Meinike to the tune of screaming brasses, ending in perfect unison decay.

Having played Nazi chasers immediately before and after the war, Robinson entered the 1950s with an implacable local enemy, native fascists wrapped in the flag and determined to revise the Constitution to exclude Communists, insufficiently repentant ex-Communists, and anyone else left of Joe McCarthy. Setting up their lemonade stand in Hollywood, they terrorized the studios into launching a blacklist that tarred Robinson for having given money to liberal causes. He returned in glory to Broadway, for the first and last time in a quarter century, but his movie work languished or depended on low-budget programmers. The year after his character in Lewis Allen's *A Bullet for Joey* (1955) stopped the Commies (never named as such) from kidnapping a Canadian physicist, he was repatriated by no less a jingoist than Cecil B. DeMille, who cast him as the traitor of the Jews in *The Ten Commandments*—ironic: Robinson was the only Jew DeMille cast in a leading role. If only he had been allowed to retain the cigar as he turns to the throng and snarls, "Moses has words, Pharaoh has spears!"

23

HUMPHREY BOGART:
FALCONS AND FASCISTS

THE BLAND TITLE *Humphrey Bogart: The Signature Collection, Vol. 2* (Warner Bros.) doesn't do justice to this irresistible set of seven films—one of the
most focused and illuminating in the Signature series. It tracks not only the
making of Bogart's stardom in the years 1941–44, after a long apprenticeship of interchangeable heavies, but also the studio's four stages of wartime
concern: denial, lampoon, flag waving, and "Marseillaise" singing. The
films, of which the crown jewel is a three-disc presentation of *The Maltese
Falcon* (including the two non-Bogart versions), are available separately,
but a chronological immersion in these movies—complete with new and
old short subjects, cartoons, blooper reels, newsreels, and a feature-length
documentary—offers an intricate lesson in history as a side effect of popular culture.

The months preceding Pearl Harbor were the best and worst of times
for Hollywood. Torn between sympathy for Lend-Lease and isolationism,
the moguls feared losing Germany, Italy, and other markets, even as they
boasted of the record profits from recent Technicolor triumphs like *Gone
with the Wind* and artistic advances by virtually every established director in town—Ford, Lubitsch, McCarey, Hawks, Curtiz, Wyler, Walsh,
Capra, even the independent patriarch Chaplin. In 1941, direct allusions
to Europe—previously addressed full bore in *Confessions of a Nazi Spy*, *The
Great Dictator*, and *The Mortal Storm*—all but disappeared from the screen.
Yet two directorial debuts altered the very look of Hollywood movies, fore-

casting the shape of a bold new cinema to come: Orson Welles's *Citizen Kane* in May and John Huston's *The Maltese Falcon* in October. Pearl Harbor would delay the fulfillment of that new cinema for four years, but the stylistic implications were adapted immediately. While Welles was regarded as an interloper from the East, easily dismissed by bean counters, Huston was a company man—one of the best screenwriters around, anticipating a winning year for his work on *High Sierra* and *Sergeant York* (both 1941) even before Warner Bros. rewarded him, at thirty-five, with his own film.

The gift had strings, of course: no stars, a limited budget, a brutal shooting schedule, and a property that had already been filmed twice, without success, in the previous ten years. Huston stunned everyone. Taking to heart the advice of his producer, Henry Blanke ("Each scene, as you go to make it, is the best scene in the picture"), he designed his shots on storyboards, editing with the camera, determined to find a filmic equivalent to Dashiell Hammett's brisk, street-smart novel. Just as these techniques would later define Huston's career, so too did the picture's intertwined themes: the group in vain pursuit of a treasure, and masked identities that obscure motive and character. Huston came in under budget and ahead of schedule, the film was a hit, and the critics saluted him as a major young filmmaker.

The impact of *The Maltese Falcon* was decisive for nearly everyone involved. Bogart was boosted to an edgy stardom that crested with his unexpected matinee-idol turn the following year in *Casablanca* (reissued in the first Bogart Signature Collection, and along with *Sahara*, made at Columbia, his only major films from these four years not included here). Mary Astor, a veteran of silent films and salacious scandals, was reborn with one of her finest roles, as was Peter Lorre, whose early coups had withered into Mr. Moto exercises. Sidney Greenstreet, a sixty-one-year-old stage actor, made a historic screen debut, waddling into the film at midpoint, and Elisha Cook Jr., who had made about twenty-five films and would appear in some seventy-five more, was launched as a cult favorite. Less flamboyant performances— by Lee Patrick, Jerome Cowan, Ward Bond, Barton MacLane, and Gladys George—also proved indelible.

Huston invented the modern detective film as vividly as Hammett had the hard-boiled novel, putting to rest the clichés of low comic relief, fade-out romantic clinches, and jovial codas, while bringing a curiously lasting facsimile of realism to 1940s movies. Arthur Edeson's photography would later be accounted as a source of the postwar school of film noir, but the cinematography specifically reflects the shadows and secrets of the characters. Visual invention is constant, in the play of light and in the character-defining angles (Greenstreet's girth shot from below, Lorre's fellating a cane shot from behind) and fluid group portraits (some of Lorre's finest moments are silent reactions as others converse in the foreground). The confrontations are deep, funny, gripping, surprising. The film opens with Spade's girl-Friday Effie, aglow like sunshine, introducing Miss Wonderly, "a knockout," who walks in with calculating steps, sizing up Sam Spade, who greets her with the fake solicitude of a banker. "I'm from New York," she says, which means "I'm not from New York." "Un-hunh," he says, which means "Sure you are." And we're off to the races, Spade genuinely bemused by the gallery of grotesques suddenly swarming into his life. The last twenty-five minutes are set in his apartment, a bravura setup that augurs the first hour of Kurosawa's *High and Low*, also staged in a living room. The intensity of the performances is matched by the virtuoso camera work, the sudden shuffling of close-ups, the choreographed division of loyalties, the gnarled, knotted ugliness of Bogart's face as he prepares to send Astor to the hangman, Astor's horrific flinch when the doorbell rings.

Warner offers a spotless print of this film and the previous attempts at *The Maltese Falcon*—a faithful adaptation from 1931 (including the forced stripping of Brigit, the phoniest episode in the novel and one denied Huston by the Production Code, spurring him to find a much better solution), undone by a lack of tempo, style, and subtlety and by Ricardo Cortez's grinning ninny as Spade; and a 1936 would-be comedy, *Satan Met a Lady*, dreadfully performed by Bette Davis and Warren William, who actually resembles Spade as Hammett describes him. It's hard to believe a mere five years separate it from Huston's film; they seem to reflect different epochs.

The other four films in the set confront World War II with varying degrees of melodrama and sentiment, yet, failings aside, remain slam-bang entertainments. Vincent Sherman's *All Through the Night* (1942), a Runyunesque comedy of Nazi Bundists (Conrad Veidt, Judith Anderson, and the matchlessly malevolent Lorre) in New York, completed shooting eight weeks before Pearl Harbor. Its slick combination of practiced farceurs and high-stakes drama, in which nice mother-loving gangsters defeat terrorists determined to bomb a battleship anchored in Brooklyn, mirrors a national turnabout as Americans and their Hollywood representatives began to accept a brutal reality that required a more potent response than Donald

Duck blowing raspberries in Der Führer's face.

Sherman, who had once directed Bogart as a vampire in *The Return of Dr. X*, was also called in to complete Huston's *Across the Pacific* (1942), about Japanese spies determined to blow up the Panama Canal. Originally the script had focused on Hawaii, but events in December mandated a new script, if not a new title—the film should have been called *Down the Atlantic*. Huston shot all except the finale, at which time he was commissioned as a lieutenant in the army and sent to the Aleutians. He claimed to have ended the final scene with Bogart in dire straits, daring Sherman to free him; true or not, the last reel is strictly boy's adventure. But the delicious repartee between Bogart and Astor is funny and sexy in this fast-moving if stylistically conventional reunion.

Lloyd Bacon's epical *Action in the North Atlantic* (1943) and Michael Curtiz's fascinating *Passage to Marseille* (1944) are among the more durable—which is to say least risible—of wartime propaganda films, confirming a rare political unity in American life. The former, dealing with the Merchant Marine, is notable for its submarine chase, the beginning of a mini-genre, and for having the Germans speak German, an efficient way of distancing the enemy. Curtiz's film, despite twaddle about Joan of Arc and the motherland, is more intriguing. Its structure violates the key principle of screenwriting, chronological coherence. The story begins in the present (call it level one), flashes back via one narrator to a second narrator (level two), who flashes back to a third perspective (level three), then works back to levels two and one, at which point Curtiz, the great action director, unveils a twenty-minute cavalcade of mutiny, anti-mutiny, bomber attack, and postbattle slaughter. Bogart plays a French journalist sentenced to Devil's Island (premonitions of Papillon) who becomes an expert gunner and cold-blooded killer—he's the hero. Lorre is a good-guy safecracker, Greenstreet a collaborator, and Claude Rains a one-eyed captain relating the overall tale. The DVD is made more savory by the addition of the one-reeler *Jammin' the Blues*, the finest jazz short ever made, and a reminder that Lester Young is what we were fighting for.

24

LET'S BE FRANK

IN ACKNOWLEDGING THE tenth anniversary of Frank Sinatra's death, Warner Bros. raised its DVD flag to half-mast with the thrifty release of thirteen films, supplemented by few (in most instances, zero) extra features. The selection covers twenty-three years (1943–65) in an often feckless Hollywood career that began in 1941, with Sinatra's uncredited vocals as a member of Tommy Dorsey's band, and ended resignedly in 1970, save for a halfhearted return a decade later. By then, Sinatra had elected to focus his creative energies on television and records. His film work is often remembered as a mere adjunct to a musician's career.

Yet for five years, between 1954 and 1958, Sinatra functioned as an actor of nerve, stature, and originality—a natural, perhaps, but also a signature personality playing against the type he assiduously perfected onstage. As a quintessential anti-hero and derisively anti-Method actor, Sinatra—his face filled out with an appealing resilience absent in his early years—embraced a work ethic that led to several ambitious movies, usually two or three a year. Alongside a couple of middlebrow melodramas, coy comedies, and a fiasco of Himalayan dimensions (*The Pride and the Passion*), the films in this period found him playing an assassin in *Suddenly*, an incomparable Nathan Detroit in *Guys and Dolls*, a junkie in *The Man with the Golden Arm*, the heir to and equal of Bing Crosby in *High Society*, a redeemable heel in *Pal Joey*, and broken men in *The Joker Is Wild* and *Some Came Running*.

As early as 1956, however, movies had begun to bore him, and tales of his terrible behavior circulated: he arrived late, not knowing his lines, refused second takes, refused to support his co-stars in their close-ups. The rest was Rat Pack frivolity, cliché dramas at which the hungrier, more serious Sinatra might have rolled his eyes (*The Devil at Four O'Clock*, 1961), unspeakably smarmy comedies (*Marriage on the Rocks* [1965], in which Deborah Kerr is outfitted as if auditioning for *Doctor Zhivago*), and worse, as Sinatra grew heavy, comfortable, and disengaged. The only remaining high points were the laconically existential detectives he played in the 1960s, chiefly the military investigator in *The Manchurian Candidate* (1962). The Warner selection is hardly a survey of high points, though it does include his best nonmusicals—two indispensable, intricately related works of the 1950s, *The Man with the Golden Arm* (1955) and *Some Came Running* (1958)—plus the ingenious if sometimes annoying postwar musical *On the Town* (1949). The others? Good lord, Elvis had better vehicles. Some early films are salvaged by musical numbers, but as the DVDs lack scene-selection menus, you may develop calluses searching them out.

Sinatra's first roles came in fussy adaptations of stage plays. He enters thirty minutes into *Higher and Higher* (1943) as a shy neighborhood crooner named Frank Sinatra, whose dreamy "I Couldn't Sleep a Wink Last Night" shows what the fuss was about. Michelle Morgan bats her eyes and Mel Torme sings like Sterling Holloway while balancing a pompadour the size of the national debt. In *Step Lively* (1944), a remake of *Room Service*, Gloria DeHaven looks, as ever, sexy; George Murphy looks, as ever, constipated; and Sinatra looks chagrined. Moviegoers in the 1940s who feared there could never again be an actor as humorless and self-regarding as George Murphy must have felt reassured when MGM found Peter Lawford for *It Happened in Brooklyn* (1947). Make a note regarding the latter: "Time After Time" is at 37:30; the film's one bolt of energy, Sinatra's duet with Jimmy Durante, is at 50:20, followed almost immediately by Sinatra and Kathryn Grayson combining anhedonia and chirping in a duet from *Don Giovanni*. Nothing at all commends *The Kissing Bandit* (1948) or *Double Dynamite* (1951), a film named for Jane Russell's double-D dramatic style, which is unaccountably buttoned up throughout the picture.

These films and the three musicals with Gene Kelly, boxed separately, come from Sinatra's monkey period—a reference not to his looks (underfed, abashed, and, well, simian) but to the phrase coined by Jerry Lewis to characterize his own roles opposite Dean Martin. Sinatra's monkey is a virgin rube who has yet to discover girls (he prefers checkers) and needs Kelly to set him straight, usually in numbers that find Kelly relentlessly mugging his condescending parodies of women. As the great Durante, whose character in *It Happened in Brooklyn* wears an apron and knits doilies ("derlies"), might have said: "Surrounded by transvestites, dat's what I am!" The colorful exertions of *Anchors Away* (1945) and *Take Me Out to the Ballgame* (1949) are leached by patriotic piety and sexual arrogance. *On the Town*, in contrast, glories in the wit of an Adolph Green / Betty Comden script, Leonard Bernstein music, and fervent direction by Kelly and Stanley Donen—yet even here, Frank looks justifiably humiliated.

After his long winter of discontent (in his 1950 television series, Sinatra wore a mustache and did cutlery commercials), the Chairman remade himself as a recording artist and triumphed with a rather ordinary performance in *From Here to Eternity* (1953). Reborn, he committed himself fully to Otto Preminger's masterly adaptation of Nelson Algren's *The Man with the Golden Arm*. Comparisons with Vincente Minnelli's *Some Came Running* begin with the fact that both are based on noted novels, though James Jones's elaborate and misunderstood 1,266-page anti-epic was widely trashed and has remained unpublished in its entirety for fifty years. (This is a job for Library of America!) In both films, style and theme are inseparable, and the plotlines reverse the literary fortunes of the protagonists and their wives. Frankie Machine, the card dealer addicted to morphine, and Dave Hirsh, the army vet, writer, and accomplished poker player addicted to self-pity, enter their respective films on buses, returning to Midwestern hometowns; in the end, violence frees them from deceptive women to face uncertain futures. In the novels, Frankie kills his connection and hangs himself, and Dave is shot down at night while leaving town and his monstrous wife. But in the films, violent death—suicide, murder—is reserved for the women.

In Preminger's film, the monkey is off Frank's face and on Frankie Machine's back—a phrase that, despite origins associated with nineteenth-century alcoholism and opium addiction, didn't gain usage among junkies until the 1940s and didn't reach the general public until Algren's 1949 novel. It became so much a cliché that Lenny Bruce killed it with his routine about an addict who joins Lawrence Welk's band and tells him he has a monkey on his back. "That's okay," the bandleader says, "we like animals in the band. Rocky's got a duck, they can play together." Yet *The Man with the Golden Arm* has dated better than the junkie films that soon followed—

including Shirley Clarke's film of Jack Gelber's *The Connection* (1960), a work that is more realistic and also more contrived. If Frankie's cold turkey is hurried, and the conventions of melodrama demand neat fixes, the film's truth resides in the sharp script and a strange mélange of performers who were never better: Sinatra, Eleanor Parker, Arnold Stang, Darren McGavin, George E. Stone, and even Kim Novak, whose vacant looks and line readings are nonetheless affecting. The virtuoso mobility of Preminger's camera, sweeping laterally and then down or up before closing in, eschewing edits, demands theatrical concentration and endurance from the actors. The patently phony sound-stage exteriors underscore their power, producing an unusual merger of theater and cinema.

Preminger's film, as written by Walter Newman and Lewis Melzer, is more of a study in the nature of addiction than is Algren's novel—heroin is only the most obvious kind. Every character is addicted to something, be it hustling, alcohol, unrequited love, failure, power, getting attention, stealing, gambling, or guilt. They will spin their wheels until they die. In addition to director and cast, the film is stylishly bound by Saul Bass's animated credits and Elmer Bernstein's sensational score, which is brazenly jazzy but—contrary to critical conventions—not jazz: there is a difference.

The big change (from the novel) introduced in *Some Came Running* by Minnelli and his script writers—John Patrick, whose most creative years coincided with Sinatra's, and Arthur Sheekman, a Marx Brothers veteran whose career was ending—concerns Ginny, played by Shirley MacLaine in the performance of her life. Jones's decision to name the novel's women after oral sex—the psychotically virginal Gwen French and the monstrously dissipated whore Ginny Moorhead—suggests an adolescent japery on par with the writer's decision not to apostrophize contractions. But Minnelli liked Ginny, and allowed her to steal the film with a baleful honesty that renders the male characters relatively impotent. Sinatra's Dave is only marginally more balanced than his pompous brother Frank (superbly played by Arthur Kennedy, who makes the character's act of adultery his only genuine impulse) and the cynical drifter and misogynist Bama Dilbert (Dean Martin, born for the role and the ubiquitous hat).

Minnelli's long takes are every bit as long as Preminger's, yet as combined with location photography and edited with inserts of emotional close-ups, they tend to replace Preminger's theatricality with frankly melodramatic inquisitiveness. In *Some Came Running*, scenes are played out in light and shadow with mad dabs and shimmers of color that spark the fastidiously designed interiors and exteriors. Minnelli captures the book's sense of moral dissolution, but ignores the relevance of the war (Jones's Dave is haunted by the price of victory) and severely underplays Dave's fall. Nor does he make Dave's instantaneous attraction to Gwen believable. As played by Martha Hyer, Gwen offers him absolutely nothing on which to hang his hopes or affection; and it's a mystery how she manages to sell his story to *The Atlantic*, which apparently publishes it the very week she pops it in the mail. If Minnelli adores the wounded Kewpie doll Ginny, he abhors Gwen and leaves her an unknowable cipher.

Minnelli dutifully shows Dave unpacking worn volumes by his five favorite writers, whom Jones successively parodies in Dave's recollections. Minnelli plays his own game of parody in the climactic shoot-out, which is entirely his own invention—a light-show chase with pursuers rising from squats as the pursued mosey along, unaware of their plight. The scene's shamelessly melodramatic excess, as if cadged from a different film, suggests an antidote to the town's staid corruption, coming right after Dave's decision to marry Ginny, which makes him little better than his calculating brother. Minnelli then cuts to the funeral and ends as Bama removes his precious hat. Ginny is in her grave. The others, isolated and adrift, are slowly running to catch up with her.

Sinatra holds these films together. In *The Man with the Golden Arm*, he is alternately jumpy and smooth, perversely innocent, whistling past the graveyard of his ambition, yet ready at the hint of an obstacle to get mislaid in drugs. His skin tingles and he is racked with guilt, and he lets us see the desperation with naked clarity. In *Some Came Running*, he is comfortable in his skin, yet no less prone to addictive retreats—alcoholic binges that change him so dramatically that Ginny stares at him uncomprehendingly, the way Chaplin's tramp in *City Lights* does at the millionaire who is his pal when drunk and dismissive when sober. The wary strength Sinatra brings to Dave is never in doubt, nor is his infinite capacity for rejection, his "sensitivity," which all but demands a kind of self-abasement. Has any other actor played quite these notes in quite this way?

25

JAMES STEWART:
NO MORE MR. NICE GUY

JAMES STEWART IS the subject of one of the odder entries in Warner Bros.' Signature Collection. Given the possibilities of Stewart's Warner and MGM work—minus the Hitchcock, Lubitsch, and Ford films elsewhere deployed—Warner might have brought to DVD such neglected worthies as *The Mortal Storm*, *Come Live with Me*, and even his most endearing instance of miscasting, *Born to Dance*. But those are prewar films. This set of six movies (available individually except for two late-autumn Westerns, *Firecreek* and *The Cheyenne Social Club*, which share one disc) explores the years 1949 to 1970, when Stewart evolved into a beloved national treasure while specializing in maniacs fixated on revenge. Stewart did most of his best postwar work at Universal and Columbia (*Winchester '73*, *Bend of the River*, *Rear Window*, *The Man from Laramie*, *The Man Who Knew Too Much*, *Vertigo*, *Bell, Book and Candle*, *Anatomy of a Murder*). Even so, this selection includes one masterpiece, Anthony Mann's *The Naked Spur*, and three historical glosses that, taken together and despite various and often robust failings, define his uncanny persona: part stuttering innocence and part bellowing fury, the twain meeting in sullen, wary silences.

The Hollywood studios lost their bearings in the late 1940s, as they lost their theaters to antitrust, their audiences to television, their writers to red-baiting, and their stars to changing tastes and independent contracts. Everything solid melted in the air, including the Production Code, a haven that became increasingly insupportable after the war. As of 1941, Stewart had

never cracked the box-office top ten, but he had grown into a reliable com-
modity. When he returned to movies in 1947, having flown twenty missions
as a bomber pilot, he confronted a new Hollywood with a sure-fire bet—Mr.
Smith reuniting with Mr. Capra for a feel-good anti-suicide Christmas pageant, *It's a Wonderful Life*. Yet that film unaccountably tanked, and follow-
ups, including Hitchcock's maladroit *Rope*, did little better.

Stewart turned his career around with *The Stratton Story* (1949), directed
by Sam Wood, a baseball blockbuster that finally landed him in the top ten,
where he resided over the next fifteen years. As a war hero, Stewart was in
no danger from HUAC suspicions or subpoenas to serve as the committee's
enabler. Wood, however, was an inquisition cheerleader, and his oeuvre has
long been ignored because of his politics and his humorlessness in dealing
with the Marx Brothers. This is unfair: his pictures merit derision in their
own right. A more-than-efficient craftsman who worked exceedingly well
with actors (except the Marxes), he balanced momentum and sentimentality with anodyne conventionalism and noble sacrifice. Judge Hardy would
have approved.

The Monte Stratton story concerns the White Sox pitcher who lost a leg
in a hunting accident, yet returned to the game. Wood's penultimate film
must have seemed very déjà vu, as he had already shed tears for *The Pride
of the Yankees* and severed Ronald Reagan's legs in *King's Row*. Stewart has a
field day: he gets to play a man half his age, confirming his boyish innocence;
marry June Allyson for the first of three times on film, patenting diabetic
cuteness; and enjoy a five-minute self-pitying freakout, portending things to
come. Unfortunately, Stewart could not pitch. Everyone in the film raves
about Stratton's fastballs, but except when a stunt pitcher is sneaked in, they
all go high and outside. Still, the actor had a point to make: like Stratton,
wounded veterans needed to find themselves.

That theme turned manic in the five Westerns he made with Anthony
Mann, his most frequent collaborator in the 1950s. Notwithstanding the
1939 parody *Destry Rides Again*, Stewart was an unlikely candidate for a
genre that John Ford and John Wayne had cornered. Yet he brought something new to it: the battle-scarred victim of treachery who overcomes obsta-
cles of nature and villainy while rediscovering his own scabbed-over core
of decency. Before Mel Gibson, Stewart may have been the most shot,
whipped, beaten, betrayed, and left-for-dead movie star in Hollywood history. *The Naked Spur* (1953) is one of the best in the series, not least for count-

ing as one of Mann's equally compelling three films with Robert Ryan. The script, by Sam Rolfe and Harold Jack Bloom, is set in the Colorado spur of 1868 (the title is a triple pun, also suggesting boot wear and motive). Stewart plays an amateur bounty hunter, tracking a murderous past acquaintance to finance the repurchasing of his farm, which was embezzled from him by his fiancée during the Civil War. The background is of less importance than the chess game involving the film's five players. Pretending to be a sheriff, Stewart inadvertently picks up a prospector (Millard Mitchell) and an amoral ex-soldier (Ralph Meeker) as he attempts to take Ryan and his woman (Janet Leigh) to Texas. Except for an Indian band that the ex-soldier forces them to massacre, no other actors appear.

The setting is vital: other than oddly angled close-ups (like the one of Leigh's face and Ryan's grizzled chin), Mann constructs every shot in a way that embeds the actors in the bluffs, caverns, and rivers of the journey—much of it slide-show beautiful. The film's decisive influence on the Budd Boetticher–directed Randolph Scott Westerns that followed is unmistakable, not only in the geography-as-fate mise-en-scène and character-driven minimalism, but in the contrast between the dour putative hero and Ryan's killer, whose every line is delivered with a charmingly addled giggle. For all the meticulousness in script, design, and performances, *The Naked Spur* is dotted with a few minor imperfections and one big mistake: the former are badly timed edits and a millisecond in which the prospector forgets his character's name; and Bronislau Kaper should have been horsewhipped for scoring "Beautiful Dreamer" every time Stewart romances Janet Leigh. Otherwise, the movie is corn-free—no romantic clinch in the startling denouement.

The other films in the collection are interesting mostly for Stewart's mulish twisting between bashful affability and cries de coeur. The disastrous failure of Billy Wilder's worshipful *The Spirit of St. Louis* (1957) has been blamed on public amnesia regarding Charles A. Lindbergh. The problem with that theory is the tremendous success of Lindbergh's book a few years earlier. One drawback may have been the picture's length. We can admire Lindbergh's flight without wanting to spend an hour in his cockpit listening to voice-over. Yet the film is often compelling if regarded as a James Stewart ordeal rather than as a biopic. In the first half, he is winning and dedicated. In the flight half, he abandons the aviator's legendary cool to screech every melodramatic ejaculation—"Ice!" "You're stalling!" "It's Ireland!" and, inevitably, "Oh God, help me!" (backed by Franz Waxman's biblical epic music).

The script is filled with flashbacks played as comedy, which befits a man of Stewart's age, not Lindbergh's (who was twenty-five and had been flying for about three years), especially since nothing is made of his childhood or background—where was his family during the big takeoff?

And where is organized crime in *The FBI Story* (1959), J. Edgar Hoover's officially sanctioned valentine to himself and his homogenous bureau? When Stewart's agent wipes out the KKK, it's because they attacked Jews (or rather "ancient devotions"), not blacks. There's no point in belittling historical inaccuracies; they are legion. The fascinating thing about Mervyn LeRoy's 149-minute, Max Steiner–scored chronicle of tabloid headlines and personal crises is how despondent it is. Vera Miles, as Stewart's wife, is as distraught as he is, and the passing years bring little pleasure and no relief from the numbingly constant criminal enterprises, even if they don't involve a single ethnic criminal or anything resembling organized crime, unless you count the reds. As one of Stewart's instructors explains, "Craftiness can solve many a criminal case, but with hoodlums you sometimes need a good, conscientious, hard-working machine gun."

That leaves the utterly inept and talky *Firecreek* (1969), a reworking of *High Noon* that not even Stewart and Henry Fonda can salvage, and the lightweight, light-wit, yet occasionally savory *The Cheyenne Social Club* (1970), leisurely directed by Gene Kelly. A tribute to America's prostitutes— each one a generous, honest, innocent, feeble-minded beauty—it gets most of its laughs from Stewart's and Fonda's double takes; in fact, Fonda hasn't been this funny since *The Lady Eve*. (The pecan-cracking gunfight is worth the trip.) After that, Stewart got by with mostly bit parts in forgettable films. Robbed of his youthful allure, he looked old, worn, and uninterested. Only his wig, shaded from brown to gray and otherwise no different from the one he had sported in John Ford's *The Man Who Shot Liberty Valence*, remained robust and full. He never took the opportunity to play a flat-out monster (as Fonda did in *Once Upon a Time in the West*), which might have extended his appeal in a new direction. But he had accomplished something all his own, incarnating hubristic madness as the underside to American can-do.

26

BORIS KARLOFF: HE'S ALIVE!

GREAT FILM ACTING results from an empathic collaboration between actor and director. However much a director guides theater actors, the performers are ultimately alone onstage. In a film, we are permitted to see a performance only as a montage pieced together by director and editor. Movie technicians can undermine a good actor as decisively as they can redeem a bad one. In *The Strange Door* (1951), one of the five twisted, mediocre films collected in *The Boris Karloff Collection*, Karloff makes a belated entrance as servant to maniacal sybarite Charles Laughton, who upstages him mercilessly with eye-rolling theatrics. Yet director Joseph Pevney gives the scene's parting close-up to Karloff, who uses every muscle in his face to milk his lines. For a moment, you think: This may be fun after all—two incorrigible hams warring over the camera. But the director, more intent on following a dreary script than the actors, allows them to go to hell in separate handbaskets, dragging the film behind them.

For an inspired communion between director and actor, one can ask for no better example than *Frankenstein* (1931), which Universal is releasing in its third DVD incarnation—this time as a two-disc "Anniversary 75th Edition" (their word order) with an excellent print, repetitive spoken and written commentaries, and documentaries. The monster's first appearance, anticipated by off-camera footfalls, exemplifies the unity of purpose. The creature emerges from a dark doorway, back first, then turns its face to the light as director James Whale, beginning with a middle-distance shot, abruptly thrusts us into its face with two jump cuts, each from a marginally different angle. Damn!

What a pleasure it is to find that after so many years and viewings, sequels and steals, documentaries and parodies (one of the first, a witless but prophetic 1933 Universal short, "Boo," is included on the DVD), the scene retains its power. Threats of camp, cliché, derision, and giggles are momentarily allayed. What do we see in Whale's scrupulously lighted and edited frames? As in the unmasking of Lon Chaney in *Phantom of the Opera*, we confront a radical makeup (by Jack Pierce), at once absurd and credible, and an actor powerful enough to make it meaningful. The producers thought the film would be about Dr. Frankenstein's attempt to preempt God; they thought the creature little more than a stunt part. That, in fact, is the approach that Terence Fisher would take a quarter century later in his color-saturated quintet of Frankenstein films made for Britain's Hammer, a series too clever and stylish to deserve its purgatory of cult insularity.

Karloff, however, made that approach impossible. With the director's complicity, he turned the film on its head. His monster is the most human and interesting being in the piece. A purely reactive figure, created from body parts and (hilariously) an unwrinkled brain, abandoned, beaten, feared, and pursued, the monster commits atrocious acts, including one of the most unspeakable of classic Hollywood murders—the drowning of an adorable child—and yet simultaneously maintains our sympathy and fear. The odds against his performance were formidable; other actors who played the role in cheapjack sequels barely register underneath the increasingly rote square-head makeup. *Frankenstein* sustains its allure as a movie that almost everyone comes to in childhood. But it doesn't stay buried in childhood. We read the 1818 novel because we know the film.

Minus Karloff, Whale's efficient staging, and the endlessly imitated art direction, the film isn't much. The script is conventional and abbreviated, the dialogue uninteresting. Most of the performances are either dated (Colin Clive's hysterical Frankenstein), dull (John Boles's stolid other man), or indifferent (Mae Clarke's confused fiancée). Dwight Frye's hunchback is amusing, but only as a commedia dell'arte genre staple—albeit one largely of his own invention. Edward Van Sloan plays two roles: Frankenstein's professor and, more interestingly, the unidentified codger in the prelude who warns the audience that it may find the film horrifying. Credulous commentators assume that Van Sloan plays himself here—despite uncharacteristic effeminate gestures, pursed lips, weird pronunciations, and googly eyes, to say nothing of the gaslight shadows. In fact, his intro is one of the creepiest things in the film. *Frankenstein* horrifies because Whale and Karloff love the monster and are amused by the havoc it wreaks.

Karloff was a forty-four-year-old veteran of bit and supporting roles (in movies since 1916) when he got his big break. He parlayed it into nearly four decades of grotesques, specializing in outsiders, fanatics, and idealistic victims of greed and ignorance. Most of his films weren't any good, but it is amazing how many of them he salvages. Even without makeup he was an odd-looking duck, with gaunt face, bowlegs, and ramrod if slightly angular posture. Yet he cut a handsome, charming figure. "Take away the neck bolts and big shoes and he was a helluva good-looking guy," the singer Rosemary Clooney once said, recalling her early days in Hollywood.

Karloff's speech patterns, despite a pronounced lisp, employed a rare musicality—long phrases that rise in chromatic increments, his shrewd timing dispatching ridiculous lines and savoring the plums. Of his early starring vehicles, the most prestigious was Fox's Napoleonic *House of Rothschild* (1934), with Karloff as the German anti-Semite, prefiguring the coming horror. Indeed, the film, highly regarded in its day and a staple of 1950s television, became a political football in the early 1940s; it has never been released to home video. More characteristic and available are the fussily art-directed mock fairy tale *The Black Room* (1935), in which he plays twins (one good, one delightfully rapacious), and the irresistibly racist *The Mask of Fu Manchu* (MGM, 1932), one of his many roles in Yellow Peril—you wouldn't call it Asian—drag, telegraphing nearly unspeakable dialogue with ariose irony, the voice rising and settling like a bassoon: "This serum distilled from dragon's blood, my own blood, the organs of different reptiles, and mixed with the magic brew of the sacred seven herbs, will temporarily change you into the living instrument of my will." (A big hand for Edgar Allan Woolf, the chief scriptwriter—one of six, three of them given screen credit.)

Much of his work, though, was strictly second fiddle, frequently at Universal, which supplies the mixed buffet in *The Boris Karloff Collection*. The little-known *Night Key* (1937) is one of the first in his series of wronged-inventor movies and probably the only one in which he is still breathing in the last reel, having survived an evil capitalist and evil gangster (the underemployed Alan Baxter, who had a premature Ralph Meeker sneer).

In *Tower of London* (1939), Karloff is the bald, beetle-browed, clubfooted Mord, who does his torture duties with the dispassion of a hotel maid. Basil Rathbone plays Crookback Richard, with a secret cabinet of dolls representing his intended victims—most memorably Vincent Price's bipolar Clarence. *The Climax* (1944) is a silly but satisfying prize, shot in Technicolor on the sets dressed for Universal's 1943 remake of *Phantom of the Opera*. Director George Waggner composed the egregious music written for the opera scenes, which include Munchkin-like chorales, but thankfully minimized the comic relief. Karloff, carrying the film on his malevolent, impeccably tailored shoulders, plays an ears, nose, and throat man who occasionally hypnotizes and strangles sopranos so that no one else will enjoy them. Curt Siodmak's adaptation incorporates elements of Edgar Ulmer's insanely visionary *The Black Cat* (Karloff preserves the corpse of his victim in a secret room) while portending the makeover aspect of *Vertigo*. The theme has something to do with music as a liberating sexual force that turns morbid and mad when suppressed.

Karloff's career and the horror genre plummeted in the early 1950s, soon to be resurrected by late-night television and Hammer films. In 1951 and 1952, Universal tried to revive grotesquerie with costume dramas in the style produced at RKO by Val Lewton, whose *The Body Snatcher* inspired Karloff's greatest performance. Where Lewton had a taste for subtlety and art, however, Universal's B-picture unit preferred secret passages, alligator pits, torture chambers, stabbings, and frothing tyrants. Turning to Robert Louis Stevenson, the studio adapted "The Sire de Maletroit's Door" as *The Strange Door*, removing most of the talk that is at the story's heart. Then it reunited Paula Corday (from *The Body Snatcher*) with Karloff in the incomprehensible *The Black Castle*, which has a ripping performance by Stephen McNally as a one-eyed Austrian degenerate.

Karloff's more spiritual qualities inspired, among several lesser works, the sublimely static reverie of childhood that is Victor Erice's *The Spirit of the Beehive* (1973, restored by Criterion and accompanied by extensive supplements). Set in Franco's arid, shell-shocked Spain in 1940, the exquisitely photographed and acted film begins with the excited arrival of a new movie to be screened in the meeting house. The film is Karloff's *Frankenstein,* and the unrehearsed reaction shots of children actually seeing it for the first time capture the magic of cinema as a modern locus for campfire storytelling. The youngest child in a disconnected family, unforgettably played by six-year-old Ana Torrent, becomes obsessed with the motiveless, liberating violence of Karloff's monster. Pursuing it in the surrounding fields and in her imagination, she makes her way out of an isolated childhood and into the budding recognition of her own identity. Those of us who came of age with Boris Karloff understand her compulsion very well.

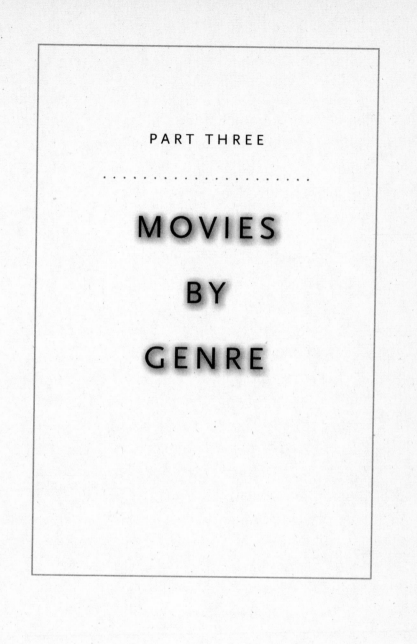

PART THREE

MOVIES

BY

GENRE

27

A LEGEND IN HIS OWN MIND

El Cid

DIRECTOR ANTHONY MANN gets the possessory credit when fans and critics speak of *El Cid*, but the film assigns that billing to its producer, the imperturbable hustler Samuel Bronston, who reinvented movie spectacles on the plains of Spain in the early 1960s. Shunning the waning studio culture of Hollywood, Bronston created his own studio in Madrid in 1958 and financed it with an intricate money-laundering operation involving the Franco government and a vindictive member of the DuPont family who didn't think losses should be part of the risk. His meteoric empire soared with *El Cid* (1961) and plummeted with *Fall of the Roman Empire*, also directed by Mann, three years later. As lawyers and prosecutors investigated Bronston's transgressions, his epics were generally shelved.

In 2007, the Weinstein Company scheduled DVD restorations of the films as part of its Miriam Collection, and in the following year released *El Cid* and *Fall of the Roman Empire* (*55 Days in Peking* [1963] and *Circus World* [1964] were delayed; the 1961 *King of Kings* is available from MGM), encouraging a reassessment of Bronston and his work. At least a partial vindication seemed likely. Bronston, who died in 1994 at eighty-five, beaten by creditors and Alzheimer's, is difficult for film lovers to hate. As he once put it, he was "insane" for movies, and by most accounts uninterested in personal wealth. He poured the vast sums of money he raised into his pictures, and Mann got him his money's worth. That's one reason people bond over *El Cid*, especially if they saw it as intended, filling the massive screen of the old, resplendent and lamented Warner Theater on 47th Street and Broadway, where it opened in December 1961. With its glorious vistas, clanking battles, luminous colors, thumping Miklós Rózsa music, and haunting climax, unfolding in 70-mm grandeur like a living tapestry, it was cinema as circus—an enveloping, emotional, big-movie event. The DVD, good as it is (a clean 35-mm transfer with stable colors, impenetrable blacks, vivid audio), can no more replicate that experience than a gift-shop poster can capture Vermeer. But it's a lovely alternative.

RKO once gave Orson Welles "the biggest electric train set a boy ever had." Sam Bronston gave Mann the whole of Spain: castles, churches, an army, an entire village of costume sewers, and an elastic check to cover such extras as swords made in the foundry that served the real Cid. In some respects, *El Cid* is the pinnacle of Mann's career, a visionary extrapolation of themes—heroism, violence, treachery, fragile alliances, and moral ambiguity—previously explored in the genre films he had made over two decades. Yet *El Cid* is different in more than size: it's a driven, humorless picture in which moral absolution is embodied in the Cid's increasing conviction that he is chosen, that if right makes might (as he prays it will before a brutal, spectacular tournament), so must might make right. He is blinding and blinded by his certainty. Gone are the charming rogues, comical asides, and ambivalent gallants of Mann's noirs and Westerns. Not entirely gone is the heroic kink, the touch of madness that defines Mann's guardians of order.

The story, based partly on Corneille's play, tells of how Rodrigo Díaz de Vivar (Charlton Heston), called the Cid (lord) by a Moor ally, defended the Christian kingdom against a Berber invasion led by a murderous, fictional fanatic, Ben Yusuf (Herbert Lom, wonderfully fanatical)—a caricature based on Yusuf ibn Tashfin, who in real life died *after* the Cid, having enjoyed many more victories on the battlefield. For all the money spent on period detail, *El Cid* is not intended as a history lesson. The film's Kennedy-era progressiveness, which comes to the fore as Rodrigo unites Christians and Moors, is undermined by the presentation of Moors and Berbers in brownface, complete with heavy eyeliner. Imperialist conventions die hard: in 1961, the good guys were tall, white, and American; the bad guys were short, dark, and wore black robes, which if nothing else made the climactic battles easy to judge.

El Cid is raised beyond that convention by its rare insistence on giving equal time to Rodrigo's domestic life, chiefly his troubled love affair with

Chimene (Sophia Loren), whose father he killed to defend his own father's honor, and his ascension from human warrior to national demiurge. The love angle is both heightened and undermined by the casting of Heston and Loren. Their individual close-ups are sensational, their two-shots less so. Heston is one of the screen's few leading men who never displayed chemistry with a woman, excepting—bada-bing—Kim Hunter in *Planet of the Apes*. Given the chance to turn the corner with Loren, he could not overcome (according to DVD featurettes) his resentment of her higher salary and vanity, though she is no more fastidiously coiffed or made-up than he. In their initial union, staged by Mann to command the fullness of widescreen, they walk, hands outstretched, to a softly lit center and nibble at each other like goldfish. But as a couple, they really come alive only when simmering in mutual odium.

At one point, the traitorous Count Ordóñez (Raf Vallone) visits the imprisoned Chimene and says, "Even all these months in the dungeon have not marred your beauty." Clearly, jailors have been smuggling in lipstick, rouge, mascara, and other concealers, and who would want it any other way? Loren's visage is easily the equal of any Spanish landscape. She and Rodrigo are larger-than-life figures, and so casually mythological that when a little girl approaches them, she is as up to par on their private lives as if they had popped from the pages of *Look*. But Mann tacks deeper than the mythology, which formally recognizes the Cid as the purest of all knights. Though his journey into greatness begins with his decision to spare the lives of a few Moors, circumstances turn him into a soldier of fortune, a paladin. An hour or so into the three-hour story, the narrative takes a remarkable turn. Rodrigo has been appointed the king's champion and rejected by Chimene. He disappears from the film for six minutes, during which the king dies and the princes, one purported to be incestuously involved with his sister, try to kill each other. The rightful new king, to whom Rodrigo swears allegiance, sends his brother Alfonso to prison.

Suddenly Rodrigo appears, riding alone, willing to kill thirteen of the king's guard to liberate the devious Alfonso. This is clearly an act of treason, but his probity is, one might say, unmoored from realpolitik. He radiates crazed individualism—not unlike the Lee J. Cobb character in Mann's *Man of the West* (1958). As a result of his action, the king will be assassinated, Rodrigo banished, and Chimene imprisoned. The complexity of Mann's portrait is clinched at the siege of Valencia, when Rodrigo intemperately decides to abandon the battle, a mistake averted by the contrite Ordóñez and Chimene. Similarly, Rodrigo's deathbed insistence on leading the final charge and his reconciliation with Alfonso are expressions of arrant pride. His indispensability does not diminish the narcissism that launches him into the realm of legend.

Within its generic requirements, *El Cid* is not unflawed, but the flaws are insignificant. To justify international financing, Bronston had to hire international players, resulting in Spaniards who speak with American, British, French, and Italian—never Spanish—accents. Several performances are memorable: Andrew Cruickshank as Chimene's burly father, Douglas Wilmer as the good Moor, Genevieve Page as Urraca (whose supreme moment is her dentalized reading of the line "After all, we would lose a city"), and John Fraser as Alfonso, who shares with Heston one of the film's finest minutes, when Rodrigo forces Alfonso to swear he is innocent of his brother's murder. Mann shot the scene with four camera setups and inserted a half-second glimpse of a Bible as a rhythmic punctuation in the editing. His assertive touch is unmistakable throughout, not least in the way he uses the castles' interior architecture.

Cinematographer Robert Krasker, who established black and white standards in Carol Reed's *The Third Man*, was no less rigorous in color, making the most of natural light, especially in the sun-dappled finish. The script, largely by Ben Barzman with contributions by Ben Maddow and possibly others, is famous for averting spectacle-speak; nor is there much in the way of expository dialogue, though Hurd Hatfield appears as a court emcee, introducing members of the royal family as though they were talk-show guests. There is, sadly, a leper named Lazarus ("I thirst!"), but what's a spectacle without a leper? Neither of the true writers was credited in 1961 because of the 1950s blacklist—Barzman's work, at least, was officially acknowledged nearly thirty years later, though his name does not appear on the DVD, which uses original film elements. The credit goes instead to Philip Yordan, Bronston's contractor and self-appointed front, and Frederick Frank, who wrote a rejected story and script. They wrote not a line of the completed film.

Rózsa's score similarly succeeds in averting cliché (narrowly much of the time, but still), favoring brasses and percussion for Rodrigo, strings for Chimene, and the full orchestra for personal and military rapprochement. Drawing on the pentatonic scale and the kinds of melodies court musicians

might have played in eleventh-century Spain, Rózsa plied the Wagnerian
system of devising a theme for each major character, spinning one against
the other in empathic counterpoint to the action. According to a featurette
on the composer (a charming raconteur), he was angry at the excision of
some of his music; yet the score is effective, with its passages that combine
silences along with supporting cues and climaxes—as in the duel between
Rodrigo and Chimene's father. No film has more diverse brass fanfares, and
not even Count Basie's band could have played them with greater precision
than the studio brass section. Bronston got what he paid for.

28

LUST FOR LIVES
Young Mr. Lincoln / Lust for Life

THE BIOPIC, A Hollywood staple, invariably says as much, if not more, about the period in which it was made as the one it depicts. The current gold rush to dig up new and old lives reflects, with rare exceptions, the Oprah-zation of popular biography in an era of shameless confession. The story arc requires the protagonist to conquer or surrender to a besetting sin. Overcoming usually means drugs or alcohol, as in *Ray* and *Walk the Line*; succumbing means greed or vanity, as in *Capote* and *Beyond the Sea*. The plot points follow a scrupulous checklist of generic clichés, including flashbacked incidents from childhood. Today's price of celebrity is analysis in the public square, and we are all analysts, though we are charged a pretty penny for the privilege.

In John Ford's *Young Mr. Lincoln* (1939) and Vincente Minnelli's *Lust for Life* (1956), two of the best biographical films from the glory days of the studios or after, psychology is apparent but not decisive. Made decades before Ritalin and antidepressants replaced gin martinis as dietary supplements, they uncannily portray what we now diagnose as clinical depression—Abe's distant reflections on the deaths of his mother and sweetheart interspersed with his blank-eyed gazes at an indifferent river and his mechanical strumming on a Jew's harp; van Gogh's exhausting alienation and slumped inertia. Yet both films are liberated from the illusion that explanations are either possible or desirable, both respect the boundaries of the knowable, and both confront larger issues, chiefly the cost in isolation that greatness demands.

Stylistically, they could not be more different. *Young Mr. Lincoln* forges a heroic if sentimental myth, and *Lust for Life* proffers aesthetic objectivity to weigh the value of an artist's failed life against the triumph of his art. Sentimentality often guarantees better box office, but is the harder sell over time. Ford's detractors are often critics who delight in explaining how a preferred filmmaker manipulates the medium to encourage fear or outrage, while recoiling in contempt at directors who induce tears. In *Young Mr. Lincoln*, Ford resolutely links national memory to the tear ducts and plays with the latter as though they were stops on a pipe organ. Might as well know that going in. The director's famously stubborn refusal to elucidate himself or his work or to admit that what he did had anything to do with art honors the audience. Art implies intellect, which is unequally distributed, and Ford demands emotion, which ruthlessly seeks out the common denominator in us all. The implication is that if he has your heart, your mind will follow, if only afterward and as justification for losing your emotional grip.

Still, the failings of *Young Mr. Lincoln*, or at least those aspects that may incline us to hold it at bay, can be lost on no one. The central incident in Lamar Trotti's screenplay is little more than Perry Mason on the prairie: the fictionalized version of a trial in which Lincoln employed an almanac to impeach a witness, here turned into a confrontation between two brothers—each claiming to be the culprit in order to save the other—and the real murderer, who senselessly blurts out his guilt when Abe puts the question. The lameness of that contrivance is made clearer by the dreary 1946 radio version (included on the Criterion DVD), which incorporates little else from the film.

Henry Fonda's Lincoln, probably the best we have had or are likely to get, makes too much of his stork legs, folding them like furniture and walking as though on stilts—in a closing scene, he lumbers over a rise during a rainstorm, looking disconcertingly like Frankenstein's monster. Fonda also overdoes the aw-shucks diffidence, as when he grabs the arm of the mother whose boys are threatened by a lynch mob (the once-radiant Alice Brady in her last role, and showing the illness that soon took her life). She pulls away and asks, "Who are you?" Instantly forgetting the extreme urgency of the moment, he does an eight-second modesty shuffle before answering, "I'm your lawyer, ma'am." At least he doesn't say, "I'm plain Abraham Lincoln"—which is how he introduces himself in his first speech. You may also object to Ford's comic relief in the courtroom, as well as Lincoln's indifference to procedural rules.

Above all, you may cringe at Alfred Newman's remarkable music, which tugs at the heartstrings Ford merely plucks. If any Ford film suggests a hyphenated authorship, it is *Young Mr. Lincoln*, thanks to Newman's underscoring of every key moment with traditional themes. His method is forewarned during the credits: "The Battle Cry of Freedom" is sung first by women, as if at a sodality meeting, then with men to beef it up before it is taken up by hanky-waving strings. New Salem is introduced with prancing square-dance music. Abe first rises into view to the somber strains of a lone cello. The death of Ann Rutledge is signaled by a transition from widening circles in a calm river to fearsome ice floes, as strings turn to darkening brasses. If Newman's music puts you off, you won't like Ford's film, and vice versa.

If, on the other hand, you surrender to the emotional power and complexity of the portrait, you may find yourself marveling at how Ford turned so tidy a script into an epic. From the opening epigram (Rosemary Benet), which indicates Abe's broken ties to his mother, to the closing shot of the Lincoln Memorial as the chorus thunders "Battle Hymn of the Republic," Ford exploits the audience's shared knowledge of Lincoln to re-create him as a colossus—a mythic beacon standing outside history, exemplifying mutual core values as well as a peculiarly un-American courage that tests its mettle with language. Twice Lincoln threatens to resolve a dispute with fighting; twice his cleverness obviates the need. And twice his life is altered by the same mother figure, though neither she nor Abe restates the happenstance that the mother of his defendants is the woman who, in the opening scene, gave him his first law book.

Ford's view of community is never entirely rosy, though here it is ludicrously homogenous: no blacks, no talk of slavery, no ethnicities at all—not even his standard yumpin-yimminy Swede or alcoholic Irishman. But violence is everywhere. At the very moment Abe doffs his hat to the veterans at an Independence Day parade, a few scamps send a military man into the dust with a slingshot. The two bullies of the piece are thoroughly unpleasant, and the convincingly crazed lynch mob includes (as Buck) the eternally unbilled Jack Pennick, a regular Ford bit player whose plug-ugly looks have symbolic resonance in this instance. The courtroom is corrupt in ways that Ford doesn't bother to emphasize; he just shows Stephen Douglas (Milburn Stone, also unbilled) ominously whispering to the prosecutor

(Donald Meek, a fly impotently buzzing around Fonda's giraffe) and the killer (Ward Bond—who else?—casually blowing smoke rings on the witness stand). Perhaps the most disquieting moment is played for laughs as Abe, during jury selection, questions and approves a drunk for conceding that he drinks, shuns the church, and enjoys a good lynching, as though all were gross pleasures without a dime's difference between them.

As usual with Ford's finest work, each shot of *Young Mr. Lincoln* is perfectly framed without calling undo attention to itself. By contrast, Minnelli's framing in *Lust for Life* takes a backseat to the manipulation of color, as Vincent simultaneously progresses as an artist and deteriorates as a man. The film is a Technicolor-coded elaboration of his mind, from the burnt umber of the Borinage—where the young would-be evangelist ministers to starving miners—to Paris, the Hague, and Auvers, where Vincent perceives hues as increasingly brilliant, inspiring, threatening, and defeating. "I have a power of color in me," he writes his brother Theo (a modulated performance by James Donald), and Minnelli rises to the challenge of his "terrible lucidity." An astonishing shot occurs the morning after Vincent arrives in Arles, when he opens the window and the light is as weighty as when Dorothy opens the door to Oz. At the last, the radiant light and color are transferred to canvases that, along with Vincent's letters, calmly read by Theo, anchor the film in more reality than is customary in biopics.

Kirk Douglas's resemblance to van Gogh is matched by the commitment of his performance. He physically recedes, especially as would-be wife to the crass and solitary Gauguin. Anthony Quinn's Gauguin makes the film snap to attention when he appears, generating a quaking apprehension regarding van Gogh's increasingly intemperate fits of temper, but he doesn't bring many dimensions to the character. Douglas dispenses with vanity altogether, playing a social misfit touched with genius, an untouchable outcast that neither he nor Minnelli insults with maudlin pleas to the audience or cheap historical ironies. Would that the same could be said of Miklós Rózsa's score, consisting largely of a ponderous eight-bar melody that he recycled more fittingly for *Ben-Hur*.

Criterion's *Young Mr. Lincoln* DVD includes a second disc with extras well worth watching, among them half of Lindsay Anderson's documentary on Ford (the early years), audio interviews with Ford and Fonda, and the Fonda segment from the BBC's Michael Parkinson program. Parkinson, the anti–Charlie Rose, rarely interrupted the Hollywood stars he featured and elicited an extraordinary archive of candid interviews. The Warners DVD of *Lust for Life* has the intriguingly dotty trailer (which takes the title literally) and inane commentary by Drew Casper, who gives a potted history of postwar America (many veterans of World War II "wondered what, if anything, victory had achieved"; *Playboy* published "well-written articles, cartoons, and centerfolds") and ignores the film. *Lust for Life* deserves better.

29

FELONIOUS MUNCH

Edvard Munch

To PARAPHRASE THE title of a classic 1960s jazz album: It's Munch's time. In early 2006, the Museum of Modern Art in New York unveiled the first American retrospective in three decades, gathering some 150 canvases and prints under the prattling title "Edvard Munch: The Modern Life of the Soul." Another 25 prints were on view at Scandinavia House, under the marginally less unlovely rubric "Edvard Munch: Symbolism in Print." His most famous work, *The Scream*, was in the news for having been stolen (for the second time), its whereabouts unknown, though the alleged thieves were on trial. And New Yorker Video released a DVD of Peter Watkins's rarely seen and thoroughly innovative film *Edvard Munch* (1976). Does this mean it's also Watkins's time? We can only hope.

The DVD arrived with a verbose copyright warning and "self-interview" by Watkins in which he defends himself against accusations of paranoia and repetition in terms that are likely to spur those very charges. Specifically, he protests the marginalization of his work, and who can deny the justice of his claim? His films don't incite controversy, but rather prompt the kind of suppression kept so quiet that no one bothers to protest the protest. Watkins isn't listed in leading directories of film directors, fellow Brit David Thomson found no room for him in his biographical dictionary, and critics sympathetic to his progressive politics seem to have ignored him—if indexes to review collections can be trusted. Even Leonard Maltin's movie guide ignores all but two of his films (*Edvard Munch* didn't make the cut). This isn't marginalization; it's blackout.

I had never seen any films by Watkins until 2005, when New Yorker released the astonishing political thriller *Punishment Park*, which in 1971 played ten days in San Francisco and four in New York before the distributor withdrew it amid a hail of critical abuse. That's hardly uncommon treatment for an independent film with a political edge—even with backing by MGM, Antonioni's *Zabriskie Point* fared little better. The surprising thing is that it stayed so far below the radar that it never achieved the bare ruin'd choirs of culthood. A reworking of *The Most Dangerous Game*, *Punishment Park* is a howl of outrage in which illegally interred dissenters and hippies can choose between decades in prison or two days as quarry for military hunters. If they survive the latter, they go home; if not, they go the way of habeas corpus. Acted by amateurs and shot with the sham objectivity of a documentary, *Punishment Park* endures as a painfully truthful reflection of that era and a parable for this one.

Watkins's initial reception in the United States had been far more hopeful. After the BBC refused to broadcast his 1965 analysis of nuclear devastation, *The War Game* (see "War/Agitprop," Chapter 71), that film crossed the ocean to win a best-documentary Academy Award. Having burned bridges in two English-speaking countries, Watkins moved his operation to Scandinavia in 1974, where he earned the ire of Norwegian television with his original three-and-a-half-hour cut of *Edvard Munch*. It's not hard to see why. One of the most probing dissections of an artist ever attempted on film, *Edvard Munch* is every bit as severe and political as *Punishment Park*, framing the artist as an indefatigable visionary trying to illuminate the lives of those who prefer the dark. In Watkins's interpretation, Munch isn't merely a radical expressionist, defying representational dicta to divulge brittle feelings of terror, longing, jealousy, sorrow, dread, guilt, and love. He is an incendiary, violating "people's tastes," undermining society's binding conventions, threatening the livelihood of painters whose work represents the image a nation wishes to see in the mirror. Every passionate stroke of Munch's brush, pencil, or knife—and there has never been an art film with so much driven brushwork—is a wound in the faith of those who "don't talk about things like that."

Although his film is no more a documentary than *Lust for Life* or John Huston's *Moulin Rouge*, Watkins combines nonfiction techniques with the asceticism and trust in amateur actors born of independent cinema. *Edvard Munch* tracks little more than a decade in Munch's long life (he died at eighty in 1944)—the years of his main artistic breakthroughs, 1884–95—within the context of remembered childhood traumas. These are not explanatory flashbacks of the kind running amok in recent biopics. They are integrated glimpses of the past woven into a narrative mosaic, and they have the effect of flattening perspective, as Munch did on canvas. Watkins complains of the strictures of what he calls "monoform" filmmaking, but he is not above creating a dramatic spine and sticking to it—in this instance, Munch's frustrated love for a married woman, Millie, or as he called her in his journals, Mrs. Heiberg.

The story is told through two narrations: the rather priggish voice of authority, recounting history, and that of Munch, taken from his writings. Not unlike the painter, who combined oils, pencil, charcoal, and every other means at his disposal in attacking a canvas, Watkins employs sundry methods, including fades to black, objectivity ("The person on the left is . . ."), time capsules ("Goering is born, Tchaikovsky dies"), improvisation, mock interviews (in the manner played for laughs on television's *The Office*), handheld photography, zooms, and especially close-ups and extreme close-ups. Visually, the film is hypnotic. The warm, faded colors have a painterly precision that complements the verisimilitude achieved by cast, costumes, and setting.

The actors, 200 amateurs who heeded a casting call, may hit false notes for those fluent in Norwegian, but none that are otherwise detectable. Geir Westby's resemblance to Munch counterpoises the use of Munch's self-portraits. Watkins likes his actors to occasionally glance directly at the camera, which he thinks breaks down the fourth wall (sometimes it does no more than suggest a Jack Benny deadpan in response to an especially baleful statistic dropped by the narrator); Westby's sullen stare eerily matches the incisive straight-ahead poses of the paintings. The director protects the integrity of his performance by giving him little dialogue. Westby is often seen walking or sitting in crowded cafés or confronting a canvas. In his verbal disputes with Mrs. Heiberg or his father, he is photographed from the side or from behind.

Two other impressive performers are Gros Fraas as Mrs. Heiberg, her mature beauty, sexual superiority, and radiant smile justifying Munch's besotted distrust; and Kare Stormark as Hans Jaeger, the troubled spokesman for free love and bohemian truth-telling—the first of several café pundits who serve to liberate Munch from the fundamentalist piety of his father. (Strindberg is also represented but not Ibsen, with whom Munch had a closer relationship.) Much of the film is concerned with the oppression of women and the chimera of free love. Jaeger—bearded, pockmarked, arrogant—expansively entertains his minions with talk of masturbation, women's rights, and adultery, but as women take up the challenge, the men are driven crazy. Watkins focuses on a few women, married but with growing portfolios of lovers, who justify themselves in interviews, as stubbornly indifferent to the whining complaints of men as Gertrud is in Carl Dreyer's film of the Hjalmar Söderberg play of that name. One Munch painting depicts a woman kissing the nape of a man's neck, an image the film sets up as crucial to Munch's infatuation with Mrs. Heiberg. The writer Stanislav Przybyszewski (who pimps his wife to prove his tolerance) renames it *The Vampire*, a title Munch lets stand, as Strindberg concedes that in any sexual coupling the man suffers the most.

Most of the film's women suck the marrow from possessive lovers or die as unmarried spinsters. An exception is Munch's fifteen-year-old sister, who died of tuberculosis, a recurring refrain in the film that leads to its great set piece: the 1885 painting *The Sick Child*, which Watkins explicates in electrifying detail. It is Munch's first statement of his brand of expressionism, which is at once objectively representational and emotionally unbound. By the time he finishes it, the viewer is virtually implicated in its creation, making the critical onslaught all the more appalling.

Although the film delivers on the artist's growth and triumph, it is strangely ungenerous in dealing with his other work. *The Scream* is never once shown in its entirety—we see close-ups of the bloody sky and skeletal face, but not the body, bridge, or water. Similarly, *Anxiety* is described, not shown; Munch's portraits of Jaeger are not mentioned. Little is seen of the continuity in the paintings that make up the *Frieze of Life*. The film is so intent on showcasing maundering Philistines, and the critical fury Munch faces at one exhibition after another, that it discloses little of Oslo's eventual capitulation to Munch, and no sense whatsoever of the riches and adoration he enjoyed for much of his life. Yet to complain that the film ignores this or fudges that is to fall into the trap that the faux-documentary invites. *Edvard Munch* is Peter Watkins's portrait of the artist. It situates Munch in a time of rampant disease and unrestricted child labor, in a family beset by death and insanity, in a world on the cusp of undefined liberation and easily tormented by cultural originality. A friend of Munch once said that he adapted "despair as his religion." A happy ending would have denied the truth of the struggle. The triumph of this remarkable film is that it indulges Munch's despair without succumbing to it.

30

HITLER'S MAGIC FLUTE

Hamsun / Hunger

IF KNUT HAMSUN had died in 1935, at seventy-six, only the pompous pastoralism that sullied his later work would have marred his reputation as Norway's beloved Nobel laureate and Scandinavia's greatest novelist. A fount of literary modernism, Hamsun—to whom Mann, Wells, Gorky, Hesse, Musil, Stein, Kafka, Gide, Brecht, Buber, Hemingway, and Henry Miller, among many others, gratefully genuflected—had, long before Joyce, laid bare the consciousness of the artist forging his soul in search of community. His egocentric misanthropy might have died with his family, friends, and publisher. Unhappily for everyone, chiefly himself, he didn't die then. Jan Troell's biographical film *Hamsun* (1997) perversely begins in 1935, more than forty years after he published his masterworks—*Hunger*, *Mysteries*, and *Pan*—and fifteen years after he clinched the Nobel with his best-selling agrarian epic *Growth of the Soil*. Troell is less concerned with Hamsun's writings than with his role as the nation's vaunted poet (a soldier salutes him as "the soul of Norway") who outlived his instinctive genius and committed the error of acting on his politics: he backed Hitler.

An Anglophobe who spent a few early years wandering around the United States, Hamsun developed a fierce hatred for Yankees, Bolsheviks, and especially Britain (in the film, he rails at imperialist carnage in India and the concentration camps in South Africa), while developing a corresponding admiration for efficient fascism. He supported Vidkun Quisling's plea for acceptance of the German invaders and offered up a few anti-Semitic nuggets that he apparently did not believe; Hitler's obsession with Jews, in fact, bewildered him. Yet even after Hamsun observed the slaughter spurred by Norway's Reichskommissar, Josef Terboven, and was brusquely ejected from Hitler's mountain aerie, he defended Hitler's actions, composing a front-page obituary for that "great warrior for mankind."

Hamsun is a long (154 minutes) and demanding film. The pace is deliberate and the dialogue elliptical, except when taken from the public record. Troell's camera rarely moves; variety and emphasis are achieved through abrupt edits, close-ups, stock footage, and short pans. The combination of a calculated tempo and accumulation of incidents jars the film's pulse. The last hour is taken up with the heavy days of Hamsun's incarceration in an asylum, yet it never bores. Troell's film, like Hamsun, who was fixated on always knowing the hour, broods over the relentlessness of time. An early close-up reveals the writer's desk clock; the final scenes are punctuated by the winding and setting of clocks. For seventeen years, until he breathed his last in 1952, at ninety-three, Hamsun whined about dying. His long-suffering family ruefully joked about his immortality pact with God. In one memorable scene, he collapses after chopping wood. He lies in the snow, knowing his time has come—and so consults his pocket watch, which drops to his side. We are invited to contemplate the watch until a fresh flurry of snow revives him, at which point he reluctantly gets up and walks home. Later, his alcoholic daughter Elinor maliciously throws his desk clock out the window. It shatters to the ground, but keeps on ticking.

Troell presumes a knowledge of Hamsun's great literary achievement, which justifies the film's gravitas and mania for detail. Yet he suggests nothing of the writer capable of mapping the absurdities of *Mysteries* or the dark burlesque of *Hunger,* except in sly references that only readers of the novels will recognize. In Hamsun's big confrontation with Terboven, for example, much of his argument is taken verbatim from a stream-of-consciousness reverie in *Mysteries.* Only his stature, not his achievement, is at stake here. "To think that the Nazis have such a magic flute at their disposal," a publisher observes.

Per Olov Enquist's exceptional script is said to be faithfully based on Thorkild Hansen's multivolume 1978 study *Processen mod Hamsun,* which has yet to be translated. (The same wartime material is replicated in Robert Ferguson's 1987 biography *Enigma: The Life of Knut Hamsun.*) Hansen's hugely successful book aroused controversy for digging up the episode that

Norway and the rest of the world had succeeded in burying. American literary encyclopedias published in the 1950s and 1960s ignore, as if by fiat, Hamsun's romance with Nazism. In the late 1960s, Farrar, Straus began publishing new and imprecise Hamsun translations, hoping to cash in on the mystical loner cache that had successfully revived Hermann Hesse—they even used similar Milton Glaser cover art. The flap copy on *Hunger* doesn't breathe a word about Hamsun's indiscretion, but the volume includes an introduction by I. B. Singer, who honors Hamsun as the foundation of "the whole modern school of fiction in the twentieth century" and blames his "tragic mistake" on his belief "that Nazism would spell the end of the leftwing radicalism which repelled him."

Troell is less forgiving, but more ironic. Much of his portrait is devoted to the embattled marriage of Knut and Marie Hamsun, a joust that went on for more than four decades. The film gets under way with a ranting argument filled with expository details: Marie had sacrificed her theatrical ambitions and the welfare of their four children to the demands of his "great mind." The Nazis, however, offered her stardom, the chance to travel through Germany reading excerpts from Hamsun's and her own stories. In the film, she is always heard reading the closing sentences of *Growth of the Soil*, which take on an increasingly baleful meaning. Marie, who died in 1969, was a far more ardent fascist than her husband and served three years in jail.

Troell cuts back and forth between Knut, forced to watch concentration-camp footage (his eyes reddening with horror), and Marie, forced to bare the most intimate details of her marriage to the detestable psychiatrist Gabriel Langfeldt, who thinks his devious probing will make him immortal. The suggestion arises that a bad marriage may have led to the Hamsuns' minor but by no means negligible contribution to the terror. Yet no explanation of their treason is possible. Hamsun disliked adulation of any kind; he knew, if no one else did, that he had no power and sought none. Two boys for whom he pleads mercy are summarily executed by Terboven, whose own suicide is gleefully dramatized: in a slimy bunker, shared with a frog, the sodden beast murmuring "Heil Hitler" while he ignites a dynamite fuse. Hamsun's thinking, despite a candid courtroom statement, faithfully enacted, is finally incomprehensible.

The film's most startling episode documents Hamsun's encounter with Hitler, which a journalist compares to Goethe meeting Napoleon. It begins with Hamsun's address in Vienna—Britain "must be crushed"—and a flight over Devil's Mountain, before he shakes hands in chilling slow motion with the devil himself. They play out a grotesque comedy. Hitler wants to discuss art—does Hamsun get his inspiration early or late in the day?—and Hamsun wants to complain of Terboven's tyranny. Hitler quakes like a time bomb before throwing him out.

The actors are splendid. Max von Sydow, in the triumphant role of his later years, disappears into Hamsun; Ghita Norby as Marie radiates the true believer's shameless gleam. As Quisling, Sverre Anker Ousdal's pasty, parchment skin exudes the viscosity associated with the name; Edgar Selge as Terboven is smarmily derisive; and Ernst Jacobi captures Hitler's chuckle-headed chipmunk look. The DVD, from First Run Features, is more problematic. A lackluster transfer is marred by a few visual distortions and skips, and the imprinted subtitles, framed in black, suggest a less than scrupulous translation. The repeated lines from *Growth of the Soil* include a meaningless reference to "dots" rather than Hamsun's "specks." Where Hamsun wrote, "All but nothing in all humanity, only one speck," the film's Marie appears to read, "She is hardly anyone among men. Only one." Still, the availability of this film—a biopic to set beside Peter Watkins's *Edvard Munch*—is a boon, requiring and justifying more than one visit.

No flaws whatsoever mar New Yorker Video's long-awaited DVD release of Henning Carlsen's *Hunger* (1966), one of the few great films based on a great novel. Working with cinematographer Henning Kristiansen, Carlsen achieved the illusion of near three-dimensionality by shooting Per Oscarsson (a vital, indispensable performance) in his inky black suit and hat against a flat gray background. When Oscarsson's character shifts to the background, the coat turns gray. Gunnel Lindblom radiates more sexual promise and longing with one glance from a window than most actresses achieve in a career. Stranded in Kristiania in 1890, Hamsun's autobiographical vagabond writer reels from starvation—he tastes sawdust, paper, and bones—yet spurns several offers of money, refusing to eat until he can buy food with the earnings from his work. Carlsen's film, as fresh as when it opened in New York four decades ago, deftly captures Hamsun's first-person desperation and humor. One choice scene of Beckettian vaudeville involves a park bench discussion of electric hymnbooks with a tramp quizzically played by Egil Hjorth Jensen. Another timeless aspect of this film is Krzysztof Komeda's John Lewis–influenced musical score. It's all of a piece and should not be missed.

31

EARLY GERMAN PSYCHOS
German Expressionism Collection

German Expressionism Collection, a 2008 DVD release from Kino collating four 1990s film restorations, two of them new to home video and rarely seen here in any form, is manna for cineasts determined to view as many titles as possible discussed in the writings of Siegfried Kracauer. It should also give pause to those who have never heard of Kracauer's hugely influential *From Caligari to Hitler*. The selection reminds us that Weimar filmmakers were as obsessed with psychotherapy as with aesthetics, not to mention crime and horror. Psychiatrists are central figures in two of the films, Robert Wiene's *The Cabinet of Dr. Caligari* (1920) and G. W. Pabst's *Secrets of a Soul* (1926), and psychological terror animates all four, including Arthur Robison's *Warning Shadows* (1923) and Wiene's *The Hands of Orlac* (1924). Be advised that these films do not provide serial thrills à la Fritz Lang, or pioneering efficiency à la F. W. Murnau, or impish elegance à la Ernst Lubitsch. The reason they—excepting *Caligari*—have faded into obscurity is that they represent an expressionism as languorous as it is shadowy and histrionic.

But stick with them. The films possess virtues entirely their own: unvarnished visions that, despite their expressionistic sway, shine with stand-alone integrity. They are postcards from a wildly inspired cultural oasis that existed chiefly in the imagination of artists skating on the edge of an abyss. Consider Werner Krauss, the incredibly prolific actor who made his name as the crab-walking, maniacally glaring, murderous psychiatrist-mesmerist

Caligari and ended up as a favorite of Goebbels, who cast him in *Jew Suss* (1940) and gratefully declared him an Artist of the State (along with Emil Jannings, to whom Krauss had often played second lead). Krauss is the head, heart, and soul of *Secrets of a Soul*, this collection's big find, an unusual triumph for the often underrated Pabst. As the tubby, impotent, middle-aged husband Martin Fellman, Krauss is hardly a matinee idol, yet we can see in this role his charm and the canny touches of realism (despite overheated emoting) that enthralled German audiences before and after he took on Caligari's primordial petulance.

Secrets of a Soul is the only film Freud ever came close to approving. As an on-screen essay details, the supreme dream catcher insisted his name not be used, but he cautiously—and, in the end, regretfully—allowed two members of his inner circle, Hanns Sachs and Karl Abraham, to serve as advisers. They were supposed to ensure some accuracy in a script that has the hero cured by the analysis of a single dream, which removes his symptoms and restores his potency: in the epilogue, Fellman turns from a clean lake, fertile with fish, to wave to his infant son. Not surprisingly, this is one of the several films that contain what Kracauer considered a characteristically Germanic expression of male fragility: a scene in which the protagonist lays his head on his mother's lap.

Hitchcock had to have seen this film, probably more than once. The obsession with knives is directly echoed in his own *Blackmail* (1929). The repeatedly frustrated climb up a bell tower is central to *Vertigo* (1958). *Spellbound* (1945) almost qualifies as a remake, though its dream sequence, designed by Salvador Dali, is no improvement on the in-camera optical tricks that Pabst created with his three cameramen. In *Secrets of a Soul*, the dream is first depicted in its entirety before being broken into component parts as the psychiatrist (played by Pavel Pavlov) solves its mysteries point by point.

At seventy-five minutes, *Secrets of a Soul* exhibits minimal dawdling. That cannot be said of *The Hands of Orlac*, which, at nearly two hours, may be charily helped along by the x2 speed button on the remote. This famous title, remade by MGM as the Peter Lorre vehicle *Mad Love* (1935), is nonetheless a savory addition to the DVD library. For one thing, it captures a sensational performance by Conrad Veidt (the somnambulant Cesare in *Caligari*) as the concert pianist Orlac, whose hands are destroyed in a confusingly expressionistic train wreck. They are surgically replaced with a murderer's hands, which Orlac suspects have a mind of their own. The script builds to a neat finish, where—at long last—the tempo matches the revelations that, though hardly plausible, are hell-bent on psychological logic and nonsupernatural criminal malfeasance. Along the way, Wiene, working with realistic sets, throws in a breadcrumb trail of Freudian symbols. Kino's presentation is more complete than the Murnau Archive's 35-mm restoration, as the producer Bret Wood added a few shots that existed only in a 16-mm print. The increased running time may go unappreciated, but Wood's scene-by-scene comparisons of the variant versions, amplified by excerpts from Maurice Renard's source novel, make for a worthy bonus.

Little needs to be said of *The Cabinet of Dr. Caligari*, an essential Cine 101 benchmark, other than that it remains unique and lively nine decades after its theatrical debut. The tale-within-the-tale framework, once harshly criticized, turned out to be a brainstorm, deepening the meaning over time. Even Kracauer, who explicated the scenarists' complaint that the framework undermined their attack on authoritarianism by making the narrator rather than Caligari insane, conceded that it achieves a larger point in establishing the madhouse as normative—a more horrific and prophetic vision of the Germany to come. Kino offers two musical scores (one conventional, the other avant-garde) that create two dramatically different viewing experiences.

If most film lovers know *Caligari*, few have seen Robison's *Warning Shadows: A Nocturnal Hallucination*, a masterly tour de force that, no less than *Caligari*, is deliriously sui generis. (Kino initially released it in 2006 to little fanfare and some derision.) The American-born Robison went to Germany to attend medical school and stayed to direct films. Shot without intertitles (the year before Murnau's similarly conceived *The Last Laugh*), *Warning Shadows* rewards concentration, though even after several screenings a few incidents remain ambiguous. Photographed by the fabled Fritz Arno Wagner, the film does *Peter Pan* one better by divorcing all the characters from their shadows. Wagner evidently had a field day coordinating the actors and their shadows in illusory poses.

Warning Shadows unfolds as a Goethean nightmare—it takes place in the early 1800s, during a single evening—as the "elective affinities" of a flirtatious wife, jealous husband, young suitor, three old letches, and three servants bounce off the walls in reciprocally thwarted assignations. A puppeteer, who doubles as de facto psychologist, arrives at the mansion that is the setting for the entire film and begs the host for the chance to perform, whereupon he liberates everyone's shadows to enact their conscious and unconscious proclivities. The film is often wryly funny—the puppeteer's wall shadows rest on the neck of one character or come nose to nose with another. There are more Freudian jokes here than in the other three films put together, as men hungrily reach for the shadows of womanly limbs—an early instance of virtual sex. The wife is superbly played by Ruth Weyher (she also plays the less interesting wife in *Secrets of a Soul*), a strikingly beautiful woman whose career did not survive the silent era. She dances in a see-through dress, sporting a log-like hair extension that seems to grow more erect as the film unreels. In direct contrast, the most peculiar of the servants (played by the great Fritz Rasp, who subsequently won recognition for his work with Fritz Lang) wears his hair split up the back and pulled forward on the sides in a kind of vulva-do. For all the sexual mischief, *Warning Shadows* is one of the few films that could be said to be about the art of cinematography: the artful manipulation of light to create the illusion of life. Even the natural daylight in the final scene is a conjuror's trick—one that hasn't grown old.

32

IT WASN'T BEAUTY KILLED THE BEAST

King Kong / Grass / Chang

"YOU'RE NOT A patch on your old man," explorer-impresario Carl Denham tells the soon martyred son of Kong, in a botched sequel rushed to theaters in the same year, 1933, that *King Kong* electrified audiences. The old man's tragedy has been replayed as farce ever since, bottoming out in the 1976 remake. The 2005 version, directed by Peter Jackson, long and fervently awaited as an escapist oasis (we have such little escape in this country), ended up unsurprisingly putting more faith in computer graphics than the characters, including the ape, resulting in a self-impressed, epical (three hours and change), and fitfully respectable patch on the original film, an authentic American fairy tale, meticulously restored by Warner Bros. as a DVD essential.

The miracle of *King Kong* is that it has survived three-quarters of a century so well. A childlike if never quite childish myth that has printed indelible images in the mind and on the culture, the film continues to elicit an emotional involvement when all we expect is to rekindle a childhood frisson. Why do we care about this giant ape, this animated puppet with monstrous nostrils and googly eyes? Why do we read so much into a transparently simple monkey-out-of-jungle fable, feeding on unstated fears of imperialism, racism, sexual repression, rape, wanton violence, civilization's discontents, Darwinian mazes, and any other theme you care to throw into the mix, with the possible exception of all that final-curtain nonsense about beauty and the beast? It wasn't beauty killed the beast. It was Denham (played by Robert Armstrong as an alter ego for the film's producer, Merian C. Cooper) and his gas bombs and the kidnapping of Kong—"We're millionaires, boys, I'll share it with all of you," he says.

King Kong could only have been made in the era before the Production Code had teeth. With its unstoppable images of wounding violence and sensual curiosity, the film employed the oldest and latest techniques of children's entertainment—puppets and animation—with a commitment that disarmed skepticism. After the original, Kong's creators reverted to "family" fare for follow-ups: the cooing monkeyshines of *Son of Kong*, the sentimental comedy of *Mighty Joe Young*, the latter combining "Beautiful Dreamer" and a burning orphanage. In the meantime, the king suffered the diminishment of a thousand (actually twenty-nine) cuts by censors who, in 1938, sniffed at RKO's triumph with far more distaste than Kong sniffed at Ann Darrow's (or Fay Wray's) white veils.

I'm of the generation that discovered *King Kong* through Channel 9's *Million Dollar Movie*, watching it a dozen times in a week. My parents, recalling it from childhood with what seemed like a subversive pleasure and hesitating between nostalgia and concern that it might not be appropriate for a nine-year-old, were relieved to find that it wasn't that frightening after all. No kidding. Not until the restoration two decades later (shown, fittingly, at New York's D. W. Griffith Theater) did we finally get to see Kong chomp—but, significantly, never swallow—natives and New Yorkers; disrobe and ogle Ann; and toss a woman out the window because she was a brunette and not a blond. Nor had we seen Denham force Ann—wearing a diaphanous dress outfitted with a belt folding into her groin like a chastity lock—to scream for her life. Without those scenes, *King Kong* is perfect kiddie material, the big lug dragged to the mean streets and attacked by fighter pilots, when all he wants to do is play with his little blond doll. The phenomenal thing about the uncut *Kong*, establishing it as a benchmark in cinematic manipulation, is the abrupt change it demands of the audience, from fear and horror at his brutal marauding to sorrow and anger at his demise. Oh, we bleeding hearts.

That this was achieved with a gorilla puppet no taller than two feet is another reason that a computer-graphics remake, even one managed by Kongophiliac Peter Jackson, who had the good sense to set his version in the 1930s, could not press the same buttons. Willis O'Brien's ingenious, painstaking stop-animation process, requiring twenty-four hand-manipulated movements and exposures per second, invites a measure of identification owing to its very crudity. The fakery inspires subliminal wonder, magnifying the wonder of the story. But O'Brien's achievement goes beyond technique. The DVD release, which includes a commentary track and a surprisingly inept gloss on Merian Cooper, boasts an excellent two-and-a-half-hour documentary on the making of *King Kong* that harps on O'Brien's influence (as do the remarks accompanying the DVD of *Mighty Joe Young*), especially as extended by the sainted Ray Harryhausen, who assisted him in animating Mighty Joe. Yet no one else has succeeded in making a puppet so anthropomorphically appealing. Harryhausen's figurines, mind-boggling as they are, are almost always senseless killing machines, comic relief, or mythological monsters brought to life for the purpose of bringing them to life. He exceeded the master in technique, not in empathy.

Also unsurpassed is Max Steiner's much imitated and analyzed score. Rachmaninoff ranks second best in manipulating three descending chords: Kong's heavy-treading theme freezes the audience before it sees a thing. This is a film with a faultless three-act structure—the voyage out; the jungle; the city—and one of Steiner's masterstrokes is to withhold music from the first section, following the credits. Once the crew reaches Skull Island, Steiner is unleashed, offering not conventional cues but a constant storytelling parallel in music, as though it were a silent film—which, much of the time, it is. (Too bad Warner doesn't provide a separate music and effects track.) Alternating Kong's theme, Ann Darrow's signature waltz, and diverse observations, he comments on every action. Used to excess, this approach is derisively known as Mickey Mousing—as, for example, in a comedy when a bassoon mimics an on-screen drunk. Steiner, however, is so omnipresent that even as he doubles the action he anticipates the responses of the audience.

Peter Jackson proves his devotion with his main contribution to this reissue, included in the massive documentary: a re-creation, combining footage from the movie with new stop-time animation, of the lost spider pit sequence. In his 2005 version, Jackson faced a more difficult hurdle in re-creating one factor that made *King Kong* a necessary entertainment in its day. The generation of Merian Cooper and his director-cameraman, Ernest B. Schoedsack, grew up during the last throes of terrestrial exploration: when everyone knew about Stanley and Livingston, about Burton, Scott, Shackleton, Peary, and Byrd; when the earth was so large it might yet harbor unknown peoples and lands forgotten by time. Skull Island enlarged on that dream, which had motivated its makers to actually take pith helmets, rifles, and a camera into the brush.

If Cooper and Schoedsack ultimately decided that the best fantasies could be secured on soundstages, they initially made their way with dramatized documentaries in the mold of Robert Flaherty, filmed in the silent era. Little seen for decades, *Grass* (1924) and *Chang* (1927) are now available from Milestone, and they stand on their own as fascinating texts as well as prototypes for Denham and company. The DVD prints look surprisingly fresh, and the new scores, played on locally authentic instruments and combining steady rhythms with scalar melodies, enliven the action. "Cute" title cards, attributing dialogue to animals (the first talking camel appeared in *Grass*, not *Road to Morocco*), mar both films; it was once assumed that the studio added them, but Cooper was the culprit. Indeed, he dismissed *Grass*, because he did not get to personalize the story by focusing on a family. For *Grass*, he and Schoedsack and a mysterious benefactress named Marguerite Harrison (whom Schoedsack despised and treated much as the Bruce Cabot character does Fay Wray) followed the Bakhtiari tribe, reportedly 50,000 strong, on a grueling annual trek for grazing land through places that no longer exist on the map, Persia and Arabia. The fourteen-minute sequence depicting the weeklong crossing of a raging river on rafts floated by inflated goatskins is as astonishing as anything in *King Kong*—and more horrific in that the drowning of animals and possibly of people (the editing is timid on this point) are real. This is followed by an ascent up 12,000 feet of an iced mountain, in all a journey of forty-eight days. If only we could see how the filmmakers obtained their footage and handled the hardships.

The power of *Grass* resides in its detachment from the people and their massive plight. *Chang*, by contrast, focuses on a family in what used to be called Siam, and is by any definition exciting filmmaking, though it is anthropologically suspect. A leopard racing through the jungle comes within spitting range of Schoedsack's camera, a tiger almost licks the lens, a herd of elephants (*chang* is Siamese for "elephant") destroys a settlement—and the people seem caught between the terror of the moment and the reassurances of the unseen filmmakers. A rapid chase, cutting between close-ups of a fleeing monkey (shouting for help, unfortunately) and a charging leopard, prefigures episodes in *The Most Dangerous Game*, the film that Cooper and Schoedsack later made on the *Kong* sets. This is action in the absence of a script, stark and unfettered, though not as gripping as a giant ape defying planes atop the Empire State Building. In the long haul, life cannot supersede imagination.

33

MASTERS AND GRANDMASTERS
The Thief of Bagdad / Icons of Adventure

REWATCHING *The Thief of Bagdad*, as released in a glorious Criterion DVD transfer, is not unlike rereading *Treasure Island*. Conceived to enchant children, both film and book requite the adult longing for formative influences that withstand disillusionment and fashion. Unlike *Treasure Island*, an exemplary display of English prose and plotting, with one of the finest first sentences in fiction, *The Thief of Bagdad* (1940) occasionally sputters, losing tempo and continuity; yet it, too, survives as a model of its kind, reveling in cinematic craftsmanship—not least the then-novel techniques of color and trick photography—and boasting one of the most magisterial opening shots in cinema. Whereas *Treasure Island*, however, was solely the work of Robert Louis Stevenson, *The Thief of Bagdad* is an auctorial anomaly even by movie standards, with so many artists and artisans—including at least six directors—working on it that only the producer, Alexander Korda, could have known how all the parts would fit. In the credits, Korda's name comes first and last; the directors are buried midway.

The first nine minutes are riveting: the opening shot of a ship bucking the waves, a closing-in on the great eye painted on its hull (the colors radiantly saturated), a cut to the eyes of the malignant wizard and vizier Jaffar (Conrad Veidt), whose face is otherwise hidden in a red turban, and then a montage to show the dock workers preparing for the ship's arrival, singing a Miklós Rózsa song that introduces the concept of purity. The sea is hard but pure and clean because men are few and far between. Jaffar descends the plank to a foreboding twelve-note theme. The first lines of dialogue establish the circular issue of power, as he asks an assistant, "Have you news for me?" "No, master."

Just about every relationship in imperialist and horror movies replays master and servant, with masters often answering to greater masters. Ahmad (John Justin), the king deposed and blinded by Jaffar, is "servant of the all highest but master of all men." Ahmad introduces himself to his beloved princess (June Duprez) as "your slave"—each is subject to the other. Jaffar, who destroys himself in attempting to win the princess's love, can only ogle her untouched loveliness as his unconscious prisoner: "Love she has yet to learn, and I am here to teach her." The contented boy Abu (Sabu), the thief of the title who prizes his freedom above all, enters into a game of master-servant exchanges when he uncorks the malevolent genie (Rex Ingram)—one of two scenes actually drawn from *The Thousand and One Nights*, in this case the third and fourth nights. Abu is about to hurl the genie into the sea when the imprisoned spirit utters the magic word: "Master!" How can a thief, previously referred to contemptuously as "master of a thousand fleas," resist that? Accused of ingratitude for his release from the bottle, the genie bellows, "Slaves are not grateful—not for their freedom!"

Abu ought to know. During a thirty-seven-minute flashback, he and Ahmad are arrested; as the narrator points out, "only little thieves are thrown in prison." Big thieves run the state, chief among them being Jaffar, who appears at one point with his sword draped by his flowing black cassock, suggesting a large tail. Jaffar turns Abu into a dog and blinds Ahmad, as his own eyes grow round and translucently blue. Ahmad's eyes, however, will "bear witness"—a phrase that reverberates in the New Testament and the Koran and was especially resonant in the twentieth century. The princess's father, the sultan of Basra (Miles Malleson, who wrote the screenplay), prefers toys to his uncontrollable subjects, and walks as jerkily as his mechanical playthings, blithely referring to the beheadings he routinely orders. He placates Jaffar by trading his daughter for a flying horse (an incident adapted from Sheherizade's tale "The Ebony Horse"); another toy will take his life. The flying horse similarly facilitates Jaffar's undoing, as Abu brings him down with the "arrow of justice."

Some of the blue-screen effects and model work in *The Thief of Bagdad* are dated, but the overall display of pastel colors, magnificent sets, and creative energy subsumes them. One episode, in which Abu claims the all-seeing eye, shows an oneiric inventiveness that spawned many images of 1950s cinema: the statue, for example, is shot in a montage of angles that anticipates Alfred Hitchcock's approach to Mt. Rushmore in *North by Northwest*. The themes of subjugation and obsession—along with the images of a giant spider and giant squid—would become equally familiar during the postwar era.

These themes and images abound in films produced by Hammer, perhaps the only studio name that reignites the adrenalin of those who began attending movies in the 1950s and early 1960s. The films were frequently censored and reviled for their violence and sexuality, inciting revulsion in England, where they were made. Here they were the stuff of Saturday matinees—not family films like *The Thief of Bagdad*, but fare for adolescent boys who could scarcely believe (I bear witness) the sadism, the colors, the bosomy extras. Four overlooked examples are collected by Columbia in *Icons of Adventure*, each of them rehearsing the same themes of master and servant, appeasement and betrayal, destructive obsession, and the decline of empire.

Terrence Fisher's *The Stranglers of Bombay* (1960), the only one in black and white and the only one lacking a shivery lead performance by Christopher Lee, is an extrapolation of the kill-for-Kali episodes in *Gunga Din* (1939), only without a genuine imperialist hero. Henry Lewis (Guy Rolfe), who is introduced patting an Indian boy's head, is merely the least objectionable of an arrogant lot of soldiers and directors of the 1830s British East India Company. The drum-playing Thuggees are fundamentalist worshippers of Kali, who is represented by a statue with Churchillian V-shaped fingers. Although they strangle indiscriminately, slit tongues, and gouge eyes, they are only marginally less appealing than the Brits, with their equally unquenchable greed and old school ties. The highlight is a Kiplingesque fight between a cobra and a mongoose worthy of a Disney True-Life Adventure, and overseen by a slave girl (Marie Devereux) who has no dialogue or credit, just famously heaving breasts.

Andrew Bushell's *The Terror of the Tongs* (1961) switches the imperialist game to 1910 Hong Kong, where the Red Tong creates suicide killers. Instead of virgins in the next world, these men get all the opium and whores they can handle the night before they go on a mission. "All passion spent," Lee's Fu Manchu–type tong leader tells them, "your spirit shall be shining and pure." The film, originally shown in American theaters in black and white, was photographed and art-directed (note the juggler who accompanies the shake dancer) with shimmering Hammer colors, solidly reproduced on the DVD. The story is strictly pulp—Captain Sale (Geoffrey Toone), whose sixteen-year-old daughter is murdered, destroys the "inviolable" Tong by storming around Hong Kong in his pea coat, unarmed but for his ready fists. The Tong have no chance; neither do any of the women in Sale's life, all sacrificed to the mission. Sale is called master in his home and the Tong leader is called master in his lair, though the latter makes it clear that he answers to grandmasters in Peking. In the absence of Devereux's yawning bosom, the film is best remembered for the way Lee leans forward and asks Sale, conversationally, in his silky bass baritone, "Have you ever had your bones scraped, Captain?"

Two thoughtfully entertaining and rarely seen pirate films, John Gilling's *The Pirates of Blood River* (1961) and Don Sharp's *The Devil-Ship Pirates* (1963), also deal with religious fanatics, but these reprehensible zealots are British Christians. In the former, they sacrifice a woman to a bay of piranhas and sentence the hero (the very un-British Kerwin Mathews) to a prison camp. Interestingly, the hero really is guilty as accused, and it is he who first appeases Lee's pirate band by offering the sanctuary of his intolerant hometown. His father, who runs the village, and the pirates are equally willing to kill everyone else for a hidden treasure. *The Devil-Ship Pirates* brings out the quislings in a British coastal town when pirates pretending to be members of the Spanish Armada convince them that England has been conquered. The governor offers them free use of the town in the hope that they are reasonable men and will go away. But there are no genies in Hammer films, and no reason for hope.

URBAN LEGEND
Blade Runner

IT'S OFFICIAL. RICK Deckard, the fatigued replicant hunter played by
Harrison Ford in Ridley Scott's latest stab at *Blade Runner* (1982, 1992, 2007),
is himself a replicant, though he doesn't know it. How do *we* know? Scott,
who likes to talk about himself with phrases like "I'm all about . . ." and
"That's what I do," says so, and he's the auteur, pal. The unicorn dream,
which made its debut in the 1992 version, is the evidence. Hampton Fancher,
who wrote the original screenplay, can insist that anyone who thinks Deckard is a replicant (or android or robot) is "stupid." Ford can deny that he ever
played a replicant. And fandom can storm Warner Bros. with pitchforks and
torches, but it won't do any good. Life is full of disillusionments.

If you don't know what I'm talking about, you probably have a (real) life,
and the thought of watching as many as five—*five*—versions of *Blade Runner*
may suggest permanent puberty or clinical insanity. Yet multiple versions
were the inducements as Warner Bros. released three packages to observe
the twenty-fifth anniversary "final cut." For most of us, one cut will do. Film
studies professors, on the other hand, will find a semester's syllabus stored
in a Deckard-style briefcase complete with handle, origami unicorn, and,
according to a press release, "a signed personal letter from Sir Ridley Scott."
That'll keep him busy—just getting the names and addresses of everyone
he has to write to.

A brief history: *Blade Runner* was one of 1982's box-office debacles,
admired for its art direction, criticized for its wan pace and narrative confu-

sion, and ridiculed for a voice-over commentary read by Ford as though he were Philip Marlow on Quaaludes. A second version was released internationally, virtually identical to the first but for the addition of a few seconds of graphic violence. Then Sir Ridley's incomplete "workprint," the movie equivalent of a first draft, made its way into cinematic consciousness, suggesting that the released film was not what he had intended. Encouraged by the demands for a better *Blade Runner*, he issued a director's cut in 1992, which disposed of the pointless voice-over and inane ending and added the unicorn. This was a big improvement, yet we now learn that the revised film was merely the director's first director's cut. Now we have what is optimistically called "The Final Cut," and it is far and away the best edition and the only one that need concern us, thanks to computer-generated images.

The irony here is in sync with the writings of Philip K. Dick, whose intricate 1968 novel *Do Androids Dream of Electric Sheep?* inspired—very loosely— the concept but not the title (which was borrowed from an unrelated novel by William Burroughs) of *Blade Runner*. The film is often vaunted as the last great special-effects extravaganza made "in camera," before the advent of computer graphics. But Sir Ridley, whose eye for architecture, costume, and smoke rarely let him down, lost track of a few more kinetic details, including a stunt double for Joanna Cassidy who wears a ludicrously inappropriate wig, a dove that takes off from a rainy deck into a clear blue sky, and inept lip-synching. These and numerous other details have now been computer-corrected: Cassidy's present-day head has been grafted to the body double's body, Ford's son has provided accurate lip movements to be melded with his father's profile, and the dove flies into man-made storm clouds.

Blade Runner never looked and sounded better, and this is a film in which looks are practically everything. It is as dependent on art direction as, say, Vincente Minnelli's *Gigi*; every inch of the screen is answered for, indoors and especially outdoors, as horizons disappear into matte paintings, smoke pots, shimmering neon, giant screens, airborne vehicles, and crowds as opaque and variously dressed as in a Halloween parade in Greenwich Village. From the justly celebrated opening shot—a grotesque metropolitan hell with fireballs shooting into the starless night—we are drawn into an alternate world. The director's small army of designers, builders, illustrators, costumers, hairdressers, and makeup artists left few details unexamined in constructing a nightmare city that lingers in the mind with greater resilience than the characters inhabiting it. Not to say that the landscape is logical or consistent. The introductory shot doesn't comport with the street details, which include Los Angeles landmarks (the film is set there in 2019), but who cares. When Sir Ridley is playing with light, bric-a-brac, architecture, and the elements (snow, rain, relentless smoke), he is at peace. When telling a story, he goes to pieces. Maybe he intended for Ford and Sean Young to play their putatively sympathetic characters as though powered by batteries, while the replicants portrayed by Rutger Hauer, Daryl Hannah, and the effervescent Cassidy are brawny with life—albeit life triggered by rage.

Other elements suggest directorial incompetence. The script seems often to have been lost amid the décor, so that no one noticed the potted dialogue, deficient characterizations, and narrative languor. With a script credited to Fancher, who was fired for refusing revisions, and David Peoples, who wrote most of the finished film, *Blade Runner* is curiously lacking in wit and rhythm; the best speech was written and recited by Hauer, as his character's dying valediction. Set pieces that should generate tension and suspense were flatly shot and edited. Deckard's pursuit of Zhora (Cassidy), which at the very least might have been Classic Movie Chase, is tired and uninvolved—more intent on a sugar-glass stunt than suspense or action dynamics. The slugfest between Deckard and Pris (Hannah) is incoherent—why *does* she insert her fingers into his nose? Hauer's Roy Batty, who provides the picture with its most grotesque violence and an unexpected burst of poetic feeling, is largely unexplored. His death is painful because we know we will have to return to dark tracking shots and elliptical dialogue between Ford and Young.

Still, *Blade Runner* is a vital movie experience because its canvas is so fully realized. It affects people who see it, not because it explores "what it means to be human" (Philip Dick does that, Sir Ridley could care less), but because it shows what it means to embrace modern urban life. Most futuristic science fiction is inherently silly—it predicts robot slaves, flying jeeps, and pillbox hats, but not cell phones or computers. The dystopias that work build on the present: Times Square on a Saturday night in a summer rain with smoke emanating from subway gratings and manholes is premature *Blade Runner*. Change the word "replicant" to "immigrant," and the movie can double as a Republican jeremiad and talking point.

Which edition to buy? The two-disc DVD includes the final cut and a three-and-a-half-hour documentary. The four-disc set has that plus the other three theatrical versions from 1982 and 1992 (a waste of time), plus some good featurettes, including two on Dick. The overpriced five-disc version adds to all that the "workprint" version (another waste of time), a solid thirty-minute short about the technical revisions made for the final cut, and that "personal letter." In offering this choice, Warner Bros. is subjecting consumers to what in *Blade Runner* is called a Voight-Kampff test: your decision divulges whether you are a human, a replicant, or a teenager.

35

CARNIVORES

Dark Sky Films

FEWER AMERICAN MOVIES are inspired by the life of George Washington than by the life of Ed Gein. The father of our country eludes its imagination, while the only famous son of Plainfield, Wisconsin, has fathered a cinematic genre in which murder and cannibalism coexist with transvestitism and freaky arts and crafts. Within three years of his 1957 arrest for murder and dismemberment, the graying, glassy-eyed little Ed was stretched into the tall, lanky, crush-worthy Norman Bates. In 1960, the year Italy produced *La Dolce Vita* and *L'Avventura*, America delivered a homicidal mama's boy and amateur taxidermist of undying appeal. The subsequent popularity of the Italian *giallo*, a stylish neo-gothic brand of slasher flick often rigged around gender confusion, showed that Monicas and Marcellos may come and go, but a fastidiously eviscerated corpse will always fill the till.

It's an Ed Gein world, or maybe it just feels that way because I have been making my way through the alternately macabre and campy catalog of Dark Sky Films, the DVD company that has taken the lead from Anchor Bay and others in offering a savory stew of low-budget American detritus, *gialli*, assorted Euro-trash, neglected television, and even a few altogether admirable movies with a bent disposition. What sets Dark Sky apart is the care it gives drive-in discards as well as respectable genre classics—care that indicates a modicum of corporate wit. One pleasing Dark Sky feature is its solo interviews, averaging fifteen minutes, with one or two participants in a given film. Instead of the usual featurette, in which pundits are edited into a counterpoint of predictable one-liners, Dark Sky's stationary camera allows the interviewee to tell his or her own story, supported by illustrative clips.

Dan Curtis's 1974 television film *Trilogy of Terror*, for example, holds a place in many hearts as a showcase for Karen Black, one of the more inventive actresses in 1970s Hollywood, and for the trilogy's third segment, a line-by-line adaptation of Richard Matheson's short story "Prey," turned into a kinetic tour de force involving a tiny Zuni fetish doll with big teeth. The Dark Sky interview with Black is no less engaging. Rolling her eyes in recollection of the crew's incompetence, she recalls the spills she had to take while pretending to wrestle the doll and offers her own analysis of the film's cult following: "Women are afraid of vaginal entry," especially by snakes, rats, and other small things, like Zuni fetish dolls. An interview with Matheson is not quite as illuminating.

The underrated *Magic* (1978), Richard Attenborough's best effort as a director, gets a bad rap because Anthony Hopkins is bizarrely cast as a Borscht Belt ventriloquist named Corky; someone remarks that Corky's father came from England, presumably to explain why Corky has an accent that doesn't comport with a performer born and raised in the shadow of Grossinger's. Yet Hopkins's performance is cannily measured and holds its own with Ann-Margret's effulgent informality, the dummy's masterly misdirection, and a thematic showbiz joke, expressed by Burgess Meredith as a crusty agent, about the pitfalls of success. The DVD does full justice to Victor Kemper's moody cinematography, and offers, in addition to an interview with Kemper, an entertaining visit with the ventriloquist Dennis Alwood and two dummies—the one in the movie and the one that didn't get the part. This is film history dressed up as vaudeville.

Dark Sky also justifies revisiting Tobe Hooper's *Eaten Alive* (1976), a mostly dismal effort as Hooper's detached style doesn't allow the characters to get beyond caricature. In this case, the interviews with director and actors are less interesting than a featurette about the film's Depression-era inspiration: Joe Ball, the owner of a Texas juke joint and a chick magnet, who fed many of his lovers—along with live dogs and cats—to his five alligators. Neville Brand's interpretation is all ranting insanity, and the rest of the cast is buried under bad makeup and mindless dialogue, but the picture isn't dull. It does, however, underscore the weird plight of its director. Imagine having only one great film in you and that film being *The Texas Chain Saw Massacre* (1974), Hooper's ingenious variation on the Ed Gein story (made the same year as a more literal telling, *Deranged*, available from MGM)—as convulsively fearsome as one of George Orwell's Room 101 tortures and a showpiece among Dark Sky's offerings, presented in a restored transfer with hours of documentary supplements. The film probably didn't look as good during its initial release as it does now. The opening seventy-second pullback, on rotting corpses wired to a grave, can now be seen as a parody of Monument Valley, with its butte-like cemetery markers, open sky, and billowing dust.

The catalog features other notable films, including Mario Bava's feverish, color-coded ghost story *Kill, Baby . . . Kill* (1966); John McNaughton's relentless *Henry: Portrait of a Serial Killer* (1990); Roy Ward Baker's funny and giddily performed Amicus compilation, *Asylum* (1972); and Jack Hill's winning send-up of pre-Gein horror films, *Spider Baby* (1964), with Lon Chaney barking the title song, Mantan Moreland waddling into a lethal window frame, and Carol Ohmart doing her imperiously sexy sashaying. Dark Sky has also uncovered several films that never had a chance here. We can only wonder about the meeting at which director Narciso Ibanez Serrador pitched *Who Can Kill a Child?*

"It's a remake of *The Birds*, only instead of birds, we use children."

"Great! But how do you get them to perch on telephone wires?"

"Well, it won't be an exact remake. We just use the idea of adorable children turning their parents into piñatas and destroying all adult life."

Made in 1976, this is one disturbing movie, previously shown in a version as violently butchered as the film's victims. Two genres are merged, each reeking of postwar paranoia: the senselessly swarming enemy, as popularized in the tales of Leiningen's ants, giant tarantulas, triffids, alien pods, and so forth, and brought to a boil in Alfred Hitchcock's *The Birds* (1963); and the beware-your-kids films that grew from *The Bad Seed* (1956) to *Village of the Damned* (1960) to *The Brood* (1979). A political framework is appended by way of grueling introductory footage showing atrocities perpetrated on children during the Holocaust and later, but the film is less intent on justifying the horrors depicted at a Catalanian vacation resort than in raising the issue of how to handle cuties with weapons, a theme that has grown strangely relevant with recent school shootings and the preadolescent assassins depicted in Edward Zwick's dismayingly superficial *Blood Diamond* (2006). Do we take preemptive action by herding them into camps, build walls around their rooms, or offer them amnesty if they'll turn in their guns and knives? *Who Can Kill a Child?* is maddening because it isn't the trash it ought to be. It is a crafty, well-paced tribulation replete with dreadful images and an unsettling denouement.

Christian Alvart's *Antibodies* (2005), a German film that played in New York for a few minutes and then disappeared after a nearly unanimous critical drubbing, also casts a baleful eye on children and merits the second chance offered by Dark Sky's double-disc edition, including an engaging monologue by Alvart. *Antibodies* borrows generic elements from other serial killer/pederast movies, from *M* to *Silence of the Lambs* to *The Pledge*, maintaining a peculiarly European approach in its perverse pride in numbers, logic, accident, and religious parable—mainly a vivid enactment of Abraham and Isaac occasioned when the film's psychopath frames the son of a small-town cop. It would be laughable if it weren't staged and played with a Bressonian confidence. Painfully brutal, suspenseful, and sharply photographed and acted, *Antibodies* will survive its detractors.

As will the late Curtis Harrington's lost film *The Killing Kind* (1973), the last of his fading-actresses trilogy—in this case, Ann Sothern and Ruth Roman. Though not as inspired as Harrington's 1971 hilarious burlesque of old Hollywood, *What's the Matter with Helen?* (available from MGM), the film has a somber deliberation that recalls his poetic debut feature, *Night Tide* (1961)—the opening under-the-boardwalk shot is an homage to the earlier film. Never actually released to theaters, *The Killing Kind* is not untouched by misogyny. Sothern plays a monstrous mother, inciting Oedipal (or Geinian) confusion in her demented son (John Savage), and the son's young targets, including a rape victim, are punished for crossing sexual boundaries. But the astute dissection of tormented families (Luana Anders is delectable as the alcoholic spinster librarian next door), the pitiless portrait of the son, and the steady legato tempo are due proper consideration.

Also perversely worth seeing is *Ricco the Mean Machine*, Dark Sky's inexplicable cover tag for Tulio Demichaeli's *Ricco* (1973), a Mafia revenge film in which Christopher Mitchum sets out to destroy the mob with his pageboy flip and a few inelegant karate chops. Remembered by a happy few for Barbara Bouchet's striptease and infamous for an on-camera castration, the film is more memorable for the performance by an almost unrecognizable Arthur Kennedy—waxen-faced behind a toupee and mustache—as Don Vito, who turns enemies into bars of soap. Kennedy ended his once formidable career with fifteen years of Italian cheapjack, yet his voice and gestures remained inimitable. Note the disdainful look he gives Malisa Longo before consigning her to the tub of acid. He even dies smirking.

RUNNING FOR A TRAIN

The General

THOSE OF US who grew up in the 1950s and 1960s, when television was awash in classic movies (*Million Dollar Movie*, *Shock Theater*, *The Late Show*, and *Silents Please* were among the first schools in cinema—just ask Scorsese, Spielberg, or Coppola), are aghast to find that our children are often reluctant to watch black and white films, let alone silent ones. Especially those deemed to be among the greatest ever made. The imprimatur of the experts turns pleasure into obligation, and suddenly the notion of sitting through a comedy that had for decades convulsed audiences takes on all the promise of reading *The Merry Wives of Windsor*—the most annoying and witless of Shakespeare's plays, yet once upon a time thought to be a riot. For anyone who has never seen a silent comedy or, worse, seen only speeded-up pie-throwing excerpts, an ideal introduction is Kino's spotless 2008 transfer of Buster Keaton's 1926 epic *The General*. Kino initially released a DVD of *The General* in 1999, which looked no better than every other version shown in theaters for decades—soft focus, faded and scratched film stock. The recent two-disc set (most of the extras concern the story's historical basis) is pristine, sharply focused, stable, and gorgeous.

Gorgeous is important, because *The General* is a peephole into history and by any definition an uncannily beautiful film. Indeed, for a first-time viewer, I would emphasize the beauty over the comedy. Many people are disappointed when they first see *The General* because they have heard that it is one of the funniest movies ever made. It isn't. Keaton did make films that are tours de force of hilarity, including *Sherlock Jr.*, *The Navigator* (both 1924), and *Seven Chances* (1925) (available from Kino, along with his other pre-MGM long and short films, all of them rewarding, many astonishingly so). *The General* is something else, a historical parody set during the Civil War. The comedy is rich but deliberate and insinuating. It aims not to split your sides but rather to elicit and sustain—for seventy-eight minutes— a smile and sense of wonder, interrupted by several perfectly timed guffaws. The film belongs to at least four movie genres: comedy, war, history, and chase. Most of it is constructed around a pursuit as relentless as any Bourne blowout, centered on a Confederate locomotive called the General, hijacked by Union spies.

The General's engineer, Johnny Grey (Keaton), spends the first half racing after it on foot, handcar, bicycle, and another train, and the second half, once he has stolen it back, in flight from the Texas, a train manned by Union troops. If the film begins as a contest between man and machine, it ultimately depicts a triumphant collusion between the two. Keaton, one of the greatest natural athletes and stuntmen in film history, loves his train as much as he does his inamorata, Annabelle Lee (played by the delightfully oblivious Marion Mack). He leaps and crawls over every inch of it, from the pilot, or cowcatcher, riding low on the tracks to the tender carrying the fuel. In Keaton's hands, the train is nothing more than a gigantic prop, an incessant inspiration to his inventive genius. Some passages are so suspenseful and minutely worked out that the gag, when it comes, is like the release of the General's steam. It gives you a chance to breathe again.

Keep in mind that *The General*, made more than eighty years ago, recounts an incident that had occurred only sixty-four years before it was shot. In 1862, a civilian Union spy, James Andrews, led a small attachment of soldiers 200 miles into enemy territory to steal an engine of the Western & Atlantic Railroad at Big Shanty, Georgia. The General's engineer, William Fuller (the basis for Keaton's character), led the chase that ended with their capture. Some were hanged, while others escaped and became the first-ever recipients of the Medal of Honor. Among the latter was William Pittinger, who published a memoir, *Daring and Suffering: A History of the Great Railroad Adventure* (which can be freely downloaded as part of the Gutenberg Project). When word got out that Keaton was making a comedy of Pittinger's story, he was refused permission to use the General, which had survived and would later—largely because of Keaton's film—be spruced up for a Georgia museum. The town of Marietta, where the story began, also wanted nothing to do with him. So Keaton moved Georgia to the Northwest, shooting the picture entirely on location. If much of our visual sense of the Civil War derives from photographs by Mathew Brady and Alexander Gardner, *The General*, for all its humor, conveys the illusion of those photographs come alive.

Keaton's best films function as a loving record of American town life, with its shops and picket fences and leisure pursuits, set against a splendor of mountains, gulches, rivers, and fields. Using Cottage Grove, Oregon, as his main location, Keaton preserved two eras: the Civil War, re-created with daunting attention to detail, and 1926 as passersby in Cottage Grove would have seen it—the costumes were of the nineteenth century, but the buildings and natural surroundings had little changed. Other Civil War films, including *The Great Locomotive Chase*, Walt Disney's dramatic 1956 telling of the same story from the perspective of the Union raiders, invariably look like Hollywood pageants. Keaton's authenticity and comedic understatement make *The General* a surprisingly modern experience. The storytelling and the gags are free of sentimentality and knockabout clichés. The four-minute battle scene is simply one of the most gripping, albeit occasionally hilarious, ever filmed.

Silent movies, especially comedies, suffer as home video. They were meant to be seen in theaters, where the audience morphs into a comedy meter, responding en masse to each gag. I've seen this film in theaters enough times to know that a few moments always elicit gales of laughter, some of them fleeting by so quickly that you may be grateful for instant replay—like Keaton's running mount onto a wooden bicycle or the scene in which he straddles the pilot and averts disaster by using one log to get rid of another. A classic minute in the history of movie romance occurs when Annabelle tries to help him fuel the train, throwing wood into the furnace. She rejects one log because it has a hole in it and tosses in a small stick. Keaton, watching this, hands her a splinter. She conscientiously throws it in the fire, at which point exasperation briefly gets the better of him, as he strangles and then kisses her—all done so quickly that she remains entirely unfazed. A standard joke in Keaton's comedies (and Charlie Chaplin's, too) is that the world of silent movies is truly silent when a character's back is turned. As Keaton chops wood, facing forward, he doesn't hear the Union army passing behind his back.

Most Keaton films have scenes that not only transcend comedy, but remind us what a resourceful filmmaker he was. In *The General*, a surprisingly long overhead tracking shot pursues Johnny and his train as they enter a smoke-filled tunnel. The most unforgettable shot, said to be the costliest filmed during the silent era, is one in which Keaton sets fire to a bridge, causing the Union train to crash into a ravine—prefiguring by thirty years the climax of David Lean's *The Bridge on the River Kwai*. The disaster might have been accomplished with a toy train and matte painting, which may be why Keaton had himself photographed poking his head through the wreckage so that no one could mistake the genuineness of the demolition. Kino's edition offers three soundtracks for *The General*, though the only successful one is the default score composed by Carl Davis in 1987. It keeps a straight face throughout, heightening without intruding on a magical film that is too brisk to bore and so absorbing that you may find yourself forgetting that it is silent.

37

ROAD WARRIOR

Trafic

JACQUES TATI'S PENULTIMATE, transcendent film *Trafic* (1971) is one of those often misperceived or neglected works by great filmmakers—others that come to mind are Leo McCarey's *Make Way for Tomorrow* (1937), John Ford's *7 Women* (1966), and John Huston's *The Kremlin Letter* (1970)—that deserve better than they got and will surely someday, however long it takes, gain their rightful stature. "Don't play what the public wants," Thelonious Monk famously advised, doubtlessly referring to critics as well as paying customers, "play what you want and let the public pick up on what you are doing—even if it does take them 15, 20 years." For Tati's film, thirty-seven years appeared to have done the trick as Criterion brought out, in 2008, a spiffy transfer that honors the fastidiously edited, razor-sharp photography by Frenchman Marcel Weiss and Dutchman Edward van den Enden.

The idea that *Trafic* is critically regarded as minor Tati is so widespread that even the otherwise illuminating DVD essay by Jonathan Romney retails its presumed failings: "a hovering tone of despair," the absence of "a clearly defined goal," "humor drawn out or diffuse to the point of near abstraction," and "[Tati] himself saw it as a step back after the accomplished vision of *Playtime*." Setting aside the probability that anything would have been anticlimactic after *Playtime*, the outsized 1967 comic marathon that bankrupted Tati and garnered little of the adulation heaped on his three earlier films—*Jour de fête* (1949), *Mr. Hulot's Holiday* (1953), and *Mon Oncle* (1958)—

this is an instance of critics paying more attention to what the director said than to what he put on the screen.

Trafic is a step to the side, not back. Its clearly defined tripartite structure is one of its key delights, along with an abundance of visual and aural gags, including a few of the best set pieces in Tati's small oeuvre (only six features, concluding with his circus quasi-documentary *Parade*, shot for Swedish television in 1974 and released theatrically a year later). Tati is said to have complained that he was forced to revive his most famous character, M. Hulot, as the only way of financing *Trafic*; if so, let us praise the commercial dictates that obliged him to give that sweetly elusive caricature of a man a satisfying and moving last act. We had seen Hulot on vacation, at home, and as an endlessly multiplying everyman. In *Trafic*, we see him at work and, just possibly, in love with a woman who, for most of the film, is his antipode.

At the end of *Trafic*, Hulot, fired from his job, walks arm in arm with the brazen Maria Kimberly (played by an American fashion model named Maria Kimberly), disappearing into the traffic of black umbrellas, as pedestrians maneuver around stalled cars. *Trafic* is a road picture that never gets where it's going. It follows Hulot's attempt to transport a camper he designed for the Altra Motor Company to an automobile show in Amsterdam. A series of breakdowns and diversions keep him and his staff spinning their wheels in Belgium until the auto show is over. But if cars get stuck, people have a way of moving forward. The picture's structure, however, works backward through Tati's movie career.

The first section of *Trafic* reflects the big-canvas style of *Playtime*, with gags steadily accruing in a frame that meshes foreground and background and favors visual pleasures over jokes, as in the stunning montage of Altra's assembly lines—a passage combining overhead shots, close-ups, and a symphony of industrial noises (buzzing, whistling, grinding gears) that recalls Joris Ivens's 1931 documentary *Philips Radio*. There is little dialogue in *Trafic*, and most of it is inconsequential, but every shot and sound effect has its reason. A casual remark about stringing measurement wires across the floor leads to a pullback in which workers high-step over them like the ponies Tati mimed in his music-hall years. When a tall Dutch executive exits his Citroën, the car settles down on its wheels, emitting a sigh of relief. A couple of tossed-off bits are redolent of Buster Keaton—one worker improvising desk drawers as a ladder, another painting a beam without moving his arm (he's on a cart rolled back and forth).

The main players make characteristic entrances. Hulot, late for work, angles his way stork-like into his office, where his attempts to draw a straight line are foiled by anyone who opens his door. Maria imperiously forces her way into every situation with the announcement "I am public relations!" Accompanied by her dog, Piton, Maria drives a tiny yellow sports car that is so small she stores one of her many hats in the spare tire compartment. Yet somehow it accommodates her vast wardrobe. She wears a different outfit in each scene, sometimes within different shots in the same scene. Another recurring gag concerns a gas station that offers customers a preposterous plaster bust of a historical figure. No one wants it, but everyone takes it—it's free.

In the second section, Tati returns to the extended comic set pieces that characterized his first two Hulot movies. These include, to the accompaniment of a radio ad pitching "a new raincoat specially for the sun," a highway montage in which the drivers, presuming themselves invisible behind the wheel, ponderously pick their noses. One nose picker is low humor and two are vulgar, but nine or ten, climaxing with two in the same shot, are golden. Amid shots of an auto graveyard is the sight of a car being towed over bumpy ground, emitting noises that sound like "Ow! Ooph! Ow! Ooph!" The most famous sequence in this section is the minute-long road accident, a benign pileup that finishes with a Volkswagen's hood flapping up and down like a giant tongue, followed by an inspired ballet of back-stretching and damage inspection, including a priest kneeling in obeisance to his motor while Hulot pirouettes through the rubble.

Yet this scene is preceded by an even more splendid twelve-minute tour de force in which Tati shows his loving assimilation of Mack Sennett: gags are offered in relentless profusion as Hulot and company are stopped at a Belgian border patrol. They are obliged to demonstrate the camper, a car that can shower and shave its occupant while barbecuing a steak. Among the cops are Fric and Frac doubles and an inspector whose raised hair is frozen in perfect imitation of Tintin. There are so many bits that you may easily miss one of the best: Hulot doffs his hat to a bride (also stopped at the border) while walking through a cloud of auto steam. When he doffs his hat again, the steam he scooped from the air the first time rises from his head.

The final sequence, set in the country, recalls the bucolic humor and tempo of Tati's first feature, *Jour de fête*, and makes generous use of the kind of gag associated with Harold Lloyd, in which what appears to be one thing turns out to be something else. In a fine two-part documentary, *Tati in the Footsteps of M. Hulot*, made in 1989 by his daughter Sophie Tatischeff and included in the Criterion release, Tati explains the difference between a visual gag that surprises the viewer, which he says is his own way of working, and one that announces its cleverness in a setup, as he says Chaplin preferred. For the defining gag in the finale of *Trafic*, he uses the latter method to trick Maria into thinking a shaggy coat is her dead dog. It's a cruel joke but funny, and has the unexpected effect of humanizing her; from that point on, her clothing is informal and constant. In the final not-what-you-think moment, Maria and Hulot wrestle over the coat, which to distant observers looks like ardent lovemaking—a metaphor for Jacques Tati's relationship with M. Hulot.

38

PRESTIGE AND PRETENSE
Pride and Prejudice

IT IS A TRUTH universally acknowledged that a movie studio in possession of a fortune must be in want of Great Books. In the studio era, the acquisition fulfilled the dual needs to borrow prestige and flaunt high Anglican taste: the first to help keep community watchdogs at bay, and the second to indulge the very pretensions that triggered Leo the Lion's roar—*ars gratia artis*. The moguls, especially at MGM, meant to entertain *and* improve minds—or at least wean them from actual books, which, great or not, kept potential customers at home.

Great Books, which for the most part were fat nineteenth-century, English language romances, offered other advantages: famous stories in the public domain; inspirational work for costumers, hairdressers, and set designers; good roles for English expats as villains. That said, the studios dipped into Western lit timidly. If MGM sought titles that emphasized the moral certainties of Carvel (Andy Hardy's hometown, not the custard stand), it was too intimidated to do as much violence to them as it did to contemporary novels, say *Babbitt* or even *Tortilla Flat*. As a result, MGM's best adaptations captured stylistic flavors that the more faithful television adaptations of our own time often ignore.

No better example exists than *Pride and Prejudice* (1940), one of five self-consciously exalted films made at MGM between 1934 and 1940 and collected by Warner Bros. as *Motion Picture Masterpieces*. (As Leo the Lion would say, "Aaaarghh!") This is one of those seriously flawed films that remain irresistible and, as subsequent adaptations prove, inimitable. Directed far too efficiently by Robert Z. Leonard, who made hundreds of silent films and almost as many talkies without creasing cinema consciousness, it was adapted partly from Helen Jerome's successful play by the odd couple Aldous Huxley and contract scenarist Jane Murfin, a veteran of the silent era. Does the film take liberties with Jane Austen? Let us count only a few of the ways. Louis B. Mayer demanded it be set half a century later so that he could use sumptuous in-house costumes; the Bennet girls seem to have moved to Meryton directly from Tara, though one of Lizzy's dresses, a shapeless tent with billowing sleeves and a black-patch top, would be unsuitable in any age. The cast is strangely mature—at thirty-one, Greer Garson isn't exactly budding, while Melville Cooper has nearly twenty years on Mr. Collins, whom he nonetheless incarnates to a T. These alterations are of little or no account. The rank sentimentalizing of Lady Catherine (Edna May Oliver, superb in her early scenes, compromised into cliché at the last) is more irksome, as is the sadly rushed ending, which betrays the first hour, though I don't mind that Mary is last seen flirting with a flutist.

Most of the plot changes are exigent—the need to dramatize information related in letters. But the omission of the Pemberley scene may be explained only by the insensible parsimony of producer Hunt Stromberg. It's not only the most dramatic chapter in the novel, with two unexpected encounters and the unveiling of an estate as the key to a man's soul, but also the most thoroughly cinematic, a rare instance in which Austen shows as much as she tells. Still, this film is more faithful to Austen than the dreary 2005 English version, which wasted its additional ten-minute running time on a credit roll and a pastoral opening, complete with bleating sheep—an obligatory element in *Masterpiece Theatre*–era adaptations. The later film's plot is closer to Austen, yet Pemberley is shot like a documentary museum tour, which suggests how limited mere plot can be when approaching a Great Book.

Austen is nothing if not acerbic and funny, her best dialogue a fountainhead for the kind of writing that would take wing a century later in the work of Wilde, Shaw, Huxley, and Coward, which may help to explain why she was so long in finding a devoted audience. (Elizabeth Bennet helpfully defines the Bush Doctrine when she asks, "Would Mr. Darcy then consider the rashness of your original intention as atoned for by your obstinacy in adhering to it?"—a line lost, alas, to the earlier film.) Austen raises characterization to an audacious pitch, almost to the level of Molière in the instance of Mr. Collins.

The 1940 film, where Austen's wit is augmented by Huxley's (including such signature japes as the Latinate medical analysis of Jane's cold), was one of the funniest chamber comedies of its day, and remains so today.

In contrast, there are few laughs and no wit in the 2005 version, where the actors giggle so derisively about each other they deprive the audience of the chance to do the same. Where Leonard's direction and the script's machinations suggest Austen's cool objectivity, the later version, directed by Joe Wright and scripted by Deborah Moggach, aimed for baleful realism, winding up with an accurately cast but dull Collins, a droopy-eyed Darcy (whose vaunted pride seems to stem from fatigue rather than class), and a Mr. Bennet whose final moment, as rendered by Donald Sutherland, laughing through tears, is Actor Studio kitsch.

The acting in 1940, including Garson's intelligent rectitude, indemnifies the film against time. Mary Boland and Edmund Gwenn as the Bennets, Maureen O'Sullivan as Jane, and surprise characterizations by Frieda Inescort as a thoroughly vicious Miss Bingley and Marsha Hunt as a comical Mary, support two ageless performances: Laurence Olivier as Darcy, underplaying as befits a character slow to show feeling but disclosing every thought anyway (the archery contest, more Robin Hood than Austen and predictable in its outcome, is a masterly comic example), and Melville Cooper's immortal Mr. Collins—tossing his tails before sitting, walking and genuflecting at odd angles, flattering with precise nasality, soaking up Lady Catherine's affability and condescension.

Of the other *Motion Picture Masterpieces*, George Cukor's *David Copperfield* (1935) remains a savory collection of impeccably cast grotesques—including Edna May Oliver, whose Betsy Trotwood has the integrity her Lady Catherine is denied. The big question raised by David, the finest memoirist in English, as to who will play the key role in his life, is unanswerable on film because his resounding centrality in the book is emphasized in his every generously observed sentence. Without David ordering events, he is merely an observer and victim of circumstances set in motion by fate and others. Cukor chose to emphasize those others at the expense of the novel's tragic soul, not to mention a good many subplots and characters. But he more than compensated with indelible types true to Dickens and to the 1930s studio repertory company. There's a reason many people don't recall who plays the grown David (Frank Lawton) or even little David (Freddie Bartholomew), but can never forget Basil Rathbone's vile Murdstone, Roland

Young's Heep of infamy, and W. C. Fields's Micawber, a miraculous transformation that shouldn't work but does, among others.

The remaining films in the set, though less successful, suggest a unity of time and place with the reappearance of the same actors, same fake sets, and same bathos and sacrificial goodness. Jack Conway's *A Tale of Two Cities* (1935) is a tale of two actors—Ronald Coleman and his unexplained melancholy (it can't be because he can't get a date), and Blanche Yurka and her inability to finish a simple coverlet despite her constant-speed-demon knitting. Coleman has the voice but Yurka has the eyes, as she leads thousands of extras to attack a matte painting. Victor Fleming's brisk if maudlin *Treasure Island* (1934) has moments, but not enough to counter Jackie Cooper's simpering and Wallace Beery's hamming.

Woody Van Dyke's *Marie Antoinette* (1938) is evidently included on a pass—though Warner might have sustained the package's literary conceit with such MGM films of the period as *The Adventures of Huckleberry Finn* (1939), *Ah, Wilderness* (1935), *Romeo and Juliet* (1936), and even *The Painted Veil* (1934) or *The Human Comedy* (1943). Still, *Marie Antoinette* looks literary, sounds middlebrow, and throws money around as only MGM's ancien régime could; too bad they didn't divert it to *Pride and Prejudice*. Norma Shearer was no more suitable as Marie than she was as Juliet, but no one had the nerve to suggest to Irving Thalberg's widow that she play their mothers. Happily, Joseph Schildkraut, John Barrymore, and an adenoidal Robert Morley are on hand to chew up that very expensive scenery.

39

AN UNHAPPY FILM IN
ITS OWN WAY

Anna Karenina

ALEKSANDR ZARKHI'S *Anna Karenina*, a 1967 Soviet film little seen in the West, exceeds expectations despite Kino's necessarily compromised transfer. For one thing, it is remarkably faithful to Tolstoy, yet dodges the mummification that results from miniseries literalness. Weighing in at a trim 145 minutes, this *Anna* canters gracefully, occasionally stopping for deluxe set pieces—the ball, the races, the opera, the train—that justify every pretty penny in its epic budget. While the novel is respectfully and often punctiliously transcribed, the film is scrupulously cinematic, elaborating on and adding to Tolstoy's symbols with an intricate color scheme and labyrinthine tracking shots devised by photographer Leonid Kalashnikov and production designers Aleksandr Borisov and Yuri Kladienko. The cast, which, if I correctly judge the accompanying interviews, was chosen counterintuitively, is superb, and in the many sequences when talk is supplanted by show, the audio slack is taken up by Rodion Shchedrin's chilling score, filtering nineteenth-century grandeur through twentieth-century dissonance.

Why is it that received wisdom regarding the great adulteresses of nineteenth-century fiction reduces Emma Bovary to a slatternly twit and ennobles Anna as a tragic victim? Tolstoy is ambivalent, or at least willing to consider all sides. According to the Internet Movie Database, Anna has been filmed twenty-six times between 1910 and 2007, but I doubt if there is a more nuanced portrayal than that of Tatiana Samojlova, often cited as the leading Russian actress of her generation, though she has appeared in few films and enjoyed only one international triumph, *The Cranes Are Flying*, in 1957. Samojlova's Anna is an aristocrat who loses her bearings in fits of love and cruelty, uncertain of what she wants beyond the slipping devotion of the lover for whom she sacrificed her son and her social standing. In the novel, she changes her mind about suicide in the second before she is crushed by a train. In the film, her fated destruction is consummated with mystical ambiguity. Her musings on love, its cost and validation, will remind filmgoers that Tolstoy's Anna served as a template for the eponymous heroine of Carl Dreyer's *Gertrud* (1964), who, by contrast, practically revels in social exile.

No less startling is Nikolai Gritsenko's Karenin. He alters the film's tempo with his every appearance, signaled by the hollow click-clacking of his shoes on parquet floors. Shoulders slightly hunched, Karenin haunts his own home like Nosferatu, his uncanny voice a petulant wail as cold and sickly as a clammy hand. His oblivious blathering at the racetrack is as oppressive as his unmoving stare in the carriage ride when Anna declares her infidelity and contempt for him. His attempts to invite pity fail miserably, as he seems incapable of pitying himself.

The story line centers, as ever, on the triangle of Anna, Karenin, and Vronsky (Vasili Lanovoy, by turns dashing, callow, and sadistic), but the parallel plots, which are often minimized or dropped from adaptations, also figure in the mosaic, making for telling edits as the story cuts from one plane to another. These concern Tolstoy's philosophical stand-in Levin (Boris Goldayev) and his devotion to his peasants and the fittingly named Kitty (Anastasiya Vertinskaya); and Anna's brother, Stiva (an honest cad, played in a shrewdly comic turn by Yuri Yakovlev), and his accepting Dolly (Iya Savvina). Although simplifications were mandated (Anna's daughter dies, once again, at birth; she thrives only in the novel), many of Tolstoy's eccentric characters are retained—including Princess Betty (willowy malice in a bird-of-paradise hat, as incarnated by ballerina Maya Plisetskaya), as well as the fly-catching lawyer, the dithering occultist, and the grotesque gossips peering through lorgnettes.

The script (by Vasili Katanyan and Zarkhi) is not without ellipses. The writers don't have much to go on in launching the Anna-Vronsky infatuation, the arbitrary nature of which is part of the point. But the absence of genuine interaction between Anna and her son until late in the film, when she sneaks home, undermines the development of her maternal desperation. The import of one of the most striking visual sequences—threshers at twilight, Levin among them, their scythes clinking like crickets as the sun recedes from the field, followed by the farmers, singing in unison—is obscure: Levin hasn't been sufficiently developed at that point.

The virtuoso peak, apparently the work of Kalashnikov, is the horse race, where swirling cameras (reprised at the film's climax), plunging angles, and fractured editing unify Anna and Frou-Frou, Vronsky's doomed horse—the casualty of a contest filmed with the teeming elation of an action block-buster. By contrast, Anna's finish is played as a claustrophobic dissent into shadows and alleys so constricted that only Samojlova and Kalashnikov's handheld camera could fit into the space where it was shot. From the first scene, in Stiva's home, the architectural warrens of massive homes are explored with tracking shots, sometimes comic, more often ominous. The showdown between Karenin and Anna is preceded by his deliberate march-ing through no less than ten rooms, one entrance after another, all in one momentous shot—a tiny but impressive harbinger of Aleksandr Sokurov's ninety-five-minute single take *Russian Arc* (2002). When Anna suggests keep-ing her son only until Vronsky's child is born, Karenin unleashes a blood-curdling "Nyet."

The film's bold use of color to telegraph emotion and delineate charac-ter inadvertently emphasizes the trouble with Kino's print. The colors lack stability, especially in part two. As the print was made available through the Russian Cinema Council, it probably represents the best there is in the absence of a full-scale restoration. Still, the shimmering lights and encroach-ing shadows do not dilute the power of the color design, fascinating through-out. The key hues are red—representing vitality, love, sex, and hope—and green, signaling impotence and hatred. In key scenes, the screen is split, so that Anna is suffused in red and Karenin in pale-green light, the shade of the wallpaper. There is a moment in the confinement scene when Karenin walks over to Vronsky, yet the color distinction abides, separating them in a way that seems at once natural and audacious.

More problematic is the sound, or the way Kino configured it. The menus require you to choose language (the English dubbing is amateur-ish) and subtitles, but the disc does not allow you to toggle between them. As the default English option has more audio presence than the Russian mono, it would be nice to switch during scenes dominated by Shchedrin's music. A second disc is filled with extras, including interviews with cast members and Kalashnikov. A section on Tolstoy includes several minutes of him strolling through winter and summer fields, arriving in Moscow, and lying on his deathbed. There is also a short documentary that emphasizes the political-philosophical import of his later work. The filmographies are rendered almost unreadable by tiny cursive print, but they contain trailers for celebrated Soviet films of the 1950s, and a splendid ten-minute lecture-demonstration on dance by Maya Plisetskaya, who is shown in an excerpt from her 1957 *Swan Lake*. In all, an illuminating package, and the most resourceful, contemplative *Anna Karenina* we are likely to see.

40

CLASSICS AND SEMI-CLASSICS ILLUSTRATED

Literary Classics Collection

FEW GREAT HOLLYWOOD MOVIES are based on genuine literary classics, while a great many are based on hackwork. If a book offers a cracking story but little ingenuity in sentence making, a first-rate picture can, as aborigines rightly suspected of cameras, steal its soul. A thousand adaptations of *Madame Bovary* leave Flaubert's novel unscathed. One excellent rendition of *The Prisoner of Zenda* renders Anthony Hope's briskly readable "classic" unread. Emma Bovary and Rudolf Rassendyll are among the prisoners of Warner Bros.' *Literary Classics Collection*, a mostly winning compilation of six films made between 1937 and 1962, with a bias toward swashbuckling. Four of them—two versions of *Zenda*, *The Three Musketeers*, and *Captain Horatio Hornblower*—revel in swordfights, while *Madame Bovary* longs for one and *Billy Budd* cowers in fear of them. No publisher would box these same novels as "Literary Classics," yet they seem less disparate as movies, perhaps because the berth between Hope and Melville is narrowed by comparably gifted actors like Ronald Coleman and Robert Ryan and photographers like James Wong Howe and Robert Krasker.

The two versions of *Zenda* bookend the five entries from the golden era of the studios and provide an exercise in contrasting styles in cinematography and acting. The 1952 Technicolor version uses the same treatment and script as the 1937 black and white film, with marginal tinkering in the dialogue. A literature major might even observe that the DVD operates as an objective correlative to the plot—a doppelganger disc about doppelgangers.

Unlike Gus Van Sant's remake of *Psycho*, however, the director of the 1952 *Zenda*, Richard Thorpe, framed his own shots: in practically every instance, they and the lighting effects are inferior to those created by director John Cromwell and James Wong Howe fifteen years earlier. The color print, though, is in better shape than its scratched predecessor.

The 1952 cast is also inferior. Stewart Granger, as Rudolf, does a creditable job and is built like a leading man, but the shorter, older Coleman has the timbre and timing of one. Deborah Kerr is a deeper actor than Madeleine Carroll, but Carroll is a princess born to the manner. Most intriguing are the two Ruperts. In the 1952 film, James Mason plays the dastardly villain who escapes punishment (out of a misguided fidelity to the novel: Hope saved him for a sequel), with his hair plastered and baritone dripping with supercilious contempt. Yet it is a conventional performance compared with that of Douglas Fairbanks Jr., often regarded as a dilettante actor, who steals the 1937 film with a curly-headed perm and a complex interpretation riddled with cynical laughter, personifying Hope's description of Rupert: "reckless and wary, graceful and graceless, handsome, debonair, vile, and unconquered." Both versions feature Alfred Newman's rousing score, and each film on its own is probably foolproof—it's *Richard III* with Clarence winning the day—but only the earlier version has the lapidary polish of a studio jewel and the casting bonus of vaudevillian Al Shean as the court conductor.

The bright idea behind George Sidney's *The Three Musketeers* (1948) was for Gene Kelly to choreograph the swordfights as dances, inadvertently prefiguring the martial arts genre. The duels are definite high points. Yet credit must also be given editors George Boemler and Robert J. Kern and stunt doubles Russell Saunders and David Sharpe, who contrive to disguise the fact that Kelly's contribution to many action scenes consists of inserts and the safer physical exertions. Kelly's line readings and forced hilarity are unfortunate—a trial run for *Singin' in the Rain*, where they were more appropriate. Hollywood is so adept at turning drama into kitsch that when confronted with great kitsch, it usually resorts to parody. Still, the film is as visually bountiful as Lana Turner in her green plumes. Lana has a few delirious moments chortling with Vincent Price, whose Richelieu pimps her out to D'Artagnan. If you're wondering how they got that past the censors, consider D'Artagnan's riposte to a remark made by Van Heflin's affecting Athos: "Then tell it to the wind of your own making!"

Vincente Minnelli's *Madame Bovary* (1949) is one of those bitter pills you have to swallow to indulge bits and pieces of prime studio craftsmanship. The story is inanely framed by the trial of Flaubert (James Mason, poorly used), who narrates the story from a witness chair, couching it in affected ostentatious reveries of such palpitating banality ("What are dreams made of? Where do they come from?") that he seems to be arguing that evil romantic novels created Emma and that he, Flaubert, functioned as little more than a secretary taking notes. Matters aren't helped by Emma's grand entrance: Jennifer Jones liveried as Betty Crocker, serving breakfast to Van Heflin's understandably befuddled Charles. After twenty minutes or so, the film periodically comes alive as Minnelli dotes on Emma's quandary, aided by Jack Martin Smith's art direction—focused around mirrors that, as in "Snow White," pitilessly reveal all—and lustrous black and white photography by Robert Plank. Visual conceits, from the eight-minute ball sequence (minimal dialogue, an aggressively mobile camera, and a climactic, vertiginous waltz) to the few seconds of the approaching hirondelle on the night Emma is betrayed by Rodolphe, realize the novel's palette of sensual detail. It's remarkable how much feeling Minnelli derives despite the demeaning narration and facilitations: Charles is too noble to operate on Hyppolite, Homais is portrayed as a village idiot, Lheureux relieved of his obsequiousness is a stock scoundrel (despite a powerful performance by Frank Allenby), and everyone is morally neutered. Flaubert was acquitted of corrupting France, but the Production Code convicted Minnelli's film before his cameras rolled. Its virtues are mainly decorative.

The final two films take place during the Napoleonic wars; other than that, they are as different as Gregory Peck and Peter Ustinov. Raoul Walsh's handsomely mounted *Captain Horatio Hornblower* (1950) begins in the doldrums (literally), but soon takes on the vigor of a sea-dog romance as the paternal captain harrumphs his way around Virginia Mayo and outfights a passel of Latin Americans who are either insane or ugly or both—they are brownface minstrels, and evidence of how quickly America's Good Neighbor Policy faded. The plot is serviceable if shameless. As soon as Peck meets Mayo, you know his wife will have to drop dead and her husband die in battle. And so they do.

Ustinov's *Billy Budd* (1962) is the most compulsively watchable film of the lot, though on a fundamental level it is the least cinematic. Based on a dramatization rather than the Melville story, it feels at times like a photographed stage play. That it works even so is a tribute to Ustinov and Robert Krasker, who insisted on shooting exteriors on a ship, creating deft images and the slight roll of becalmed waters (by contrast, the ship in *Hornblower* is as steady as a highway); an intelligent adaptation by Ustinov and DeWitt Bodeen of a Louis Coxe and Robert Chapman play; and stunning performances by Ustinov as Vere, Terence Stamp as Billy, and Robert Ryan as Claggart.

Stamp, making his movie debut, combines unearthly beauty with a gift for line readings that sound entirely unpremeditated. But the great Ryan—dark, coiled, implacable—makes this film something to watch and watch again, his every close-up defying a single interpretation and consequently justifying Billy's misreading. True, the script simplifies Melville's ethical concerns: it invents another victim, ignores Billy's silence about a potential mutiny, and, most annoyingly, concludes with patriotic zeal. Yet in Ryan and Stamp (whose commentary track is the set's best extra, along with Tex Avery cartoons, relevant radio broadcasts, and a travelog about postwar Britain), the film illuminates Melville's tale of horror and pitiless moral purview: "Struck dead by an angel of God! Yet the angel must hang!"

41

A ROSETTA STONE FOR THE 1950s

Ben-Hur / The Man Who Fell to Earth / Bad Timing

WILLIAM WYLER'S *Ben-Hur* (1959) and Nicolas Roeg's *The Man Who Fell to Earth* (1976) are oddly companionable. Both are based on novels that track the travails of fish out of water, strangers in strange lands, messiahs, aliens treated badly by the natives but triumphant in the long run. Both are protracted, self-important, and fatiguing, yet remain in their best moments visually and aurally sumptuous. These films now have something else in common: they are redeemed as exemplary DVDs, which fail to make them better movies but do amplify their finer points. This isn't just a matter of the tails—documentaries, interviews, commentaries—wagging the dogs, which have never been more brightly spruced. DVDs encourage and demand skill at fast-forwarding; they prompt you to watch episodic films episodically. Watching *Ben-Hur* all at once is like sitting down to a ten-course meal and finding that every course consists of potato dumplings except for the seventh, which is strawberry shortcake. That would be the chariot race. Segmented viewings of *The Man Who Fell to Earth* counter its stubborn lack of dramatic thrust. The profuse extras reconstruct the deconstructed films so that the viewer, who may once have dismissed them as kitsch, can now participate in the business of creating kitsch.

The DVD producers indicate what they would like us to make of these time capsules by the selection of annotations. The talking heads—a cast of thousands—assembled to praise *Ben-Hur* speak almost exclusively about the making of the film; Roeg and his collaborators are concerned almost as exclusively with themes, characters, and ideas. They've got it reversed. *The Man Who Fell to Earth*, attempting to mean everything, means nothing, but glimmers with superb camera work, dazzling editing, bravura performances, and the annihilation of chronological time—a Roeg specialty, more effectively employed in his slightly more realistic follow-up, *Bad Timing* (1980). *Ben-Hur*, for all its logistic marvels, works as a useful roadmap to the evasions of the 1950s. It is a landmark, a Rosetta stone, marking the beginning of the end of Hollywood piety and a doting farewell to nineteenth-century melodrama.

Criterion's recent DVD of *Boudou Saved from Drowning* (1932) includes an old television interview with its director, Jean Renoir, offering a quaint moment of illumination. Renoir is explaining that he used a certain lens to bring Paris locations into the story, yet he apologizes two or three times for bringing up a vulgar detail of technique. Technique, after all, is his problem, not that of the viewer, whose sole concern ought to be characters and narrative. Now we are all authorities on computer effects, matte paintings, divisions of labor, and every other aspect of what goes on behind the scenes. The storyteller has been usurped by the manner of his telling. *Ben-Hur*, though praised in terms that might make anyone feel like an alien ("the thinking man's epic," "one of the ten best films of all time," "profound dialogue"), is in fact venerated for its colossal accumulation of backstage anecdotes and its influence on twenty-first-century films that, even in the realm of cinematic refuse, occupy a lower order: *Gladiator*, *Revenge of the Psith*, *War of the Worlds*.

Sometimes the gossip and films correct each other. Much is made of Wyler's decision to shoot Jesus only from the rear, but the DVD's inclusion of Fred Niblo's superior, shorter, more faithful, and silent 1925 film reveals that he went Wyler several limbs better, showing only Jesus's arm. Niblo even positioned an enormous kneeling extra to hide Jesus's face at the Last Supper. Gore Vidal's claims of authorship are similarly undermined. He insists that *Ben-Hur* is trash on which he was forced to labor (while lamenting his lack of credit), that he wrote several drafts of the initial scene between Ben-Hur and Messala and scripted everything before the chariot race, at which point Christopher Fry came aboard. He boasts that Wyler wanted him and Fry to share the credit that went instead to the original writer, "one Karl Tunberg." Yet the hapless early screen tests (with Leslie Nielsen as Messala) show that scenes Vidal claims as his were 80 percent

written years before he was hired. Wyler and Heston credit Fry (the director fought unsuccessfully to get him an unshared credit) without even mentioning Vidal.

The 1959 film is less a tale of the Christ than a spectacle cleverly navi-
gating the political minefields of the day. Its themes include the threatened
extinction of the Jews, the value of passive resistance, the evils of informing,
and Jewish-Arab solidarity. Hollywood liberalism meets Christian conser-
vatism without rustling anyone's feathers, an achievement more awesome
than racing chariots, battling pirates, or vanishing leprosy. Messala might as
well be lecturing Marlon Brando in *On the Waterfront* when he says, "Telling
the names of criminals is hardly informing," except that Messala is evil and
Ben-Hur (the hyphen, incidentally, was added by MGM in 1925, apparently
fearful that people might think the hero's full name was Benjamin) doesn't
buy it. All these themes are in Lew Wallace's unreadable novel, but were
tweaked for modern customers, as was Ben-Hur's refusal to join the Jews for
Jesus movement. He's grateful that his family no longer has leprosy, but we
leave him kissing his mezuzah. Also absent is any hint of debauchery—gone
are the topless petal-strewing gals of the 1925 film, gone is the treacherous
Iras, who kills Messala in the novel and vamps mightily in the silent film.
Instead, we have chasteness and violence, a lesson not lost on Mel Gibson.

The shooting star that announces the Savior's birth in *Ben-Hur* prefigures
the hurtling vehicle that brings David Bowie to ground in *The Man Who Fell
to Earth*. The films also share an emphasis on water and thirst. (Hemingway
lovers may be reminded of another fish-out-of-water tale, "Wine in Wyo-
ming," about a French vintner who attempts to ply his trade in Prohibition
America.) While Ben-Hur is undeterred from his mission by a love of horses
and vengeance, Bowie's Thomas Newton is sidelined by affection for gin,
sex, and television. Reading into Newton's appetites an indictment of modern values is like reading into *Ben-Hur* a parable of sacred devotion. The
themes are vast, general, and elastic, adding up to a justification for filmmaking zeal. "America is so beautiful," Newton observes, and the New Mexican
desert shot by Roeg fits the bill. The film also sounds good, with a score that
includes Louis Armstrong, Bing Crosby, and, in a climactic burst of inspiration, Artie Shaw's "Star Dust"—the power of the latter compensating for
the diminishing of power as the script hurtles into a no-man's-land of the
inexplicable. Oddly enough, the film is devoid of drugs and 1970s rock, but
as a warning against demon gin, Carry Nation could not have said it better.

Roeg, as always, piles on the symbols and the sex—so scrupulously that as Candy Clark's character ages, her midsection and pubic hair are made-up to reflect the change in life. As for the symbols, we learn from an interview with screenwriter Paul Mayersberg that the mysterious figure who watches Newton fall is supposed to represent the author of the piece, which could mean Roeg or novelist Walter Tevis. Has anyone else ever come to that conclusion? And has anyone ever recognized Newton's gazing on a dock as homage to Gatsby, who he in no way resembles? Noting that the critics thought the film made Clark's character out to be antifeminist, Mayersberg says, "She's living with an alien, for Christ's sake. That beats most women's lives, doesn't it?" Roeg and his writers, here and in *Bad Timing*, toss in poems, paintings, names, book jackets, photos, and anything else that might amplify one theme or another, while ignoring characterization and plot. Why doesn't Newton take off in his rocket? Why is his lawyer thrown out a window? Who are the bad guys? Why are we watching excerpts from *Love in the Afternoon* and *Billy Budd*? Don't ask, and they won't tell.

The coherent, shorter, and more effective *Bad Timing* is hoisted on the petard of Art Garfunkel's lax posing (one wouldn't call it acting), especially in concert with an overwhelmingly inventive, nubile Theresa Russell, who should have gone on to greater things than increasingly recondite Nick Roeg films. But here, too, there are scenes that compel giggling: the staging of the final fornication, the troubled detective who is supposed to serve as a—take a deep breath—doppelganger. The extras, among them interviews with Russell and Roeg, help but aren't necessary. *The Man Who Fell to Earth* is unusual among DVDs in its determination to make a case for the source material as well as the film. The package includes Tevis's 160-page novel plus an audio interview with the novelist (who never mentions the movie), and behold: the rational, dramatic book has the qualities the film lacks but none of its virtues—the explosions of sight, sound, and emotion beyond the writer's ken. The two add up to a more effective work than either one alone.

42

JOHN HUSTON'S NOVEL APPROACH

Under the Volcano

IT IS AN axiom of cinema: second-rate and worse books tend to make the best movies. Immortalized in auteurist filmographies are the likes of Ethel Lina White (*The Lady Vanishes*), Alan Le May (*The Searchers*), and Mario Puzo (*The Godfather*), whereas Willa Cather, William Faulkner, and Eudora Welty have not fared well at the multiplex. Still, personal and even visionary films adapted from slavishly admired literary works do exist, and John Huston made an impressive number of them, probably more than any other director. Nearly half of Huston's thirty-nine feature films, not counting his wartime documentaries (good as they are) or his acknowledged and unacknowledged collaborations (bad as they are), are based on significant literary works—novels, plays, stories. Only four (*The Bible*, *Moby Dick*, *The Red Badge of Courage*, and *The Man Who Would Be King*) predate the twentieth century, which is copiously scrutinized in the others.

Some of these films have supplanted source material that was once highly regarded (*The African Queen*, *Key Largo*); others helped to establish or raise the stature of their sources (*Treasure of the Sierra Madre*, *Fat City*). Huston's best films, beginning with his first (*The Maltese Falcon*, 1941), survive on a parallel plane to that of the originals, all reflective of Huston's craggy sensibility, which, essentially agnostic and existential, is predicated on a conviction that heaven and hell exist not in the clouds or along the Styx but in what we make of the world. It prizes moral courage over physical derring-do, while sneering at moral certainty. Kafka wrote that the victorious man inflicts more damage on the world than the world inflicts on him. This is a speculative notion but one that Huston, the most concretely centered of storytellers, illuminated time and again. Few of his heroes get to taste victory, but they die trying.

Criterion has now released one of his most neglected, nitpicked, and misunderstood films, *Under the Volcano* (1984), in a two-disc DVD that does justice to Gabrielle Figueroa's brightly sinister photography. A thoughtful gathering of commentaries, documentaries, and interviews reconsiders the film and its relationship to Malcolm Lowry's novel. Just in time: in a year, 2007, that saw much ado about the fiftieth anniversary of Jack Kerouac's *On the Road*, nary a toast was raised to commemorate the fiftieth anniversary of Lowry's death or the sixtieth of his masterpiece, itself a road trip fueled by stimulants and religious delirium. In fact, Lowry's novel, which is set in Mexico and recounts the last day (the Day of the Dead, 1938) of a consul named Geoffrey Firmin, consists mostly of hallucinations, flashbacks, allusions, metaphors, symbols, and signs—printed signs, including a movie poster.

Huston, working with a daringly efficient script by Guy Gallo, tossed almost all of that by the wayside. He retained a few symbols, including a sickly green poster of Peter Lorre in *The Hands of Orlac* (*Mad Love*), peering over the consul's shoulder in the grim Farolito whorehouse, and even added one of his own: a carnival reenactment of Don Juan in hell. But for the most part, the director and Gallo drew a scalpel down the novel's body, extracted key plot elements, and arranged them chronologically, ruthlessly discarding one of the four central characters (M. Laruelle) and hundreds of pages of background material (including, alas, the references to Joe Venuti and 1920s jazz), retaining only the consul's wartime disgrace and his wife's adulterous fling with his half-brother Hugh.

The remarkable thing is that Huston managed to construct a moving, plausible, and faithful interpretation of Lowry's vision in the absence of his prose (which the novelist once described as "flowery and often glowery") and the intricacy of his method. Immeasurably aided by Albert Finney's devouring performance as Firmin, which remains one of the most involving and comprehensive depictions of alcoholism or addiction ever brought to the screen, Huston's *Under the Volcano* is ultimately worthy of the consul, even if in other respects it is a diminishment of the novel. The clarity of Huston's direction and the confidence of the film's tempo, buoyed by a colorful supporting cast, fastidious art direction, and a crafty Alex North score, belie the small budget.

In an audio interview included on the DVD, Huston makes clear his ambivalence about the book. He disapproves of literary froufrou. He accuses Lowry of hiding behind showiness, which he insists ultimately undermines the work's effectiveness. He is mistaken, but his error is hard won. In reducing *Under the Volcano* to the plight of Geoffrey Firmin, Huston reveals that touching protectiveness toward his heroes that characterizes his most durable work. Gallo's script factors in the political treachery of the time by introducing a Nazi bureaucrat but undermines the personal treachery by cutting out one of Yvonne Firmin's adulteries, granting her a surprising, saintly forbearance (nicely captured in Jacqueline Bisset's delicate performance). Yet Gallo and the picture's three producers, in their commentary tracks, express ambivalence about the degree to which Huston fixated on Firmin.

Huston's literary films, especially those in the magical last act of his career, between 1972 (*Fat City*) and 1986 (*The Dead*), are partly defined by critical adjustments to the original works. Huston never merely transposed a story from one medium to another. His thematic consistency—often conveyed in dark, willful humor—allowed him to pay homage to the stories while making them over. *The Man Who Would Be King* (1976), perhaps his masterpiece, is more resourceful, weird, and hilarious than Kipling. *Wise Blood* (1979), though largely faithful to Flannery O'Connor's short novel, makes vital changes that define the difference between the writer's Catholic vigor and the director's agnostic humanism. He boldly transformed Joyce's *The Dead* from a work of estrangement to an elegy.

Much of the strength in *Under the Volcano* stems from Huston's recognition that Firmin's alcoholism has a courageous facet. It represents a way of staying alive in an insane, toppling world. Firmin achieves clarity in mescal drunkenness, even though it requires his denunciation of a submissive diplomacy (he has renounced his consulship) and of Yvonne's love, which he concedes is the only thing that makes life worth living. Yet in choosing hell, represented by the Farolito ("the paradise of his despair" in the novel), Geoffrey is permitted a moment of grace—a heroic last stand as, impotently swinging a machete, he denounces the murderers and thieves who have hijacked Mexico. His rage and "dingy" death are his deliverance. They are also Yvonne's death sentence, something she predicted in one of her letters, unread by Geoffrey until he discovers them in the Farolito: "If you let anything happen to yourself, you will be harming my flesh and mind." Lowry transposed their deaths, introducing Yvonne's mishap before Geoffrey's murder, but Huston made a better choice, connecting the dots as Geoffrey's defiance liberates the white horse that runs down Yvonne, allowing the possibility (which Bisset, in her DVD interview, acknowledges was an aspect of her interpretation) that Yvonne may exist only in Geoffrey's mind.

Huston was in top form staging their first scene together, as Geoffrey, pontificating in a cantina, thinks at first that Yvonne must be a mirage and shrugs her off. He retained throughout the humor that resonates in the novel (especially the hapless comings and goings of the transcendent fifth chapter). But he was most stimulated in the film's final thirty-five minutes— more than a quarter of the picture, drawn from the nightmarish closing chapter, staged in the Farolito. His thrilling control of the material echoes Lowry's strategic achievement: to make the reader return from last page to first (indeed, the first chapter, recounted a year after Firmin's death by M. Laruelle, is unintelligible until the rest of the novel has been digested). Huston's *Under the Volcano* similarly closes a circle, inclining the viewer to reexamine the film, beginning with the daring opening scene, a long, silent, stumbling and otherwise behaviorally revealing walk through the morning festivities by the consul, armored in dark glasses and incongruous tuxedo. Huston insisted that the Farolito whores be played by genuine Mexican prostitutes, and their authenticity evidently inspired him, because, shot for shot, it is one of the most riveting, wrenching sequences in his canon, insolent and cold and agonizing.

43

LIGHTS! CAMERA! TALK!
Tennessee Williams

PERVERSITY LOOMS OVER the very idea of the *Tennessee Williams Film Collection*—and not the perversity of the playwright who locates poetry, nostalgia, and the weight of the world in the hearts of gigolos and the fading actresses who keep them in Brylcreem. When a Hollywood studio packages, in the guise of homage, adaptations that are notorious for disemboweling the honored works, I hear their author rolling over and haplessly sighing, in the manner of *Night of the Iguana*'s Reverend Shannon, "Fantastic." It's surprising, then, to find so much pleasure in a collection that helps to define its time if not one of its most vaunted writers. As an anthology of extravagant emoting, it's hard to beat.

Williams may be destined for immortality, but the Age of Tennessee is long gone. From 1945 (*The Glass Menagerie*) to 1961 (*Night of the Iguana*), he was the very soul of Broadway; as the theatrical magic waned, he peaked in Hollywood with the release of seven wildly uneven films between 1958 and 1962. The franchise was finally detonated in 1968 by a rank adaptation of *The Milk Train Doesn't Stop Here Anymore*, fittingly retitled *Boom*. The eight-disc Warner Bros. collection includes a 1973 Canadian television documentary (*Tennessee Williams' South*) and six films—fewer than half the number turned out in the 1950s and 1960s.

In the absence of sensationalism, talk is talk. We can only marvel at how much talk movie audiences were ready to digest in the late 1950s, when the talkers were physically attractive, happy endings were guaranteed, and everything that wasn't fit for television was controversial. Williams gave equal time to mastication and masturbation, to psychoanalysis and cannibalism. Few plays in his canon are bereft of someone who buys or sells companionship. Yet his talk requires virtuoso assurance, which to Hollywood meant going English or importing from Broadway, even as the talk was adjusted downward for audiences west of the Hudson River.

Although critics were riled by the censorship imposed on each movie, Williams has enjoyed no cinematic revival in the years since censorship abated. In one case, *Sweet Bird of Youth* (1962), censorship partly improved on the original, turning an unbelievable denouement into acceptable melodrama. In another, *Baby Doll* (1956), the absence of censorship (until it was too late, though Cardinal Spellman's ranting did frighten Warner Bros. into yanking the film from theaters) seems remarkable. Elia Kazan directed *Baby Doll*—an original Williams screenplay based on characters introduced in his one-act *27 Wagons Full of Cotton* (subtitled a "Mississippi Delta Comedy")—on location with an improvisational enthusiasm that suited its inspired cast. More than a comedy, *Baby Doll* displays Williams and Kazan letting loose and having fun, a feeling their work rarely indulges. Yet 1950s audiences drowned out the laughs with heavy breathing. Carroll Baker's thumbsucking virgin in a crib, and the shaggy cuckold joke played around her, smacked of pederasty at a time when the word "virgin" had only recently found its way into a Hollywood movie. A genuinely witty performance was lost in the lust, even as Baker's Baby Doll defended her intellect: "I've been to school in my life. *And* I'm a magazine reader."

Karl Malden, hilarious with and without dialogue (he moves like an addled rooster), exercises an unexploited comedic gift as Baby Doll's arsonist husband; Eli Wallach, making his film debut, oozes revenge and fake seduction, a twinkling light in each of his otherwise obsidian eyes. Mildred Dunnock's dotty old maid inserts third-act pathos, justified only by her skill. The film is long: too much sneaking in and out of doorways, too much enraged husband with a rifle. Still, Kazan's nimble camera, Boris Kaufman's photography, and the actors, especially the luminescent Baker, carry the day. One privileged moment has no talk at all—just the Malden and Wallach characters staring at each other and scratching their heads on a staircase.

Kazan also directed *A Streetcar Named Desire* (1951), which, despite the deletion of a key line from the play ("We've had this date with each other from the beginning"), is an indelible film. The restored, crisply digitalized transfer captures Marlon Brando and Vivien Leigh at their peak, and demonstrates how much movement can be generated in stagy settings. This edition includes a feature-length documentary about Kazan, an appreciation of composer Alex North, outtakes, and a 1940s Brando screen test—a splendid package.

The splendor is mitigated in the other films, though the only downright unwatchable entry is *The Roman Spring of Mrs. Stone* (1961). Based on Williams's one novel, it is more static than the plays—inserted shots of the Spanish Steps do nothing to alleviate José Quintero's stodgy direction or a script that teases self-parody (loneliness "is one of the great mysteries of the human heart"). Vivien Leigh muses that "beautiful people make their own laws," but her commitment to the role isn't enough to make it credible, especially given the deadly earnestness of an embarrassingly miscast Warren Beatty (Leigh, it has been said, refused the more appropriate Alain Delon because he was prettier than she) as her Italian gigolo with two Italian words, "ciao" and "prego," and a high-pitched accent that veers between Bela Lugosi and Topo Gigio. That leaves Lotte Lenya, as the bloodsucking pimp in a red boudoir, the chance to steal the film in a warm-up for her more convincing turn a year later pursuing James Bond in *From Russia with Love*.

Richard Brooks directed *Cat on a Hot Tin Roof* (1958) and *Sweet Bird of Youth*, and deserves credit for keeping the former moving even though it isn't moving toward anything worth reaching. For all the blather about mendacity, the film is about why Paul Newman won't sleep with Elizabeth Taylor, and no answer is provided. He must be really angry to resist those engulfing arms and all they are attached to. The play locates the problem in homosexuality and adultery; in the movie, adultery is just a whim and homosexuality not even that. Taylor is riveting, in her snugly tailored slip; even so, it's easy to imagine how much more provocative Barbara Bel Geddes must have been onstage, with her meowing voice and pouting virtue. Newman works hard with his sabotaged part, though he occasionally forgets how much pain he's supposed to be in. Best are the heavies: Burl Ives as tyrannical Big Daddy and Madeleine Sherwood as a screamingly obnoxious Sister Woman. *Cat* merits credit as an exceedingly rare postwar film that despises children on principle, as though they were all bad seeds.

Sweet Bird of Youth, on the other hand, benefits from the bowdlerization of a bad play, with characters named Chance, Heavenly, Alexandra Del

Lago, and Fly ("just like the fly, sir"), and a finish in which the gigolo hero waits to be castrated while asking the audience "just for your recognition of me in you, and the enemy, time, in us all." Sorry, Chance, if someone threatens castration, flight first, poetry later. By leaving Chance (Newman recreating his stage role) with merely a broken nose *and* his girl, Brooks salvages most of the good dialogue and crafts a more satisfying curtain than Williams's strenuous masochism. Indeed, *Sweet Bird* almost has the heart of a good B feature. If only the director hadn't fleshed it out with cornball split-screen flashbacks scored to the swelling strings of "Ebb Tide"—among them, actress Del Lago's Norma Desmond close-up, which sent her fleeing from Hollywood. Yet Brooks improves on the original by adding one scene, merely described in the play, involving Boss Finley (Ed Begley), Miss Lucy (the reliable Sherwood), and an Easter egg, chiefly because Begley revs up the film every time he appears. Chosen by God to be governor and baring a smile that could curdle milk, he demands repudiation—and Brooks almost gives it to him, as Mildred Dunnock, playing yet another dotty old maid, departs from Tennessee diction to tell him to go to hell. Geraldine Page plays an abbreviated version of the role she created (a screen test, included on the DVD, offers a powerful taste of her stage interpretation), but her climactic phone call is intact and, yes, worth the price of admission.

Williams's final Broadway-to-Hollywood success, *Night of the Iguana*, renders unto Tennessee his due while rendering almost as much to the movie gods. As directed by John Huston, the first twenty-seven minutes are terrific—all back story and built for speed. Instead of intrusive flashbacks, Huston uses the preliminary plot points as an excuse for cinematic vim centered on three great performances: Richard Burton as Reverend Shannon, perhaps the most compelling work of his film career; Grayson Hall as the group leader of the vacationing biddies chaperoned by Burton; and Sue Lyon, who was always better than expected in her abbreviated teenage career. This much is played as comedy, albeit of a cruel sort. But then the play kicks in and the talk is relentless, often handily delivered by aging Ava Gardner as the sexually avaricious Maxine and porcelain-skinned Deborah Kerr as an unlikely forty-year-old virgin. The film improves on the play by updating its original 1940 setting, losing its Nazi family, and smartly illustrating the sermon that cost Shannon his church. But then it has to go and add a silly riposte to the Grayson Hall character (in the play, Shannon calls her a dyke and she slaps him; in the film, she doesn't know what a dyke is and he's too compassionate to explain), and an aberrant attempt at martyrdom by Maxine, who is obliged to utter such expletives as "Jehoshaphat!" and "Just a flipping minute!" In the real world, Huston would soon enter a few years in the wilderness, emerging with several of his best films; Burton would never reclaim his mantle; and Williams would settle off Broadway, trying to make sense of an era that had discovered sex but had tired of talk.

44

MAXISERIES

A Dance to the Music of Time /
Fabio Montale

ERICH VON STROHEIM, the director of the legendarily mutilated 1924 masterpiece *Greed*, based on Frank Norris's novel *McTeague*, was forty-five years ahead of his time when he tried to release the film in its original form as a nine-hour adaptation. In 1969, after a British miniseries based on John Galsworthy's *The Forsyte Saga* crossed the Atlantic, and PBS committed itself to more of the same—under the self-parodying rubric *Masterpiece Theatre*—a nine-hour *McTeague* might have been just the thing for Sunday evenings.

Yet even now, filmmakers of Stroheim's stature ignore the miniseries format, leaving the eternal (in every sense of the word) costume drama to a largely ponderous crew of television journeymen. Exceptions abound, of course: Rainer Werner Fassbinder's fifteen-hour *Berlin Alexanderplatz* (1980), a riveting demonstration of how a great filmmaker can make a classic from a classic, and the best British series—among them *I, Claudius* (1976), *Brideshead Revisited* (1981), and *Tinker, Tailor, Soldier, Spy* (1979)—play as well today as they did two and three decades ago. But something went wrong in the offices at PBS, where, excepting an occasional visit from Dickens, literary interpretations gave way to fruitless cycles of drawing-room mysteries; it's probably no coincidence that Miss Marple is now the same age as those doo-wop bands PBS keeps recycling.

In consequence, two commendable if flawed series, *A Dance to the Music of Time* and *Fabio Montale*, have made their American debuts on DVD. In the case of *Fabio Montale*, reticence on the part of PBS and cable is fairly easy to understand. It was made for French TV and thus requires a willingness not only to read subtitles but to accept language that most stations bleep. If the title doesn't ring a bell, Fabio is the reflective, nostalgic, endangered cop hero of Jean-Claude Izzo's Marseille trilogy, which has attracted a growing following, spurring Koch Lorber to import these 2002 adaptations of the Fabio novels—*Total Chaos, Chourmo*, and *Solea*. The star is the 1960s heart-throb Alain Delon, now an eminence grise, no deeper than in his prime but still forceful enough to hold the screen with minimal effort. At sixty-five, he was ten years too old for the role, which doesn't bother the many gorgeous women half his age, who blithely seduce him. This is almost always a bad move: loving Fabio usually means dying for Fabio. A cabal of Mafiosi, politicians, assassins, and fellow cops out to get him wind up settling for his friends. By the third entry, a comic inevitability intrudes: whenever Fabio tells someone he will take care of him or her, that person may as well take last rites.

The director José Pinheiro did a stylish job in adapting the material, making Marseille as central a character in the films as the city is in Izzo's novels. Exquisite telephoto and helicopter shots of the harbor serve as transitions, and the rhythmic cutting between gleaming sunlit afternoons and nighttime alleyways adds to a sense of dislocation where anyone can be killed, including several very likable characters. A few cornball touches (pointless flashbacks and voice-overs) and a near-total negation of Izzo's insistence that racism is at the core of Marseille's chaos remind us that television is television, even in France. On the other hand, when Fabio tells a young woman that he has named his bar Solea, she says, "Like the Miles Davis record." Ah, France.

These are *policiers* in which character trumps forensics, in which a sense of loss—the body count is appalling—is earned along with Fabio's certainty that all villains, no matter how high in the chain, are puppets manipulated by invisible masters. Delon is given a fine Hollywood-style entrance: Fabio appears alone in the street, his coat buffeted by the wind, before he single-handedly settles a hostage crisis. By the third installment, his invulnerability is badly tattered. Koch Lorber's bare presentation should have included an introductory essay: no one who hasn't read *Chourmo* will figure out the title (slang for galley slave). The image is window boxed, which looks fine on a traditional monitor but is much reduced on widescreen. The colors are intense.

Acorn Media's penny-pinching approach to *A Dance to the Music of Time* (1997) is more regrettable, because Anthony Powell's incomparable twelve-novel cycle, even when reduced to seven hours (a fraction of the time allotted Robert Graves's Claudius novels or Evelyn Waugh's *Brideshead Revisited*), cries out for a bit of help—and not just an insert that randomly identifies a mere fifteen characters. You may want to consult Hilary Spurling's skillful handbook *Invitation to the Dance* or, better yet, the novels themselves as a way of tracking characters and references, though the four parts of the series do not cleave to Powell's four seasonally organized trilogies.

Hugh Whitemore's seriously pruned adaptation, as co-directed by Christopher Morahan and producer Alvin Rakoff, is sufficiently dynamic to surmount the charge that it is merely an illustrated abridgment of an essentially unfilmable work. Whereas much of Powell's humor resides in the punctilious tempo of his deceptively Wodehousean prose, the humor in this endeavor is entrusted to great character actors—John Gielgud (St. John Clark is pretty much reduced to one hilarious speech), Alan Bennett (a hirsute Sillary, sounding slightly more than necessary like a refugee from *Beyond the Fringe*), Carmen du Sautoy (Tuffy Weeden as a castrating gargoyle), Edward Fox (an aged and rouged Uncle Giles), Michael Williams (Ted Jeavons with a Hitler mustache and satyr grin), and Paul Brooke and Zoë Wanamaker (the ill-fated critic McLintock and his ominous Bo-Peep wife), among many others. Paul Rhys brings a raw nerveless edge to the alcoholic Charles Stringham, and no one who sees this adaptation can ever read Powell without seeing and hearing the North Country insolence of Adrian Scarborough's pitch-perfect Quiggin.

One difficulty with the material, which as a study in time extends Shakespeare's seven ages to the brink of television's *Seven-Up*, is that the central character and narrator, Nick Jenkins—a bastion of normality even when engaged, like everyone else, in the cycle of musical beds—is too remote to generate dramatic interest. Three actors divide the part, including James Purefoy and the always persuasive John Standing, but they are asked to do little more than alternate expressions of bemusement and confusion. Happily, the two most extreme characters—the unforgettable, incessantly recurring Widmerpools—are vividly amplified to a point just short of caricature. Simon Russell Beale plays Kenneth Widmerpool from public school to death, his fat bespectacled face a catcher's mitt for carelessly flung food. Not even Widmerpool deserves a wife like Pamela Flitton, the greatest femme fatale since Lady Macbeth, who is suspected of committing suicide so that the last of her many lovers can enjoy a spot of necrophilia. Miranda Richardson's performance secretes venom.

But the adaptation makes some strange choices. It opens with Nick's mistress, Jean Templer (Claire Skinner), greeting him in the buff, which naturally sends him into a reverie about school days. The nudity seems to have no purpose but to command instant attention (it does that) and perhaps to hold the audience through the introductory material by implying similar shocks to come. Using Jean instead of Powell's cold workmen, dancing around a fire like the quartet in the Poussin painting that sets Nick's memory dance in motion, is as gratuitous as altering Proust's madeleine to an Oreo. More mysterious is the decision to stage all the events of 1946–47 in the mid-1950s. Among the admirable directorial touches are carefully chosen locations, including Venice, and a sadistically mordant series of parallel sudden deaths, each ending with an eyes-open stare. The music and art choices are sensible. The depiction of the Blitz is as frightful as in any feature film. And the closing, with Jenkins intoning a passage from Burton's *An Anatomy of Melancholy* while watching a home movie of Widmerpool (who at last morphs into Quasimodo), high-stepping in a loincloth before phallic stones known as the Devil's Fingers, is ingenious. The series is challenging, addictive, at times obscure, and extremely powerful.

45

WHO'S AFRAID OF AL JOLSON?

The Jazz Singer

"MY FLESH CREPT as the loud speaker poured out the sodden words, the greasy sagging melody. I felt ashamed of myself for listening to such things, for even being a member of the species to which such things are addressed." So wrote Aldous Huxley in 1929, after seeing *The Jazz Singer*. Half a century later, David Thomson was no less horrified: "It is as if printing had been invented to fill labels on ketchup bottles: That sound on film . . . should have been born on the lips of a Lithuanian Jew blackface minstrel encouraging his mother to love him." Huxley and Thomson reserved most of their derision for the film's monstrous sentimentality, a fair point—though some of us would suggest, ever so gently, that Jolson made an art of monstrous sentimentality: a cunning, pandering, madly riveting art. Those who disdain the film as racist are chipping at thinner ice. *The Jazz Singer* is a middle-brow but serious inquiry into ethnic identity. Given the status of race as the number one theme in American life and culture, we could hardly ask for a more fitting choice to inaugurate sound on film than a Lithuanian Jew blackface minstrel—except maybe Bert Williams, a Bahamian Negro blackface minstrel, but he was dead.

Warner Bros. released, on the occasion of its eightieth anniversary, a three-disc DVD edition of *The Jazz Singer* (1927), which doubles as a tribute to the Vitaphone Corporation and its efforts to synchronize sound on film. The elaborate package, with many hours of extras and printed inserts, offers no comments on race or any other idea beyond the wonders and perfidies of technology. That, too, is fitting. It's far easier to trace historical facts than the historicist factors that define social mores. Make of this vital survey what you will: it's a veritable four-credit course on an indelible juncture in the evolution of American popular culture.

Directed by Alan Crosland, *The Jazz Singer* made its bones as the first feature film with synchronized dialogue (about two minutes' worth). There had been short films with dialogue and long ones with synchronized music and sound effects, but nothing like this. *The Jazz Singer* turned the industry on its ear, and Jolson's contribution can hardly be overstated. His vitality, inseparable from his ego, was tuned to a vocal, terpsichorean, and comedic pitch that nullified the need for microphones, scripts, or other actors. He was an evangelist of popular entertainment. Wound up in song—windmill arms, rolling eyes, swaying hips—Jolson was unyielding, like someone grabbing you by the lapels and shaking you up and down till you cry uncle. Some people found this easy to resist. Luckily for the four Warner brothers, especially Sam, who dedicated himself to putting sound on film, much of the American public couldn't get enough.

This was astonishing on several levels. In a time of endemic anti-Semitism, the most famous American showman—rivaled in celebrity by Charles Lindbergh, Babe Ruth, Paul Whiteman, and few others—was a Jew who wore his Jewishness on his sleeve, and a curiously empathic blackness on his face. (Jolson's black alter ego, Gus, was at once a racial caricature and the smartest, wisest, funniest man in every situation.) In one of the ironies surrounding *The Jazz Singer*, Jolson got the role of Jakie Rabinowitz / Jack Robin only after George Jessel, who originated it onstage, out-priced himself and Eddie Cantor turned it down. Samson Raphaelson had based the play on Jolson's life as a rabbi's son who left home as a boy to work as a burlesque stooge and minstrel. That's pretty much Raphaelson's plot, as it would be of the 1946 biopic *The Jolson Story*.

As a drama of assimilation, *The Jazz Singer* updated one of the oldest stories known to man (the Bible uses it a lot): How to make the leap from immigrant to citizen? How to balance old traditions and new? Raphaelson's uniquely American twist stemmed from his recognition of minstrelsy—in its eighth decade when his play made its debut—as a kind of ethnic tunnel. Jolson himself recalled entering the tunnel as an insecure Jew, finding a performance style through the invincible anonymity of blackface, and exiting as a fully assimilated American entertainer. *The Jazz Singer* scrupulously avoids using blackface for comic relief or nostalgia. When Jackie / Jack finally blacks up in his dressing room, the effect has a metaphorical purity; he doesn't know who he is, and putting on the wig and cork provides temporary comfort. He smiles at his gentile lover as he puts on the mask that will make him a star even as it renders him invisible. In the end, he is no more himself filling in for his dying father on Kol Nidre than he is in minstrel drag. "Mama, we have our son again," the cantor says with his dying breath. Cut to the Winter Garden: Jack Robin, in blackface and on bended knee, sings of another "Mammy" in another way.

The DVD package is far more than this film. It offers an original, well researched and edited eighty-five-minute documentary, *The Dawn of Sound: How Movies Learned to Talk*, marred by the annoying de rigueur present-tense narrative style (and equally fashionable use of "transition" as a verb) and total neglect of the advances in sound film going on in Europe at the same time. There are a predictably factual commentary, relevant short subjects (highlights: Jolson's "Plantation Act" and a vehicle for the black Original Sing Band, directed by Buster Keaton, though you'd never guess), a radio broadcast of *The Jazz Singer*, facsimile booklets, and Jolson trailers, including misleading previews for his best film, *Mammy* (1930), and his most surreal, *Wonder Bar* (1934)—forthcoming, we can only hope.

But the real prize here, an excavator's paradise, is a selection of twenty-four Vitaphone shorts from 1926–29, an extraordinary quarry of remote entertainment styles. Note that they do not include the 1926 musical numbers that introduced Vitaphone's system (as a prologue to *Don Juan*, presumably being saved for another release) or the elaborately directed short films that followed well into the 1940s. Instead, these are mostly obscurities, some long available, others thought lost or deteriorated beyond repair. Though the performers are exclusively white (unlike the later Vitaphones), they cover a lot of territory, and though they are often referred to as vaudevillians, most of them were not—no more than Jolson, who never even played the Palace.

In addition to several true vaudeville luminaries—Elsie Janis, Burns and Allen, Van and Schenk, Blossom Seeley and Bennie Fields, the Foys, Trixie Friganza—there are performers and bands from New York nightclubs and revues otherwise lost to history. Standouts include Shaw and Lee (dour comedians in bowler hats exchanging double takes after *every* line) and a sketch with William Demarest, who does two Keatonesque pratfalls.

Gary Giddins

The songs are consistently among the very worst of the period, possibly reflecting a rights issue, but music buffs will enjoy seeing twenty-year-old Russ Columbo fiddling and singing falsetto with Gus Arnheim's band, and arranger George Stoll leading a quintet and doing a fair Joe Venuti imitation on violin. Warner Bros. should have included commentary or at least dates and personnel listings for these films.

One short is a major discovery, *The Happy Hottentots*, directed by Bryan Foy and starring the legendary "jazz" dancer and stuttering comedian Joe Frisco, who does not stutter here. This is the only short among these early Vitaphones with multiple stage sets and a plot, and is so obscure that even Frisco's biographers omit mention of it. Tying together several inside-showbiz gags to a memorable finish, and conveying with gallant exasperation the hard, repetitive, squalid, and unappreciated world of low-rent vaudeville, *Hottentots* teams Frisco with two unbilled partners: fellow vaudevillian Billy Callahan, who wears black gloves because of severe psoriasis, and the well-known comic actor Billy Gilbert. Frisco is remembered today for still-repeated witticisms and unlikely walk-ons in a novel (*The Great Gatsby*) and movie (*The Sweet Smell of Success*). It is a joy to finally see him work for more than a few seconds and in one of the funniest one-reelers to survive the Vitaphone—not to be missed.

46

PENNIES FROM HEAVEN
The Threepenny Opera

IN AGREEING TO film *Die Dreigroschenoper* (*The Threepenny Opera*), G. W. Pabst was not only poised to adapt Berlin's theatrical sensation of 1928: a sharp parody of John Gay's 1728 parody *The Beggar's Opera*, by Bertolt Brecht (and his uncredited assistant Elizabeth Hauptmann), with music by Kurt Weill. He was confronting a work conceived as a specifically theatrical experience, and had to choose between making a photographic record of a cultural milestone and discarding the milestone stuff to reinvent the work from the ground up, analyzing its components in filmic terms—this at a time when sound on film was still in its mewling stage. Released in 1931, the movie was only modestly successful with the public, though much admired by critics other than Hitler, who banned it two years later. For the next three-quarters of a century, it languished in the unpleasant limbo of lifeless washed-out prints with scratchy sound and grind-house splices, and its reputation faded accordingly. That's all changed with Criterion's two-disc DVD edition.

While Pabst's other films of the period—*Pandora's Box* (1929), *Kameradschaft* (1931)—were successfully revived, *The Threepenny Opera* remained a historical curiosity, valued only for preserving Lotte Lenya's fabled rendition of "Pirate Jenny." The picture was often derided as murky or fogbound and as a compromise; it was said to dilute and even betray Brecht, either because of censors or the director's fastidiousness. The DVD, taken from a stunning 2006 German restoration, forces a reassessment, instantly discrediting the idea that Pabst sought to create Victorian realism with decorative mist. There is no fog whatsoever—not a wisp. The startling clarity of the image allows us to appreciate why filmgoers in 1931 cheered Fritz Arno Wagner's expressively mobile cinematography. We can now enjoy Andrej Andrejew's elaborately droll art direction: the broadly feigned (which is to say Brechtian) "exteriors," filmed indoors, and the crammed interiors that recall the digs of Miss Havisham.

The issue of fidelity to the text is more complicated, but with one very big exception, the ultimate decisions redound to Pabst's credit. The exception pertains to the score, nearly half of which was dropped—including most of the middle-act numbers: "Ballad of Sexual Dependency," "Pimp's Ballad," "Polly's Song." One major character, Lucy, was also discarded, mandating the loss of "Jealousy Duet," though Pabst and company might have tailored that number no less delectably for the remaining rivals, Polly (Carola Neher) and Jenny (Lenya). The lost songs rob the piece of Weill's great music and some of Brecht's finest verse. Still, Pabst retained eight songs and used instrumental interpolations of two others. He improved on the play by changing the order of the four showstoppers, so that they build to a rousing climax. "Mack the Knife," magnificently hissed and gargled by Ernst Busch's street singer, opens and closes the movie.

The film's midsection is paced with the two declarations of feminine independence, Polly's "The Barbara Song" (mistakenly identified as "Polly's Song" in the DVD booklet) and "Pirate Jenny," which is also sung by Polly in the play but was assigned by Pabst to Lenya, whose Jenny sings it with dead eyes, as if her veins pumped iced water—except during the chorus, which she warbles like a bird. The song remained with Jenny in later stage revivals, in part because it makes more dramatic sense as a portent of Jenny's revenge than as Polly's wedding entertainment. The "Cannon Song," a merry recollection of imperialist adventurism at its most barbaric—indeed, cannibalistic—is saved for last and made all the more powerful for it. Which brings us to the big question: Is The Threepenny Opera Pabst blue ribbon or Brecht red banner? Brecht unsuccessfully sued the production, and sympathizers have assumed that he was protesting the undermining of his theatrical innovations and Marxist rhetoric.

Well, as Criterion's many commentators (including Eric Bentley in a fine made-to-order documentary) point out with choir-like harmony, this is manifestly preposterous. In creating a movie, Pabst—who never considered photographing the stage play as a serious option—had to find his own way to suggest Brecht's epic artificiality and galvanizing didacticism. Pabst rejected placards to announce songs, but he had the street singer narrate brief transitions and bannered the fakery of the thing with sham backdrops, surreal lighting, snake-like camera moment, and stylized performances, chiefly by Rudolf Forster, whose Mack the Knife struts and poses like a coiled muscle.

Brecht's play cuts from Peachum's beggars' establishment to Mack's marriage to Peachum's daughter Polly. Then it tracks Peachum's revenge, enlisting the corrupt police chief, Tiger Brown, and Brown's daughter Lucy, and climaxes with Mack on the gallows. The hanging is miraculously averted by a last-minute reprieve from the queen. Peachum then reminds us that in real life the queen rarely intervenes and exhorts us to combat injustice. In the film, Mack goes into hiding, entrusting his gang to Polly, who proves her mettle by buying a bank and dressing up the hooligans as board members right out of *Little Caesar*. After a near-anarchic Coronation Day march by the beggars (a silent, gripping confrontation and pure cinema), a liberated Mack makes Tiger Brown and Peachum his partners. Thus the underworld, big business, and law collaborate to fleece the poor. Mack and Brown reminisce about the good old days, turning desert peoples into steak tartare, and the street singer resumes "Mack the Knife," singing of people who live in the light or dark, as the common folk shuffle off into the shadows and fade to "Fin."

The film's ending is more powerful than the play's, and the strange thing is that despite his protestations, Brecht himself wrote this revised final act in his rejected screen treatment. Pabst kept more faith with him than either man ever acknowledged. The film improves on the play in other ways. I've seen two productions and heard cast albums of three others, and they all suffered from cloying, self-conscious attempts at irony and vulgarisms deemed daring, even as genuinely daring elements of the work were defanged. The film deepens the material by adjusting its tone, not once but (at least) five times.

By delaying our first encounter with Peachum, the first section is concerned exclusively with Mack's silent courtship of Polly; the feeling is slow and ominous, with long tracking shots, strange angles, mirrored reflections, and portentous body language. The second section introduces Tiger Brown (Reinhold Schunzel: "You actually . . . caught a burglar?") and concerns the wedding. This episode is played as comedy, combining familiar bits from burlesque, vaudeville, and Mack Sennett—bits as old as the hat that rises from its wearer's head as if in surprise or the champagne cork mistaken for a gunshot. Nowhere is the marriage of high and low better represented than in the wedding of Mack and Polly, complete with a nervous vicar, much of it proto-Ionesco. The third section introduces Peachum and the business of paupering, which is defined as creating in others the unnatural desire to part with money. Peachum, as played by Fritz Rasp (interviewed at length in one of the disc's supplements), has a whining buzz-saw voice and a demeanor that conveys the eternal vigilance of the hypocrite. The scene displays Langian efficiency, fast and objective. The fourth section details the paupers' march with the crosscutting and quiet buildup of a silent movie. The final section celebrates the happy ending in the scrupulously sterilized bank, shot close up and with little movement—the better to let "Cannon Song" work its mischief.

Criterion also includes the French version of the film, shot by Pabst on the same sets on the same days. The print is gray and tinny, but watchable. Florelle is charming as Polly, but boulevardier Albert Préjean is, at best, Mack the Butter Knife. Gaston Modot injects some life as Peachum, and Antonin Artaud hilariously overacts his one important line. It's the same film with none of the tension. Also included is a visual essay comparing the two versions, a photographic montage, and a solid commentary by David Bathrick and Eric Rentschler. According to Fritz Rasp, Hitler outlawed the film but accepted a copy as a fiftieth birthday gift. One imagines him in the bunker, humming "Mack the Knife" over and over and over.

47

HABIT FORMING

The Busby Berkeley Collection

IN 1931, FOUR years after *The Jazz Singer* had popularized synchronized sound and only two years after *The Broadway Melody* won the best-picture Academy Award, the movie musical was considered a dead duck at the box office. MGM was so distraught at the public's indifference that it halted production on its most lavish revue, *The March of Time*, reportedly turning much of the footage into banjo picks. The audience had soured on those long, plotless, self-important diversions that tended to show off a studio's players as stilted, insincere, pompous, and untalented—hard to do even when you're trying. Sit through MGM's *The Hollywood Revue of 1929* or Warner Bros.' *The Show of Shows* (1929), if you dare; they stalled and killed many a career. The dance numbers looked particularly silly, arrayed on a proscenium arch, the dancers swinging their arms in hapless arcs; and popular music sounded better on radio—better songs, better singers, better sound.

Two movies changed all that, and ushered in a golden decade of lush, inventive, sexy, funny, irreverent musicals that, at their best, managed the neat trick of offering intoxicating escapism while nailing the class consciousness and class fantasies rife during the Depression. The first was Frank Tuttle's *The Big Broadcast* (1932), which paid tribute to France's innovative director René Clair, using surreal optical tricks and animation and linking the music to the story. Its commercial draw was a bevy of radio singers, led by Bing Crosby playing an alcoholic lout named Bing Crosby, performing their signature songs. A public already enchanted by their voices lined up to see their faces. Paramount's film was popular enough to spawn a series, yet eventually disappeared.

The second was Warner Bros.' *42nd Street*, which followed a few months later, in 1933, and had an altogether different history. Nominally directed by Lloyd Bacon with a strange cast—one star (Warner Baxter), one fading star (Bebe Daniels), two untested juveniles (Dick Powell and Ruby Keeler), and a fleet of character actors—and a brand-new score, it vivified the musty clichés of backstage musicals urgently enough to sustain its story, and then exploded with climactic choreography that made the camera its true star. In the last reel, *42nd Street* abandoned the stage in favor of pinwheels and kaleidoscopes, zooms and overhead shots, mini-dramas fraught with sex and violence, all animated by the fairly novel idea that this was a *movie*: to hell with stages.

The choreographer was a thirty-seven-year-old philandering, alcoholic Broadway veteran with the memorable nickname Busby, who had already proved his cinema bona fides with three Eddie Cantor hits made for Samuel Goldwyn: *Whoopee!* (1930, Ziegfeld's Broadway hit eroticized by the camera), *Palmy Days* (1931, leggy calisthenics in the gym), and *The Kid from Spain* (1932), mostly directed by Leo McCarey though it begins with a reel of purest Busby Berkeley, depicting a girls' dorm in which dozens of beds circle a swimming pool and the day's main activity is showering. After *42nd Street*, Berkeley became king of the Warner soundstage, a swashbuckler of the giant crane, the commander of a legion of alabaster-skinned, casting-couch beauties who didn't necessarily require any talent beyond finding their marks and smiling on cue. A Busby Berkeley movie was an idiom unto itself. Audiences happily whiled away the moments with Ruby Keeler's adorably clumsy dancing and Dick Powell's already dated tenor (and high-rise pompadour), along with barking Ned Sparks, flustered Guy Kibbee, flustering Hugh Herbert, and the rest, waiting for the outlandish dance numbers, now saved for the end.

There comes a point in the rediscovery of the previous generation's sexual expression when double entendre loses its doubleness. At that point, we are left to marvel at how really perverse our parents or grandparents were. Forget about swimming through dozens of open-scissor female legs or male voyeurs arrayed on their tummies shaking their heads or other obvious indications of omnivorous, ambidextrous, and neutered sexuality (as one simpering fellow remarks in *Dames* [1934], "Mr. Ounce does not approve of females"): what is going on with all those midgets, diapers, and spanking? The historical record fails to support the idea, advanced by the song "42nd Street," that American men in the 1930s referred to their shorts or trousers by the nineteenth-century locution "panties." As Berkeley became more confident, so did the sexuality of his stars—including such antidotes to Keeler's doe eyes as the hot-blooded sarcasm of Ginger Rogers and the hot-blooded everything of the ebullient Joan Blondell, whose right breast makes a lofty entrance in *Dames*. In real life, she married Dick Powell, which certainly makes him more interesting in retrospect. In *Footlight Parade* (1933), Berkeley found his perfect (one-time-only) double in James Cagney, as a dancer and choreographer whose mile-a-minute charm ratchets up the romantic urgency in a film too long on buildup, but ready to deliver with "Shanghai Lil."

Berkeley's rapid decline in the late 1930s (notwithstanding his inspired salute to phalluses and decapitated heads in 1943's *The Gang's All Here*) is usually attributed to his personal failings. More likely, the next generation simply cringed in embarrassment. It took a more detached generation to rediscover him—the postwar baby boomers, who may have found Busby incomprehensible during childhood TV infusions but eventually figured him out with the help of natural herbs and hallucinogens. The transformation of *42nd Street* into a 1970s Broadway extravaganza defanged him once and for all. Or not. A myth that clings relentlessly to these films, endlessly iterated in talking-heads featurettes, defines them as mindless or mind-blowing entertainments, respites from Depression woes. In fact, the musical numbers brim over with stirring reminders of hard times, sometimes ironic (Ginger Rogers draped in a necklace of giant gold coins singing "We're in the Money"), sometimes angry (bonus marchers restored to dignity in "Remember My Forgotten Man"). The stories say "Let's put on a show," but the musical numbers illuminate the desperation behind the melodrama and farce.

For that, Berkeley can take only part of the credit. Warner Bros. has collected five films and a bonus disc as *The Busby Berkeley Collection*, but it could have legitimately released them as *The Harry Warren / Al Dubin Collection*. They are the forgotten men in this series, though it is impossible to overstate the importance of their remarkable songs. Berkeley's style and, for that matter, musical conventions of the 1930s required taking a song and playing it repeatedly for the duration of a choreographed number. In later years, musical directors would allow arrangers to "open up" songs, extending them with variations and interludes. But in the Warner musicals, the songs had to hold their own. Harry Warren's lingering melodies achieved both novelty and pleasurable familiarity with their surprising rhythmic figures and contrary melodic ideas.

Warren employed triplets, for example, to inject a happy spirit ("I don't know if it's cloudy or bright") or a dour one ("remember my forgotten man"), and routinely combined eighth notes, dotted eighths, and sixteenth notes to create rhythmic ripples in most of his songs in these films ("I must have you every day, as regularly as coffee or tea"). "You're Getting to Be a Habit with Me" is a splendid example of two dissimilar melodies alternating in a song. Dubin, the man who rhymed "scanties" and "panties," caught the mood of the project exactly with lyrics like "Ev'ry kiss, ev'ry hug seems to act just like a drug," or with the relentlessly mooing "you" every three bars throughout "Shadow Waltz." He and Warren were never more masterly than in "Lullaby of Broadway" (from *Gold Diggers of 1935*), countering the main strain's mellow swing with a whole-note passage, "Gooood niiiight, baaay-beeee." These songs are based on melodic hooks that circle back on each other and don't wear out their welcome, allowing Berkeley to go for broke at leisure, raising the terpsichorean stakes from one chorus to the next.

Warner Bros. DVDs are justly praised for treating studio archives with the care that Criterion puts into its international collection of classic films, and *The Busby Berkeley Collection* is exceptional. It includes smashing prints of *42ⁿᵈ Street*, *Gold Diggers of 1933*, *Footlight Parade*, *Dames*, *Gold Diggers of 1935*, and a twenty-one-number anthology, originally prepared for laser disc, which isolates musical scenes and adds excerpts from four other 1930s Berkeley pictures, including *Wonder Bar* (1934)—though not the infamous blackface fantasy "Goin' to Heaven on a Mule," which is now considered too insensitive even for history. And that's just the main course. A savvy selection of short subjects and cartoons fills out each disc with rare opportunities to see the ingenious bandleader Don Redman, who almost single-handedly codified big-band jazz orchestration, seven-year-old Sammy Davis Jr., the neglected songwriter-performer Harry Barris and his wife Loyce Whiteman, an Adam and Eve parody with June MacCloy and Leon Errol, Harry Warren, and many vaudevillians—in all, quite a trove.

48

SMILIN' THEM TO DEATH

Hallelujah | The Green Pastures |

Cabin in the Sky

AFRICANS, KIDNAPPED AND enslaved in the New World, soon learned to "signify"—to communicate with one another in a way that wouldn't rile massa, for whom a different kind of communication was necessitated, as summed up by the grandfather in the opening pages of Ralph Ellison's *Invisible Man*: "I want you to overcome 'em with yeses, undermine 'em with grins, agree 'em to death and destruction." We forget that massa, too, had need to signify. Bounded by fundamentalists and Puritans, he could no more exercise his wild side or express irreverent attitudes toward sex, religion, and race than blacks could stump for empowerment or date massa's daughter. Black slaves had their say by making music of Exodus and desire. Whites had theirs by pretending to be black slaves: nature's dim-witted eternal children who said the darndest things.

This is a severe simplification, but in examining the ongoing if mutable allure of minstrelsy, we tend to focus on racist stereotypes as vehicles for hatred, when in fact they also served as vehicles for freer, if not necessarily free, speech. As blackface minstrelsy slowly, slowly lost its appeal, it was successfully supplemented by the all-black theatrical pageant, written and produced by whites and presenting an America in which there were no whites and, consequently, no racism. Not that the black communities they envisioned didn't have problems—like choosing between de Lawd and Lucifer, prayer and gambling, obeisance and transgression. These pageants, most famously Marc Connolly's 1930 Pulitzer Prize winner, *The Green Pas-*

tures, which sent a generation of white critics into paroxysms of teary gratitude, did triple duty. They indulged in heresies by ascribing them to Negro
folk culture; furthered the national illusion that even in their segregated
neighborhoods stock Negro types made their way through life yassing (but
with no thought of death and destruction); and thrust talented black performers into the limelight.

Warner has released DVDs of three of the most celebrated all-black musicals (Fox owns the other two from the same period, *Hearts in Dixie* [1929]
and *Stormy Weather* [1943]), which originally came out in seven-year installments: King Vidor's *Hallelujah* in 1929, William Keighley's version of Connolly's *The Green Pastures* in 1936, and Vincente Minnelli's *Cabin in the Sky*
in 1943. An all-black cinema had thrived in black communities since the
silent era, producing low-budget musicals, dramas, and westerns. These,
however, were major studio releases from MGM and Warner, distributed
in full knowledge that Southern white theaters would boycott them. Yet
they made money in their day, and continue to startle and entertain, though
Warner Home Video understandably worries that some will take offense.
In a written warning that can't be skipped or fast-forwarded, the company
disavows images it acknowledges as "wrong then and wrong now"; it provides commentaries by black scholars, characterizing racial stereotypes as a
part of history we need to confront.

You can understand the qualms. Is it really okay to take pleasure in Man-
tan Moreland as one of the funniest movie comedians of his day, or are we
obliged to watch grimfaced as he gets more mileage from the line (in *Cabin
in the Sky*) "I was the one that thought up flies" than any actor had a right
to? You have to wonder when a commentator has the moxie to characterize
Louis Armstrong as a great musician who incarnated an Uncle Tom image.
Yet the twenty-first-century disbelief that greets these movies stems from
our awareness that today they would be enacted by the intelligent design
crowd. They all depict a fundamentalist religious dichotomy between good
and evil, rationalizing a literal interpretation of the Bible by crediting the
viewpoint to Negro children or Negro illiterates (Eddie Anderson's Little
Joe, in *Cabin in the Sky*, signs his name with an X). The high priest of Israel
in *The Green Pastures*, who takes God's name in vain to further a political
agenda, is Pat Robertson without the shit-eating grin.

Hallelujah is a remarkable film, not only for the subject and cast but
because King Vidor shot much of it on location in Tennessee and Arkansas,

providing a documentary authenticity in his depiction of cotton farming, baptisms, and shotgun housing. So what if two songs, including a putative old-time spiritual ("Waiting at the End of the Road"), were written by Irving Berlin? At the center of the film is the dynamic Nina Mae McKinney, the first potential black sex symbol—reportedly sixteen when the film was made. McKinney's career soon vanished, as Hollywood offered no more black Jezebels until Lena Horne's brief movie fling fourteen years later. Still, here she is, wearing her heart, or a pair of dice, on her bodice, a black variation on the woman in the bulrushes, luring a too easily enticed farm boy away from God before dying in a muddy ditch. Her nightclub dance, justifiably compared by commentator Donald Bogle to Elvis's moves in *Jailhouse Rock*, is a raucous delight, and the film's theme of rehabilitation seems especially pointed now, when rehabilitation is so out of fashion. The DVD includes two 1930s shorts with McKinney and the untouchable teenage Nicholas Brothers, born to sport fedoras and determined—especially speed-demon Fayard—to avoid every cliché in devising endless variations on a basic time step.

The Green Pastures, which also features a Nicholas Brothers short and the infamous "Rufus for President," with Ethel Waters and seven-year-old Sammy Davis Jr., begins with risible references to "very simple, devout people" who are "humble" and "reverent," but comes powerfully alive in the broad harmonies of the Hall Johnson choir. Set in New Orleans, which began when "the whole world wasn't nothing but a mess of bad weather" and where a child is warned against growing up to be a "transgressor," the story moves quickly to heaven—a combination fish fry and prayer meeting. De Lawd, wittingly incarnated by the striking Rex Ingram (even more witting as Satan in *Cabin in the Sky*—he was versatile), creates Earth to provide firmament for his custard. Religion is the custard of the people.

Eddie "Rochester" Anderson is very funny as Noah, but most of the minstrelsy here is designed to disguise such heresies as God not bothering to listen to prayers, and a conclusion (cleverly borrowed from the poorly married prophet Hosea) in which a newly invented soldier named Hezdrel converts God from wrath to mercy. *The Green Pastures* postulates the moral growth of God—something you can only suggest through the eyes of Negro children. Even so, minstrels do have their limitations: Connolly depicts God but not Jesus, who is clearly no relation. De Lawd doesn't know who Jesus is or where he comes from, though He looks awfully beatific watching the crucifixion from His seat in heaven.

Cabin in the Sky, Minnelli's first film, deserves a more learned commentary or documentary than it gets. The DVD does offer a major audio-only extra: the excised five-minute Louis Armstrong version of "Ain't It the Truth," previously available on records, though it fails to explain how the number figured in the screenplay. Had Armstrong's number been included in the original film, he would have stolen the show—it was the picture's most ambitious orchestration and production. As released, Armstrong, though fourth-billed, appears only in a wondrously funny scene set in Hades with Ingram, Moreland, Willie Best, and other competing black comics. The original idea was to cut from Hades to Armstrong's performance, which begins with a swinging vocal, followed by a trumpet solo and coda that leads to a blazing orchestral episode and finale, brimming with high notes. As Armstrong's trumpet reprised the melody, the scene would shift to Earth, where Lena Horne's Georgia Brown would sing the same song while luxuriating in a bubble bath.

That idea was scotched by the Breen Office, which, overstepping the mandates of the Production Code, could not abide a beautiful black woman in a tub, but her scene was filmed, and a clip is included in the montage that accompanies the recording. Unfortunately, the DVD does not include the unedited audio performance of Duke Ellington's "Going Up." His appearance in the film, all too brief and prominently featuring trombonist Lawrence Brown, is nonetheless a moment of glory—one of many. Minnelli is so spellbound by the talent at his disposal that the film plays as vaudeville basted by dramatic vignettes. Ethel Waters and Lena Horne have their best turns ever in film musicals, as do Eddie Anderson ("Life's Full of Consequences") and the incomparably silky John Bubbles. Two complementary tap numbers play variations on the stereotype of the grinning, gravity-defying Negro dancer. First Bill Bailey (whose kid sister was Pearl) does a relatively conventional buck-and-wing to "Taking a Chance on Love." Then, in one of filmdom's all-time showstoppers, Bubbles, singing and dancing to the self-effacing minstrel anthem "Shine," turns that characterization on its head, as he spins (note the one-legged turns, à la Peg Leg Bates) the material into an expression of narcissistic thuggery, smiling the entire community into death and destruction.

49

VAUDEVILLE

Bing Crosby: Screen Legend Collection

FOR THE PAST fifty-plus years, you had about as much chance of seeing a complete print of a 1940 Bing Crosby vehicle called *If I Had My Way* as you did of the initial nine-hour version of *Greed* (1924)—which is to say no chance at all. Admittedly, there wasn't much demand for it. Still, while *Greed*, the lost grail of cinematic obsession, was permanently sacrificed to greed, Universal held on to what a company archivist assured me was a "pristine" interpositive of *If I Had My Way*. The studio just didn't want anyone to see it. (More about that in a moment.) Now, however, you can buy the complete *If I Had My Way* for under six bucks, or a fifth of the retail price of *Bing Crosby: Screen Legend Collection*. This is one of Universal's generous if elemental (not even a chapter index, though English and French subtitles are included) DVD clearance packages. Previous offerings collected horror films and enough Abbott and Costello to induce psychosis.

The Screen Legend series aims to soothe the savage breasts of movie-obsessed completists. Each volume dips into the sediment of great careers for five pictures, many long forgotten and deservedly so. In addition to Crosby, other volumes resurrect obscurities by Cary Grant and Rock Hudson, which will requite the curiosity of those determined to see a tuxedoed Grant posing in drawing rooms before he learned to act, and Hudson aglow with Man-Tan as a Baghdad freedom fighter back when insurrections were a good thing. Thus, the Crosby set wins by a tonsil. Its low point is the naval recruitment orgy *Here Come the Waves* (1944), an incessant Mark Sandrich musical with Betty Hutton as twins, though only one is as annoying as the real Betty Hutton. The joke is that Crosby plays a Frank Sinatra–style crooner, clutching a microphone pole as a swooning woman is carried off on a gurney. Unhappily, Crosby's weakness for blackface is exercised in a duet of "Accentuate the Positive" with dim-bulb Sonny Tufts—especially galling given the segregation that divided the armed forces.

Frank Tuttle's *Waikiki Wedding* (1937), a megahit in its day, spurred interest in all things Hawaiian with its score ("Blue Hawaii," "Sweet Leilani") and scenic shots by master cinematographer Karl Struss. Dated by low humor involving a pig, it is polished by Tuttle's imaginative staging and a neat mixed-identity plot device designed to fool viewers along with leading lady Shirley Ross. *Double or Nothing* (1937), sluggishly directed by Theodore Reed, leavens another millionaire-with-a-munificent-plan story with intermittent rewards, like Crosby's swinging "Smarty," comic relief by his real-life pals Andy Devine and William Frawley, a scat-singing Singband (women in black satin dresses), and Martha Raye's azure-tinted faux striptease "It's On, It's Off." Of greater interest are the two films Crosby made at Universal as an independent agent and co-producer with director David Butler: *East Side of Heaven* (1939) and *If I Had My Way*. The former is a minor but swift-moving screwball musical festooned with inside showbiz jokes and a splendid cast led by Crosby and the incorrigibly bright-eyed Joan Blondell, with Mischa Auer, Jerome Cowan, and assorted friends, including Matty Malneck's band and the erstwhile speakeasy hostess Jane Jones as a singing chef. Bing plays a purveyor of singing telegrams who gets stuck with an infant (surely the oddest box-office attraction of the era, Baby Sandy, who retired at four). He whiles away the time with a good James Monaco / Johnny Burke score and several clever lines.

The mystery of the butchered *If I Had My Way* gets to the nub of why it was made. Crosby and Butler shared a love of old show business, on which they were raised, especially vaudeville and minstrelsy. Crosby's films are littered with references to that era—*Double or Nothing* features an interpolated vaudeville show. For this picture, they contrived a story that allowed them to preserve on film a few figures who had long since faded from view, especially the legendary minstrel Eddie Leonard, whose three-minute "Ida" is his sole filmed legacy. When the film was sold to television in the late 1940s, it was cut to eighty minutes from ninety-four to accommodate ads—not because of Leonard's blackface number, as was often assumed. The vaudeville numbers and cameos were cut along with a solo by Bing's fourteen-year-old co-star Gloria Jean, then being groomed to replace cranky Deanna Durbin. In an interesting footnote to postwar hysteria, Jean's career was torpedoed in 1946 when she sang her signature rendition of "The Lord's Prayer" in London; the press accused her of criticizing the British war debt with the words "forgive us our debts as we forgive our debtors." In time, the missing minutes were thought lost: even the personal copies of Crosby and Gloria Jean lacked sequences, though her copy was several minutes longer than his.

So now we have a pristine print. Great film? Hardly, but it is a highly entertaining mixture of lend-lease politics, showbiz lore, and social wish-fulfillment à la Capra. Support is provided by Charles Winninger, Allyn Joslyn, a squirrel named Crack, and another good Monaco and Burke score; on the minus side, there is the ceaseless mugging of El Brendel, the fake Swede of vaudeville who—go figure—never stopped working or sucking the life out of every scene he was in. Crosby is thoroughly appealing as Gloria Jean's temporary guardian—warm but casual, skirting the temptation to jerk tears. For anyone interested in ancient show business, a frisson is provided with the one-line walk-ons by Grace La Rue, Trixie Friganza, and the man who established transvestitism in American entertainment (and also had a Broadway theater named for him), Julian Eltinge. He jokes about smoking cigars while dressed as a woman; for all the professional pearls and chiffon, turns out he was as closeted as evangelist Ted Haggart. Blanche Ring probably should have done a cameo, too, instead of singing "Rings on My Fingers," shaking like jelly.

Eddie Leonard, however, is magical: unlike "Accentuate the Positive," his blackface is too much a part of historical ritual to offend. I doubt that even those who are offended can fail to admire his artistry. Here are the original moonwalk, the yodeling croon that attracted attention when minstrel Emmett Miller was revived on records several years ago, and the rhythmic panache of the 1890s. Crosby introduces Leonard as "sixty-four years young," but he was probably seventy and would be dead within the year. He makes this film a significant time capsule, evoking the racial conflation of otherness and respect that prolonged minstrelsy in that era, when it averted vicious stereotypes. He is a missing link.

50

TECHNI-GLORY

The Tales of Hoffman /

Rodgers & Hammerstein / Gregory Hines

THE THREE-STRIP TECHNICOLOR process, introduced in the 1930s, flourished for nearly twenty years, bringing to fulfillment the notion of painting with a camera. Doomed by its bulky system of prisms, the high cost and broiling lights, and subsequent innovations that resulted in simpler, more natural-looking color cinematography, the process left an uneven legacy of movies defined by aggressively splashed and deeply saturated hues. The three strips, each representing a primary color, dyed the filmstrip, thus defining the contrasts—the way a painter might juxtapose a bright red coat and a bright blue sky. Its main drawback and most lasting virtue were one and the same: the luscious artificiality that, combined with soundstage fakery, banished realism.

The effect is symbolized for many by the moment when Dorothy opens a sepia door onto the paint-box hysteria of Oz. But even in natural surroundings, a master cameraman like Leon Shamroy could turn reality into a measured likeness, as in *Leave Her to Heaven*, the 1945 thriller that sustains attention primarily as a visual coup. By the early 1960s, filmmakers as different as Jerry Lewis (*The Ladies Man*) and Michelangelo Antonioni (*Deserto Rosso*) were painting sets and spraying lawns to drench images in color. Today's color photography is so accomplished that almost any effect is possible, including wistful replication of Technicolor's heyday, as in Todd Haynes's *Far from Heaven* (2002). Yet it isn't the same. The three-strip process

produced an effect hovering between rank vulgarity and sensual dazzle—
Hollywood's dreamscape.

Digitalization can effectively reproduce and amplify (sometimes exces-
sively) the palette. If DVDs can't simulate the experience of Ava Gardner's
visage lighting up a thirty-five-foot screen, precise color restoration has
redeemed more than a few middling films. For example, if Paramount's
The War of the Worlds (1953), a George Pal production directed by Byron
Haskin, had been shot in black and white, it would survive, at best, as a
cold war curio, albeit a prophetic one in its focus on the military-religious
complex. This is a picture in which a Catholic priest freely barges in on a
tactical base, and Gene Barry shouts at soldiers caught in the Martian holocaust, "I'm looking for some Pacific Tech professors!" The moral (scored by
a choir singing "Amen") is that God dispatched the invaders because "we
have followed too much the devices and desires of our own hearts." (Not
as far-fetched as the Spielbergian vision that sacrifices New Jersey to make
Tom Cruise a better dad, but not far from the Jerry Falwell / Pat Robertson
sermon explaining 9/11 as His punishment for abortion and gay sex.) As
photographed by George Barnes, the film pops off the screen, the lighting—
particularly during night scenes—calibrating every tone as carefully as the
depth perception. Frying eggs in real life are pale imitations of those sizzling
under Barnes's eye. The prologue, a newsreel conceived in homage to the
subversive scenario of Orson Welles's radio version, is practically three-
dimensional.

Paramount has also cut a deal with the John Wayne estate to release
movies that had been removed from the market for a quarter century, produced by Wayne's Batjac Company. It hardly needs to be said that Technicolor was almost as decisive in boosting Westerns as musicals, especially
in the 1950s when the old masters John Ford and Howard Hawks made
the switch, and their preeminent heirs, Anthony Mann and Budd Boetticher, expanded the palette. John Farrow's *Hondo* (1953) stands up almost
as well as the films Ford and Hawks made with Wayne during the same
period—though, as with all of Wayne's own productions, it spouts gratuitous commandments about patriotism and rugged individualism that the
older filmmakers would have blue-penciled. Originally shot in 3-D *Hondo*
suffers from too many objects hurled at the viewer, but the cinematography
by Robert Burks (Hitchcock's photographer at the time) and pioneer Archie

Stout (who shot one of the definitive Technicolor showpieces, Ford's *The Quiet Man*) is scrumptious, and the chemistry between Wayne and "plain" Geraldine Page, making her movie debut, redounds to the benefit of both. Still, Westerns were obliged to shoot the world as it exists; musicals labored under no such compunction.

Few canvases are more intricately color-coded than that rendered in the Michael Powell and Emeric Pressburger masterpiece *The Tales of Hoffman* (1951), brought to DVD by Criterion. In this instance, the British filmmakers began with a recording of the Offenbach opera in modified form, conducted by Sir Thomas Beecham. The film was designed as a visual complement to the playback, and nary a frame fails to glitter and shine. The décor and actors are drunk with color (the makeup as well as costumes); the story is told with the radical deployment of rapid cuts and camera tricks; and the divide between formal dance and casual movement is painstakingly breeched. A horror film about debased love with a bleak conclusion countered by its overwhelming sensuality, *The Tales of Hoffman* unfurls in a stream of out-landish visuals—many of them unforgettable, including Moira Shearer's dis-located head and Robert Helpmann's malevolent face.

True, it is an opera; true, it is a dance; yet it is ultimately the purest kind of filmmaking, where music and motion correspond to the rigors of Hein Heckroth's design, Christopher Challis's camera, and Michael Powell's eye and tempo. The use of Technicolor here lacks Hollywood's deep-focus precision—middle-distance shots fade—but the scheme is erotically charged, and the material suits and even demands the riot of color. Flames appear to charge from Hoffman's head in the Prologue, real sets and drawings are used interchangeably, foregrounds are adorned with dreamy hangings, and water infuses the sky. Arriving thirteen years after the Criterion laser disc, which restored the "Antonia" episode, the DVD uses the same 125-minute print; the 138-minute original may not exist, but fans will be disappointed to find that the extras do not include a rundown of what is missing.

Meanwhile, 20th Century Fox has released expansive two-disc anniversary editions of the Rodgers and Hammerstein musicals *State Fair* (1945), *Oklahoma!* (1955), and *The Sound of Music* (1965), and they haven't looked this good since they were first unspooled. On the other hand, they are Rodgers and Hammerstein musicals—a genre that fills millions with pleasurable anticipation and a few miserable churls with acid reflux. I can speak with authority only for the latter, who bewail their humorlessness, their condescension toward rustic Americans and all other cultures, their pretense of taking on serious subjects, and their touristy approach to romance, not to mention all that corn as high as an elephant's eye. Two more insolated Manhattanites than Rodgers and Hammerstein never lived, and yet they rarely deigned to write about what they knew, unlike George and Ira Gershwin (notwithstanding Catfish Row), Cole Porter, or Jule Styne. Everything R&H touched turned to dessert.

Yet they were tuneful fellows, and even those who could care less about whether Curly will ever get it on with Laurey or Judd or whoever may find their capillaries swelling to "People Will Say We're in Love," as well as the radiant Eastman Color photography of *Oklahoma!*—courtesy of the great Robert Surtees. The disc also includes the Todd-AO version of the film, which a documentary seems to favor, though the colors are dim by comparison. As Julie Andrews joyously notes, everyone loves *The Sound of Music*, the happiest of all musicals involving Nazis except for *The Producers*, and, to be sure, Robert Wise's opening travelogue (a reprise of his overhead opening in *West Side Story*) is breathtaking, as are a few stagings of songs (not including "Climb Every Mountain," "So Long, Farewell," and several others). You may have to retire to find time to watch all the extras, a sampling of which I found more enjoyable than the movie.

The best of the bunch is *State Fair*, the only R&H score written for the movies, and shot by Leon Shamroy with a three-strip richness more caloric than the songs, including "It Might as Well Be Spring"—one of their very best. I wish that number had been assigned to Dick Haymes and not that lip-synching, ravishing bride of Technicolor Jeanne Crain. The film benefits from cheery performances by Charles Winninger, Vivian Blaine, Dana Andrews, Harry Morgan, and Donald Meek, and from showbiz talk, something R&H did know about. Yet they had to go and ruin things with an endless paean to Iowa that is characteristically demeaning (I speak as an erstwhile Iowa resident). The close-up of Crain at 19:10 exemplifies the Shamroy touch—her lips, scarf, and complexion and the night sky are all imbued with deep, tactile colors, as if by a brush. The DVD also includes the atrocious 1962 remake, an example of color photography sagging into anonymous flatness. But as it is sort of free, you can go directly to 49:30 for its sole compensation: Ann-Margret's disrobing and dance frolic.

By the 1980s, the musical was as defunct as the Western—every exception tending to prove the rule that movie genres can thrive only as long as performers give them authenticity. In that sense, John Wayne is as much a long-ago representative of the West as Wyatt Earp. If a dancer as skillful as Fred Astaire were to emerge from the bowels of Broadway, Hollywood would roll its eyes in disbelief and indifference. For proof, consider the charismatic tap virtuoso Savion Glover, who apparently can't get arrested west of the Rockies. For a brief moment, however, Gregory Hines demonstrated at least the potential for a new kind of dance film built around the virile insistence of tap and the post-Technicolor verisimilitude of urban color cinematography.

Columbia released Hines's two key films—Taylor Hackford's *White Nights* and Nick Castle's *Tap*—and though neither is entirely winning, they are better as DVDs, which allow you to fast-forward to the good parts. Hackford's film (1985) is a souvenir from the evil days of the Soviet Union, burdened with a plot so contrived that Helen Mirren looks embarrassed at having to recite her expository dialogue. Ah, but then there are those opening eight minutes, a Mikhail Baryshnikov number ending with a faux suicide by hanging, Hines's subsequent vodka-induced autobiography in dance, and their long-delayed and entirely satisfying pas de deux—reasonable trade-offs for cold war platitudes. For dance lovers, *Tap* (1989) is a must-have disc, as much for the extras, which include interviews with veteran dancers, as the film. Sammy Davis Jr., in his last movie, turned in his best film work since *Porgy and Bess*. The old-timers' tap "challenge," despite too many reaction-shot cutaways, is one of the most savory face-offs on film and includes a stunning summation of his life's work by Harold Nicholas. Savion Glover, in his teens, radiates charm and smarts, marking his unfulfilled cinema promise with one number. But this is Hines's film, and he carries it on his pugnaciously sloping shoulders and in his cynical, lidded eyes. His dancing expands on the attitude and elegance of John Bubbles while charging into a new realm—percussive, assertive, and uncompromising, not least in his nostalgic regard for a fading tradition. The plot holds no surprises, but the camera has a few, including a pan of the hoofers' office, papered in photographs that track the history of black entertainment, an area Technicolor completely neglected.

51

CASTING DOUBTS

Fiddler on the Roof / Presenting Lily Mars

IN THE HEYDAY of the studio assembly line, musicals were so much a part of the mix that they ranged from A-list spectaculars to D-list programmers, something for every taste and budget. Most were Hollywood originals, though many had theatrical pedigrees or existed solely to exploit stars of radio and swing. Similarly, we now have hulking Broadway adaptations like *Dreamgirls* and *Chicago*, sentimental biopics like *Ray* and *Walk the Line*, hip-hop melodramas like *8 Mile* and *Hustle & Flow,* and occasional oddities like the underappreciated *Idlewild.* What we don't have are movie musical stars. No Astaires, Kellys, or Eleanor Powells; no Crosbys, Garlands, or Sinatras. Instead, we get actors stretching their way into musicals and using stunt doubles for the more rigorous dance moves. Does anyone anticipate a series of Jennifer Hudson musicals? The manager of a superstar hip-hop artist recently explained that he will no longer allow his client to appear in musicals because they would stereotype him.

DVD releases of a major 1971 musical, *Fiddler on the Roof,* and a minor 1943 musical, *Presenting Lily Mars,* show that problems of casting have long befuddled the genre. Norman Jewison's *Fiddler* reeks of money, ambition, and profundity, though it is hardly an unalloyed success. I always approach *Fiddler* with trepidation, in part because it exacts a transitory emotional toll I can neither explain nor transcend; I sob profusely. My more rational ambivalence concerns the Jerry Bock / Sheldon Harnick score, which is certainly tuneful and possibly immortal, but awfully kitschy when it sacrifices its Middle European harmonies and rhythms for corn-fed Broadway cheeriness—in some respects, the template for *Fiddle* was *Oklahoma!* One example: in the song "Miracle of Miracles," the melodic phrase for the lyric "God has made a man today" sorely misses the Judaic ingenuity of Gershwin, Kern, Arlen, or even Porter (think of "My Heart Belongs to Daddy"), and at this point it's hard to remember if "Sunrise, Sunset" invented bar mitzvah music or was a product of it. The best songs, most of them boasting skillful counter-melodies, like "Tradition," "Matchmaker," "If I Were a Rich Man," and "To Life," have failed to gain a significant musical life outside the show.

What I miss in the film is the irreverence, the surprising hilarity, of the original 1964 Broadway production, as embodied in Zero Mostel's ability to create the illusion of spontaneity even when each gesture was polished to a shine. There were no tears then. The expulsion from Anatevka was moving, but the entire production radiated the explosive heat of Broadway-meets-Yiddish-theater adrenalin, which did wonders in cutting the syrup. Even the then-novel absence of an overture signaled something fresh and nervy. The shift from brazen comedy to universal pathos probably began when Herschel Bernardi, a veteran of Yiddish theater, took over the part—his niceness became the rule. The movie emphasizes the sentiment, pre-ferring history over folklore, cutting down on Chagall's magic realism in favor of scenes that show Red riots in Kiev and a flashback of Tevye's most rebellious daughter as a small child. *Fiddler* may be the Jewish *Roots*, a tie to the Russian travail, but it was also a paean to the transcendence of Jewish-American entertainment. Yet in almost any production, *Fiddler* is critic-proof and goyim-venerated.

Jewison's film works on several levels. Despite the two-minute opening sunrise, its three hours are rarely laborious. Isaac Stern's splendid fiddling during the opening credits sets a high standard for the score, which John Williams orchestrated forcefully. The cast is mostly excellent, especially Topol, a sly Tevye with a back broad enough to carry the film, excelling at the recitative and keeping one eye on God and the other on the camera. Leonard Frey (as the poor tailor), Paul Mann (as the rich butcher), and Rosa-lind Harris (as the eldest daughter) all deliver. The film's primary failing is in failing the Jerome Robbins choreography—dances are shot waist-up. Rather than build to a climax, the "To Life" episode spins into incoherence and then simply stops, with a freeze-frame; even the bottle dance, one of Robbins's peak achievements, is staged unimaginatively and curtailed. Still, the desire for verisimilitude has its rewards, as do the rhythmic editing by Antony Gibbs and Robert Lawrence and the photography by Oswald Morris, who, like Jewison, is nothing if not literal-minded. I'm not certain that the antiseptic shtetl they built in Yugoslavia is any more realistic than the stage set built for Broadway's Imperial Theater in 1964, but the vistas are lovely.

Making Tevye dramatically authentic was probably an easier call than that facing MGM and a twenty-year-old Judy Garland, who in 1943 had all but exhausted an adolescence of capers with Mickey Rooney. She had already appeared in fifteen feature films, including an adult role in 1942's *For Me and My Gal*, when the producer Joseph Pasternak bought Booth Tarkington's 1933 novel *Presenting Lily Mars* as her follow-up vehicle. It's the strangest musical in her resume, and consequently a cult film. Clearly, MGM did not see her as a contemporary woman (*For Me and My Gal* is set during World War I). Yet, with Norman Taurog directing, the studio compromised, bringing the story to the present while deciding that the music should be extra-light operetta—perfect for Deanna Durbin, then at her peak, but all wrong for the greatest song belter since Al Jolson. Then someone had another thought: this swing thing that had been going on for a decade still had life to it. So guest appearances by the Bob Crosby and Tommy Dorsey bands were added. Then someone else, reportedly Louis B. Mayer, complained that the picture looked kind of chintzy, so why not reshoot a grand finale, reviving a good old MGM tune from 1929, "Broadway Melody"? As a result, *Presenting Lily Mars* is three films in one, and as no one likes all three parts, it's usually dismissed as a dud.

I sing the praises of part one, the first forty minutes, played unexpectedly for laughs, with Judy doing mustache-twirling readings of Lady Macbeth and a refugee from *Way Down East*, as several sibling moppets imitate her every melodramatic excess. Van Heflin works on his double takes, Spring Byington fussbudgets, and a weird little girl plays and sings for Lily's grand entrance—a little girl who grew up to be the flame-haired jazz singer Annie Ross. Garland never looked better, though she blows the hair off her brow a few times too many. The next hour is a cliché-packed retake of *42ⁿᵈ Street*, as Judy wins Heflin's heart and a role in his dreadful stage show featuring her rival, played by the Hungarian operetta star Marta Eggerth, who sings most of the regrettable songs, one of which Garland parodies (wasting the

Crosby band). Heflin begins to look as though he were earning every penny of his salary, and just when you have surrendered to disbelief, along comes part three—the finale: Judy unchained, though forced to dance as much as she sings. A year later, she would get the film she deserved, *Meet Me in St. Louis*, but in the next quarter century she would not make as many films as she had in the six years before *Presenting Lily Mars*. She, too, had surrendered to verisimilitude.

52

HOW JAZZED CAN YOU GET?

Passing Through | A Great Day in Harlem |
Blues in the Night | Pete Kelly's Blues

THE SCENE

IT WOULD BE easier to grouse about the paucity of great—or good or tolerable or watchable—jazz-themed feature films if Hollywood had done any better by classical music or rock. It hasn't. Most American musicals, from *The Jazz Singer* and *The Broadway Melody* to *Moulin Rouge* and *Dreamgirls*, are concerned with the backstage tribulations of show folk, and employ stock story lines on which to hang the songs. Of all the movie genres, the glossy musical has died the stoniest of deaths, not because they are no longer made but because they have lost their rote, casual allure. People too young to be courted by AARP may find Busby Berkeley's calculus of female body parts or Fred and Ginger's between-dancing spats or the Technicolor trippiness of Fox and MGM burlesques to be a realm as foreign as Oz. Camp will take you only so far down the yellow brick road. Even I, a diehard fan of musicals, am dumbfounded by Esther Williams.

Jazz has long been an important part of the mix, and we must be grateful for what we have in the way of jazz footage on film and videotape. The twisted relationship between movies and jazz predated the sound era, when jazz was usually invoked as an ominous indication of wayward flappers, dissolute roués, and other lost souls. After the war, jazz continued to represent the underbelly of the human experience. Three instances, among countless others, will suffice as examples. First, Frank Capra's *It's a Wonderful Life* (1946), in which Jimmy Stewart is obliged to imagine idyllic Bedford Falls as if he had never been born. The place has gone to hell, particularly the friendly neighborhood bar, which in his absence has been invaded by bullies, rummies, hookers, and . . . Negro jazz. Second, the humid saxophone glissando that became ubiquitous in melodramas of the 1950s. Whenever a doll gets flirtatious or has too much to drink or wanders into a bad part of town, cue the alto—a sultry, ascending little lick, jazz's putative contribution to moral unrest. Third, a quite good Peruvian movie by Armando Robles Godoy, called *The Green Wall* (1970), about an office drone who leaves the noisy congestion of Lima for the verdant purity of the forest. When he is exulting in nature, the music is imitation Bach; when he's in the nerve-shattering city, the music is imitation Modern Jazz Quartet.

A counter-tradition also exists, in which Hollywood uses jazz to represent vitality and good times. As jazz musicians achieved radio stardom, it was good business to banner them on movie marquees, and not just for intermission floor shows; a filmed cameo was the only way most people got to see them. When Duke Ellington appeared in the leaden blackface Amos and Andy vehicle *Check and Double Check* (1930), for less than three minutes, black audiences flocked to local theaters, though the film was widely panned as offensive. Significantly, Ellington wanted Bing Crosby and the Rhythm Boys to handle the vocal part, but as the producers would not allow white singers to share the stage with a black band, a mike was set up for the trio to sing behind a curtain and three band members lip-synched their chorus for the camera, prefiguring the climax of *Singing' in the Rain*.

The racial issue remained toxic throughout the 1930s and 1940s, as jazz became a familiar element in big-budget musicals. Black specialty numbers were routinely isolated from the plot so that they could be excised when the film was distributed in the South. In 1936, Crosby invited Louis Armstrong to appear in *Pennies from Heaven*, which established him as a "specialty" performer in movies; and in 1937, Berkeley ignored the color line to feature the Benny Goodman Quartet (Goodman and Gene Krupa, white; Teddy Wilson and Lionel Hampton, black) in *Hollywood Hotel*. As the Swing Era waxed, however, almost all the good movie gigs went to white bands—often dull ones—ignoring the excitement and showmanship of Jimmie Lunceford, Chick Webb, Andy Kirk, and the 1930s Basie band. Basie wasn't invited until 1943 (*Reveille with Beverly*). Black bands were usually relegted to shorts, including the Vitaphone masterpiece *Jammin' the Blues*, a diamond amid that copany's dozens of white-band novelty acts.

The 1950s brought biopics of Swing Era bandleaders, and what a weird crew that sub-sub-genre produced: Glenn Miller, Benny Goodman, Red Nichols, Gene Krupa, Eddie Duchin, each the subject of the same story line. An arrogant rube arrives in city, is tamed by a woman, overcomes indifference or ridicule, triumphs, grows too big for his britches, dies or makes big comeback. *The Glenn Miller Story* includes an immortal line: asked to describe his revolutionary approach to music, Glenn explains, as if contemplating nuclear fission, "To me, music is more than just one instrument. It's a whole orchestra playing together!" After that sorry appproach faded, *Sweet Love, Bitter* (1967) originated the theme of the troubled black jazz genius, in this instance a saxophonist called Eagle, whose travail is told from the vantage point of an enlightened white friend.

By that time, Hollywood soundtracks, which had often employed jazz and jazzy touches, had passed through a happy moment when actual jazz composers were hired to compose scores: in Europe, Louis Malle invited Miles Davis to improvise the music for *Elevator to the Gallows* (1957). Thelonious Monk enlivened Roger Vadim's 1959 *Les liaisons dangereuses* (1959), Martial Solal added grace notes to *Breathless* (1960), by Jean-Luc Godard, who used jazzier scores by Michel Legrand for *A Woman Is a Woman* (1961) and *Band of Outsiders* (1964), as did Agnès Varda in *Cleo de 5 à 7* (1962). An especially bold jazz-themed film, *All Night Long* (1962), directed in England by Basil Dearden from a script by the American writers Nel King and the blacklisted Paul Jarrico, cleverly stages a retelling of Othello in an afterhours Soho jazz club, while a fierce storm rages outside. An ongoing jam session, played by Charles Mingus, Dave Brubeck, and several noted British musicians (including Johnny Dankworth and Tubby Hall), paces, spurs, and ultimately determines the (in this instance) near tragedy. *All Night Long* was neglected in this country. But the burgeoning independent film movement in New York had also claimed jazz. In 1959, Mingus's bass and Shafi Hadi's saxophone provided a spare pulse for John Cassavetes's *Shadows*, which, like *All Night Long*, explored mixed-race lovemaking; David Amram scored Robert Frank's *Pull My Daisy*; and Freddie Redd created a classic quartet score (with saxophonist Jackie McLean) for Jack Gelber's off-Broadway hit *The Connection*, filmed by Shirley Clarke in 1963.

Even Hollywood got the bug, as Henry Mancini (*Touch of Evil* in 1958,

High Time in 1960, and especially the 1958–60 television series *Peter Gunn*)
and Elmer Bernstein (*The Man with the Golden Arm* in 1955, with on-screen
participation by the Shorty Rogers Giants; *Sweet Smell of Success* in 1957,
with on-screen participation by the Chico Hamilton Quintet; and *Walk on
the Wild Side* in 1962), among several others, introduced jazz voicings and
rhythms. But it was Robert Wise, now widely associated with the films
West Side Story and *The Sound of Music*, who went to the actual jazz well. In
1958, he recruited John Mandel (and an all-star Gerry Mulligan ensemble)
for *I Want to Live*, initiating Mandel's long, fruitful film career, and the following year John Lewis, the pianist and director of the Modern Jazz Quartet, for *Odds Against Tomorrow*—these are two of the most masterly of all
jazz-inspired scores, rivaled perhaps only by the one Duke Ellington wrote
in that same period for Otto Preminger's *Anatomy of a Murder* (1959). Benny
Carter, one of jazz's most fabled innovators as an instrumentalist, composer, arranger, and trailblazer in integrating the Hollywood musician's
union, worked on many scores, ghosting for famous film composers (and
often appearing on screen in nightclub scenes as a kind of tip-off), but did
not get to put his own name on a film until the 1960s. By that time, several
jazz composers were at work, including Mal Waldron, Lalo Schifrin, and
Quincy Jones. Yet by the 1970s, after the success of films like *The Graduate*
and *Easy Rider*, jazz disappeared in favor of rock scores or licensed recordings with which the audience was already familiar.

Historical jazz films enjoyed a small and uneven revival in the 1980s
and 1990s. *Jazzman* (1983), by Russian director Karen Shakhnazarov, who
also made a powerful film about terrorists, *The Rider Called Death* (2004),
depicts musicians risking their freedom to play jazz in the Soviet Union
of the 1920s, and deserves more attention than it has received. Bertrand
Tavernier's *'Round Midnight* (1986), a darkly romantic and Parisian vision
of American jazz musicians driven abroad, lives on in the startling performance by Dexter Gordon, as an actor—his abilities as a musician had begun
to wane by the time it was filmed. Clint Eastwood's *Bird* (1988) is a formidable work, unnecessarily free with some of the facts and often as bleak
as Charlie Parker's increasingly tenuous hold on life; but as an uncompromising and unsentimental portrait of a great black artist and an interracial
love affair, it remains a genuine Hollywood breakthrough. Unlike Robert
Altman's wretched *Kansas City* (1996), in which joyful 1930s jazz musicians
are arrayed as the saving grace in a community so drunk on corruption and

self-importance that Harry Belafonte's vile mobster all but talks his victim to death. Two films that broach the subject of contemporary jazz focus mostly on amateurs, with salutary results. Frank D. Gilroy's *The Gig* (1985), a melancholy comedy, captures the enthusiasm of lunchtime musicians. Gary Winick and Polly Draper's *The Tic Code* (1999), though concerned with autism, conveys the love of jazz among grade-schoolers. Both films offer male bonding and jazz as a reason for living.

LOST AND FOUND

DESPITE THE ATTENTION given jazz films (notably in Krin Gabbard's 1996 book *Jammin' at the Margins: Jazz and the American Cinema*), one of the most illuminating and innovative American movies about the interaction of jazz and urban life was virtually lost for thirty years, until 2008 screenings brought it a renewed if limited attention. Larry Clark's *Passing Through*, a product of the black filmmaking resurgence at UCLA in the 1970s, was Clark's master thesis project, first screened in 1977, the same year as Charles Burnett's thesis film, *Killer of Sheep*. Burnett served as one of five cameramen on *Passing Through*; Clark served as one of five sound assistants on *Killer of Sheep*. *Passing Through*'s revival at the Brooklyn Academy of Music and the Museum of Modern Art (no DVD thus far) may have reflected the critical interest generated by the 2007 DVD release of Burnett's film, but it is a profoundly different kind of work—dark, incantatory, violent, angry, short on humor, and long on music, which it employs with an intricate and defiant commitment. Initially shown privately and at community fundraisers, *Passing Through* was screened at Cannes and other festivals, winning a special jury prize at Locarno. At home, it won an Oscar Micheaux Award from the Black Filmmakers Hall of Fame for its groundbreaking integration of jazz and narrative, yet it slipped so deeply into the cracks of obscurity that most considerations of jazz on film ignore it.

Shot in bleak, flat colors, emphasizing reds and blues, *Passing Through* is a picture of its time, capturing not the quotidian pleasures, frustrations, and telling anecdotes mastered by Burnett (who made his own wily jazz-and-community short film, *While It Rains*, in 1995), but rather a seething rage that renders narrative structure a sputtering montage of jump cuts, time warps (including a flashback within a flashback), dissolves, sepia-toned recollections, stock footage of imperialist atrocities, and plot twists that prefigure David Lynch—all scored to music that registers emotional upheavals with the precision of a tuning fork. You don't have to be a jazz fan to find *Passing Through* compelling, but it helps. Clark understands the distinctions between bebop and hard bop, borderline avant-garde jazz and full-body avant-garde jazz. He uses those distinctions to telegraph the mood of the characters and story, combining original music with excerpts from classic jazz recordings.

The plot, scripted by Clark and actor-writer Ted Lange from Lange's story, concerns an accomplished Los Angeles tenor saxophonist named Eddie Warmack (television actor Nathaniel Taylor), who returns to his neighborhood and band after serving a prison sentence for killing a white thug who blinded his friend and bandmate Skeeter (Bob Ogburn Jr., the father in the opening scene of *Killer of Sheep*). Hoping to restart his career, Warmack refuses to sign with the gangsters who recorded him in the past and vainly attempts to create a musicians' cooperative. This attempt alone is enough to trigger a deadly reprisal, which he avenges with the kind of efficiency that had animated blaxploitation films a few years earlier. Yet this isn't audience-rousing agitprop. Although we've learned from a startling flashback that Warmack is capable of cold-blooded murder, he is no Shaft or Super Fly. The line he crosses is morally conflicting because it seems to have a salubrious impact on his art.

Warmack's professional woes are inextricable from personal ones. Betrayed by his former lover Trixie (Sheryl Thompson), he takes up with a shy if fiercely independent graphics designer, Maya (Pamela B. Jones), who is assigned to do a magazine layout on him. The overlong middle section of the film is a rain-drenched series of overlapping vignettes, most of them played out in his cheap hotel bed, documenting the rise and fall of their relationship. At the same time, Warmack is intent on finding his grandfather and mentor, a musician and community seer known as Poppa Harris. As played by the legendary eighty-seven-year-old Clarence Muse—the director, writer, lawyer, songwriter ("When It's Sleepytime Down South"), and incredibly prolific actor who played the usual retinue of porters and butlers but without the slightest degree of servility—Poppa is the film's moral and mystical center, a teacher who trained Warmack to hear the universality of music. So it is mystifying to learn that this vigorous old man, seen only in flashbacks or as a corpse, bequeaths to Warmack the cryptic memo that unleashes his vengeance.

Passing Through is dedicated to the pianist, composer, and teacher Herbert Baker, who had recently died in a highway accident, and forty-two other musicians, some very famous, others utterly obscure, all associated closely or indirectly with California's black postwar jazz scene. Central to the film is the pianist and composer Horace Tapscott, who appears as himself and who conducted all of the film's new music. Tapscott, a resolute and influential artist who apprenticed many musicians, including several who went on to gain far more fame than he did, was in some respects a model for Warmack—minus the violence and jail time. In 1968, he composed, arranged, and conducted a peculiarly undervalued jazz masterwork, *Sonny's Dream*, a concerto-driven album by the West Coast alto saxophonist Sonny Criss. It should have launched his national reputation, but Tapscott devoted himself instead to his Watts-based Pan Afrikan Peoples Arkestra, using jazz to further community outreach and recording only for independent labels.

The film opens with a nearly six-minute musical prologue, most of it a piano improvisation by Tapscott filmed in hazy red hues and closing with a freeze-frame that cuts to a blue train, presumably the one bringing Warmack home. Throughout the film, Warmack's temperament is gauged by Tapscott's music and by the archival excerpts—Eric Dolphy's burbling bass clarinet, for example, to emphasize his alienation. In one magical scene, Warmack stands at a curb waiting for a lift, as the soundtrack plays a festive theme by Charlie Parker, conveying a sense of historical pride and communal self-reliance; this was the avant-garde jazz of the 1940s, now imparting a folk-like foundation for the blatantly expressionistic jazz of Warmack's generation. The plot of *Passing Through* helps to explain the music's emotional spasms; the music spurs the narrative arc.

Still, Clark's film is caught in a contradiction that undermines its depiction of the music business. On the one hand, Warmack's musicians acknowledge how parched they are for work—although rock and soul barely intrude in the film, they complain that they can only earn a living if they play commercial music dictated by the corrupt record company. On the other, that same mobbed-up company is apparently willing to murder to win a monopoly on avant-garde jazz, a laughable waste of its energy. *Passing Through* is the kind of film in which every appearance by a white person is ominous, and footage from Attica, Birmingham, and Africa is used to keep the outrage at a boil. But the film's power resides elsewhere, in its portrayal of a particular place and time. It captures an era when many musicians saw themselves as benign rebels whose music could bind and enrich the community and sustain its pride; and it imagines how that belief in music's healing power could be throttled into vigilante justice.

GROUP PORTRAIT

ONE OF THE best jazz documentaries has been expanded to more than twice its length on DVD. The sagging shelves of jazz docs, numbering in the hundreds, include many that are more musical, biographical, educational, political, philosophical, theological, and emotional than Jean Bach's unstoppable 1994 hour *A Great Day in Harlem*—but none that are more entertaining, and none that more casually dismiss the issues of racial and musical stereotypes as hopelessly square distractions. Bach's film is steeped in personalities, faces, generosity, and humor that, despite countless inside references guaranteed to warm every jazz lover's cockles, also captivates otherwise indifferent civilians. Just as a zoology degree is unnecessary to empathize with the migratory habits of penguins, an appreciation for the differences between the tenor saxophonists Coleman Hawkins and Lester Young (one of *Great Day*'s fleeting subtexts) is not a requisite for catching the infectious awe in which they are held.

A veteran radio producer and hostess of jazz-themed parties, Jean Bach had no filmmaking experience when she conceived the idea to interview on camera everyone associated with the most celebrated of jazz photographs: the 1958 gathering, on the stairs and stoop of a 125th Street brownstone, of nearly five dozen musicians, all but two (the totally obscure Bill Crump and the section man Scoville Brown) renowned in jazz. Few of the musicians were specifically summoned for the shot, which was conceived by the art director of *Esquire*, Art Kane, whose career in photography it inaugurated. Instead, a general invitation was issued for a 10 A.M. shoot. No one knew for certain who or how many would show up. In the event, fifty-eight did, though one, Willie "the Lion" Smith, wandered off right before the shutter was snapped.

As the musicians, who represented a great deal of jazz history, congregated at the appointed place at what was for them an early hour (one commented that he didn't know there were two 10 o'clocks in the same day),

Kane stood across the street with his camera strap around his neck, figuring a way to pose them. Some of the work was done for him by the process bassist-photographer Milt Hinton describes as water finding its own level: musicians unself-consciously grouped themselves by instrument–drummers schmoozing in one place, trumpeters or pianists in another.

The picture that *Esquire* published, with everyone facing front except Roy Eldridge, whom Dizzy Gillespie (tongue distended) made laugh at the fatal moment, and Mary Lou Williams and Marian McPartland conversing, became—increasingly, as one participant after another died—a religious totem, a symbolic, flat, sunlit mural marking a time when jazz's past and present could be contained in a wide-angle snapshot. The very serendipity of the project integrated legendary innovators with journeymen: soloists and singers, leaders and sidemen, section men and studio players. Other gatherings of equal note (Jimmy Carter's 1978 White House jazz festival, for one) have taken place, but produced no portrait of comparable power; the many outright imitations of Kane's grouping almost always project unintentional parody.

Bach began interviewing survivors in 1989, and her talking heads advance the narrative in standard ways while giving the film its humor and heart, because she favors the characteristic over the informational. Much of the running time is taken up with short biographical appreciations, but again, these function less as potted history lessons than as mutual appreciations. The words "idol" and "idolize" are heard constantly as musicians pore over the photograph and reminisce about the magnitude of colleagues. Imagine fifty-eight writers brought together and talking about how wonderful they all are—the very idea is laughable (PEN tried that once in New York, and you continue to hear tales of unresolved hard feelings). But all Bach, often heard but never seen, has to do is mention Hawkins or Young or Mary Lou Williams or Red Allen or Thelonious Monk or Rex Stewart or (the preternaturally beautiful) Maxine Sullivan to elicit sighs of admiration, illuminating anecdotes, and unadorned wonder.

When *A Great Day in Harlem* first appeared, those of us who had grown up with the Kane photograph were astonished within the opening seconds, as the black and white image morphed into color movement. Milt Hinton had shown up not only with his still camera, but also with a silent movie camera. What's more, Willie "the Lion" Smith's teenage protégé, pianist Mike Lipskin, brought his own camera and, standing near Kane, snapped

away. In addition, Kane had kept rejected shots, and by a cosmic coincidence, CBS in 1957 had broadcast *The Sound of Jazz*, America's finest hour
of televised jazz, featuring many of the musicians gathered in Harlem. The
cutting between all those shoots and the amateur and TV footage brings the
great day to life in a way that is spookily intimate, thanks to the unfailingly
impressive editing by Susan Peehl. The entire documentary, directed by
Matthew Seig, glides by at a sagacious tempo. Most documentary filmmakers foster the pointless illusion that they are shooting talking heads in her-
metically sealed confines, stopping the camera because the rumble of a truck
is barely audible in the distance. Not here: this film breathes with unfussy
naturalness—someone walks behind an interview subject, the sound briefly
fades, an off-camera question serves as a transition. So what?

When I first reviewed *A Great Day in Harlem*, in 1994, my one complaint
concerned its length. Much as I value the old showbiz adage "Always leave
them wanting more," I wanted to hear about every musician in the photograph, not just a few. The new double-disc DVD goes a long way in fulfilling
that wish, though it unaccountably omits "The Spitball Story," the prize-
winning twenty-minute addendum edited from original interview footage.
(A few minutes are included in the Gillespie section on the second disc.)
Other absences are equally hard to figure: the lack of credits on the new
featurettes (presumably Seig and Peehl are responsible); the lack of optional
English subtitles (infrequent subtitles are included at the filmmakers' discre-
tion); and identification of the musical pieces heard in the original film. Yet
nearly four hours of new material has been added, combining old and new
footage, making this an irresistible package. A forty-three-minute film on
the making of *Great Day* amounts to a sequel, edited with comic aplomb, as
Bach and team recount their travails in finding money and musicians, dealing with bad memories, long digressions, and physical ailments (we learn
more than we need to of Art Blakey's loss of hearing). An interview with
pianist Bill Charlap and drummer Kenny Washington, who weren't alive
when the photograph was taken but function as representatives of the next
generation, is enlivened with good stories and Washington's dead-on mim-
icking of Jo Jones. Other supplements deal with Art Kane, who took his life
at the height of the movie's initial success (apparently because of a hospital's
misdiagnosis), and a montage of imitations of Kane's photograph, stimulated by the release of *A Great Day in Harlem*.

The best addition is on the second disc: fifty-eight brief though often discursive verbal snapshots of each person in the photograph. Most of them range from two to five minutes, and you can access them in two ways: by using arrow keys to light up an individual in the photograph, or (more quickly) through an alphabetical listing. These small bits are very much in the style of the film—look to jazz encyclopedias if you want the facts—and focus on expressions of admiration, characteristic anecdotes, and idiosyncratic asides. Oddly, Bill Crump is misidentified, though we now know that he was a Buffalo-based saxophonist who in later years worked in West Coast bar bands, including that of Nellie Lutcher. Some of the best portraits concern the Lion, Young, Gillespie, Eldridge, Blakey, Gerry Mulligan, Max Kaminsky, and best of all Sonny Rollins, who sits for a relatively extended interview. The great day becomes a great party.

MINING THE MISERY

THE CYCLE OF gangster movies launched by Warner Bros. in the early 1930s often included scenes in speakeasies with anonymous musicians in the background. Anatole Litvak's *Blues in the Night* (1941) and Jack Webb's *Pete Kelly's Blues* (1955) reversed the perspective. These Warner gangster pictures are told from the point of view of idealistic white jazz musicians, determined to play their music despite rude audiences and mob interference. In the last reel, they win the day with inadvertent or vengeful help from mob apparatchiks, thereby saving themselves from the arms of the law. It isn't clear what saves them from other mobsters. Nothing can save them from the racial smirk of history.

Litvak and Webb had to confront—as did all jazz-related pictures made in the studio era—the embarrassing fact that they were obliged to dramatize black music as represented by white actors. *Blues in the Night* handles it by having the white band thrown in jail, where, in a segregated cell, the uncredited actor Ernie Whitman announces that everyone's got the misery, and to prove it, the uncredited singer William Gillespie moans "Blues in the Night"—written by those sons of the blues Harold Arlen and Johnny Mercer. The blacks seem to be truly miserable, but the whites are overjoyed to hear authentic misery, especially their leader, Jigger (Richard Whorf), who spends the rest of the film attempting to compose "Blues in the Night," which is never performed in its entirety. The film's credits omit another racial crossing: Jack

Carson plays a trumpet player whose work is (mostly) dubbed by Jimmie Lunceford's eminent lead trumpeter, Snooky Young. Lunceford's orchestra briefly appears as a New Orleans band, though his rigorous brand of swing is as close to New Orleans style as, say, "Blues in the Night" is to blues.

All of this would be borderline offensive, especially given the vaunted singing by the band's canary, Priscilla Lane, who couldn't swing from a trapeze. But the film is salvaged by many things, among them Litvak's speed, Ernie Haller's stylish (noir-like) photography, a sporadically witty Robert Rossen script (which reaches its apex in a spot-on parody of Mickey Mouse sweet bands), and the cast, including two Group Theater veterans—informer Elia Kazan (a live wire) and martyr Howard Da Silva (a short fuse). The other players include Lloyd Nolan (the chief gangster), Betty Field (the slut fatale), Wally Ford (the gimpy eunuch), and Peter Whitney (the hulking bassist). *Blues in the Night* features lots of talk about who's in or out of "the groove," as well as a few montages by Don Siegel, including an obligatory insert of blacks picking cotton and lifting bales, and a surreal alcoholic hallucination that liberally borrows from German expressionism. The band, with Whorf miming the piano playing of Stan Wrightsman, isn't much, but the climactic shoot-out in the rain is generically sound. Note: the DVD includes Gjon Mili's sublime *Jammin' the Blues*, a Lunceford short, and three Looney Tunes—two with "Blues in the Night" woven into the scores, and the third, "Swooner Crooner," a replay of the rivalry between Bing Crosby and Frank Sinatra that relates crooning to fertility.

The vastly superior *Pete Kelly's Blues* is handsomely transferred to an otherwise skeletal disc: too bad—the film deserves a commentary track if only to annotate the mostly superb music and the many inside jokes about jazz and Prohibition. Indeed, the film, despite its shootings, dipsomania, and insanity, often plays out as a comedy. Jack Webb originated Pete Kelly on the radio (for a three-month run in 1951), having already scored on radio with *Dragnet*. For *Pete Kelly's Blues*, he surrounded himself with old friends: his usual writer, Richard L. Breen; the Disney production designer and a fellow Dixieland addict, Harper Goff (who is in the film, playing banjo for Janet Leigh), and army buddy Dick Cathcart, who plays the trumpet solos that Pete Kelly mimes. Webb set out to re-create 1927 Kansas City in Technicolor and widescreen. As directed in his long-take style, the picture allows the musical numbers to play without interruption. The homage to blacks and misery is taken care of in a precredit sequence that depicts a 1915

New Orleans funeral—the camera stands as still as the mourners for a solid minute, as real-life trumpeter Teddy Buckner plays a hymn—for a musician whose cornet falls out the back of the hearse. A few years later, Kelly (Webb), in short pants, wins that same cornet in a New Jersey crap game. By the time the opening credits roll, twelve years have passed.

One of Webb's conceits was to cast against type: thus Lee Marvin is Mr. Nice Guy, a clarinetist whom little Pete coldcocks twice; sweetheart Janet Leigh is an heiress and sexual predator; Andy Devine, then of TV's *Andy's Gang*, is a tough but honest cop; singers Ella Fitzgerald and Peggy Lee are, respectively, a gin-mill owner who sings and a gangster's moll who sings and goes mad; and ordinary guy Edmond O'Brien is a ruthless mob boss and would-be band booker—a type he parodied a year later in the Jayne Mansfield breakthrough *The Girl Can't Help It*, though at times he seems to be doing the parody in *Pete Kelly's Blues* (in which Jayne Mansfield appears as a cigarette girl). A memorable character is the club owner, Rudy (Than Wyenn), who counts the anchovies on the pizzas, manufactures champagne with a seltzer siphon, and samples customers' drinks as they exit the kitchen to make certain they are diluted with water.

Webb's performance, though often mocked, is mostly effective. Bow-tied and low-key, he moves with casual self-possession, handles props with focused deliberation, and spits out a stream of memorable one-liners. He stages almost all of his scenes so that he is facing forward, usually tucking his hands in his pockets, as he clearly doesn't know what to do with them in the absence of props. (An example is the scene in which the Lee Marvin character says he's leaving Missouri while Webb allows his hideous sweater to do the emoting.) The film's colors sparkle, and the long takes work like tableaux, sometimes tricked up with canny camera movements—Hal Rosson's camera covers a four-minute hotel bedroom scene with Webb, Leigh, and a canary in a single shot, and handles Peggy Lee's major mad scene in five unbroken minutes. Talk about editing in camera: no inserts, no over-the-shoulder conversations. Poorly reviewed in its day, *Pete Kelly's Blues* made money, revived the Dixieland craze, influenced a host of Roaring 20s films and TV shows, including at least two more gangster films with musicians in the foreground (*The Joker Is Wild* and *Some Like It Hot*), and, thanks to Ella's riveting performance, made a 1950s hit of the 1924 song "Hard Hearted Hannah."

53

BATTLING NAZIS WITH SAMBAS

Saludos Amigos / The Three Caballeros

BEFORE ANTONIO CARLOS Jobim, there was Ary Barroso; before "Desafinado" and "The Girl from Ipanema," there were "Brazil" (originally "Aquarela do Brasil") and "Bahia" (originally "Na Baixa do Sapateiro"). During World War II, Barroso's songs, composed in the late 1930s, launched Brazilian popular music around the world. They were taken up by dozens of jazz and dance bands and pop singers. Yet unlike Jobim's songs, which took flight after North American jazz musicians discovered them, Barroso's intricate compositions were imported by an unlikely popularizer, Walt Disney, working at the behest of an unlikelier master, Nelson Rockefeller—the ambitious Coordinator of Inter-American Affairs who proposed to weaken the Nazi position in South America with a Good Neighbor movie policy.

Rockefeller enlisted Disney in 1941 with a guarantee of $150,000 against losses, as part of a wide-ranging Hollywood reach-out. He promised Orson Welles twice as much to fly south and shoot a film, but then abandoned him; Welles, whose reputation never entirely recovered, exacted a modicum of revenge by casting a Rockefeller look-alike as the treacherous nutcase who calls everyone "fella" in *The Lady from Shanghai* (1947). Disney, true to form, never had to claim the guarantee. He produced two films that made money: the short, uneven compilation *Saludos Amigos*, which premiered in Rio in 1942 and in Boston the next year, and the astounding seventy-two-minute feature film *The Three Caballeros*, which premiered in Mexico City toward the close of 1944 and in New York early in 1945.

Disney's two films enjoyed even greater popularity south of the border than at home, but have never accrued the stature of his other animated classics. Rockefeller's offer came at a time when Disney was at a creative crossroads. His animated features had not always earned back their costs, and between *Bambi* (1942) and *Cinderella* (1950), he focused on an odd medley of works. This period might be characterized as the Mary Blair era, after the art director whose unusual color schemes and dramatic watercolor effects gave these works a particular style that was further developed in Disney's fairy tale hits of the early 1950s. Yet the films that established her skills were hit-and-miss anomalies: propaganda (including the outstanding *Victory Through Air Power* [1943], which remained unavailable to the general public until its DVD release); compilation films that emphasized music; and projects that combined animation and live action—beginning with these two Latin films.

Live action and animation had been successfully wed in the silent era—it was the selling point for the Fleischer Studio's "Out of the Inkwell" cartoons (beginning in 1919) and, a few years later, Disney's less memorable "Alice Comedies." But no one made the process work in Technicolor until *Saludos Amigos*. Traveling through South America with his wife and sixteen artists and musicians, divided into groups to take in the different countries, Disney brought three 16-mm silent cameras. He used that footage to bind the animated stories in *Saludos Amigos* as well as for a half-hour 1942 documentary, "South of the Border with Disney," which is included (along with two Latin-themed Donald Duck cartoons) on a DVD that represents the first pairing of Disney's Latin animations since a munificent 1995 laser disc. The low-grade film stock gives the picture a nostalgically pleasing ordinariness, as it looks no better than the home movies suburban dads would be shooting a few years later, after the war.

The film's early sections are mostly as expected: anthropomorphic views of animals and objects, Donald exploring Lake Titicaca, Goofy doing a gaucho bit on the pampas (employing paintings by the gaucho artist F. Molina Campos), a boy-airplane weathering a storm to deliver the mail. These are nicely done and occasionally funny, but nothing like the last segment: "Aquarela do Brasil" combines Barroso's undying, harmonically daring song with an interpolation of a popular wartime samba, Zequinha de Abreu's "Tico Tico no Fubá," which, though composed twenty-five years earlier (Abreu died in 1935), remained unknown beyond Brazil until Disney brought it home. Framed by Blair watercolors and sung by Aloysio Oliveira, this sequence also introduces the lively parrot José Carioca, voiced by the actor and bandolim player José Oliveira. Carioca gets Donald blind drunk on *cachassa* while calmly puffing on his cigar.

While *Saludos Amigos* unleashed two songs that became national obsessions, it was merely a rehearsal for *The Three Caballeros*. For the first film, an uncredited Carmen Miranda served two days as a consultant. In the second, her more beautiful sister Aurora, though never a star in her own right, danced to samba rhythms that Carmen had been turning into box-office gold since her 1940 Hollywood debut in *Down Argentine Way*. A major musical by any standard, *The Three Caballeros* boasts sixteen songs, though only five are noted in the credits. Again, an omnibus structure enfolds discrete tales: Donald gets a box of presents from his South American friends, including a film projector and screen that he clambers into as easily as Buster Keaton does in *Sherlock Jr.* The opening sections concern "strange birds," including a penguin that would rather live in the tropics, an aracuan (a woodpecker-like creature that also triggers the DVD menu), and a flying donkey.

Things begin to jump with the reappearance of José Carioca, who takes Donald to Bahia, where the music includes Dorival Caymmi's "Have You Ever Been to Bahia," and Mary Blair's drawings predominate. As Barroso's "Bahia," with its vamp, two-part melody, and lavish chords, is supplanted by his pulsing samba "Os Qunidans de Yaya," Aurora Miranda dances into view, giving Donald bestial palpitations. Soon other dancers are performing against the animated scrim, for a widely imitated and tenaciously adult sequence. Carioca describes one dancer as a *malandro*, declining to explain the term as Portuguese shorthand for gigolo. After Aurora kisses Donald, the film cuts to silhouetted dancers who morph into fighting cocks, the transitions signaled by crashing cymbals and lightning blasts. This is one of Disney's most impressive musical sequences. The live-action photography by Technicolor specialist Ray Rennahan is realized in perfect accord with the processing effects.

Then it gets better still, in Mexico, with the introduction of the third caballero, the rooster Panchito (voiced by Joaquin Garay), who joins Donald (invariably voiced by Clarence Nash) and Carioca for Manuel Esperón's entrenched title song, "The Three Caballeros," furnished with an audacious English lyric by Ray Gilbert. Except for a patronizing Christmas interlude and a gringo ballad (Disney's Charles Wolcott was a talented music director and a dreadful songwriter), things go into overdrive as the gay caballeros prove how gay they can be, at one point dancing in drag with live-action female legs.

After Donald ogles bathing beauties at Acapulco Beach (actually the Disney parking lot filled with sand), Doña Luz enters as a disembodied head, singing Augustin Lara's "You Belong to My Heart," which would soon be a major hit for Bing Crosby. The influence of Busby Berkeley is everywhere—floating heads, freewheeling hallucinations—especially during the stunning "Jesusita," as Luz dances at the apex of countless Donalds who grow into giant phallic cactuses. The staging echoes that of "The Lady in the Tutti Frutti Hat," from Berkeley's *The Gang's All Here*, released the previous year (and including "Brasil," snatched from *Saludos Amigos*). The hyperinventiveness is dazzling. As the caballeros finish their song, Panchito holds the last note for twenty seconds, giving the animators time to pile on nearly a dozen sight gags—an irresistible capper for an irresistible film.

However, this is one of Disney's most disappointing DVDs. The films are in excellent shape—colors brighter than in previous incarnations, images stabilized. But the 1995 laser-disc edition of *Saludos Amigos* and *The Three Caballeros* was one of the most comprehensive and insightful packages in the annals of home video: bolstered with hundreds of drawings (many Blair watercolors), photographs, storyboards, a detailed explanation of how animation and live action work, newsreel and studio footage, advertising materials (including the clever trailers), radio broadcasts, an informative flyer, and fastidious reconstructions of two cartoons slated for the films but never completed. Even the box was artfully designed. The DVD dispenses with everything but "South of the Border with Disney" and a ninety-second interview snippet. Is all that supplementary work now consigned to a studio vault? *Caballeros* libre!

54

DOG DAYS

Lady and the Tramp / Hayao Miyazaki /

Max and Dave Fleischer

AS EVERY PARENT knows, most family entertainment is no such thing—it's more often preschool entertainment, a much easier sale; or adolescent entertainment, which for boys tends to emphasize toilet jokes and special effects, and for girls sexual dilemmas with a Nancy Reagan punch line. Niche marketing, like global warming, is a slow, inviolable process, melting consensus and leaving the Beatles as the only bulwark against complete cultural disunity. Let's blame Michael Eisner. You remember him: imperious CEO of the Disney empire, who chased Jeffrey Katzenberg from the magic kingdom; attempted to emulate Uncle Walt on television and rendered his base audience comatose; banned wine from Euro-Disney; outsourced animated features to Pixar; and went an extra step by declaring two-dimensional cartoons obsolete. My own theory consigns decline and fall to the release of *The Hunchback of Notre Dame* (1996), based on two remarks by my then seven-year-old. As Frollo waxed insane before the fireplace, thinking of Esmeralda, my daughter asked, "Why is he so angry?" You try and explain. At the end, when Quasimodo—depicted as cute but pimply—united Esmeralda and Phoebus in marital harmony, she asked, "Is he their pet?"

At least the film united us in dismay. We had previously shared a delight in many classic Disney and Katzenberg-generated pictures. More than any mogul since the young David Selznick, Disney, despite the arrogance of his possessory credits and the suburbanization of his once-anarchic (think of the original Mickey Mouse) cartoon characters, helped to stabilize the nineteenth-century mostly English tradition of inherited works—*Alice in Wonderland, Peter Pan, Twenty Thousand Leagues Under the Sea, Treasure Island*—passed from one childhood to the next. His best animated features were morally rigorous, mixing suspense, comedy, romance, and adventure with smart musical support, state-of-the-art animation, and artful composition. Where did it all go wrong?

The Disney of *Snow White and the Seven Dwarfs* and *Pinocchio* understood that fairy tales are self-contained dramas, rife with malevolence and death. Subsequent generations of parents decided that the villains who chilled *them* would traumatize their own children. Worse, those tenderized children eventually took charge of the Disney studio and replaced visual comedy with trendy wisecracks, terror with melodrama, innocence with sentimentality, and illumination with didacticism. Disney's recent DVDs lay out the terrain. *Lady and the Tramp* (1955), a pinnacle of Walt's dominion, has lost nothing to time. *Chicken Little* (2005), a 3-D Pixar impersonation, died before it was hatched. Three films from Japan's Studio Ghibli—Hayao Miyazaki's *My Neighbor Totoro* (1988) and *Howl's Moving Castle* (2004) and Yoshifumi Kondo's *Whisper of the Heart* (1995), written by Miyazaki—for which Disney produced American dubbings, inadvertently prove that 2-D animation is far from dead and that emotional commitment will always trump technique.

Lady and the Tramp, Disney's first Cinemascope cartoon feature, is exemplary despite a story buried in banality. The confident tempo channels Chaplin: the animators knew exactly how far to take any expressive template—adorableness, slapstick, calamity, serenade—before switching to another, though 1950s timidity mandated a lot of gibberish about storks and birds and bees to get around the unmentionable word "pregnant." The ethnic humor is tame (unless you are a rat, a Siamese cat, or a maiden aunt, in which case protests may be warranted), the drawing accomplished, and the subtext invigorating as it motors over the pros and cons of freedom and servitude. Lady, a cocker spaniel who looks at times like the Scottish actor Alastair Sim, and other dogs of the haute monde love nothing more than to be collared and licensed, though they draw the line at muzzles. Tramp, a scrawny mutt, makes the case for the open road, the unfenced world at large, the liberation from licensed behavior. In the end, Lady convinces him that life on the homestead is best and Tramp proudly sports his collar and offspring, the result of one all-nighter, which begins memorably with vino and spaghetti and causes so much concern in the dog world that two canine neighbors propose marriage to save Lady's honor.

The film is mired in two controversies, one of which is explored in a making-of documentary. Unlike Disney's previous cartoon features, *Lady and the Tramp* was based on an original story, much of it developed in the 1930s by animator Joe Grant. He created Lady, her milieu, and the cats, but failed to supply a love interest, something Disney recognized when he read about a devious bird dog in a story by Ward Greene. Having fallen out with Grant, Disney deprived him of all credit (claiming Lady was inspired by his own dog) and paid Greene to write a novel based on the script of the uncompleted film so that he could pretend that the film was adapted from the published story.

The other controversy concerns the music and the Eisner regime. Peggy Lee, who wrote the lyrics to Sonny Burke's melodies and voiced four of the characters, was represented by a farsighted agent who included a proviso guaranteeing her royalties from future sources of distribution, like home video. When the studio refused to acknowledge her claim, Lee sued for $25 million and was eventually awarded $2.3 million in a judgment twice appealed by Disney and twice upheld by the courts. Her name doesn't appear on the DVD box, though she receives her due in the documentary. If anyone deserves a possessory credit, she does—her treatments of "Siamese Cat Song," "La La Lu," and "He's a Tramp" are the film's wittiest touchstones and highlights of the 1950s Hollywood musical. Oliver Wallace's score enfolds them and the other tunes, including "Home, Sweet Home," with fastidious elegance.

Chicken Little, by contrast, is a noisy, long-winded, witless, insincere amalgam that will displease children of all ages. One can imagine the writers trying to outdo each other with inside jokes that have all the freshness of *Saturday Night Live*. It's not worth mentioning except as an indication of how alienated its creators are from the verities that once made Disney a dependable brand. That position is now enjoyed by Pixar and, since the international success of Miyazaki's *Spirited Away* (2001), Studio Ghibli.

Hayao Miyazaki's films unwind at a far more leisurely tempo with relatively little comedy and a strangely derivative approach to music (he loves the lumbering, lyrical, heavy strings of 1950s film scores). They feature humans as opposed to anthropomorphic animals—especially girl humans of about fourteen years of age. Perhaps the main quality of Miyazaki's world is its spirituality. In American fantasies, spiritual elements are either explained away or experienced only by children; in Japan, spirits, ghosts, wizards, and witches are an accepted part of the landscape, and the wasteland that divides childhood and adulthood is more illusory than real. Evil exists but is mutable, not absolute, and is often defeated by universal trust—a belief in the uncanny.

Of the three DVD releases, *My Neighbor Totoro* has the most conventional plot. As their mother recuperates in a hospital, a father and his two daughters move into the country where a benign forest monster and his eight-legged Catbus solve their dilemmas. What is unusual is the children's fearless embrace of adventure; deliberate comic timing of a sort that recalls the movies of Blake Edwards; and adult concurrence with childhood imagination. As always, there is the sheer beauty of Miyazaki's images. Yoshifumi Kondo's *Whisper of the Heart* is unique in my experience in that, notwithstanding a few fantasy episodes that could have been handled by computer graphics (or double exposure), the film might have been shot live with real actors. Set in and around a junior high school in West Tokyo, it depicts a budding romance between a girl who wants to write and a boy who wants to build violins, set against the lost love of an old artisan. In this instance, the early promises of the supernatural are muted, and though the faces occasionally suggest the teenage girls in Archie comics, the sense of place is persuasively specific. One of the boys, frustrated by the heroine's complaint, says, "I don't speak girl code!" Miyazaki and Kondo clearly do.

Howl's Moving Castle is a more divisive work, a magnificently illustrated and intricate adventure packed with assorted parts from children's lit, especially *The Wizard of Oz*. It features a prince turned into a scarecrow, a shapeshifting hero with courage but without a heart, and, doubling the tin man, the eponymous castle—a clunking, patched-up ship waddling on chicken claws, with portals that can be tuned, like a television set, to various modes of reality. The castle and other machines suggest the unmistakable influence of the 1950s Czech animator Karel Zeman. The wizard is an evil (or not) sorceress who wages war, the heroine a young milliner turned into an old crone (but whose age is shown to be in constant flux, depending on the emotional context of any scene), and the setting a fictitious fin de siècle Europe beset by wizards, witches, mollusk-like assassins, and terrifying airships that strafe city after city with firebombs. The problem is the final fifteen or so minutes, which are so repetitive and complicated that the story seems to unravel. Still, I wouldn't want to have missed all that precedes them.

We don't have to access contemporary Japan to experience the cartoon rebelliousness that Disney quelled. The pioneering comics artist Kim Deitch rigorously investigates that very theme in his ingenious, funny, and deeply moving 2002 comic-book novel *Boulevard of Broken Dreams*, which tracks the fortunes of animation from individual visionaries to meretricious assembly lines, with delusions of theme park grandeur as the abiding punch line. For individualism at its most feverishly kinetic, we can refresh our souls with the intensely musical, insanely spontaneous, Jewish-urban sensibility of the Fleischer brothers, Max and Dave, who paved the way for and briefly rivaled Disney, usually making hipper, riskier cartoons—until the Production Code reined them in and Paramount, the Fleischer Studio's distributor, engineered a takeover and kicked them out.

In 1914, Max Fleischer invented the Rotoscope, which linked a motion picture projector to an artist's easel, allowing the artist to trace, frame by frame, live movement as a source for animation. A few years later, he introduced Koko the Clown in the surreally imaginative "Out of the Inkwell" series, pioneering the combination of fluid animation and live-action footage, usually of Max in the process of drawing Koko. Dave, who soon became the studio's key director, began as Koko's model. With the advent of sound, the brothers pioneered musical synchronization, including the bouncing-ball "Screen Songs" and the Talkertoons, which introduced their most durable creation, Betty Boop; Betty began animated life as a dog and soon morphed into a short-skirted coquette, inspired by the singer Helen Kane (who unsuccessfully sued) and deliciously voiced by Mae Questel.

The studio's trademark irreverence, musicality, ethnicity (black music, Yiddish jokes), and restive resourcefulness meshed in such 1932–33 Betty Boop classics as "I'll Be Glad When You're Dead, You Rascal You" (Louis Armstrong's disembodied head stalks Betty and Koko), "I Heard" (bandleader Don Redman shares the vocals with Questel), and two benchmark tours de force with Cab Calloway, "The Old Man of the Mountain" and "Snow White." In the last, Questel's Betty, informed of her imminent decapitation, sings Charles Harris's 1903 lament "Always in the Way," after which Cab, Rotoscoped as a dancing goblin, wails "St. James Infirmary" in hell. Unlike Disney, the Fleischers preferred animating humans to animals, so when, in 1933, they were able to get rights to the comic-strip sailor Popeye, they seized the day. The complete Betty Boops, pre- and post-Code (garter belt gone, skirt lowered, maternal duties added), were collected on laser discs in the 1990s, but have yet to enter the DVD era. Popeye, however, is back, correcting a far longer absence from center stage.

With "Popeye the Sailor Meets Sindbad the Sailor," we are reminded that the Fleischers also pioneered the use of Technicolor: this two-reeler is noted for hallucinatory colors, three-dimensional animation, a lively theme song, and almost exhausting vitality. It's one of sixty Popeyes, programmed in the order of their initial release, on *Popeye the Sailor, 1933–1938*, a four-disc set made possible by the resolution of a long-standing conflict between the newspaper syndicate that owns the strip and Warner Bros., which now owns the Paramount cartoons. Also tucked into the set among the featurettes are Fleischer animations from the silent era, notably nine "Out of the Inkwell" epics, with Koko misbehaving on Max Fleischer's drawing board. The absence of music is regrettable, yet the Koko animations exude the joy of discovery, as do several older vault treasures, including a 1916 Mutt and Jeff exploit with dialogue balloons and a plot later recycled frequently by Laurel and Hardy.

Popeye represents a pinnacle in Depression animation and comedy, working diverse variations on the eternal triangle with Olive Oyl, the fickle femme with concave chest and linguini limbs, and Bluto, the bruiser with a huge body, tiny head, and revolting manners. Moral support is provided by Swee'Pea, a cap-wearing infant of uncertain origin, and Wimpy, a poster boy for fast-food super-sizing. These cartoons often embody the antithesis of Rotoscoping, preferring rubbery creatures given to rapid metamorphosing. Dave Fleischer exhorted his animators to punch up each scene with a gag. And the Popeyes deliver; they may not be as consistently subversive as the pre-Code Betty Boops, but the best of them are faster and funnier. The Fleischers offered an anti-Disney view of life: gleefully violent, habitually jazzy, low-rent, and gloatingly unreal. The characters are plugged into a cosmic jiggling rhythm, their mutterings too subliminal to lip-synch. As a baleful sign of the times, note that the box warns: *"Popeye the Sailor, 1933–1938, Volume One* is intended for the adult collector and may not be suitable for children." Say whaa? Also, while due regard is paid the voice of Popeye, Jack Mercer (dig him scatting "The Spinach Overture"), little is said of Mae Questel, who patterned Olive Oyl on Zasu Pitts, flattening the vowels at the end of lines and singing like nobody's business. Without Olive, Popeye is just another spinach-crazed gob.

55

UNCLE WALT'S
PRAIRIE HOME COMPANION
True-Life Adventures

WALT DISNEY'S *Legacy Collection*, which packs its archival desiderata in stately double-disc tin boxes with hours of celebratory extras, has collected all fourteen of the *True-Life Adventures* released to theaters (and later televised) between 1948 and 1960. Also included are a few nature films that fell outside the True-Life rubric; relevant episodes of the TV show *Disneyland*; tributes to the men and women responsible; advertisements for theme parks; and best of all, "Filmmaker's Journals" that, among other things, merrily 'fess up to much but not all of the series' fakery—as if we knew it all the time. Hurrah, with reservations. These are among the more controversial items in Disney's canon, and time has not unraveled the agony from the ecstasy.

The True-Life series was supposedly inspired when Disney looked at wildlife footage commissioned to aid the artists drawing *Bambi* (1942), and figured nature documentaries might make for inexpensive entertainment. The idea was to take the reels and reels of raw footage, organize them with thematic story lines—prairie, desert, arctic, jungle, ocean, and so on—and punch them up with dramatic musical scores. Distributors thought he was mad, but audiences flocked to see these films, and multiple Academy Awards fell into his lap. Much of the footage is riveting: gorgeous, suspenseful, violent, amusing, illuminating. Disney recognized the power of wonder as well as the thriftiness in shooting nonunionized animals, and few (grumpy naturalists aside) can remain entirely unmoved by these Technicolor zoological templates for *The Lion King* and *Finding Nemo*.

On the other hand, it isn't nice to fool with Mother Nature or exploit the credulity of children, and Disney's ventures into the wild did plenty of both. Mother can take care of herself (except where theme parks blight the ecosystem), but children can handle only so much prevarication. Grown-ups lied about the tooth fairy, Santa, Washington's cherry tree, Indians, and plantation-loving slaves, and then—et tu, Uncle Walt?—they lied about the lemmings. To this day, millions of people believe those endearing arctic rodents are genetically suicidal, taking to the sea like Ishmael, as a substitute for falling Cato-like on, say, pointy twigs. Disney didn't invent that myth, but he dramatized it in *White Wilderness* (1958), with narrator Winston Hibler's voice of scientific rectitude explaining that the lemmings jump over cliffs because they think the sea is just another rivulet to cross in their endless quest for Lebensraum.

Trouble is, lemmings don't inhabit the part of Canada where the picture was shot, and so they were imported and photographed on a turntable to create the illusion of large numbers. When the lemmings refused to leap from the parapet, helpful naturalists tossed them over and filmed their lifeless floating bodies. Beyond first-degree lemming murder, the main crime here is that it was done for a series that, from the first short subject, *Seal Island* (1948), claimed to be "completely authentic, unstaged, and unrehearsed," "straight from the realm of fact"; as Walt put it: "Nature is the dramatist. There are no fictitious situations or characters." The illusion took root. According to the Oxford English Dictionary, the earliest usage of "lemming" as a "person bent on a headlong rush" stems from 1959, a year after *White Wilderness*. The upside is that disillusioned naturalists in the 1980s were stirred to do serious lemming research that disproved the legend. In that spirit, it would have been noble if Roy Disney, Walt's nephew and the godfather of these DVDs, had sat down with a true-life scientist to itemize what is and isn't kosher about True-Life Adventures.

As it is, Disney does offer welcome candor in the "Filmmaker's Journals," demonstrating, for example, how many animal noises were made with inanimate appliances, not unlike sound effects on old radio. Much of *The Living Desert* (1953), the hugely successful first True-Life feature, is shown to have been shot on a soundstage. The films aimed for something new: they combined genuinely innovative close-quarters nature photography with plotlines similar to those of Disney cartoons. The dexterous editing in several instances—the infamous hoedown by two scorpions, for one—recalls talking-dogs shorts of the 1930s, except that few of us had ever seen a scorpion, square dancing or not. In fairness, a certain amount of creative latitude is telegraphed in the titles, and it is impossible to look at these films through mature eyes and not see the editing tricks, the endless tracking shots (as if the cameraman knew exactly where that snake was headed), the underground visits with gophers and ants, and the relentless anthropomorphism. Did you know that otters are "carefree vagabonds" and "merry madcaps" for which "life is a continuous, carefree water ballet"? It's a True-Life fact!

James Algar, the director and co-writer of the series, spoke frankly about not only imposing narrative situations on the miles of footage (some of it freelanced), but employing film school techniques, like point-of-view and over-the-shoulder shots. He set out to follow the Disney mandate of educational entertainment and succeeded so well that he created the entire field of nature films in which humans are never glimpsed. Such recent box-office bonanzas as *Winged Migration* and *March of the Penguins* are not far removed from the Disney prototype. When Morgan Freeman intones in the latter film that a penguin's loss of an egg is "unbearable," we are having yet another True-Life Adventure.

In two respects, at least, Algar's science is insistently if somewhat coyly accurate. First, though the narrator never mentions evolution or Darwin (no need to offend Tennesseans, still celebrating their triumph of the will in the Scopes monkey trial), the word "develop" is used constantly to explain why one creature has blubber or fins or a woolly hide. Indeed, evolution is the theme that unites the series, perhaps to a fault. It is employed to justify the destruction of the "unfit"—"cripples and weaklings"—while imposing humanistic qualities. Nearly every courtship, regardless of species, is described in the same terms: the female is a "damsel" or "fair lady," and the male has to endure violent combat to win her. The second respect is conservation, another word you don't hear, though the point is clear: the wonders of nature will prevail only "as long as man shall leave her work untouched." The Disney Studio harbored romantic liberals in mouse ears.

The most hoked-up of these films, such as *The Vanishing Prairie* (1954) or *Perri* (1957), may still engross young children, and the footage is usually beguiling even when the narration is turgid: "It seems like a coyote can't make a move these days without someone giving the alarm"—that "someone" is a member of the Beaver Vigilance Committee in *Beaver Valley* (1950). The best of them are enthralling. These include *The African Lion*

(1955), which, notwithstanding a makeshift conceit about the lion ruling its domain, is a robust record of jungle creatures visited with eye-popping intimacy, though the geography is finessed (Kilimanjaro is and is not on the horizon in shots that are supposed to depict the same area); and *Secrets of Life* (1956), which, according to Roy Disney, was inspired by the volcanic *Rite of Spring* animation in *Fantasia* (1940). The secrets include a six-minute sequence, without narration, of ravishing botanical time-lapse photography.

Many scenes are as remarkable for their cinematic as their natural power. A comparison of backstage photography of alligators in the Everglades, where they are shown to be benign, with their appearances in *Prowlers of the Everglades* (1953), where Wagnerian music and canny cutting transform them into vampiric nightmares, shows how spurious True-Life dramatization could be. That doesn't mean it isn't effective. The battle between the wasp and the tarantula in *The Living Desert* is as tense as, say, King Kong versus the dinosaur, doubly so for being real—even if it was instigated in a studio cage. Some of the natural monuments and wide-open vistas are captured as magnificently as anything by Ansel Adams (who shot some of the same landscapes). At such moments, when the heavy musical cues and pandering narration are merely intrusive, you may want to cut the volume and slip into an iPod. Overall, the *True-Life Adventures* justify these spruced-up DVD restorations, issued in four volumes: *Wonders of the World*, *Lands of Exploration*, *Creatures of the Wild*, and *Nature's Mysteries*. They display the diversity, beauty, horror, and ingenuity of the natural world, which, despite suicidal lemmings and giddy hoedowns, is no lie.

56

MEN WITHOUT MOLLS

Gangsters Collection, Vol. 3

WARNER HOME VIDEO has released its pre–Production Code movies by gender. The *Forbidden Hollywood* series focuses on women who indulge in sexual bravado or maternal sacrifice. These films ask us to identify with women as free souls who instigate affairs, exploit male assistants, and assault the citadels of power, mounting one gatekeeper after another, though in the end they would rather die than have it known that the spawn of their street-walking days is the district attorney. With few exceptions (Barbara Stanwyck in *Baby Face*, Jean Harlow in *Red-Headed Woman*), a whore's ambition is no match for a mother's love, even pre-Code. On the men's side, we are often asked to identify with gangsters, until they bite the dust. Four of the six films in *Gangsters Collection, Vol. 3*, are pre-Code variations on the theme of the heavy who is more sympathetic than the forces of law and propriety. The other two cover similar ground while strenuously out-running the censor by resorting to patriotism or parody.

In all these brisk, cheerfully immoral films, women continue to enjoy sexual freedom, but only as calculating hussies whom the protagonist will abandon as soon as the good girl enters the picture. Another difference between male-dominated films and those gathered in *Forbidden Hollywood* is that the molls in gangster films get their faces slapped, hair pulled, rumps kicked, and bodies tossed into hallways or out of doors. Also, gangster films spend almost as much time in lavatories as in boudoirs—it's a guy thing. In the 1960s, Jack Warner, the last old-time mogul to rule a Hollywood studio, regarded the gangster films that had put him and his brothers on the map with chagrin. They were movie pulp, pandering to the public's unslakable thirst for sex, violence, and stylish irreverence. While Paramount went continental and MGM sought class, the Warners drank from the working-man's trough, where ethnic groups simmered without quite melting.

The uncommon common man was exemplified by two unexpectedly fascinating yeggs: Jewish Edward G. Robinson and Irish James Cagney. Both men grew to resent the characterizations that made them famous, but audiences didn't pack theaters to see them expand their range; they came to watch them assert and defy authority. Notwithstanding the fatal climaxes of *Little Caesar* and *Public Enemy*, the characters often got away with it, as Robinson developed comedic chops and Cagney showed that tough guys danced and sang. The directors, including the journeymen in this collection, knew that the key objective was to keep pictures moving fast and to wind up with a knockout. The beauty of the pre-Code era is that it inspired vibrancy as well as moral combativeness. When that era was first revived in the 1980s on cable (thank you, Ted Turner), audiences raised on the Production Code could scarcely believe that the studios had ever been able to get away with candid depictions of casual sex, impulsive violence, and Depression iniquities. An audience raised on Internet porn will be less impressed by revealing lingerie or dialogue such as: "You've been rubbing noses with movie stars." "Call it noses if you like." Yet time has not gentled the buoyant cynicism of these movies, which prize gambling, petty crime, prostitution, and extortion over corruption, piety, prejudice, and unkindness to children and small animals.

In the earliest picture in the package, Alfred E. Green's *Smart Money* (1930), Robinson plays Nick, a small-town barber with a lucky streak and the hubris to match; given a stake to take on big-city poker players, he gets fleeced. To use a frequently parroted phrase in these films, he also "gets wise to himself," fleeces them back, and creates a gambling empire. Defending the honor of the woman he loves, he accidentally kills his best friend (Cagney). Betrayed by that woman, he is sentenced to ten years. So much for the hero, rendered sympathetically by a lean if fat-faced Robinson, who employs a nervous giggle and boyish vanity to transform himself into an exceedingly likable popinjay. His every comic gesture compensates for the formal stagnation of filmmaking in an era when the slightest camera pan called attention to itself. Cagney is co-billed despite a small role, which allows him a few silent reactions that make up for the paucity of lines. The film bypasses mere insinuation: Cagney musses Robinson's hair and says, "Mother knows best." Robinson replies, "She'll be gone in a couple of days and then you can be my sweetheart again, dearie." *Smart Money* would make a perfect double feature with Robinson's late-career poker movie *The Cincinnati Kid* (1965), though the critical moment in the earlier film pivots not on a card game but on a D.A. who, insisting that ends justify means, frames Robinson and orders his men to break into his casino, smashing windows with hatchets like barbarians storming the last refuge of civilization. Led off in handcuffs (a black comrade from the barbershop tells him, "I loves you, Mr. Nick"), Robinson remains a portrait in indomitable pizzazz.

In Roy Del Ruth's *Lady Killer* and Lloyd Bacon's *The Picture Snatcher*, released three years later, Cagney's inborn electricity sparks the relatively supple camera moves of 1933. His characters are complicit in gambling, robbery, and other crimes, but he is allowed to win the girl and complete exoneration. *Lady Killer* begins as a near remake of *Smart Money*. After Cagney's unemployed usher is conned by Mae Clarke and Douglass Dumbrille (showing more nuance than his usual scoundrels), he turns the tables by taking over the mob and Clarke. Then things take a twist: while on the lam in Los Angeles, talent scouts find him on skid row and pave his way to cinema stardom. The satire of studio life in *Lady Killer* (a Michael Curtiz–like director insists, "In all my pictures, everything must be real . . . light the moon!") is milder than that of newspaper ethics in *The Picture Snatcher*, a comedy inspired by the notorious 1928 New York *Daily News* photo of murderess Ruth Snyder frying in the electric chair. Cagney toys with a reporter played by Alice White, who sends him out her bedroom window so she can welcome her fiancé (Ralph Bellamy) with the line "I was in bed thinking about you." Lavatory scenes include a Cagney bath with lavender ("Am I gonna stink pretty") and his hiding out in a ladies' room already occupied by White, who leads him to a stall for more privacy. His character betrays everyone, triumphantly.

Bacon, one of the most dependable of the Warner Bros. directors, made a sub-genre specialty of gangland comedies. He completed three with Robinson, which exemplify unapologetically barefaced low humor. *A Slight Case of Murder* (1938) was included in *Gangsters Collection, Vol. 2*, and *Larceny, Inc.* (1942) followed in *Gangsters Collection, Vol. 4* (a Robinson bonanza, with

Michael Curtiz's sizzling boxing flick *Kid Galahad* [1937], Anatole Litvak's daft, gynecologically titled *The Amazing Dr. Clitterhouse* [1938], and Roy Del Ruth's burlesque *The Little Giant* [1933]). But the middle feature, *Brother Orchid* (1940), is in a class by itself. When Cagney's would-be reporter quits crime in *The Picture Snatcher*, a goon asks, "Whatcha gonna do, open a flower shop?" That's pretty much what Robinson's Little John Sarto does in *Brother Orchid*, when an unsuccessful hit lands him dazed in a monastery peopled by geriatric flower children: a perfect hideout, he reasons. The key visual joke is Robinson tromping around in his monk's robes, puffing on a cigar—an image more appropriate to Looney Tunes. The ending would be risible if it didn't richly exemplify Production Code hypocrisy. After sacrificing his moll (Ann Sothern) to a right friendly rancher (Ralph Bellamy, of course) and turning in his former henchman (Humphrey Bogart, of course) for muscling in on the flower trade, Little John happily incarcerates himself in the monastery, at peace at last.

The two films directed by the strangely morbid Archie Mayo are the most bizarre of the lot. In *The Mayor of Hell* (1936), Cagney plays a crooked ward heeler who sets out to reform a reformatory run by a pathologically violent director (Dudley Digges). The film borrows from Dickens and Brontë and anticipates Anthony Burgess, as the punishment visited on the delinquents is more appalling than their crimes. The fine performance by Allen "Farina" Hoskins is notably free of racial stereotyping. The same cannot be said of the treatment accorded his character's father or the Jewish inmate, who is elected reformatory treasurer.

In *Black Legion* (1936), one of Bogart's first starring roles and a singularly expressive one, no black or Jewish characters appear, although the legion (despite an opening disclaimer) is based on a real offshoot of the Ku Klux Klan, centered in Michigan and Ohio. The targets are first-generation Americans, chiefly Polish and Irish, denounced by the gleefully sadistic mob as anarchists, but the film focuses on their tormentors: blue-collar immigrant bashers, nourished by hard times and a shady businessman who hides behind the flag. Despite stagy direction, the film is a stinging rebuke of that peculiarly American breed of hysteria mongers, from Coughlin to Limbaugh, who exploit the fears of nativist bullies. The script by Abem Finkel (better remembered for his work on *Jezebel* and *Sergeant York*) and cult-novelist William Wister Haines (whose acclaimed 1934 Depression novel *Slim* has been inexplicably out of print for nearly sixty years; he also co-wrote John Ford's *The Wings of Eagles*) includes a March of Time spoof, a pre-Code tramp (Helen Flint) who mysteriously evaded the censors, and invocations of Lincoln and the Constitution. Bogart's decent guy, transformed by a mob into a madman who destroys himself and his family—the exquisite Erin O'Brien-Moore, as his wife, gets many a shattered close-up—while killing and flogging innocent people, is treated as a victim. But that's true of most gangster films.

57

ELEMENTARY

Charlie Chan / Michael Shayne

IN AN ERA besieged with recycled characters launched like political campaigns (Spider-Man, Batman, the Hulk, Jason Bourne, the insane killer Jason Voorhees, the insane killer Michael Myers, the insane killer Freddy Krueger, the *Die Hard* guy), let us recall franchises of yore, the 1930s and 1940s, when beloved familiars made their way to theaters so frequently and economically that little fanfare was necessary. Among those revived by DVD from the vaults of 20ᵗʰ Century Fox are the detectives Charlie Chan, as in *Warner Oland Is Charlie Chan, Vol. 3*, and Mike Shayne, as in *Michael Shayne Mysteries*. Amazing how well they stand up.

The Chan set assembles leftovers, unlike the earlier collections, which were configured thematically: volumes 1 and 2 feature Earl Derr Biggers's Chinese-Hawaiian detective stumbling over murders in four countries (1934–35) and at four cultural or sporting events (1936–37), all expediently located on the Fox lot—think Epcot with stock footage. These volumes include the most admired pictures in the series, with Charlie visiting Paris, Egypt, the opera, and the Olympics. Four of Oland's earliest outings as Chan have maddeningly disappeared, bringing us to the fine motley of volume 3, beginning with Oland's second Chan film, *The Black Camel* (1931), his only surviving picture based on a Biggers novel and the only one filmed on location (in Honolulu). Bela Lugosi helps out as a crystal ball gazer, and Dwight Frye plays an apprehensive butler, adding a twist to the original story, which was loosely based on the murder of Hollywood director William Desmond

Taylor. The other Oland films consist of a visually lively investigation of the occult, *Charlie Chan's Secret* (1936), in which Charlie shows his skill in forensics and gunplay; and his final outings—*Charlie Chan on Broadway* (1937), with a strong supporting cast and an arbitrary but unguessable villain, and the routine *Charlie Chan in Monte Carlo* (released after Oland's death, in 1938), where the bumbling of Keye Luke and sloe-eyed beauty of Kay Linaker (better known for writing *The Blob* twenty years later) provide much-needed relief from Harold Huber's pidgin French.

The ringer in the carton is *Behind That Curtain* (1929), the first talkie based on the Chan stories and a slow-moving antique that nonetheless has much to recommend it, including the unusual presence of an Asian actor, E. L. Park, in the title role. When Fox began releasing its Chan and Mr. Moto films on DVD, the company included featurettes with Asian American commentators, as if demonstrating permission to recycle movies in which characters with Asian roots are played by such Occidentals as the Swedish-born Oland or the Hungarian-born Peter Lorre. We now live in a time when racial politics limit actors to roles permitted by birthright—a long way in the wrong direction from the era, forty-plus years ago, when Ruby Dee played Cordelia to Morris Carnovsky's Lear. Yet no one can get too exercised about Oland's Chan, who is always the smartest, bravest, and most courteous man in the room. Next to the murderers, the most derisively treated characters are the white cops, especially the racist ones (like the William Demarest character in *Charlie Chan at the Opera* [1936], who calls Charlie "Chop Suey"). The bowing and scraping attributed to Chan is something of a charade and not without a touch of condescension. The deliberate diction with which Oland recites an endless supply of aphorisms recalibrates the tempo of scenes to suit him, often forcing the other characters to suppress impatience. Chan's signature "Thank you so much," recently appropriated by Kyra Sedgwick's Brenda Johnson on television's *The Closer*, can be especially acidic, as in *Charlie Chan's Secret*, when a cop bawls him out for letting the presumed killer escape.

In *Behind That Curtain*, Chan is a supporting character, brought in toward the end to gather evidence and shoot the malefactor. Park, making his only film appearance, is so amateurish and unlike Chan (no words of wisdom) that he nervously looks toward the camera, as if seeking direction. His presence manifests the detective's utter remoteness from a real Chinese man. Chan is a minstrel construct in the American tradition of humbling otherness. It would be unthinkable to revive him today without an Asian American actor, but even he would have to channel the physical and verbal politesse that gives Chan his solitary disposition. Oland was savvy enough to play a stereotype while simultaneously—often in close-ups that counterpoint casual conversations—puncturing it.

Another fascinating aspect of *Behind That Curtain* is that it represents an exceedingly rare instance of a screenwriter (Sonya Levien, whose later work ranged from *Drums Along the Mohawk* to *Bhowani Junction*) taking an intricate detective story (the Biggers novel of the same name) and removing the elements of mystery fiction so that all that remains is a backstory, tracked chronologically. Instead of the detective compiling clues to find out what happened to Eve Durand (Lois Moran), the film follows her strange travail, which depicts a cleansing view of the desert that looks backward to T. E. Lawrence and forward to Paul Bowles, and could be intelligently adapted today. Actor Warner Baxter, who plays Eve's lover, and director Irving Cummings had just come off a great success with *In Old Arizona*, and Fox was willing to spend serious money. As in many early talkies, scenes are haltingly enunciated, visually inert, and performed as if the actors were sedated, but location shots of the desert, notably a caravan trekking across the horizon, and the streets of San Francisco are impressive. So is Boris Karloff, in little more than a bit role, milking the line (see if you can do it) "The desert gives and the desert takes away" for a full six seconds.

Between 1940 and 1942, Fox made seven films starring Lloyd Nolan as Brett Halliday's Mike Shayne. As concise detective pictures proved to be among the most dependable of B features—cheap to make, easy to take— Fox added Shayne to a roster that already included Chan and Moto. Like them, the Shayne films usually ignored the novels; but rather than create original stories, the scriptwriters adapted novels featuring other characters, from the forgotten Great Merlini to the immortal Philip Marlowe. Fox initially released a DVD of the third in the series, *Dressed to Kill* (1941, not to be confused with a 1946 Sherlock Holmes entry of that name), distinguished by its theatrical milieu, dry wit, and a double denouement in which Shayne's fiancée jilts him. The company then boxed four more on double-sided discs as *Michael Shayne Mysteries*, mysteriously leaving the final two—including *Time to Kill* (1942), a fairly faithful adaptation of Raymond Chandler's *The High Window*—for another day. These films have a peculiar charm, thanks to subtle period references, droll dialogue, solid supporting performances,

and Nolan's interpretation of Shayne. *Sleepers West* (1941) is a splendid
example of shaggy-dog B-movie plotting.

Halliday is no longer read, in part because he turned out too many novels and created a factory of scribes to turn out even more. His two-fisted,
Irish, cognac-swilling, and usually Miami-based Shayne was duly revived in
a postwar movie series, as a TV show, and as the name of a magazine. But
if Shayne proliferated as relentlessly as the Hardy Boys, Halliday was no
slouch at plotting and settings, exploring the environs of Miami and New
Orleans and working into his stories the latest techno-gadgetry. His first
Shayne novel, *Dividend on Death*, appeared in 1939, and the first Shayne
movie, loosely based on it, appeared the next year. It may have been Hollywood's first venture into the hard-boiled.

Better make that poached. Lloyd Nolan could throw a convincing hay-
maker and rejoinder, but he was always too normal, too average to fit a
stereotype. Everything about him was distinct—voice, face, laugh, and line
readings—but most distinct was his lack of distinction. He stole scenes by
standing around and looking very real, as though a human being had somehow sneaked into a passel of actors. No one was better at making small talk
sound like small talk. Intentionally or not, he captured the casual, almost
incidental virility of the Halliday character. Watch Nolan's characteristic
entrance in *Sleepers West*, as he strolls through a train station (a rare location
shot in Inglewood) twirling a key chain, amiable, unhurried, unconcerned,
stopping at a magazine stand, bantering, meeting an old flame, bantering
again, and heading for his train, giving no sign that he's on a case. Unlike
most B-movie sleuths, Shayne wasn't burdened by a slow-witted pal or
excessive comic relief, because Nolan was naturally witty—his voice is a
tranquilizing foghorn, nasal yet musical, and his laugh a jaunty, teeth-baring
sneeze. He was by no means handsome, but he had charm and knew how
to wear a fedora.

Sleepers West, based on a previously filmed 1933 Frederick Nebel novel
called *Sleepers East*, takes place almost entirely on a train traveling from Den-
ver to San Francisco. The plot is close enough to that of the admired 1952
Richard Fleischer thriller *The Narrow Margin* to suggest a template, except
that Shayne is trying to protect a woman who will testify for rather than
against a defendant. His method is to ignore her. A gangster tells Shayne:
"My name is . . ." Shayne: "Carl Izzard." Gangster: "How'd you know?"
Shayne: "I don't know. You just look like a fellow who'd have a name like

Izzard." The story line is repeatedly interrupted by scenes of a conductor determined to keep the train on time, rumor-mongering porters (a who's who of black comic actors, including Mantan Moreland, Sam McDaniel, and Ben Carter), and an accidental, seriously inebriated romance between the witness and a fleeing husband (Louis Jean Heydt), who has had a Flitcraft-type epiphany that his life is boring. Trust the movie to ultimately braid the strands.

If not for the Production Code, *Sleepers West* would have been a B classic. The performances are so disarming, you may actually be surprised when the husband returns to his wife, and the witness transforms herself from alcoholic playgirl to bright-eyed waitress. You don't mind because the witness is played by Mary Beth Hughes, a blond and buxom Shayne-series regular who worked all the time but rarely enjoyed parts this good. She almost always left more of an impression than the female leads—in this case, the appealing Lynn Bari. Hughes is reduced to flinging lamps in *Blue, White and Perfect* (1942), a retrospectively astute film because it was made a few weeks before Pearl Harbor and released a few weeks after, and has Shayne (and apparent gigolo George Reeves) on the heels of Nazi diamond smugglers. The film is set entirely on a Hawaii-bound ship with everyone traveling under aliases, and the last-act patriotic reversals have a prophetic post-Pearl ring. *Michael Shayne, Private Detective* (1940) and *The Man Who Wouldn't Die* (1942) are more conventional mysteries, complete with standard issue brainless cops—strange that no one protested this custom of prewar and wartime detective movies. After the war, cops were merely corrupt.

58

TO COIN A GENRE
Kino's Film Noir

IN THE PAST decade, film noir has become the preferred genre in movie publishing and DVD releases. I count well over fifty volumes on the subject, a number that indicates diminishing returns as bookshelves buckle under encyclopedias and anthologies of film noir essays, publicity stills, poster art, and quotable dialogue; not to mention tomes on film noir directors, writers, composers, cameramen, and actors—with particular attention paid to those who played femmes fatale. Meanwhile, DVD companies release whatever suitable movies they own, along with some that aren't so suitable, because film noir is more than a genre: it's a marketing tool for the mostly black and white urban thrillers of the 1940s and 1950s. It provides a veneer of cerebral approval in a day when such native phrases as "crime films" or "gangster films" no longer do the trick. Thus we have Warner noir, Fox noir, MGM noir, Criterion noir, and Hammer noir.

This enthusiasm is partly a French lingo thing, representing an *amour fou* for movies with stylish *mise-en-scène* by directorial auteurs. Unlike Westerns, musicals, science fiction, and every other genre, film noir didn't exist as a banner in the years it peaked as a style. As a result, many elements that have come to characterize film noir—high-contrast chiaroscuro lighting, expressionistic staging, hard-boiled stories set deep in the underworld, location shooting, themes of sexual betrayal and innocence undone—evolved in a more competitive than formulaic environment, as filmmakers outdid each other in the relatively unmonitored world of low-budget second features.

French film critics coined the term *film noir* to denote the similarities between Hollywood's 1940s wave of brutal crime films and the pulp fiction that had appeared in France under the rubric *Série Noire*. Yet not until the 1970s did American critics and filmmakers begin to fetishize the style, which at its best produced imaginative, fast-moving, disturbing films, fraught with incidents and ideas that slyly undermined the Production Code; in addition, they proved to be a testing ground or a preferred idiom for filmmakers who later emerged as A-picture directors or cult figures, among them John Huston, Fred Zinnemann, Billy Wilder, Anthony Mann, Robert Wise, André De Toth, Jules Dassin, Sam Fuller, Richard Fleischer, Otto Preminger, Joseph Lewis, and Nicholas Ray. The excitement of rediscovering these films was intensified by the fact that they had initially received little critical attention—film noir was practically a virgin field.

Kino, a company best known for distributing arcane international titles and refurbishing dozens of silent films, including the Edison archive and masterpieces by D. W. Griffith, Buster Keaton, Fritz Lang, and F. W. Murnau, has long poked around in the noir field. Now it has packaged ten films in two collections that define the phrase loosely enough to include movies that range beyond the confines of American crime, suggesting hyphenated genres such as propaganda-noir, current-events-noir, British-noir, and even women's-romance-noir. These discs have hardly any extras—not even closed captioning—but the prints are solid and the selection is intriguing if not entirely first-rate. *Film Noir: The Dark Side of Hollywood* includes *Hangmen Also Die!*, *Railroaded*, *The Long Night*, *Behind Locked Doors*, and *Sudden Fear*. *Film Noir: Five Classics from the Studio Vaults* has *Contraband*, *Scarlet Street*, *Strange Impersonation*, *They Made Me a Fugitive*, and *The Hitch-Hiker*.

The only directors represented with two films, one in each set, are Fritz Lang and Anthony Mann. Lang made a dozen Hollywood pictures that could be defined as classic noir. *Hangmen Also Die!* (1943) is not one of them. It was a fictional attempt, scripted by Bertolt Brecht, to re-create the 1942 assassination of the Nazi butcher Reinhard Heydrich and the unspeakable reprisals that followed, which eradicated the town and population of Lidice. (Douglas Sirk's *Hitler's Madman*, also from 1943, was based on the same incident.) No contemporary film, let alone one starring Brian Donlevy as the Czech hero, could have lived up to those events, but Lang's picture has aged well. Photographed with glistening precision by James Wong Howe and scored by Hans Eisler, it recalls his early serial-like German pictures in which plot is unfolded in layers and nothing is as it seems. As such, it offers a stylistic link between the expressionistic pulp Lang helped to invent and many medium-budget Hollywood successors, including Lang's sublimely perverse *Scarlet Street* (1945, discussed in Chapter 22, "Edward G. Robinson, See").

Mann is similarly represented by an anomaly and a classic noir. The former is the little-known *Strange Impersonation* (1946), a sixty-eight-minute poverty-row tour de force about a woman scientist who rebuffs her fiancé in favor of self-experimentation with an anesthetic she is attempting to perfect. She pays the price by losing her face, her personality, her fiancé, and very nearly—and on more than one occasion—her life. Of course the whole story is a dream, but unlike other dream movies, including Lang's *The Woman in the Window* (1944), Mann doesn't pretend to hide it. In the first scene, the scientist (Brenda Marshall) lectures her colleagues that anesthesia may stimulate dreams. Mann uses the dream as license to realize the protagonist's suppressed paranoia regarding the beauty and aspirations of her blond assistant (Hillary Brooke): she envisions a newspaper headline that reads, "Girl Scientist's Death." The film's style becomes more radical as the plot becomes more preposterous. Yet at heart, it remains a woman's picture in which the femme fatale haunts another woman. The man is a worm who doesn't even get the chance to turn.

By contrast, *Railroaded* (1947) is quintessential postwar-noir and Mann's breakthrough as a hard-boiled observer of criminal sociopaths. Jane Randolph plays the operator of a beauty shop that doubles as a bookie joint; her paramour, John Ireland, is a vicious thug who meticulously perfumes his bullets and strokes his gun barrel. When she arranges for him to rob her betting parlor, everything goes haywire and Mann pulls out all the stops. He stages a brunette-on-blond catfight under Ireland's amused gaze and shoots the syndicate boss's office as a tableau of deep shadows, glaring table lamps, and the unexpected touch of bountiful bookshelves. He is equally deft at contrasting the dark relationship between Randolph and Ireland with a cop's daylight courting of a good girl, and he subtly incorporates references to the war as part of the fabric of social dissolution.

Postwar-noir was obsessed with documenting the psychological depression that followed so quickly on the heels of victory. Despite the GI Bill, affordable housing, the spread of suburbia, and the middle-class fantasies per-

petuated by that recent invention television, the bottom half of double features countered the affluent piety of Cinemascope spectacles with a vision
of America beset by ennui, hysteria, and guilt. Two of the Kino selections
document a similar decline in morale in England. Michael Powell's *Contraband* (1940) features the first star of German expressionism, Conrad Veidt,
as a Danish sea captain who has to navigate the cellars of Soho, amid Blitz
blackouts, to foil a spy ring. He prevails, but London is clearly at sea. Alberto
Cavalcanti's superior *They Made Me a Fugitive* (1947), with a gripping performance by Trevor Howard, also descends into the underground, but the spies
have been replaced by organized crime, the blackouts by the black market,
and the heroic ship captain by an unemployed and victimized war hero.

Dislocation and desperation characterize the remaining films. In the
semi-noirish *The Long Night* (1947), Anatole Litvak's unnecessary remake of
Marcel Carné's *Le jour se lève*, the narrative structure is splintered, as the recollections of one night give way to flashbacks within flashbacks—a strange
movie convention of the period, also explored in *Passage to Marseilles* and
The Locket. Budd Boetticher's *Behind Locked Doors* (1948) is a minor programmer, interesting as a prophetic examination of the fear of madness, as a
detective goes undercover in an asylum—a plot device later adopted by
the Swiss novelist Friedrich Dürrenmatt in *The Quarry* and by Sam Fuller
in *Shock Corridor*. The dialogue is unintentionally mirthful: "I've told you a
dozen times not to abuse the patients!"

Far better are the two 1950s films. In David Miller's *Sudden Fear* (1952),
Joan Crawford suffers the penalties of female success while tormentor
Jack Palance is undone by the latest in fear-inducing technology: home-
recording devices. In Ida Lupino's nail-biting triumph *The Hitch-Hiker* (1953);
a malevolent William Talman turns America's ribbon of highway into a hell
on wheels. Lupino, a cult figure twice over as actor and director, is overdue for DVD resurrection. The half-dozen films she directed from 1949 to
1953 consistently tackled controversial themes from a woman's perspective:
unmarried mothers (*Not Wanted*), rape (*Outrage*), women's sports (*Hard, Fast
and Beautiful*), debilitating illness (*Never Fear*), and bigamy (*The Bigamist*). Yet
her most effective film, *The Hitch-Hiker*, is a testosterone-heavy exploration
of what two ordinary guys (you can't get more ordinary than Frank Lovejoy
and Edmond O'Brien) discover themselves capable of under threat from a
psychopath. Lupino maintains the suspense at fever pitch.

The noir revival of the 1970s and 1980s produced several savory films, including at least one undeniable masterpiece, Roman Polanski's *Chinatown* (1974). But most of them were either stylistically or thematically self-conscious, as they attempted to revive the attitude and look of the classic noirs or, as in *Chinatown*, set the story in the perilous past. The Kino selections are strengthened by the conviction with which they reflect a terrifying present.

59

NEW GRUBB STREETS

Film Noir Classic Collection, Vol. 4

WARNER HOME VIDEO released the eagerly anticipated DVD collection *Film Noir Classic Collection, Vol. 4*, with ten films instead of the usual five, and while one might presume that a fourth volume must verge on barrel-scraping, these films have earned their devoted cult following and merit broader dispersal. Nor will this set stem the tide: several major noirs are tied up in legal knots and many others await restoration. Noir is practically a bottomless pit. The period covered here is 1946 to 1955, but seven of the ten were initially released in 1949 and 1950, a dramatic high point for noir and the careers of its directors. These filmmakers, working in a then-déclassé genre with diminutive budgets and short shooting schedules, were goaded by ambition and fevered inventiveness. They wanted to prove themselves worthy of climbing the ladder to A pictures, with all their attendant glamour. Some succeeded, making better pictures in better circumstances, while making trade-offs in the process.

Consider the prostitutes in Fred Zinnemann's 1949 nail-biter of post-war America, *Act of Violence*, and his Oscar-endorsed 1953 epic of prewar America, *From Here to Eternity*. In the former, Mary Astor plays a worn-out, middle-aged hooker whose pathetic attempt to justify her life ("I had my kicks") is an indelibly haunting refrain. In the latter, Donna Reed's bar girl is presented as a well-scrubbed "hostess," as though more expensive movies attracted a better class of customer that wouldn't put up with the grime of reality, even when borrowed from a best-selling novel. On the other hand, the lovemaking scene on the beach in *From Here to Eternity* gathers adrenalin from Deborah Kerr's hungry gaze at Burt Lancaster's off-camera crotch—an indulgence permitted only to prestige actors and films with budgets large enough to include a beach.

The chiaroscuro photography that typifies the B films, turning familiar localities into shadow-streaked cells, was doubly fitting. They were made on the dark sides of the studios, bound by Production Code rules but permitted faux-documentary peeks into the nation's grubbiest corners. Despite impressive location exteriors filmed around Southern California, New York, Boston, and elsewhere, realism is not really the point. Nor is the plot, although the twists and turns keep us guessing. Most of the stories are no better than magazine hack work. The art is in the style, the gloss, the way directors, photographers, editors, and actors use composition, lighting, cutting, and improvisation to make sequences a little different than usual—though occasional process shots remind us how conventional the conventions were. Cinematic panache imparts its own substance.

Act of Violence is a perverse variation on *Les Misérables*, in which the Valjean character, Van Heflin's Frank Enley, has remade himself as a model citizen, his face reflecting the cheery contentment of postwar upward mobility. But he has a terrible crime in his past that has not been expiated. The Javert figure, Robert Ryan's Joe Parkson, tails him across the country—by appearances a scowling, crippled madman bent on brute justice. In the end, Joe's face will radiate serenity, but only after he chases his quarry into an underworld that is more Virgil than Hugo, with Astor's whore as the sibyl. This stuff is no more or less profound than it sounds, yet Zinnemann, cinematographer Robert Surtees, and the terrific cast impart a reverberant significance that supersedes the literary ostentation. That applies to most of the films in the Warner set, including the one paired with *Act of Violence*: John Sturges's scrupulous, Boston-based, forensics-themed *Mystery Street* (1950), in which Ricardo Montalban's police detective encounters racism, upper-crust contempt, Harvard, and a dingbat landlady played by Elsa Lanchester in pursuit of the man (a particularly malevolent Edmon Ryan) who killed a pregnant hooker played by Jan Sterling.

Nicholas Ray's *They Live by Night* (1948, but shelved for a year) and Anthony Mann's *Side Street* (1950) are an ideal double bill, less because both feature Farley Granger and Cathy O'Donnell as a troubled couple than for putting out front the competitive tension of noir filmmaking. Ray's film opens with a benchmark helicopter shot of fleeing thieves, but Mann out-does him with a breathtaking introductory helicopter shot that peers straight down on the Empire State Building and transforms the city into a steely Grand Canyon. Both films deal with makeovers. In Ray's film, O'Donnell metamorphoses from an introverted plain Jane into an opalescent beauty. Mann turns Granger from a caricature of sunlit innocence into a man on the run, trapped in the canyon, frightened, beaten, mangled, and last seen on a gurney being loaded into an ambulance as a cop narrator assures us, "He's gonna be all right." Mann's eerie car chase is a stunning commentary on urban constraints; indeed, the film holds a unique place in his oeuvre for dramatizing a young man's making the mistake of a lifetime—unlike his subsequent Westerns, in which the hero's mistake is buried deep in the past.

Still, *They Live by Night* is the better film, a painfully instinctive love story that captures the feeling, time, and tempo if not the plot of Edward Anderson's marvelous Depression novel *Thieves Like Us*. Ray intensifies visual symbols (Howard Da Silva's thief has a glass eye instead of a deformed foot, as in the book), shoots in close quarters, dispatches the gang to focus on the lovers, and breaks for a musical number—Marie Bryant, of *Jammin' the Blues* fame, leading a band with trombonist Vic Dickenson. He also allows O'Donnell's Keechie to avoid the novel's holocaust. Robert Altman's anti-noir, anthropological 1974 remake also spares her; only Arthur Penn's *Bonnie and Clyde* (1967), itself a loose variation on the theme, adhered to Anderson's pitiless example.

All these films are relatively familiar. The real gifts in this collection are the rarities: André De Toth's *Crime Wave* (1954), John Farrow's *Where Danger Lives* (1950), John Berry's *Tension* (1949), and Jack Bernhard's z-budget *Decoy* (1946). Much pleasure is to be had here, not least in the lovely form of Jean Gillie, whose femme fatale in *Decoy* may be the nastiest of them all. She takes such unseemly pleasure in firing a gun. Shot for shot, beginning with gas jockey Dub Taylor impersonating Doris Day, *Crime Wave* delivers a succession of jolts as a slightly bent but very tall cop (Sterling Hayden) solves a series of penny-ante burglaries in which the unlikely couple of Gene Nelson (the dancer from *Oklahoma!*) and Phyllis Kirk (the beauty in De Toth's *House of Wax*) are trapped. They are surprisingly good, as is everyone else—cultists will happily note the presence of Timothy Carey and Hank Worden—in a film that is at once intimate and oddly objective, employing location interiors as well as natural lighting and sound though shot mostly at night. De

Toth, whose noir masterpiece *Pitfall* (1948) is one of the films caught up in legal wrangling, even manages to subvert a sentimental curtain line.

Claude Rains appears in *Where Danger Lives* for all of six minutes, as Robert Mitchum mutates from a princely doctor and fiancé to Maureen O'Sullivan to a slow-on-the-uptake boy-toy for the ever-pouting Faith Domergue, who has psychiatric problems. Mitchum is finally reduced to groveling semiconsciousness as Domergue is consumed in what is likely the second-best (after *Touch of Evil*) border-town sequence ever made. Except for its atrocious André Previn score (a coy alto saxophone plays the same smarmy riff every time a bed is shown), *Tension* is an idiosyncratic delight, with Audrey Totter giving the performance of a lifetime as an extremely unfaithful wife. The first scene is pretty steamy by any standard: she turns a trick in her husband's all-night drugstore. Eventually, the husband (Richard Basehart), upset with her and possibly with the soda jerk who likes him too much, reinvents himself with a foolproof disguise devised with his glasses (he takes them off). He immediately meets Cyd Charisse, cast rather counterintuitively as the girl next door. You have to see this one to believe it.

The remaining films are in on a pass: Don Siegel's South American adventure *The Big Steal* (1949); and Lewis Allen's remake of *The Mouthpiece*, tailored for Edward G. Robinson as *Illegal* (1955) and recycling a few of the anecdotes told of real-life 1920s mob lawyer William Fallon. By the 1950s, those lawyerly stunts (drinking a vial of poison held in evidence, and then secretly having his stomach pumped) seemed so incredible that Warner found a grizzled attorney to attest to their accuracy in a television promo, included on the DVD. Don't miss co-star Nina Foch's commentary track on *Illegal*, a picture she despises. On costuming: "My breasts are not my largest feature." On Lewis Allen: "He was a nice man. He just wasn't a director." On co-star Jayne Mansfield: "I never was fascinated by sex symbols. They always just made me nervous. It may have been jealousy. I don't know. No, I don't think so." She continues in that vein for eighty-eight minutes.

60

THE DEADLY FORTIES

I Wake Up Screaming /

When Strangers Marry

I WAKE UP SCREAMING is one of the most beautiful of all black and white movies. Nearly every detail, other than a few amateurish process shots, suggests the glossy perfection that exemplifies what André Bazin famously called "the genius of the system." How else to explain the transformation of prosaic melodrama into a highly influential exercise in sculpted lighting? On paper, the casting of Betty Grable and Victor Mature is no more promising than the unfathomable title. Director H. Bruce Humberstone and cinematographer Edward Cronjager were prolific hacks who began in silent pictures and ended on television, their careers defined by indiscriminate efficiency and intermittently shrewd visual coups. Producer Milton Sperling and screenwriter Dwight Taylor were initially known primarily for musicals.

Yet they created a film almost abstract in its attention to pools of light—a stylish display of technique that enhances a sentimental murder mystery in which exposure of the killer is secondary to the uncovering of sexual obsession and envy. The chiaroscuro police grilling in the first scene may indicate a typical postwar crime thriller, but *I Wake Up Screaming* was made in 1941, the year Orson Welles and John Huston directed their first films. If it lacks the substance of *Citizen Kane* and *The Maltese Falcon*, and it does, it rivals them in shoring up plot with procedural panache, a gleaming surface that came to characterize Fox's B product.

The unusual look of *Screaming* derives from a combination of conventional camera placement and innovative lighting. Humberstone has a few neat camera moves, but for the most part he directs straight on, eschewing the upward and downward angles that distinguish Huston's film and preferring flat pictorial design to the deep-focus dimensionality of Welles. Instead, the film stock glistens: the blacks are so opaque you half expect to see your own reflection in them. Shot after shot is composed with erotic meticulousness—not just set pieces like the interrogation, in which shadows are necessary to postpone the disclosure of a character's identity. Consider the shot at 7:02 when, amid the backs of men leaving a hotel, Elisha Cook Jr. briefly turns around and the light shines from his face and white collar. Or Laird Cregar's entrance eleven minutes later, like a ghost on the far side of a glass pane, inside of which Carole Landis is waitressing, doubled by her own reflection in the glass. Or Grable's quickstep into a perfect close-up at 31:29, to say nothing of the several glamour shots of Grable and Landis, their cheeks lit up like alabaster. One of the odd things about the story is the frequent breaking in to boudoirs without warrants or keys. As Mature wakes up in the middle of the night to find Cregar staring at him from a cushiony chair, Cregar is centered between a panther painted into the décor over his right shoulder and a photo of Landis to his left, shimmering in its frame.

During preproduction, I Wake Up Screaming was talked about as a project for Reuben Mamoulian and (in what would have been his American debut) Jean Renoir. But their participation would have meant a more costly film. Humberstone, who had shown a penchant for clever lighting in movies like Charlie Chan at the Opera and Sun Valley Serenade, promised to abide by studio frugality. Darryl Zanuck insisted that the setting be changed from the Hollywood of Steve Fisher's 1941 novel to New York because he was opposed to portraying sleaze in his company's town. This meant replicating Broadway on the lot, including a nightclub large enough to stage the Rose Bowl, and gauche rear projection when actors ventured outdoors or into a car.

The lighting mitigates the dull interiors, especially hotel rooms, and so do the actors. Did anyone ever look better in hats than Mature and Grable? He is particularly lively, holding his own with the looming, velvet-voiced Cregar. An indication of Mature's extra-thespian appeal is a swimming scene with Grable (not yet the army's favorite pinup girl): the camera lingers more on his legs than hers. At one point, the producer feared making a Grable film without a musical number, so a very bad one was shot and deleted—it is included as a DVD extra. Even so, the score proved innovative, if repetitious, in its own right, consisting chiefly of three tunes, each assigned to a character: Alex North's "Street Scene" (Fox's unofficial anthem) for Mature, "Over the Rainbow" for Grable, and an ominous Cyril Mockridge theme for Cregar.

Dwight Taylor's smart script begins by alternating flashbacks from the perspectives of Mature and Grable, the camera tracking from one to the other. The dialogue includes Grable's advice to her doomed sister, "If you lose your looks, you lose your entire bankroll," and Cregar's memorable response to her ingenuous question "What's the good of living without hope?" "It can be done." Previously known for such scripts as *Top Hat* and *Rhythm on the River*, Taylor went on to write Sam Fuller's Communists-in-the-subway-noir *Pickup on South Street*. In adapting *I Wake Up Screaming*, he combined elements of *Pygmalion* (Mature bets that he can make a star of a waitress) with themes other writers would explore years later in *All About Eve*, *Sweet Smell of Success*, and *Touch of Evil*. Most of his script faithfully replicates ideas in Fisher's novel, though he adds a feminist aspect as Grable takes charge of the sometimes demure Mature, conking the villain with her shoe, sawing through handcuffs, and sneaking out a fire escape, remarking, "I wasn't a campfire girl for nothing!" Taylor's ending improves on the novel. It mercifully lacks Fisher's closing line (the Mature figure greets the Grable figure with the words "Hello, mommy!"), and elaborates on the bent cop's shrine to the sexually unobtainable, while adding a meek suicide and a tortuous speech in which the villain convinces his victim that evil really does have its reasons.

The Fox DVD missed a bet in not offering *I Wake Up Screaming* as a double bill with the 1953 remake, *Vicki* (*Laura* had taught Fox something about titles)—a mostly miscast version, set once again in New York, but worth seeing for the hair-raising performance by Richard Boone in the Cregar role. In 1960, Fisher published a revised version of his novel, producing an uneasy concoction of name dropping from the two eras. In the intervening years, he had worked on other pictures (*Johnny Angel*, *Dead Reckoning*, *Lady in the Lake*) in the noir genre he had inadvertently helped to launch. What he could not do was get anyone to film his Hollywood story as a story of Hollywood.

William Castle is mostly remembered for the self-promoting ballyhoo with which he sold the medium-concept, irony-laced horror movies he directed and produced for the adolescent market in the late 1950s and early 1960s. The best of them (*Macabre*, *House on Haunted Hill*, *The Tingler*, *Mr. Sardonicus*) are uproariously tasteless, especially the incomparably nasty *Homicidal*, Castle's attempt to one-up Alfred Hitchcock in the wake of *Psycho*: it begins with the evisceration of a justice of the peace, and extends gender-bending to the casting of a performer whose sex he refused to reveal—television actress Joan Marshall, working under the gender-neutral and, for anyone who remembered the waxworks impersonations of George Arliss, in-joke pseudonym Jean Arliss.

By that time, Castle was an old hand at cribbing from Hitchcock and others, having turned out more than three dozen cheapie crime thrillers and Westerns between 1943 and 1956. No one is likely to peruse them in search of a neglected auteur, yet at least one of his early films is an almost perfectly gauged gem, a bellwether noir suggesting how frightening the postwar era might be. Initially released by Monogram in 1944, *When Strangers Marry* was rereleased five years later with the less witty title *Betrayed*, which now tarnishes most if not all existing prints. One of the charms of the original title is that it fails to prepare the audience for a sixty-seven-minute exercise in murder, deception, paranoia, sexual intrigue, and sweaty psychosis—though it does point up the thematically relevant wartime shortages and confusion that led to hasty couplings and forced acquaintanceship in hotels and on trains. For obscure legal reasons, the film hasn't been available on home video, though prints circulate freely among collectors.

Millie, a waitress from Ohio (Kim Hunter), arrives in New York City for a delayed honeymoon with a man (Dean Jagger) she encountered three times before marrying, and has not seen in the month since their apparently unconsummated wedding. Instead, she runs in to a rejected beau (Robert Mitchum in his first major role) who thinks she is in town in response to his written proposal. Eventually, the mysterious, close-mouthed husband appears, using an alias. As Millie rebounds between the two, she finds herself at the center of a murder investigation, with nothing to rely on but her instinct. Before reaching New York, while sharing a sitting room with strangers on a train, Millie marvels at her marriage, using the words "strange," "stranger," and "strangeness." She's on her own, and so is the audience—adrift in a routine thriller made memorable by elliptical dialogue, shrewd visuals, odd tangents (including a startling episode in a Harlem bar, the dancers and musician sadly unknown, invisible even by Monogram standards), and understated yet physically forceful performances. The strangeness swells, as does the music, while she makes her way through a murky Gotham that could exist only on a Hollywood soundstage short on props and extras.

Somehow, the chump-change budget, courtesy of the cheapjack producers the King Brothers, allowed for a Dimitri Tiomkin score. Otherwise, *When Strangers Marry* provided a lucky apprenticeship for most of its participants. The rather commonplace story was concocted by George Moskov (who worked on Edgar Ulmer's *Green Fields*). The superbly efficient script is credited to the obscure Dennis J. Cooper (later a writer for TV's *Superman*) and the controversially prolific Philip Yordan—just getting started, a year before he wrote Monogram's breakout hit *Dillinger*. Castle had been directing for only a year, yet it's hard to imagine any director coaxing better work from his soon-to-be-A-list cast. As the ex-suitor, Mitchum, who had previously labored as evil (often uncredited) cowpokes, discloses the range of his seductive ease and brittle unpredictability, qualities that would secure him an undying grip on the noir universe. Jagger, then the veteran of thirty films, including the title role in *Brigham Young* (1940), had not yet found a part that required much nuance; here, to compensate for a necessarily underwritten character, he has to convey, with little help from the script, the elliptical charm that captivated his wife and prompts her misgivings. The naturalness of both actors is matched by the skillfully unaffected twenty-one-year-old Hunter, who had just been brought to Hollywood to appear in Val Lewton's *The Seventh Victim*. Her first smile at Mitchum jolts the film into action.

Hunter isn't the only thing Castle took from Lewton. He recruited (also from *The Seventh Victim*) the scrawny character actor Lou Lubin for an effective bit as a bartender and witness, and imitated the characteristic Lewton walk down a lonely street—in this instance through an archway in Central Park—where each sound shrieks and every silhouette menaces. Castle took far more from Hitchcock, including the vain projection of himself into the movie (in a photograph that triggers the film's best joke). The framework echoes *Suspicion*; a Coney Island mentalist recalls Mr. Memory in *The 39 Steps*; and imagined shouts suggest the innovative soundtrack in *Blackmail*.

But *When Strangers Marry* doesn't feel derived. The most impressive moments, like the acting, are intrinsic to the material: the economical two-shot close-ups of opalescent faces against stark black backgrounds; an aborted claustrophobic drive to Louisville; the stroll from 137th Street and Lenox to 128th and St. Nicholas; odd bits of business and dialogue, like Mitchum sharing a steam bath with a homicide detective (Neil Hamilton), and the detective later telling Hunter after she names the killer, "Don't be too hopeful"; and Jagger's musing on the way a lifetime's habits can be undermined in a single moment (yet another variation on the Flitcraft passage in Dashiell Hammett's *The Maltese Falcon*). Even now, it would be criminal to describe the denouement, except to say that it cunningly turns the screw and merits a second life on DVD.

61

WHO IS HARRY LIME?

The Third Man

CAROL REED AND Graham Greene's masterpiece *The Third Man* opened in London in 1949 and came to New York early the next year in a version butchered by its nervous American distributor, David O. Selznick. He sheared anti-Americanisms and other passages he thought too European or mature or cynical or whatever for those of us living on what one character calls "the other side." During the next forty years, the print quality declined with endlessly compromised television airings that had not the slightest effect on its standing as one of the best-loved and most admired pictures ever made. *The Third Man* has been a perennial favorite on home video ever since Criterion presented its 1999 restoration of the film as produced by Alexander Korda, followed eight years later by a two-disc edition. The print is visually the same on the latter, though the audio track was juiced and the supplementary material is generous if uneven: an excellent feature documentary and a 1968 U.K. television hour on Greene, pedestrian commentary tracks.

The two-disc packaging is much improved. It no longer depicts Orson Welles on the cover, a ploy that exacerbated a phony controversy about the film's authorship and gave away the plot—as will this review, incidentally. I point this out in recognition that not everyone has seen *The Third Man*, though it is often thought of as one of those cultural landmarks that, like *Hamlet* or Beethoven's Fifth, are hard-wired into our DNA. Newcomers ought to have the pleasure of credulously following the murder investigation and Holly Martins's astonishment when, as Greene writes in his treatment-novella, "a window curtain was drawn petulantly back by some sleeper he had awakened and the light fell straight across the narrow street and lit up the features of . . ." Well, you know very well whose features are lit up.

Set in Vienna in 1947, the film is a thrilling contradiction. Misery, menace, and horrific crimes play cheek by jowl with inspired comedy and Anton Karas's hauntingly buoyant zither music—which transformed a beer-garden entertainer into the most profitable Austrian composer since Johann Strauss II. *The Third Man* is often characterized as perfect, which seems fair. Greene's script, improved by Reed, who devised the unforgettable closing scene over Greene's objections, is Aristotle-pure; even throwaway lines (and there aren't many) divulge increased significance on repeated viewings. Robert Krasker's photography, coached by Reed's blueprint of off-kilter angles, continues to astonish. Vincent Korda's set design fastidiously complements the bombed exteriors and personalities of the characters—counterintuitively in the case of Harry Lime, whose bedroom is disarmingly feminine with its delicate fixtures, vanity table, and quilt.

Beyond the leads, consider how many frissons are triggered by the supporting cast. Whatever else it is, *The Third Man* is a supreme gangster film, and there is no more peculiar motley than the Lime gang. Ernst Deutsch's Kurtz has the face of a marionette: either droopy-eyed or all crinkly and slit-mouthed. Sigfried Breuer's slicked-hair dandy, Popescu, shifts mid-sentence from cavalier to murderous. Erich Ponto's aged Dr. Winkel peers at Holly through a mirror, stepping forward ominously to correct the pronunciation of his name. Each delivers reverberant line readings, sometimes just a word—"Advice," "Keep ze pack," "Viiink-el."

Paul Hoerbiger, a veteran Austrian film star, spoke no English and learned his lines phonetically. As the porter, he appears to fumble his way through them while muttering in German and sustaining masterly comic timing, whether confusing heaven and hell or whirling to address Holly, standing behind him. "Dere vas a turd man"—cue zither! Bernard Lee, later famous as M in the Bond series, is splendidly droll as Holly's devoted reader, socking him with one hand and picking him up with the other. Confiscating love letters, he tells a distraught Anna, "That's all right, Miss. We're used to it, like doctors." Wilfred Hyde-White, playing a distracted civil functionary, constantly leads by the elbow a perpetually pissed-off but silent mistress. Herbert Halbik, who never acted again, raises holy hell as Hansl, the little boy with banshee voice. And so forth, down to the smallest role. When Anna is arrested, the Soviets are accompanied by one member of each of the other governing forces: the American is embarrassed; the Brit admits he doesn't know what "protocol" means; the Frenchman reminds Anna not to forget her lipstick. Lee Strasberg is said to be an extra in this scene, but I can't spot him.

The lead players were never better. It's something of a mystery why the film is always referred to as an Orson Welles vehicle. True, his Harry Lime has the two most memorable speeches. He wrote one (with a cuckoo-clock punch line) and took credit for the other (about dots on the carnival midway, written by Greene), and his charisma was never exploited more ingeniously—not even in his own films—than in his sensational, silent entrance, suddenly lighted in a doorway, wearing a rather paternalistic smirk. Yet the tension is ratcheted for an hour before his arrival by Trevor Howard's understatement as the major hoping to put him in a foolproof coffin, Alida Valli's surprisingly unglamorous despondency as Anna, and Joseph Cotten's superbly clueless Holly, a performance measured in nuance and delicious wit as deep as his adroit, slightly Southern baritone.

Holly represents Greene's first evisceration of the "quiet American," the well-meaning innocent abroad whose drunken arrogance embarrasses Anna, whose bumbling leads directly to the murder of the porter, whose fate is to kill "the best friend I ever had." The one theme that emerges in parallels throughout the story is betrayal—in an era of informers, *The Third Man* is rife with what Holly calls dumb decoy ducks. Harry induced Anna to betray one of his associates, and Holly is persuaded to do as much to Harry, but only after two didactic lessons in villainy. The first, purely evidentiary, isn't enough; like most of the world, Holly lacks the empathy to imagine suffering until forced to look at it. He is given a moral pass by many commentators, including those heard in the DVD commentaries, who regard his execution of Harry as a mercy killing. I suspect Reed and Greene had another paradigm in mind: the adoring Judas.

Holly gets to hold a gun on his friend only after he has tried unsuccessfully to exorcise his memory. He is the perennial schoolboy dupe, awed by a magnetic leader who knows how to do things, who makes life exciting, who has the perfect head to sport a homburg. Before leaving for Europe, Harry left Holly holding the bag and stole his girl. Even with Harry presumed dead, Holly can't return the favor. Dead Harry is more vivid to Anna than living Holly. She advises him to find himself a girl, as though he were a harmless adolescent. But harmless he is not. Like the hero in one of his Westerns, Holly is out for revenge, first against the major who slanders his pal, then against his pal. Bleeding and cowering like a wounded cub, Harry may nod for Holly to put him out of his misery, but the film isn't so forgiving. Like Anna, it leaves Holly in the cemetery alone, to contemplate his own motives.

Morality in *The Third Man* is very public-school British, very Greene, very E. M. Forster saying he hoped he would have the courage to betray his country rather than a friend. The opening narration (recited by Reed as though he were recalling an incident from way back) lays it out. Like the start of *Madame Bovary*, it suggests that we are in the hands of a narrator relevant to the story. Yet apart from being a former smuggler, the narrator is an anonymous figure retelling an anecdote he may or may not know firsthand, and instantly disappears from the story. As in *Bovary*, the effect is to go from outside to in, from bemused indifference to growing horror. Even Greene, however, must have been astonished by the topsy-turvy morality with which the world greeted *The Third Man*. Harry Lime, who murders children by stealing and diluting penicillin, charmed the audience as relentlessly as he did Anna. He returned in a radio series (starring Welles) and a television series (starring Michael Rennie), as an admirable rogue who ultimately does the right thing. The sequels are long forgotten. The original is, after six decades and counting, ageless.

JOKER

Ace in the Hole

ONE OF MANY memorable lines ground between the teeth of Kirk Douglas, as the fallen journalist Chuck Tatum in Billy Wilder's trenchant *Ace in the Hole*, is a faux-axiom: "Bad news sells best, 'cause good news is no news." In 1951, when the film was released to critical brickbats and public indifference, Americans could remember when good news sold better than anything—from the summer of 1942, when the Allies began to turn the tide, through September 1945, when Japan surrendered unconditionally. Regular bouts of good news fueled the nation and the newspaper business. Yet the big party, with strangers kissing in the streets and all that, was amazingly short-lived. Within a year, a psychological depression took up where the economic one left off, as the military looked for a new war to fight, Churchill pointed to an Iron Curtain, atomic bombs blasted Bikini, Commie hunters blasted the Constitution, and Hollywood (goodbye, Mr. Mayer, don't let the door hit you on the way out), for the first time in fifteen years, released a slew of caustic movies that challenged the most vaunted principles of American life.

In the early 1930s, the Production Code helped to stem the surge of movies that questioned the national commitment to justice and morality. The postwar scourge of the left attempted to do the same, but while it temporarily silenced or displaced many filmmakers, it couldn't develop an actual code to prevent depictions of racism, organized crime, and adultery. Even if it could have, the noir-ish overcast of the times was far less specific, pointing to a blanketing boredom, ennui, suppressed hysteria, and vague guilt, plus a surfeit of material goods piled on top of hidden fault lines and pitfalls. Criterion's DVD of *Ace in the Hole* looks as fresh as a Jon Stewart montage of media high jinks. The "human interest story" with which Wilder's corrupt journalist hopes to spark America while rescinding his banishment from a New York paper is news of a kind that is neither bad nor good. It is fake news, comic book news, binge news that everyone can follow. The fact that two men wind up dead, murdered after a fashion, is almost beside the point. They die to fulfill the demands of the tale, but their deaths bring neither absolution nor what the twenty-first-century press likes to call "closure."

Credit Wilder for having the nerve to make a picture that wasn't subtle enough to qualify as un-American. It's outright anti-American, but in a good, equal-opportunity way that can please neither the left nor the right—it doesn't even acknowledge a left and right. Almost every character in *Ace in the Hole* is a heel, a crook, or a milquetoast; the best of the rest are merely superstitious. Within days of a disastrous premiere, Paramount withdrew prints in order to reopen the film with a more festive title, *The Big Carnival*—a moronic change, but not an inapt description of a movie that unfolds like a George Grosz pen and ink nightmare brought to life.

As Chuck Tatum explains, the narrative he will weave is based on a true incident that took place in 1925, when the failed attempt to rescue an explorer trapped in a cave attracted legions of tourists and won a Pulitzer for newspaperman Skeets Miller. When Tatum tells that story, his face is lit in a grotesque mask of greed, as if in homage to Erich von Stroheim. Tatum, a misanthropic alcoholic (he doesn't drink "much," just "often"), stuck on a newspaper in Albuquerque, chances upon a similarly trapped explorer, Leo (Richard Benedict), a veteran who passes the time singing "The Hut Sut Song." Like any good hack writer, alert to cliché and sentiment, Tatum braids various details, including an ancient Indian curse and grieving parents, with his own inventions, among them the inadvertently homicidal insistence that the rescuers will—must—take a week to dig Leo out.

Part of Tatum's plot depends on Leo's presumably distressed wife, Lorraine, played with the precision of a diamond drill by Jan Sterling. In truth, Lorraine is a bottle blond of dance-hall provenance, eager to jump the first bus out of town until Tatum convinces her that she is sitting on a gold mine. Tatum sees in her sullen, slatternly smile all the radiance of a gorgon, along with his own worst instincts. Wilder presses the point by giving her alarming close-ups as she closes in on Tatum, rousing a violence that will ultimately do him in. Even less appealing is the bent sheriff, played by Ray Teal, who carries around a pet rattlesnake when the only rattler he has to worry about is Tatum. The sheriff is so gross that Tatum scores points with the audience by roughing him up. But Tatum has no soft edges—even his apparent last-minute moral turnaround is subject to questions of motivation. This is Douglas's most merciless performance, and Wilder toys with the actor's volatility in having his character shown up by people he otherwise dominates: the news kid Herbie (Bob Arthur), who verbally bests him, and the editor, Mr. Boot (nailed by Porter Hall), a weedy yet impressively unimpressed man who shows up in Tatum's room sharing the frame with an oversized crucifix.

Wilder gives Tatum a singularly witty entrance and one of the most memorable exits in film history, but he doesn't allow the audience much intervening relief from the guy's nastiness. In some respects, the faceless tourists who flock to the makeshift fairground are more repellent than Tatum and his stooges. They are represented by one couple, the Federbers. Tatum calls them "Mr. and Mrs. America," and Frank Cady, in the role of Mr. Federber, is the image of the farmer in the painting *American Gothic*. The Federbers, unable to see the bars that are their natural habitat, are oblivious to the predicament of hopeless entrapment—Leo in his cave, Lorraine in her marriage, and Tatum in Albuquerque. Only Lorraine walks off. The last we see of her, she has missed her bus and is begging for a ride, an indication of her future.

A decade earlier, Orson Welles had told the story of a newsman who launched a war to sell papers: nothing in *Ace in the Hole* was new in 1951. Yet no other newspaper film, including those made much later—*Absence of Malice* (1981), *Broadcast News* (1987)—speaks so directly to the low esteem in which the press is now held. It augurs a future filled with phrases like "feeding frenzy" and "news cycle," of hyperbolic clichés like "tsunami" and "kudzu," of useful nouns turned into kapowie verbs like "impact" and "transition." In 1951, *Ace in the Hole* seemed merely unfair, overstated. Wilder, not yet associated with ribald hilarity, was known chiefly for three of the darkest movies made between 1944 and 1950, *Double Indemnity*, *The Lost Weekend*, and *Sunset Boulevard*. Even by those standards, *Ace in the Hole* crossed a line. After its failure, he kept his vitriol in check until 1964, when the sexually audacious *Kiss Me, Stupid* fared just as badly.

Ace in the Hole may be unfair, but it is hypnotic filmmaking and one of

Wilder's peak achievements. The uncharacteristic aerial shots are magnificent, as are the contrasts between sun-drenched desert and foul cavern.
Charles Lang's cinematography and Hugo Friedhofer's dissonant score
match the material. Criterion has done a thorough job in restoring an overlooked prize, complementing a stunning transfer with archival interviews
of Wilder, Douglas, and co-scenarist Walter Newman, plus a solid commentary track by Neil Sinyard and a four-page tabloid "extra," with fine essays
by Molly Haskell and Guy Maddin—a touch worthy of Wilder.

63

SALVAGE JOBS

Affair in Trinidad /

The Garment Jungle

A TROUBLED MOVIE production, parented by too many writers and directors, usually ends in catastrophe. So it is no small thing when a director swoops in to salvage a debacle. *Affair in Trinidad* and *The Garment Jungle*, two narrowly averted disasters from the 1950s, released simultaneously on DVD, are signed by Vincent Sherman, who first won his spurs as the uncredited salvager of *Across the Pacific* (1942), directing the last reel after John Huston went to war. If Sherman's name fails to ring a bell, several of his films should: *The Hard Way, Old Acquaintance* (both 1943), *Mr. Skeffington* (1944), *Nora Prentiss*, and *The Unfaithful* (both 1947). Made in his great decade as a Warner Bros. contract director, they helped define the careers of Ida Lupino, Bette Davis, and Ann Sheridan. But those films also earned him an unwelcome reputation as a women's director, although the soapiest of them concern tough, loveless women and boast an acidic wit that is no less apparent in his 1942 Humphrey Bogart wartime farce *All Through the Night* or his 1949 Errol Flynn self-parody *The Adventures of Don Juan*. All are impeccably crafted with brisk editing and expressive angles, shadows, and tracking shots. Histrionic urgency and plush physical texture in Sherman's films counter far-fetched or routine scripts.

Sherman began as an actor, first on stage and then in the movies, where he turned to screenwriting before landing the unlikely directorial assignment of Bogart's 1939 vampire movie *The Return of Dr. X.* The 1950s were hard years, marred by the blacklist and unsuitable projects, and after a few misfires in the early 1960s, Sherman turned to television. He died in 2006, a month short of his 100th birthday.

At ninety, Sherman published a kiss-and-tell-and-kiss-again memoir, *Studio Affairs*, recounting his romances with leading ladies throughout the course of his marriage (his wife was "modest, devoted, intelligent, and genuinely sophisticated"), including a liaison with the cinematically incandescent but privately lovelorn Rita Hayworth. In 1952, Hayworth had returned to Hollywood and Columbia Pictures after her four-year marriage to Aly Khan, and studio chief Harry Cohn ordered her to appear in a retread of her signature hit, *Gilda*, to be called *An Affair in Trinidad* and directed by Sherman. The studio had everything but a script and, despite many attempts, never did get one worth shooting—eight writers added their two cents, four of them earning on-screen credits.

The plot gets underway with the discovery of the murdered, estranged husband of a nightclub dancer, Chris Emery (Hayworth), and is so incoherent that we never find out why he was killed or by whom, or why they were estranged, or why he summoned his brother to Trinidad, or why the brother is numbingly bad-mannered and one-dimensional as played by Glenn Ford, Rita's flame in *Gilda*. The story goes downhill from the discovery, incorporating elements of Alfred Hitchcock's *Notorious* without its sexual compromise, and (more intriguingly) anticipating the climax of Hitchcock's *North by Northwest* as the tuxedoed, silk-spoken villain (Alexander Scourby) discovers that his fiancée Chris is a spy and prepares to dispose of her from his plane. For added color, Juanita Hall plays a maid who speaks in the lingo of fortune cookies: "When one day is over, another day begins." "It is the prerogative of a good and loyal servant to be impertinent."

Hayworth is the only reason to see this film, and if you need a better reason, *An Affair in Trinidad* isn't for you. Sherman knew this. He moves things along so quickly that the film survives as a moody valentine to unblushing star power. Audiences certainly knew it: *An Affair in Trinidad* actually outgrossed the far superior *Gilda*. At thirty-four, Hayworth's fresh face had taken on an edgy wariness, indelibly captured in a close-up as she stands smoking on the veranda, the light barely revealing her—unlike Glenn Ford, who shares the scene lit up like a spark plug.

When Hayworth danced, she was transformed (see *You'll Never Get Rich*, *You Were Never Lovelier*, *Cover Girl*), and Sherman gave her two terrific numbers, choreographed by Valerie Bettis, who appears riotously as the alcoholic floozy Veronica, uttering the film's inside joke: she wishes *she* could dance like Chris. In dance, Hayworth is no longer in character. She is redeemed, or, as an obsequious club owner played by Steven Geray tries to explain, "She is not just a woman, some woman. She's Woman with capital W!" Saul Chaplin arranged two undervalued songs by Lester Lee and Bob Russell: "Trinidad Lady" overlays bop triplets on a mild calypso rhythm, and "I've Been Kissed Before" is a tauntingly swinging tune overdue for rediscovery. In these numbers, Hayworth (who flawlessly lip-synchs vocalist Jo Ann Greer) goes way beyond the glove-removing tease of *Gilda* for a skirt-hiked, knees-bowed, energetic ritual of terpsichorean eros—plot points be damned.

After *An Affair in Trinidad*, Sherman was shunted aside by the blacklist as studio heads and producers refused his calls. Other than one film in Italy, he didn't direct for five years. His first post-exile credit began as a reluctant favor to Harry Cohn, who had fired Robert Aldrich from a film provisionally called *The Garment Center*, and asked Sherman to finish the job. It was unpleasant taking over another man's picture, particularly one starring Lee J. Cobb, whom Sherman had known years before (even before the Group Theater) and who had been a friendly witness for the House Un-American Activities Committee.

But Sherman went forward, retooling the script and extricating a rounded performance from Cobb; by his own account, he directed 70 percent of the film released as *The Garment Jungle* (1957). He credited Aldrich with several good scenes and wrote that he expected a secondary credit, not the sole credit that Cohn gave him. Aldrich is generally presumed to have directed the action scenes, but it was Sherman who revised the plot to make plausible Cobb's dress manufacturer, who hires thugs to thwart the union and then has to answer to the moral disillusionment of his son, played by Kerwin Mathews. Sherman also added domestic touches that were unheard-of in 1950s Hollywood—a father changing his baby's diapers, his wife breastfeeding the child in a bar. But trying to assign authorship is beside the point: *The Garment Jungle* is a surprisingly lucid, powerful film.

It belongs to a cycle of 1950s gangster films about union organizing, including *On the Waterfront*, *Salt of the Earth*, *Slaughter on Seventh Avenue*, *Chicago Confidential*, *The Big Operator*, and several others, reaching a nadir in the James Cagney all-dancing, all-shooting musical fiasco *Never Steal Anything Small*. In each, mobsters commit atrocious crimes, martyring union leaders, and are ultimately brought to justice by the workers. *The Garment Jungle* is set apart in its careful approach to the business side of the equation. It is filled with pointed details: the phony wood-paneled offices, the dreary hallways, the general tumult, the juxtaposition of a showroom adorned with models and a sweatshop of underpaid sewers.

It is less distinctive in its craven avoidance of ethnicity. Mafia? There is no Mafia. The only Italians in the film are good guys: Tony, the floor manager (a nicely nuanced performance by Harold J. Stone), and Tulio, the union martyr—charged with slithery energy by Robert Loggia, in his first film. The Jewishness of Cobb's character is as muted as his name, Walter Mitchell (he must have been used to that after playing Willy Loman). The chief killer, embodied by a relentlessly malevolent Richard Boone, is called Ravidge. Solid performances—including Gia Scala at the peak of her brief career and wild-eyed Joseph Wiseman, who could turn a line of lackluster dialogue into a sonata of ulcerous torment—add to the tension, which rarely falters from the opening *in media res* close-up of two partners shouting to the violent finale. A few location inserts demonstrate a feeling for the period and milieu, especially as the film moves to an uneasily quiet four-story walk-up on the Lower East Side, counterpointing the wealth of the manufacturer's home and the clamor of the garment center. If the finish is a fairy tale, it comes only after Boone's madman wipes up the floor with Mathews's prodigal son—a vet just returned from Korea. We don't believe the sitcom ending, and we're not meant to. The jungle has simply undergone a turnover, union or no union, from one set of bosses to another.

MOB MENTALITY

Mafioso / Excellent Cadavers

THE NEARLY CONCURRENT DVD releases of Alberto Lattuada's *Mafioso*, from Criterion, and Marco Turco's *Excellent Cadavers*, from First Run, make for a complementary treatment of the Sicilian Mafia as an indestructible force of evil. Americans have adopted mobsters as cultural house pets: as urban outlaws, dapper rogues, fairy tale capitalists, and House of Atreus incendiaries, depending on one's metaphorical preference. These two films—a dark comedy from 1962, featuring a perfectly judged performance by Alberto Sordi, and a documentary from 2005—go beyond catch phrases and soap opera to capture the chilling reality of an institution that appears to be as secure as the church, even though for a long time it was hardly acknowledged at all.

Mafia movies, like Mafia prosecutions, were redefined in the 1950s by two commissions. First, the 1951 televised Kefauver Committee hearings concluded that organized crime existed, despite suspiciously stubborn denials by the FBI. The stars of the proceedings were Frank Costello's hands— the mob boss had somehow convinced the committee and the broadcaster not to show his face. A better symbol for the manipulations of an invisible puppeteer could not have been invented. The cinematic response was instantaneous, as a stream of films appeared about the secret empire. Unlike crime films of the 1930s, which focused on individuals, these movies looked at the larger enterprise: *The Enforcer, The Big Heat, The Big Combo, On the Waterfront, The Miami Story, The Phenix City Story, The Brothers Rico, Chi-*

cago Confidential, New York Confidential, The Garment Jungle, Underworld USA, and dozens more. They often avoided ethnicity, steered clear of the word "Mafia," and ended with Mr. Big taking a fall. "I'm glad what I done to you," Terry Malloy chides Johnny Friendly in On the Waterfront—all it took was a stand-up guy or sit-down stoolie.

Even so, J. Edgar Hoover persisted in characterizing the mob as a chimera, unlike the bank robbers he had dispatched in the happier days of the Depression. Hoover had to moonwalk, however, after the mob bosses convened their own 1957 commission in Apalachin, a previously sleepy municipality in upstate New York. The local police intruded, sending sharks in sharkskin suits scurrying into the nearby woods. Denial was no longer an option for the FBI, though it was the Treasury Department's Bureau of Narcotics, not Hoover's white men in gray suits, that soon compiled the first bestiary of connected men, kept under wraps until its publication in 2004 as Mafia. This time the cinematic response was more violent and morally baroque, animated by a realism that the Production Code could not entirely repeal. Compare Richard Widmark in the pre-Kefauver Kiss of Death (1947) and Eli Wallach in the post-Apalachin The Lineup (1958). Both played psychopaths who push wheelchair-bound seniors to their death. In the former, the victim is a harmless woman, and the death of the predator restores social order; in the latter, the victim is a kingpin, and the death of the hit man who pushes him over the balcony railing of a skating rink resolves nothing. Richard Wilson's underrated Pay or Die (1960) tells the true story of the fearless Italian American police lieutenant Joe Petrosino, who visited Sicily in 1909 seeking information to expose the secret society. He was promptly assassinated: end of movie.

The Italian film industry, which had ignored the Mafia to this point, now began to acknowledge its barbarity, if somewhat obliquely. In the late 1950s, Francesco Rosi began his career by exploring the rituals of organized crime in La Sfida (1958, shot in Naples for fear of offending Sicilians, though the Naples mob, the Camorra, would soon rival the Mafia's reputation for viciousness) and the bumbling I Magliari (1959, starring Sordi). He found his own voice in Salvatore Giuliano (1962), using documentary meticulousness to trace the rise of a mob chieftain in the postwar years as the Allies cemented a Mafia-government coalition—a theme briefly explored in Excellent Cadavers.

That same year, Sicily's underground was further breached in two comedies set in the present: Pietro Germi's flat-out hilarious *Divorce Italian Style*, in which the rule of the dons is a given and pandemic blood lust is played out in a burlesque of marital honor; and Lattuada's *Mafioso*, in which the comic elements are, at first, disarmingly unclear. If *The Godfather* is a blood-soaked epic that leaves residual recollections of star-powered romance, nostalgia, and humor, *Mafioso* is a comedy of manners that leaves the chill of unappeased horror. It drolly meanders for half its running time, a beautifully played character study efficiently told but without an apparently urgent objective. The viewer is encouraged to feel superior to the naive Nino (Sordi), until Nino and viewer alike are placed literally in the dark—a plane's cargo hold, en route to New York to commit a crime for which neither he nor we are prepared.

Lattuada makes it clear from the beginning that Mafia tentacles reach well into the north. Nino has lived in Milan for eight years as an efficiency expert in a factory. He now chooses to take a long-delayed vacation, bringing his wife and children to meet his family in his native Sicily. His boss gives him a package to be hand-delivered to Don Vincenzo (Ugo Attanasio), which turns out to be an American-made golden heart that will adorn the church's Madonna and also contains coded instructions for a death warrant. Nino is a fish out of water, except in the zone afforded by his family and by his vanity, never more so than when shipped to New York, oily and over-dressed—though he briefly feels at home as he looks up at the astonishing skyscrapers and sees a poster for a Sophia Loren film. The favor Don Vincenzo demands of him is filmed as a dream, a few hours on the other side of the looking glass. Nino and we know nothing of his target, but the deed is compromising all around. *Mafioso* is constructed like a snare, supported by the sumptuous photography of Armando Nannuzzi and a wonderfully mottled score by Piero Piccioni, who mixes idioms and amplifies ill omens with electrical rumbling.

Excellent Cadavers is not for the faint of heart or the cheery of disposition, yet unlike Matteo Garrone's diligently segmented yet panoramic study of the bloodthirsty Naples mob, *Gomorra* (2008), a fictionalized elaboration of Roberto Saviano's terrifying journalism, Marco Turco's documentary sees a way out. His film argues that the Mafia, which during a two-year period in the early1980s left 300 slaughtered bodies on the streets of Palermo, could be eradicated. It almost was, according to Turco, when two magistrates, Giovanni Falcone and Paolo Borsellino, combined their resources to launch the maxi-trial that placed more than 400 Mafia suspects before a judge and, despite interference by the Italian government, ultimately won convictions. Reprisals were swift. In 1992, Falcone and Borsellino were murdered, months apart, in explosions that observers likened to nuclear blasts. Silvio Berlusconi's government then undid much of what had been accomplished, even dismantling the witness protection program. Today the Mafia is said to extort tributes from 80 percent of Sicilian businesses, to say nothing of its role in the international heroin trade.

Much of the archival footage in *Excellent Cadavers* is appalling, including dozens of photographs by Letizia Battaglia, who appears on camera at seventy and recalls the almost daily calls she received to cover various murder sites. Her pictures of bodies surrounded by grieving widows and curious onlookers are ghastly; in one, a severed head is set upon a car seat. Given the film's strengths, its missteps are particularly regrettable. Turco's film is based on a book by Alexander Stille, who is inexplicably on camera throughout, lugging a shoulder bag, occasionally pretending to read or write. He also serves as narrator but lacks authority in that role—he doesn't deign to explain that the title is mob slang for the bodies of political officials. Yet the film tells an intricate story with a great many names (First Run ought to have provided a dramatis personae), and it is coherent and dramatically sound. Falcone and Borsellino emerge as genuine heroes, as stoic as they were tenacious. Asked if he is afraid, Falcone, who looks disconcertingly like Alberto Sordi, tells a reporter, "Living with one's fear, without being conditioned by it, that's courage. Otherwise, it's not courage but recklessness." *Excellent Cadavers* is one of the saddest films I've ever seen.

65

WARS TO END WARS

All Quiet on the Western Front /

49th Parallel

IT'S EASY TO forget how good *All Quiet on the Western Front* is, the film (1930) and the novel (1929). Both have been antiwar staples for so long they've become almost invisible, relics from an era when its theme—war is madness visited on the young by delusional old men—had novelty. In Homer, warriors instigate war; in Tolstoy, war is a product of historical forces; in Crane, war tests personal courage. World War I changed all that, engendering a battlefield literature of futility, outrage, repentance, and self-pity. Its warriors belong to a generation that was characterized as the greatest by no one and as disillusioned by everyone. As Erich Maria Remarque's sacrificial hero, Paul Baumer, says, "We are forlorn like children, and experienced like old men, we are crude and sorrowful and superficial—I believe we are lost."

   The novel's invisibility stems from its odd reliability as high school fare, a tribute to the A. W. Wheen translation, which no one has thought to update in eighty years. The film has weathered less well, and not just because it lacks an ongoing adolescent base: the acting is sometimes creaky, the rhetoric verges on cant, the complexion is black and white. Yet, like the translation, it survives with untouchable grandeur, free of remakes and endlessly influential. Enduring aspects are particularly evident in light of Clint Eastwood's bravura diptych *Flags of Our Fathers* and *Letters from Iwo Jima*, released in the same year (2006) as Universal's DVD of Lewis Milestone's picture. Like *Flags*, *All Quiet* corrosively examines home-front patriotism;

like *Letters*, it is told from the viewpoint of the enemy.

Universal's bright transfer of *All Quiet* arrives in an otherwise skeletal package—you'd think the novel's ongoing utility and the film's historical importance would mandate at least a featurette. As an ironic addendum, though, Criterion offered at the same time a two-disc edition of Michael Powell's *49th Parallel* (1941), which also narrates its story through the eyes of German combatants. What a difference a decade made. Milestone looked back in horror. Powell's Germans, with one exception, aren't young boys who struggle to keep their humanity, but the devil's playthings. His film was designed to encourage America to enlist in the war and kill, kill, kill. Indeed, Powell's argument is virtually the same as that advanced by the vile schoolmaster in *All Quiet*, whose rhetoric whips his students into gung-ho froth. Perhaps mom and dad don't want them to go, he remonstrates: "Are your fathers so forgetful of their fatherland that they would let it perish rather than you?" Not a nurturing lot. Those responsible for *49th Parallel* also ask us to recognize that the fatherland is in peril, especially Canada: what red-blooded Canadian or American boy could fail to relish punching out a Nazi? Punching is the recourse of choice here—as it is, for that matter, in *Plan 9 from Outer Space*. The trouble with propaganda is that however well-intentioned or justified, it leads to remorse and levity.

Remarque's short, declarative sentences are a triumph of journalistic precision, packing more images of physical revulsion and mental anguish than the novel's modest length would indicate. Milestone's film also pursues accuracy, but is more self-conscious in its search for style. His innovative use of cranes and other techniques ensures a striking visual mobility; the scenes of trench warfare, as soldiers charge into machine-gun fire, have lost nothing to time—the battle scenes are stunning and emotionally taxing. Milestone uses rapid editing to isolate and satirize members of mobs. His tracking of Kemmerich's boots augurs Steven Spielberg's girl in a red coat in *Schindler's List*. Twice, his camera passes through gates, from one space to another. It subdivides the screen in the scene where Paul and his friends study a poster, the men reflected in a mirror so that they seem to be standing to its right. It stops altogether for ninety long seconds, showing only unmoving shadows as we hear the postcoital conversation of Paul and a woman he has bought with food. Today's directors might not hesitate to show the decapitated lance corporal ("He runs a few steps more while the blood spouts from his neck like a fountain"), but no one could improve on

Milestone's indelible depiction of Remarque's soldier whose "body drops clean away and only his hands with the stumps of his arms, shot off, now hang on the wires." Milestone's subsequent career was a mixed bag, including racist wartime humbug in the 1940s (*The Purple Heart*), but in 1930 he was the right man for the job.

Maxwell Anderson's script is, despite a few too many soulful meditations, a textbook example of how to adapt a famous novel. Remarque's story employs Conradian breaks in time and internal meditations. Maxwell broke the story down to its components, arranging them chronologically to emphasize the surreal descent from classroom to shelled trenches. Much is missing, but much is preserved. Had the film been made a few years later, after the imposition of the Production Code, the violence, homoerotic barracks life, incontinence, and casual sex would have all disappeared.

The acting is mostly solid, especially the broken-nosed Louis Wolheim, who is incapable of a false moment. Lew Ayres makes a yeoman attempt to hold the picture together as Paul, but his hysteria ventures into the range of Colin Clive on amphetamines. For most of the young actors, *All Quiet* topped their careers, including Ben Alexander (thin and haunted, nothing like the overweight partner to Sergeant Friday on *Dragnet*) and William Bakewell as Paul's friend Albert Kropp. I interviewed Bakewell years ago. At the time *All Quiet* was shooting, Universal was also making a financially disastrous musical revue, *King of Jazz*, with Paul Whiteman. Bakewell recalled shooting the war by day and hanging out with Bix Beiderbecke, Bing Crosby, and other party animals at night. Call it the magic of old Hollywood, but watching *All Quiet on the Western Front*, you forget they were anywhere near a studio or California.

49th Parallel was an important film in its day; it jolted the British film industry, made the case for American intervention, and cemented the team of Powell and writer-producer Emeric Pressburger. But it's one of their lesser works. Scripted as a conventional thriller, in which six Nazis stranded in Canada attempt to cross the 49th parallel into the United States, murdering and looting until they are winnowed down to the leader, it offers few thrills. The tension is diluted by unstoppable agitprop and stereotypical characters, of which the most risible are Laurence Oliver as a jovial French Canadian trapper who takes his nasal accent to the brink of cuteness and never returns, and Leslie Howard as an English twit who reads Mann and camps in a teepee with a Matisse and a Picasso.

Still, the film makes the most of location vistas, including an opening montage tracking the titular parallel, and stupendously good photography by Frederick Young, rendered in the digital transfer with a high-definition level of detail. A few performances are outstanding: those by Eric Portman as the Nazi true believer, Finlay Currie as a stationmaster, and especially two actors who incarnate aspects of Lew Ayres's distress, proving that even in a prowar exercise the memory of *All Quiet on the Western Front* could not be entirely quelled—Anton Walbrook as the leader of a German Canadian Hutterite commune and Niall MacGinnis (who wouldn't get another film opportunity this good until *Curse of the Demon* in 1957) as a reluctant Nazi who would rather bake bread for the Hutterites. The accompanying disc includes an excellent fifty-minute television film from 1982 on Powell and Pressburger, audio recordings of Powell dictating sections of his autobiography, and Powell and Pressburger's "The Volunteer," a witty forty-five-minute promotional film for the Fleet Air Arm, in which Ralph Richardson—wearing Othello drag in one scene—tells the story of his incompetent dresser Fred, who becomes a wartime volunteer, saves a plane, and wins a medal from the king, smiling the whole time. War: what fun!

66

LOVE THE WARRIORS

Overlord / The Guns of Navarone /

The Caine Mutiny

WAR IS HELL; writing about war is Homeric. The settings, fighters, and armaments change, but the fervor, terror, heroism, cowardice, agony, resentment, egotism, majesty, relief, pain, death, joy, love, corruption, humor, and insanity abide, as does the overweening desire to mythologize war's grotesquerie. Unlike his progeny, though, Homer didn't bother with scoring political points. Neither pro- nor antiwar, he offered no special succor to those appalled or elated by it. For that, we've got liberals, conservatives, and, for lack of a better term, libratives—those who count receipts before taking sides.

Three recent DVDs—one a first-time release and two rereleased in improved editions—partake of mythmaking, and two of them document librative ambivalence. Like politicians who praise our troops to distinguish themselves from politicians who hate our troops, the Hollywood entries deride war but love warriors. *The Caine Mutiny* (1954) and *The Guns of Navarone* (1961) are products of World War II, the Hollywood blacklist, and producer Stanley Kramer's tradition of moral certitude, which favors equivocation as the essence of artistic vision. But first, consider the virtually unknown *Overlord*, a 1975 film by Stuart Cooper, an American who lived in England and worked mostly in television. The film, which won festival prizes but not distribution in the United States, was produced by the Imperial War Museum, which gave Cooper unlimited access to its immense collection of World War II footage. Working with Christopher Hudson, he scripted an anecdotal story about an everyman soldier who is called to service and trained for D-Day (Operation Overlord), where he is an immediate casualty.

During the war, John Huston and other filmmakers courted controversy by staging scenes for putative documentaries. Cooper did the opposite, using footage taken from the RAF, Germans, London Fire Brigade, newsreels, and other sources to fill out the surreal, terror-filled tableau that frames his soldier's painfully ordinary travail. Some footage is familiar from nonfiction films, notably the great British documentary *The World at War*, made in the same years as *Overlord*, yet takes on an intensified urgency in this context. Instead of illustrating a historian's narrative, the film paints the maw into which men are channeled like debris in a sluice. The fireworks that represent fierce nighttime battles and the bomber-bay shots of descending missiles landing in step-by-step patterns punctuate the steady tramping of feet into harm's way. Purely as a technical achievement, *Overlord* is remarkable: cinematographer John Alcott (Stanley Kubrick's cameraman) worked with 1940s lenses to match scripted scenes to the archival material, and Jonathan Gili's editing is so precise you cease to distinguish what is real and what is staged. This illusion would mean little if Cooper and his lead actor, Brian Stirner, had not succeeded in creating an illusion of layperson realism; comical, lyrical, and artsy interludes notwithstanding, the film exudes a quiet confidence that seems to eschew the professionalism it embodies.

Overlord is not about heroics, yet the archival footage is testament to the heroics that would win the war. The everyman, Tommy, is an object lesson in the depersonalizing techniques, older than Homer, that reduce soldiers to sacrificial lambs, cannon fodder—"Die of boredom, die in battle, what's the difference?" As the military machine gets bigger, the men get smaller, until—as Tommy observes—there is nothing left. Two moving sequences introduce women: an aging prostitute (Lorna Lewis) with aggressive eyebrows tries to seduce Tommy in a movie theater showing the Nazis goosestepping to "The Lambeth Walk," and an innocent but astute young woman (Julie Neesam) engages his imagination with a kiss until the film abruptly returns him to the bumping reality of a transport truck.

Cooper explains, in a commentary track, that the repeated, fuzzily prescient image of a soldier shot down while running toward the camera was inspired by a Robert Capa photograph. That image is one of several intended to lift *Overlord* to the level of myth in which Tommy's death is as preordained as the invasion's success. A good deal of material is covered in eighty-three minutes, not all of it understandable without the commentary and other addenda provided by Criterion. Watching it cold, you may not recognize shots of Dunkirk or know what the strange barrel rolling out of the sea is (a failed invention intended to destroy mines, called the Panjandrum), among other fleeting images. The DVD explains all, and when you watch the film again, its clarity is fairly overwhelming.

By contrast, nothing is clear in *The Caine Mutiny* or *The Guns of Navarone* but the desire to create rousing adventure, thumpingly scored to the martial music of Max Steiner and Dimitri Tiomkin. Kramer assigned *Caine* to Edward Dmytryk, the once promising B filmmaker and member of the Hollywood 10, who sought to rebuild his career after doing time and naming names. Herman Wouk's novel was so widely read that Kramer insisted on a Classics Illustrated treatment, moving quickly among the most famous incidents—the tow line, the missing strawberries, the typhoon, the trial, Captain Queeg's breakdown, and the bizarre turnabout in which the defendant's lawyer lectures his client on Queeg as a misunderstood hero.

The novel is dated less by the operatic melodrama—it's still quite readable—than by smaller things, like Wouk's prudish refusal to indulge in "billingsgate" or his racist stereotyping of black stewards, including one named Rasselas. The movie improves on the book in that regard: actor James Edwards's steward doesn't "yassuh" anyone. For the rest, the film might have been written by the *Caine*'s heel, Keefer, the villainous intellectual who finks at the trial. The script gives Queeg a speech requesting understanding from his crew and noting his pet dog, a probable dig at Richard Nixon's Checkers broadcast. But that bit of mockery, shared by Keefer and the filmmakers, is just a diversion; the speech ultimately justifies the pro-Queeg climax, removing what little ambiguity Wouk offered. The film also de-ethnicizes Barney Greenwald, robbing him of motivation and the novel's most memorable line: "I owed [Queeg] a favor, don't you see? He stopped Hermann Goering from washing his fat behind with my mother." And it makes Willie a man by marrying May, who is a more interesting, independent, near proto-feminist character in the novel.

The whole point of using Willie as the story's anchor is neutered by Robert Francis's one-note performance of a one-note character—purely a mama's boy, not the slumming nightclub pianist and would-be professor of the book. This allows the outstanding foursome of Humphrey Bogart, Van

Johnson, Fred MacMurray, and Jose Ferrer to kick out the jambs, keeping the ship afloat despite extreme fracturing of the hull. Dmytryk's direction is pedestrian, capturing none of Willie's awe or Wouk's conceit that the *Caine* mutiny was a modern myth, known "throughout the service."

The Guns of Navarone doesn't hesitate to proclaim its fake mythic status, beginning with James Robertson Justice's plummy narration. As the critic Christopher Frayling points out in an interview that is the best of the new DVD extras, the film is constructed out of Greek legends, from the Minotaur in the labyrinth to Jason and the Argos. It was produced by Kramer's former partner and script writer for *High Noon*, Carl Foreman, who fled the HUAC hearings to reestablish himself in London; he assigned the direction to J. Lee Thompson, and neither of them would do anything nearly as good again.

The direction of a complicated film is certainly efficient, and the grand adventure, however improbable, continues to hold up. Yet possibly because the producer was disinclined to waste expensive location footage, the action slows at times to a crawl, like an unedited documentary. Some scenes have no tempo at all. Foreman, who wrote the script, added thumb suckers about the dread ironies of war, but in the nuttiest scene he throws the bathwater out with the baby, as Gregory Peck, in perhaps the worst line reading of his nobly uneven career, lectures David Niven on his responsibility to the team effort. Niven's response is priceless: you can't tell if his character is chagrined or if Niven himself is wondering what the heck got into Greg. Either way, this is the kind of antiwar film that could double as a recruiting tool. *Navarone* is a librative theme park, each episode another ride.

67

THEATER OF THE ABSURD

Merrill's Marauders

DURING THE SLAUGHTER of Japanese troops at Burma's Walawbum in March 1944, members of the 5307th Composite Unit (Provisional), better known as Merrill's Marauders, hurled—in addition to mortars, grenades, bullets, and shells—various epithets, including the allegation that Hideki Tojo ate excrement. According to a Marauder staff sergeant, the Japanese yelled back, "Eleanor eats powdered eggs!" Whether this rejoinder was intended as an assessment of Mrs. Roosevelt, K-rations, or both, it portended a wit rarely encountered in descriptions of the Burma campaign, and nearly impossible to render on film. Samuel Fuller's war pictures are besotted with gallows humor, but even he would have been hard pressed to use this story (had he heard it), suspending the audience's suspension for a collective "Hunh?" The powdered eggs remark heralded a dying fall: 800 Japanese soldiers died at Walawbum, as opposed to 8 Marauders. The Marauder casualties were of a different kind: a third of them succumbed to disease, psychological breakdown, starvation, exhaustion, and a ferocious sense of betrayal. Still, as the Warner Bros. DVD of *Merrill's Marauders* (1962) reminds us, Fuller's compromised yet uncompromising movie is by no means deficient in hunh? moments.

At least four such moments exemplify Fuller's emphasis on mental dislocation in war. A dying soldier who screams, "Did they get Lemchek?" *is* Lemchek. A group of exhausted men suddenly realize they can't tell what day it is or the difference between A.M. and P.M. The keeper of a much-coddled mule—named Eleanor (!)—volunteers to carry the mule's load and dies under the weight. Sergeant Kolowicz (played by the leathery Claude Akins), waking to a bowl of rice extended to him by a very beautiful, very old Kachin woman, doffs his hat and blubbers inconsolably. Another Fullerian moment was perhaps designed primarily for the unit's survivors. How would anyone else know that the actor playing Brigadier General Frank Merrill's attaché, credited as Vaughan Wilson, is actually Major (later Lieutenant Colonel) Samuel Vaughan Wilson, a Marauder who served as the film's technical adviser and narrated the trailer? That knowledge gives his character's valedictory lines an extra kick: "Do you know what I'm going to do after the war? I'm going to get married and have six kids. Then I'm going to line them up and tell them what Burma was like, and if they don't cry, I'll beat the hell out of them."

Merrill's Marauders was not a project sought by Fuller. He wanted instead to film his own World War II story, *The Big Red One*. But Jack Warner held it out as a carrot, so Fuller left for the Philippines with a company of Warner contract players, mostly from its television Westerns, including Ty Hardin, Peter Brown, and Will Hutchins. The cast was led by a middling star, Jeff Chandler, whose prominent cheekbones had pigeonholed him as an Indian chief. Chandler's striking performance should have upped his stature, but he suffered an injury to his back while filming and died before the movie was released, a victim of medical malpractice and front page news at the time. The gifted cinematographer William Clothier specialized in Westerns and war films, but was not an ideal choice for this Cinemascope project; his vistas are a bit too enchanting. And hack composer Howard Jackson came up with nothing but martial clichés, though Warner supplemented them with its library of stock music by Max Steiner and Franz Waxman, who wrote the great score for the studio's first pass at the story, *Objective, Burma!* (1945).

In the end, Warner took the film away from Fuller, insisting on the ludicrously upbeat ending of a thoroughly irrelevant marching band. But it makes no difference: by its final scene, the film—a box-office success—has decisively undermined every illusion of military glory. From the first shots, which follow a nicely cobbled historical setup using newsreel footage and animation, Fuller shows the Marauders up against something more frightening than combat. As Marauder Charlton Ogburn Jr. wrote in his 1959 account *The Marauders*, on which the film is based, "The major enemy was not the Japanese themselves, but your own apprehensions." Fuller's dialogue begins with apprehensions: "Another bend in the road," a soldier says. "Wonder what's behind this one."

It was not an easy story to tackle—not for Warner Bros, and not for the army, which had been torn between honoring (reluctantly, after a congressional hearing) the extraordinary bravery and fortitude of the Marauders and quashing the resentment of its members. Colonel Charles N. Hunter, who assumed command after Brigadier General Merrill suffered a heart attack, protested that the force of nearly 3,000 volunteers—initially formed with the code name Galahad—had been "expended to bolster the ego" of General Joe Stilwell, the American commander of the Chinese-Burma-India theater. That may explain why military history pays little interest to Hunter, though he was responsible for much of the unit's success. In Fuller's adaptation, which is filled with his usual nicknames (Bullseye, Chowhound), Hunter becomes Lieutenant Stockton, or Stock (adeptly played by Ty Hardin). One of the film's most intriguing qualities is the relationship between Merrill and Stock—father-son with an undercurrent of homoeroticism. Stock undergoes a sea change from gung-ho obedience to obstinate fury.

Yet for all the painstaking historical touches—leeches (but no tigers or elephants, present in Burma but too expensive to unleash in the Philippines), the tapped Japanese radio wire, the "balletic" dances of death (in Ogburn's description), and the oddly shaped concrete fuel tanks at the dynamic rail-head battle—this is a movie beyond history, locked in its own absurdist treadmill. Despite the documentary opening and the abrupt all's-well finish, *Merrill's Marauders* has no beginning and no end. It's about a trial of endurance without reward. The Marauders excited the public during the war, partly through the luck of alliteration. The volunteers who made up Galahad, including several sociopaths and others who won release from prison to join up (Galahad prefigured *The Dirty Dozen* school of wartime adventure), were formed as the 5307th regiment. That designation was changed to 5307th Composite Unit (Provisional) because the leadership of a mere regiment was considered unsuitable for a brigadier general. A *Time* reporter, James Shepley, came to the rescue, calling them Merrill's Marauders—a name the press could understand.

In 1944, when Raoul Walsh began shooting *Objective, Burma!*, the Marauders offered an obvious inspiration for a fictional film about American paratroopers on a mission to blow up a radar station, unaware that they have become an expendable diversion. Walsh's fine film wasn't just fiction, it was fantasy. Paratroopers? Not a single soldier dropped into Burma from the air. Allies consisting of men with names like Nebraska and Gabby? Burma was a mostly British-Chinese operation. *Objective, Burma!*, banned in England by an angry Winston Churchill, wasn't the first instance of Hollywood's oddly possessive attitude toward Burma: in the Poverty Row programmer *Bombs over Burma* (1942), a Chinese woman and a two-fisted American bus driver save the country from a British spy.

By war's end, Americans looked sheepishly at the Marauders, as the army tried to play down the length of their tour and the grueling casualties, especially mental ones. It also suppressed John Huston's documentary *Let There Be Light*, about psychiatric illness in the armed forces. Fuller shows how the successful occupation of Walawbum turned out to be the first of three missions, the second and third added without warning or respite. Within five months, the Marauders fought five major conflicts and thirty-two skirmishes, walking 750 miles in relentless heat through polluted swamps and rivers, along jungle trails, over razor-backed ridges, and on tight mountain trails from which their pack mules fell into the ravines below. They survived on minimal K-rations and with no change of uniform. Of the nearly 3,000 Marauders, only 200 were present at the final objective, the airbase at Myitkyina, after which the unit was quickly disbanded. Subsequent honors, including Bronze Stars and the Distinguished Unit Citation, satisfied few.

Fuller had not intended to film the harrowing second half of the story, the political and psychiatric aftermath. Yet can it be mere coincidence that he set his very next picture, *Shock Corridor* (1963), in an insane asylum beset with victims of war and racism—a theme he amplified years later in his masterpiece, *The Big Red One* (1980)? Warner Home Video could have done a lot more with this DVD; most movies that get commentaries and featurettes don't deserve them. *Merrill's Marauders* does.

68

IN SEARCH OF LOST TIME
Muriel / La belle captive

ALAIN RESNAIS'S *Muriel, or The Time of Return* (1963) has languished below the radar of most film lovers, even those who came of age with the *Nouvelle Vague*. Arriving on the heels of the director's two international sensations, *Hiroshima Mon Amour* (1959) and *Last Year at Marienbad* (1961), Resnais's third feature film wore out the patience of those who had perhaps too enthusiastically accepted the portentous incantations of the former and the silky inscrutability of the latter. Bored with metaphysics, they didn't recognize the unsparing humanism of this, his masterpiece. Even *Muriel*'s admirers, during the film's brief New York run in the fall of 1963, stigmatized it as obscure and, worse, a movie that had to be seen twice to be appreciated. That issue, at least, is mooted by Koch Lorber's DVD release. *Muriel* is an indispensable film. You can now watch it as often as you like.

A reputation for difficulty is almost impossible to undo. The sad reality is that as people get older, they are less inclined to tackle works of art shrouded in warning labels. The Joyce industry succeeded chiefly in stamping a majestically entertaining writer as radioactive. By any standard, however, *Muriel* has gotten a bad rap. Though it rewards intimacy, it does not require the exegesis it seems effortlessly to generate. A degree in Bergson is unnecessary; a relationship with the novels of Alain Robbe-Grillet is entirely optional. *Muriel* is an expression of painstaking realism, configured with wit and in the generic trappings of a thriller. As Truffaut noted, a more helpful grounding for Resnais's film would be a familiarity with Hitchcock.

The plot is fairly straightforward. Hélène (Delphine Seyrig), a prematurely gray widow on the verge of middle age, lives with her stepson, Bernard (Jean-Baptiste Thierree), a traumatized veteran of the war in Algeria, in the coastal city of Boulogne-sur-Mer, which is rebuilding itself from the rubble of World War II. Barely eking out a living by selling antiques from her apartment (Bernard complains, "You never know which period you'll wake up to in this flat"), she borrows money and compulsively gambles it away. Bernard, haunted by his role in torturing to death an Algerian prisoner named Muriel, pretends that he is dating a girl of that name while hoarding evidence—on film and tape and in journals—of his war crime, which he blames in part on another soldier. Hélène's life is also shadowed by war, particularly by the older man who saved and abandoned her twenty years ago, her first lover, Alphonse (Jean-Pierre Kérien), whom she impulsively invites to visit. He arrives with his young mistress, Françoise (Nita Klein), passing her off as his niece. Alphonse, a habitual liar, attempts to leach onto the town and Hélène's affections while escaping his failed business and marriage. His brother-in-law comes looking for him, ultimately crushing Hélène's illusions.

Those who can't tolerate *Muriel* argue that the story line is needlessly racked by its circuitous treatment. In fact, the treatment is everything—and more than four decades later, it remains innovative, persuasive, and illuminating. The script, by publisher, novelist, and poet Jean Cayrol, leaves nothing unsaid but forces the viewer to participate in its emotional turmoil by eliding everything that isn't necessary. The integrity and falsity of relationships and the way the trappings of the past stifle the present are magnified by ingenious cutting that, like a musical work, waxes and wanes in tempo.

In the novels of Robbe-Grillet, consciousness is sublimated to objective description, which gave his script for *Last Year at Marienbad* a heartless, game-playing beauty. With *Muriel*, Resnais uses narrative omniscience to suggest the interior lives of his characters. The first sequence is startling. A prelude to the main action, it depicts Hélène politely waiting out her last customer (as her stepson makes coffee), so that she can rush to the train station to greet Alphonse. The scene lasts all of thirty-five seconds, and in the first twenty-four there are twenty-four cuts of uneven duration, speeding up with Hélène's anxiety to be on her way: recurring shots of the customer's gloved hand holding open the door, the customer's coat and hat and face, the kettle, the antiques, Hélène drawing on a cigarette or closing a tape measure. The shots reflect the point of view not of the characters, but of the director laying out the tableau; yet the tempo and images perfectly convey Hélène's impatience.

The next forty-eight minutes are like an adagio movement, detailing the events of that evening as Hélène brings Alphonse and Françoise home, introduces them to Bernard, and bizarrely informs Alphonse that she has a date (like the dope addict she apparently once was, she needs a fix at the casino), as Bernard similarly invites Françoise out for the evening and suddenly abandons her to sit by himself in a bar. This section closes as Alphonse, pretending to be asleep in a chair in Hélène's bedroom, reaches for her hand. The story is conveyed with a boding suspense: Alphonse and Françoise arrive with the slick artificiality of honeymoon killers (nervously cold, he is never seen without an overcoat or scarf), and Bernard's weirdness leaves gaping mouths whenever he speaks.

The following morning is announced with a shot of Bernard on a horse, riding along the coast like Lancelot in search of a Muriel he can save, only to be greeted by an old man who asks if Bernard can procure for him a mate for his goat. The subsequent sequence is an allegretto tour de force of comings and goings, elliptical dialogue, missed cues, failed connections, new characters, vague wanderings, passing sex, quotidian actions and musings, and an unspecified passing of time. Tortured by her misgivings about Alphonse, Hélène turns to her forbearing companion, a developer named Roland de Smoke (Claude Sainval), who tries to comfort her. "Love affairs are like dinners," he says, "some guests behave, others don't."

The extraordinary denouement includes, among other incidents, a lunch at which Alphonse is exposed, the rendition of an old music-hall song counterpoised with shots of the soulless new buildings in Boulogne, a rash murder, an explosion, and Hélène's self-exile from her home. In the end, she makes a halfhearted attempt to follow Alphonse, who—like the ghost of shame and misery—sneaks off on a bus bound for Brussels, while his wife arrives at the abandoned apartment and walks through the rooms, now as empty as the streets in the closing sequence of Antonioni's *L'eclisse*, released the year before.

The stylistic exuberance, amplified by Sacha Vierny's color cinematography and Hans Werner Henze's ominous musical incursions, would mean little if the characters did not resonate so vividly. *Muriel* belongs to the genre of films and novels that sets out to map the way we live, and its concern for lives caught between an insufficiently explored past and uncertain future remains compelling. The specific situations entailing colonial wars, the lure of anaesthetizing habits, and the shoals of a constantly deconstructing present are as timely as sin. *Muriel* is a marvel of unblinking compassion, detailing lives we cannot fail to understand better than we might like.

The same cannot be said for Robbe-Grillet's *La belle captive* (1983, also from Koch Lorber), but if your idea of a good time is to watch the radiant Gabrielle Lazure writhing naked or in a white diaphanous gown, then your idea comports with mine and you may get a bang out of this 1983 Euro-trash vampire spy movie amplified by metaphorical jokes taken from Magritte paintings. With music by Schubert, Ellington, and an accordionist, and metallic colors by photographer Henri Alekan, *La belle captive* shows that the novelist knew how to make a film, and may even encourage curiosity about his other films, which never received much of a reception here despite his literary celebrity in the 1960s. The substance, however, is an old routine: the nightmare that never ends. The borrowings range from Kafka and Arthur Schnitzler (*Traumnovelle*, the source for *Eyes Wide Shut*) to Fritz Lang's *Woman in the Window*, Boris Karloff in *The Devil Commands*, Mario Bava's *Lisa and the Devil*, Kubrick's *A Clockwork Orange*, and who knows how many other cultural leavings. The others, though, do not have Lazure, whose sensuousness makes Robbe-Grillet's indulgences worth indulging, even as they remind us that—contrary to literary prejudices—he was the *Marienbad* artist who stagnated. Resnais, who came to international prominence with his devastating tour of abandoned concentration camps, *Night and Fog* (1955), written by Jean Cayrol, was the one who matured by marrying bravura technique to grubby anguish and moral desolation. He followed *Muriel* with the existential thriller *La guerre est finie* (1966), laying bare the futility of politics as a continuation of war by other means.

69

A SOVIET GUIDE TO CUBA

I Am Cuba

MIKHAIL KALATOZOV'S *I Am Cuba* is justifiably treated as an object of veneration in Milestone's cleverly simulated cigar box, supported—along with interviews, slide shows, and a pamphlet—by two exceptional feature-length documentaries that provide context while raising as much dust as they settle. The only resolved opinion about *I Am Cuba* is that it did for cinematographic bravado what, say, Fred Astaire did for dance, and is just as pleasurable. Never has antique agitprop proved more intoxicating, and the DVD format offers an ideal way to experience the film. The viewer is now empowered to stop and replay the big moments, of which there are far too many to properly absorb in one sitting. The star is Kalatozov's camera, which, though almost exclusively handheld, seems at times to have a mind of its own as well as supernatural means of mobility.

The accompanying documentaries—Vicente Ferraz's *The Siberian Mammoth* (2005) and the fastidiously titled *A Film About Mikhail Konstantinovich Kalatozov in Two Parts* (2006), by Kalatozov's grandson Mikhail Kalatozishvili—explain some of the magic and demonstrate how it was presaged in Kalatozov's earlier films, made at the dawn of sound. This detracts not at all from the emotional satisfaction of the movie's visual beauty, wit, and power. *I Am Cuba* may represent a feat of engineering, in which scrupulous planning and rehearsal allowed the running camera to be passed from one operator to another or from a crane to a cable, yet the technique invariably serves the substance—an idea that was fiercely contested when the film premiered in Cuba and Moscow in 1964.

We can't possibly look at the picture with 1964 eyes—but then whose eyes was *I Am Cuba* intended for, anyway? It was made to solidify the relationship between Cuba and the Soviet Union, as a generously financed collaboration between Mosfilm and ICIAC (Cuba's national film industry). Yet the Soviets didn't offer the Cubans financing to document their own revolution. Instead, they sent two celebrated figures in Russian cinema: Kalatozov and his despotic, virtuosic director of photography, Sergei Urusevsky, who had opened the international market to Soviet films in 1957 with their first collaboration, the hugely successful *The Cranes Are Flying*. Kalatozov put together a Cuban-Russian crew, spent a year studying the island, and shot *I am Cuba* for fourteen months.

Unlike *The Birth of a Nation*, *Battleship Potemkin*, or *Triumph of the Will*, *I Am Cuba* is not a nationalist call to arms. It is the work of foreigners, misty-eyed with naive romanticism, determined to glorify what they presumed to be a relatively bloodless revolution that was souring before their eyes. In 1962, as they scouted locations, recruited crew members and actors, and prepared a script (by Yevgeny Yevtushenko and Enrique Barnet), the United States was buzzing the island with low-flying planes, amid threats of a naval quarantine in response to the installation of Soviet missiles. Kalatozov was reportedly appalled by American attempts to stifle the new Cuba, and saw the film as his personal protest. By the time he started shooting, in February 1963, the victories of 1958 were dimmed by ongoing summary executions and the heedless expropriation of land.

When the film was first shown the next year, Cuban newspapers ridiculed it as "I Am Not Cuba." The narrative refrain of "Soy Cuba," spoken by a woman with a childlike voice, generated laughter in the theater, as did the deliberate tempo and the outlandish camera moves. Urusevsky, in particular, was blamed for subordinating content to image. In the accompanying *The Siberian Mammoth*, a Cuban participant, looking back, concedes, "Maybe we didn't understand their temperament. They sure didn't understand ours." *I Am Cuba* fared no better in Moscow, where the filmmakers were attacked for formalism and for showing Americans having a good time in Havana. The screenwriters agreed, to a point: Barnet was disappointed that the project had grown artificial and condescending; Yevtushenko allowed, in a TV interview included on the DVD, that the script was its weakest aspect. The film was buried in the archives (one print in Russia, one in Cuba) and forgotten for three decades.

In 1992, Tom Luddy of the Telluride Film Festival tracked down a copy and showed it as part of a Kalatozov tribute. Milestone secured rights from Mosfilm, and with Martin Scorsese and Francis Coppola lending their names as co-presenters, the film made its New York premiere in 1995. The reviews were ecstatic, despite a bit of thumb-sucking about whether it is permissible to bask in the erotic gleam of thrilling filmmaking when the agitprop is sentimental, simplistic, even jejune: the *Waiting for Lefty* finish, impressively staged with 5,000 soldiers massed in a victory march, invites us all to join the revolution—we won't actually be killing any people, just the past. The most amusing episode in *The Siberian Mammoth* occurs toward the end, when the director informs the Cubans who had worked on *I Am Cuba* that it has been rediscovered and acclaimed a masterpiece in the United States. These crew members had remembered Kalatozov with great affection, but considered the film a dead letter. They find its resurrection astonishing, baffling, bemusing, and pleasing. Even so, the veteran head of ICIAC can't help but note that when the film might have meant something to Cuba, it was ignored; now that it is an artistic heirloom, it is treasured.

If the overall perception of this heirloom was transformed from superfluous formalism in 1964 to rousing innovation in 1995, perhaps it has changed once again a dozen years later, when it would be even more simplistic to mistake *I Am Cuba* for history or politics or naturalism. Revolution is a legitimate, universal theme, and in *I Am Cuba* it is treated with four sequential tales that could hardly be more familiar: a young woman is exploited by capitalism into a life of prostitution; a sugarcane farmer is rudely kicked off his land by a landlord; a young revolutionary student is shot down in cold blood by a police assassin; and a farmer who wants to live in peace joins the revolution after his home is bombed. In other words, agitprop isn't far removed from melodrama, and melodrama's only defense resides in the power of the telling.

The astonishing tracking shots are like great Faulknerian sentences that continue lucidly for hundreds of words. The one that begins on a hotel rooftop with a rock and roll band and a bikini contest, with a swimming pool way off in the distance, is as funny as the material it encapsulates: the camera descends the side of the building, makes its way through a deck party, and follows a sashaying beauty into the swimming pool, diving in after her as the music goes glub-glub. By contrast, the shot of a funeral cortege begins on the ground and ascends to the top of a building, tracking through a cigar-making shop where a flag is hung out on the balcony, and continues out past the balcony, looking down at the crowd like an omniscient yet help-less god. The screen fades to black, and the revolution follows. Kalatozov and Urusevsky didn't look for realism: they filmed an unmusical old man as a singer because of his looks (Carlos Fariñas wrote his famous "Canción Triste" for that scene). They diverted a waterfall because it didn't fall in the best light. They refused to film on days when the sky was cloudless and dull. Everything they did intensified the feeling of the story, and the story requires no apology. Yesterday's rum and Coca-Cola is today's Cuba Libre.

THE REDMEN ARE COMING

Indianerfilmes

In 1965, East Germany's nationalized film studio, DEFA (Deutsche Film Aktien Gesellschaft, currently parked in the archives of the University of Massachusetts), took envious measure of its West German counterparts. West German films didn't often cross the Atlantic, but their widespread European acceptance earned international recognition for the stars who did—Curt Jürgens, Maria and Maximilian Schell, Hardy Krüger, Horst Buchholz, Romy Schneider, Gert Fröbe, and others. Their secret was no secret: the West turned out border-crossing entertainments, while the East pursued social consciousness, a hard sell with or without a wall.

So DEFA turned to cowboys and Indians. In a sense, it was reexploring German pop-culture roots. The American West had long generated an intoxicating sway in Germany. The immense popularity of German novelist Karl May and his heroes, Old Shatterhand and Winnetou, preceded by two decades the writings of Zane Grey and made the Wild West as much a German preoccupation as European royalty was for Hollywood. Annual celebrations in May's honor encouraged hundreds of thousands of Germans to dress up in feathers and leather, as if they needed prompting to indulge their inner noble savage. In the early 1960s, West Germany co-produced a series of May adaptations that proved extremely profitable, influencing Italy's 1964 breakout Sergio Leone Western, *A Fistful of Dollars*, which clinched the adaptability of the genre—costumes, settings, manners, and all.

West Germany, however, made Westerns for Westerners, employing down-on-their-luck American actors (Lex Barker played Old Shatterhand) and dubbing English-language versions. DEFA, its audience confined to the Soviet bloc, made Westerns for Easterners. Crossing the Atlantic was not an option; the studio wanted to create stars in its own market. For its first venture into a pop genre, DEFA recruited a Czech director, Joseph Mach, and a little-known Yugoslavian athlete turned actor who could do his own stunts and sport a wig that, on bad-hair days, might have served Ali MacGraw. He became the biggest star in the history of East German cinema—also the only major star. If you've never heard of Gojko Mitić, you obviously didn't spend much time on the dark side of Checkpoint Charlie.

The Sons of Great Bear (1966) minted money, kicking off a new genre, the Indianerfilme, and establishing a franchise that ultimately produced twelve lucrative movies between 1966 and 1982, all starring Mitić and shot in widescreen saturated colors on the great plains of Montenegro, Romania, Bulgaria, Uzbekistan, and Slovakia. Interiors were shot in East Germany. One remarkable aspect of this series is how obscure it remains outside the Eastern bloc. First Run now offers three entries on DVD separately or in a box as *Westerns with a Twist*, and twisted they are—enough to bait the palette for more. Indianerfilmes spurned the clichés of Karl May along with those of Hollywood. Loosely interpreting historical events, they present the Indians as heroes, Mexicans as morally compromised bystanders, and whites as greed-addled barbarians, except for the peaceful ones who align themselves with the gallant red man. But that's hardly a twist; these films were made in an era when Hollywood reveled in pro-Indian apologias, including *Cheyenne Autumn*, *Tell Them Willie Boy Is Here*, and *Ulzana's Raid*. Two far more interesting twists are worth considering.

The first is political: there are reds and there are reds, and it is difficult to read *The Sons of Great Bear* as an indictment of the West when the issues suggest presentiments much closer to home. The main villain is a white man who calls himself Red Fox (he has red hair), and the cavalry for which he scouts could as well be Soviets rounding up its apolitical Indian citizens—one of the first whites we see drools at the sight of a gold nugget. The film's style is airless and claustrophobic, suggesting an artificial closed-in environment even when it races on horseback across open terrain. There is no weather in this film, no breezes or baking sun, not a ripple in what passes for the Missouri River. Elliptical cutting elides geographical or spatial coherence. East Germans are meant to identify with the Indians, not the cavalry.

"I come as lord of the prairie," Tokei Ihto (Mitić) tells a commander, who responds, "You come as a spy, and we hang spies here."

The second twist is aesthetic. The three films selected by First Run include the first two in the series—*The Sons of Great Bear* and *Chingachgook: The Great Snake* (1967)—which are at once intriguing and unintentionally funny. Whole sequences suggest an escapade choreographed by a drugged-out Bob Fosse and directed by his connection. The third DVD and eighth film in the series, *Apaches* (1973), is therefore entirely unexpected. Sharply directed by Gottfried Kolditz, who took control of the franchise for several years, it is a sobering and original take on the bloody Ulzana raid of 1885, albeit set during the 1840s Mexican War. If the earlier films are bizarre cold war relics, *Apaches* is by any standard a very good Western, perhaps a great one. Even Gojko Mitić, a male model in his first films, delivers a performance.

The initial Indianerfilmes could never have been shown in the West except as Saturday matinees for the same undiscriminating children who ate up *Hercules* and *Rodan*. You can't watch the first two without giggling. For one thing, everyone speaks German, although Indians are forever raising their hands and solemnly intoning "How" or "Gut! How." Action scenes, few and badly staged, unfold with existential disorientation—the massacre that begins about thirteen minutes into *The Sons of Great Bear* has the opponents riding up from every possible angle, with two empty horizon shots thrown in for Lent. The music is wonderfully inappropriate—drums that are more Art Blakey than Sitting Bull, trombone solos, a chorus by saxophones, lots of xylophone. Some of the white war talk is at once contemporary and historic: discussions of insufficient reinforcements and armaments, demands that the enemy be spoken of only in nonhuman terms, which is better than lines like "My brother Wolfchief is quieter than summer-parched soil." The Indian camp is a paradise, full of life and babies and feather pinwheels. The interior of a wigwam, though authentic-looking from the outside, is as big as the fort and more handsomely appointed, with perpendicular walls and plenty of light.

Chingachgook is a pretty faithful adaptation of Fenimore Cooper's *The Deerslayer*, except for two sidesplitting Indian dances, including a June Taylor overhead shot. Directed by Richard Groschopp, and with Rolf Römer as a beanpole blond Deerslayer, it loses the character of crazy Hetty and the barge attack that inspired Mark Twain's hysterics in *Cooper's Literary Offenses*, but it doesn't stint in establishing white traders, not Indians, as the inventors of scalping as a business. One odd touch is the casting of Judith, who looks like the Deerslayer's twin, imparting an incestuous edge to their stillborn romance. The film lurches between drama and comedy (Chingach-gook does a Three Stooges getaway as rival Indians pile on top of him), as does the score, which offers Dixieland and a snippet of "Empty Saddles," suitable for lines like "I'm a bit of a hunk, but if she weds another, I'll kill him." The Indian chosen to break Chingachgook is called Red Buffalo (he does not have red hair), and the astute ending sends the heroes in one direction and the British and Judith in another, as the cabin representing free homesteading goes up in flames.

Apaches is, by contrast, a measured and focused look at betrayal and revenge, with impressive attention to historical detail, including costumes and wickiups. The betrayal is a bloody massacre in which women, children, and men are scalped by military command, an event drawn from the Camp Grant massacre of 1871, though very few of those hundred or so victims were men. The staging of this scene prefigures the massacre of Civil War irregulars in Clint Eastwood's *The Outlaw Josie Wales* (1976). Mitić is properly stoic as Ulzana, and well supported by Milan Beli as the murderous Johnson and Colea Răutu as an arthritic but wily old Indian, Nana. The film ends with Ulzana's temporary victory, in full knowledge that Captain Crook's cavalry will soon arrive. History wasn't kind, but the 1973 sequel, *Ulzana*, may have a different take; it remains for First Run to unveil. The prints of these films are in good shape, though the running times are several minutes shorter than advertised on the DVD cases and the framing is tight, sacrificing information on the right side. Still, the colors are bright, the audio is effective, and the movies fill in a Western gap few of us knew existed.

71

RECALLING THE FUTURE
OF NUCLEAR WAR

The War Game / Culloden

ALL MOVIES ARE about the present, especially those set in the past or future. Hairdressers working on Hollywood Westerns in the silent era or in every decade from the 1920s to the present attempted verisimilitude by researching period photographs, and yet they all ended up with do's that define the decades in which they sheared, curled, and set. You could not ask for a better display of 1930s fashion than *Things to Come*, or of 1960s vogue than *2001: A Space Odyssey*. Of course, if a movie is any good, it will decipher the past and adumbrate the future even as it captures its own day. Peter Watkins's *The War Game* (1965) derives its enduring power by attempting, if not always succeeding, to do precisely that. Consider the film's resourceful use of tense. Watkins's forty-seven-minute film depicts the *possible* effects of a nuclear war as shown through faux-documentary footage and interviews with survivors whose travails, according to intertitles and a narrator, replicate the firebombings of Dresden and Tokyo as well as the bombings of Hiroshima and Nagasaki. In short, what will be has already been. Sort of like Ed Wood Jr.'s *Plan Nine from Outer Space*, in which Criswell assures us that we'll be seeing exactly what happened in the future.

Decades later, the effectiveness of *The War Game* depends on the degree of fear in the land. During the years in which nuclear war receded into a memory-lane jaunt, motored by détente, the film may have played as a period piece, quaint in its use of amateur actors looking into the camera and saying, no, they never heard of radiation or Strontium 90. It's different now, as Pakistan and India play the war game with multiplying nuclear warheads, going for the gold against North Korea and Iran, while Americans, notified by their leaders that collateral damage in Iraq is only about 40,000, evolve from color-coded terror to outrage over gas prices to lynch-mob fury over Wall Street bonuses.

Watkins is antiwar of any kind; or rather, he pleads for recognition of what war entails. His most terrifying shots, achieved with a shaky camera, grisly makeup, and wind blowers, tell us that this is what we can expect, since the same conditions existed in Europe and Japan during the last war. It is one thing to read about a firestorm and learn of the body count and another to see it, even in a recreation done on the cheap, albeit rather ingeniously, for British television. *The War Game* was of a piece with its time, when movies about nuclear devastation were solid commercial bets between the late 1950s and mid-1960s. But they were all rather antiseptic. *The World, the Flesh and the Devil* and *On the Beach* nattered on about how lonely it would be for survivors (even dead bodies mysteriously vanished); *Fail Safe* sacrificed New York to melodramatic equity; and the incomparable *Dr. Strangelove* taught us to stop worrying—how lovely are mushroom clouds rising to the strains of Vera Lynn. Watkins, however, shows an accretion of small details, from shattered teacups to blinded children to burnings and shootings and riots and the complete breakdown of society.

When he submitted his short film to his BBC masters, Watkins was the hottest young filmmaker in British television. A year earlier, he had made the prize-winning *Culloden*, a no less censorious you-are-there recreation of the British slaughter of Bonnie Prince Charlie's Scottish Highlanders. A portrait of corruption, incompetence, and retaliatory bloodthirstiness verging on genocide, *Culloden* showed Watkins to be a resourceful, tenacious, angry young man with a gimlet eye for demonstrative faces. The Brits loved it: they could look 1746 square in the eye without flinching. Yet the BBC flatly refused to broadcast *The War Game*. According to Patrick Murphy's essay and commentary, included with the DVD, detractors complained that Watkins had slandered not only the civil service but the English people, who, far from panicking, would surely behave in a nuclear holocaust with the same fortitude they displayed during the Blitz.

Perhaps they would. *The War Game* is too outraged to explore the character of the people or detail the times in which they live; its Kent is a claustrophobic village removed from the Beatles and other aspects of popular culture that would dominate Watkins's next film, the eerily prophetic *Privilege* (1967). The men and women on the street are none too bright, and news from abroad is as absurd as an Ed Wood or Joel Schumacher movie. In Watkins's telling, English and American bishops at an Ecumenical Council at the Vatican signed off on the following statement: "The church must tell the faithful that they should learn to live with, though not love, the nuclear bomb, provided that it is 'clean' and of a good family." If the portrait is neither full nor fair, it makes the undeniable case that neither the people nor their leaders were prepared for the devastation that pop paranoia constantly promised.

A more revealing film than *The War Game* might have been made about its reception. Watkins denounced the censorship of his work, creating enough publicity and indignation to secure a feature film release. The Brits refused to show it for twenty years, but America welcomed it with neighborly cheer, giving it the 1966 Academy Award for best documentary feature—a double stretch given its length and speculation: isn't a fake documentary, by definition, a fake documentary? It was a different story when Watkins turned his gaze on the New World. Having endured brickbats for *Privilege*, in which rock and roll is treated as the opium of the welfare state, and *The Gladiators* (1969), in which war is reduced to a sporting event overseen by distant commanders, he visited the American Southwest for *Punishment Park* (1971), imagining the desert as a firing range in which dissidents are the ducks. No Oscars for that; not even distribution.

The Cinema of Peter Watkins is an important series from Project X in collaboration with New Yorker Video, restoring the work of one of the few filmmakers whose vision is shored up by a sense of mission. It's a mistake, however, to pigeonhole Watkins simply as a scolding voice of the left. He's an artist in a way Michael Moore can never be, having no need to curry favor, flatter the audience, or celebrate himself (except in a few liner note treatises). Watkins is offensive because he is pitiless in handling the dystopian tactic of stretching bad news to the breaking point. Even Aldous Huxley and George Orwell found silver linings. Not Watkins. The historic recreations of past and future in *The War Game* and *Culloden* prohibit gleams of hope, and Watkins is not the sort to hold our hands and whisper, "It's okay." It's not okay, and sometimes art consoles us by telling us that.

INDEX

· · · · · · · · · · · · · · ·